THE INFERNAL LIBRARY

THE INFERNAL LIBRARY

On Dictators, the Books They Wrote, and Other Catastrophes of Literacy

DANIEL KALDER

Henry Holt and Company New York

Henry Holt and Company
Publishers since 1866
175 Fifth Avenue
New York, New York 10010
www.henryholt.com

Henry Holt® and 🎔® are registered trademarks of
Macmillan Publishing Group, LLC.

Illustration credits: p. 78, Mussolini (Keystone-France/Getty); p. 114,
Hitler (Time Life Pictures/Getty); p. 139, Cultural Revolution poster (David Pollack/Getty);
page 197, Franco and Salazar (Associated Press); p. 220, Gaddafi (Epsilon/Getty); p. 241,
Brezhnev (East News/Getty); p. 292, Castro (Sven Creutzmann/Mambo Photo/Getty); p. 319,
Rukhnama (ullstein bild/Getty)

Library of Congress Cataloging-in-Publication Data is available.

ISBN: 978-1-62779-342-1

Our books may be purchased in bulk for promotional, educational, or business use. Please
contact your local bookseller or the Macmillan Corporate and Premium Sales Department at
(800) 221-7945, extension 5442, or by e-mail at MacmillanSpecialMarkets@macmillan.com.

First Edition 2018

Designed by Kelly S. Too

Printed in the United States of America

1   3   5   7   9   10   8   6   4   2

To Leon and Annie Henderson

While nothing is easier to denounce than the evildoer, nothing is more difficult than to understand him.

—Fyodor Dostoyevsky

The writer is the engineer of the human soul.

—Josef Stalin

I am not a writer.

—Adolf Hitler

CONTENTS

Tradition and the Individual Tyrant

This is a book about dictator literature—that is to say, it is a book about the canon of works written by or attributed to dictators. As such, it is a book about some of the worst books ever written, and so was excruciatingly painful to research.

This is why I did it.

Since the days of the Roman Empire, dictators* have written books, but in the twentieth century there was a Krakatoa-like eruption of despotic verbiage, which continues flowing to this day. Many dictators write theoretical works, others produce spiritual manifestos, while still others write poetry, memoirs or even the occasional romance novel. Indeed, the best-selling book of all time attributed to a man rather than a deity is the work of a dictator: *Quotations from Chairman Mao Tse-tung*. However most of these books are entirely unread today, or are treated as jokes, despite the fact that their authors once enjoyed record-breaking print runs, (literally) captive audiences and the acclaim of intellectuals who should have known better. Since many of the authors were mass murderers of some note, the

---

* NB: I use the term *dictator* here and throughout the book in its widely understood sense of a leader not overly fond of free elections but very keen on having his own way.

almost complete disappearance of their texts and subsequent lack of interest in them struck me as something of an oversight. Surely it was worth taking a closer look at these works; perhaps they would provide insight into the dictatorial soul. If not, they might still serve the historian as portals into worlds of suffering, offering glimpses of the ultra-boredom of totalitarianism, a condition endured by hundreds of millions of people for generations.

Dictators usually live lives that are rich in experience. They wield the power of life and death over millions and frequently live like small gods—for as long as they can get away with it, anyway. Certainly, their lives are much more interesting than those of most authors. With all this power and unique knowledge, the dictator of even a small and geopolitically insignificant country should thus be in a position to write at least a moderately interesting book, even if by accident. And yet to a man, they almost always produce mind-numbing drivel. I wanted to know why.

I was struck by the fact that many dictators begin their careers as writers, which probably goes a long way toward explaining their megalomaniac conviction in the awesome significance of their own thoughts. I noticed also that the dictatorial canon was a real thing: the despots of the twentieth century were aware of what their rivals were saying and doing, and were often familiar with each other's major texts. Dictator literature thus spawned a tradition of its own, a bit like the one T. S. Eliot describes in his seminal essay "Tradition and the Individual Talent," only infinitely more tedious. A deep study of dictators' works might enable me to map devastating wastelands of the spirit while also exploring the terrible things that happen when you put writers in charge.

Many people regard books and reading as innately positive, as if compilations of bound paper with ink on them in and of themselves represent a uniquely powerful "medicine for the soul." However, a moment's reflection reveals that this is not even slightly true: books and reading can also cause immense harm. To take just one example: had Stalin's mother never sent him to the seminary then he never would have learned to read and never would have discovered the works of Marx or Lenin. Instead, he would have been a drunken cobbler like his father, or perhaps a small-time gangster in Tbilisi. He would still have spread misery, but on a much smaller scale—and the twentieth century might have been considerably less awful as a result. Likewise, the collision between increasing levels of literacy and the holy books of humanity has not led to mass outbreaks of people focusing on the peaceful bits to the exclusion of the dangerous bits. On the contrary, many people find the dangerous bits quite inspiring, and a lot of killing and repression has ensued as a result. Literacy is a blight as well as a blessing, and dictator books are particularly worth studying in this context as unlike holy books, which inspire good deeds as well as evil, their impact is almost entirely negative and so demonstrate, in pure form, just how bad books can be. Their legacy is much less mixed than that of religious works.

Finally, I did it because nobody else had done it. I saw the mountain. I climbed the mountain. By the time I was nearly halfway up, it was much too late to go back down.

What I did not anticipate was how much the world would change while I was writing this book. When I began writing short articles about dictator literature for the *Guardian* in 2009, many ossified regimes dating back to the Cold War were still standing, and I felt that I was describing a largely historical phenomenon. Then came the Arab Spring of 2011, and for a brief moment, politicians, journalists and think-tank pontificators were speaking and writing with breathtaking naïveté, as if a new era of freedom and democracy had dawned wherein dictatorships would increasingly be consigned to the dustbin of history. I didn't believe this for a moment—authoritarian regimes are considerably more common than liberal democracies, after all—but I did think that this book, which was by that point in its early stages, might be dead in the water. It might be a while before the counterreaction kicked in, making my theme timely again.

How wrong I was: the counterreaction kicked in almost immediately. Authoritarian rule made a spectacular comeback in the Middle East, while deepening its grip in Turkey and Russia, and it was holding up pretty well in China, Iran, Saudi Arabia and any number of other countries besides. Vast swathes of humanity were becoming less free. By the time I reached the end of the book it was clear that something unnerving was happening in the liberal democracies of the West also, that we had entered an age of disintegration in which the complacencies of the post–Cold War order no longer applied. A generation with no memory of that half century of paranoia and fear had entered adulthood; antiestablishment politicians and ideologues were challenging the ruling classes with increasing confidence; hitherto fringe ideas were going mainstream; nationalism was making a comeback; radicals were bandying about the word *socialism* as if it were some exciting thing that had never been tried before; and some members of the elite, horrified by the revolt of the plebeian classes, were openly questioning democracy.

In short, it was all starting to look a bit like the moment when everything started to go terribly wrong for the twentieth century. That said, I couldn't shake the feeling that the populists, ideologues and radicals of this era were much less well read than those of a century ago. They didn't seem to realize that a lot of their arguments and ideas were not new, and appeared to be largely unaware of the details of all the wondrous social and political experiments that had already failed so badly.

Far from being dead in the water, I now started to see the themes of my book unfolding all around me. And as I write these words, that's pretty much where we stand today.

This is the story of how it all went down the first time around.

THE INFERNAL LIBRARY

THE
DICTATOR'S CANON

Lenin

*Vladimir Lenin, author and revolutionary mastermind
who liked to have priests shot*

Lenin, the father of dictator literature, was born Vladimir Ilyich Ulianov*
in 1870 in Simbirsk, a provincial outpost in the southern Volga region of
the vast and ineffable Russian emptiness. This former fortress town had
been established a century earlier as a bulwark against the heathen tribes
on the fringes of the empire, but was now a sedate place, equipped with a
church, schools, factories and a class of local nobles profiting from the
labor of their tenant farmers.

---

* Lenin used dozens of pseudonyms throughout his career. For the sake of clarity, I call him
Lenin throughout.

Alexander Ulianov, the local inspector of schools, was one of these fortunate nobles. He was fortunate, too, in that his youngest son, Vladimir, was a pious, studious youth, loyal to the tsar; good at Greek, Latin and chess; and very fond of books, a particular favorite being Harriet Beecher Stowe's *Uncle Tom's Cabin*. The southern Volga region had a history of insurrection—a century earlier, a peasant named Yemelyan Pugachev had declared himself tsar and led an armed uprising against Catherine the Great—but nobody looking for a potential revolutionary leader who would transform the course of history would have glanced twice at the school inspector's boy. He seemed set for a stable, respectable career in a stable, respectable profession—as a lawyer, say. Indeed, Lenin himself became officially "noble" at the tender age of fifteen, inheriting the status upon his father's death in 1886. A year later, his elder brother, also named Alexander, attempted to blow up yet another Alexander, Tsar Alexander III and that possible future as a stalwart member of the provincial bourgeoisie disintegrated.

Lenin's brother believed that by murdering the tsar, he could force backward, autocratic, tyrannical Russia closer to revolution, ushering in a new era of liberty and justice. Of course, there were a few problems with this strategy, the foremost being the lack of any empirical evidence that it could ever possible work. After all, neither the French Revolution nor any of the other revolutions that occurred in Europe in the mid-nineteenth century had ushered in eras of glorious reform, let alone utopias. On the contrary, they had resulted in periods of terror and/or sustained counter-revolutionary repression. As for Russia, the previous tsar, Alexander II, had abolished serfdom in 1861 and subsequently pursued a course of moderate social and political reform for two decades. This was not enough for Russia's most notorious terrorist organization, the People's Will, which demanded more, and faster, while dedicating much energy to finding ways to kill him. Eventually they succeeded: the tsar was shredded by a bomb thrown by a member of the People's Will on March 1, 1881, the very same day he signed a proclamation announcing the creation of two legislative commissions comprised of indirectly elected representatives.

Following Alexander II's assassination, the people did not rise up, and the tsar's successor, Alexander III, pursued a course of reaction and repression. Multiple arrests and executions later, the People's Will had ceased to exist. Regardless, Alexander Ulianov believed that the best way to bring about revolution was to repeat the previous failed attempt and so joined a group that purported to be a continuation of the People's Will. The apocalyptic-millenarian desire for radical, instant change overwhelmed reason, and unfortunately for Alexander Ulianov, it also overwhelmed any sense of subtlety, strategy, or general conspiratorial best practices. Doubtless it seemed an amusing idea at the time to blow up Alexander III on the sixth anniversary of blowing up Alexander II, even if one might also reasonably expect the Okhrana, the tsar's secret police, to be on high alert that day. The assassination of Alexander III was thus penciled in for March 13, 1887,* and Alexander Ulianov duly set to work on the bombs, but his grand dream of reducing the tsar to a smoking pile of bone, singed meat and gristle was to go unrealized as the Okhrana uncovered the plot, and Alexander Ulianov and his coconspirators were arrested before a single bomb could be tossed.

The regime showed mercy toward most of the would-be terrorists, but not Ulianov, who claimed responsibility not only for the explosives but also exaggerated his role as a leader of the assassination attempt in order to save his comrades. During the trial, he even went so far as to declare that the laws of science and evolution made terrorism inevitable and that he was not afraid to die for the cause. The court obliged him: he was hanged.

And shortly afterward, Lenin, the hitherto studious schoolboy, started to assemble a new self out of the forbidden works that lined his brother's bookshelves.

RUSSIA HAD ITS own radical traditions, and Lenin read the works of indigenous revolutionaries before he discovered Marx. Here are some of the movements and thinkers that influenced him:

Populism: The belief, popular among Russia's radical intellectuals in the 1860s, '70s and '80s, that the nation's salvation depended on a revolutionary uprising by the peasantry. In 1873–1874, fueled by a messianic (and condescending) impulse, thousands of members of the youthful intelligentsia became Populists, and "went to the people" on a crusade

---

* According to the Gregorian calendar, that is—in nineteenth-century Russia, the Julian calendar was still in use, and so for Alexander Ulianov and his coconspirators the date they had chosen was the more poetic-sounding March 1.

to raise the consciousness of the noble savages while also instigating an uprising. Some Populists also believed that national salvation could be hastened by eating black bread, dressing up as peasants, living among peasants and adopting the traditions of the peasant commune. In fact, the ancient modes of rural life were already disintegrating, and the peasants, disturbed by this bizarre behavior of their social superiors, were often hostile toward the Populists. Rather than rise up, they either responded with indifference or reported the young revolutionaries to the police. Disappointed, some Populists turned to violence as a means of accelerating the revolution.

Sergei Nechaev: In 1869, Nechaev founded the People's Retribution (or "Society of the Axe"), a revolutionary organization predicated on two main concepts: first, that the leader was absolutely correct about everything all the time, and second, that "day and night [the revolutionary] must have but one thought, one aim—merciless destruction." Nechaev subsequently strangled and shot an insufficiently loyal member of his microscopic organization, believing that this would bind those who remained to him more closely. Instead, the People's Retribution fell apart, and Nechaev, widely dismissed as a homicidal lunatic, died in prison. However, his *Catechism of a Revolutionary* (1869), which he coauthored with the anarchist theorist Mikhail Bakunin, survived as an inspirational text for radicals overawed by its romantic nihilism—"The Revolutionary is a doomed man. He has neither his own interests, nor affairs, nor attachments, nor property, nor even name. Everything in him is absorbed by a single, exclusive interest, by a total concept, a total passion-revolution"—and total dedication to the idea that any means were justified so long as they advanced the ends of revolution as expressed by the maxim:

> Moral is everything which contributes to the triumph of the revolution.
> Immoral and criminal is everything that stands in its way.

Pyotr Tkachev: An intellectual influence on the People's Will and sometime collaborator with Nechaev, Tkachev has been referred to as "the first Bolshevik" due to his enthusiasm for revolution as soon as possible, his insistence that Russia was better suited to revolution than western Europe, and his belief that, following the revolution, the country should be ruled by a minority dictatorship run by revolutionaries who would ruthlessly suppress dissent through violence—all of which would eventually happen under Lenin, of course.

He also advocated the "complete leveling of all people in their moral and intellectual capacities" in order to destroy competition and inequality of outcomes among people. Ever the charmer, following a stint in prison, Tkachev told his sister that everyone over the age of twenty-five should be killed, as they were incapable of self-sacrifice.

Nikolai Chernyshevsky: A journalist dedicated to preaching socialism, democracy, the rights of women and minorities and other radical (for the time) causes, Chernyshevsky wrote his political novel *What Is to Be Done?* in 1863, while imprisoned in Saint Petersburg's Peter and Paul Fortress. Evidently underwhelmed by the story's wooden characters and tedious didacticism, the imperial censors permitted its publication. According to historian Orlando Figes, this was "one of the biggest mistakes the Tsarist censor ever made: it converted more people to the cause of revolution than all the works of Marx and Engels put together." So rapturous was the novel's reception that at least one overexuberant critic compared Chernyshevsky to Jesus, while Marx himself studied Russian so that he could read the book and correspond with its author. Lenin was so impressed by *What Is to Be Done?* that he read it five times one summer and even carried a photograph of Chernyshevsky in his wallet. He was particularly inspired by the austere, monastic self-discipline of one character: the ultrarevolutionary Rakhmetov. This ascetic abandons all physical comforts and selfish pleasures and lives only for the cause. He lifts weights, eats raw meat and even sleeps on a bed of nails to distract himself from thoughts of an alluring widow. Lenin duly quit chess, music and the study of classical languages and took up weight lifting. He may have skipped the bed of nails part, but otherwise he agreed with Rakhmetov: revolution was all.

Thus, in a very Borgesian way—only without any of the irony, sophistication or playfulness—Chernyshevsky's creation infiltrated the physical world and *What Is to Be Done?* became the "Tlön, Uqbar, Orbis Tertius" of nineteenth-century socialism, remaking living, breathing people in the image of its two-dimensional characters. Just as the imaginary planet invented by a secret society in Borges's fantastical tale gradually supplants reality, so Lenin, infected by Chernyshevsky's word virus, rebuilt himself in the image of a preposterous imaginary character, becoming a living avatar of revolution.

By the time Lenin started attending the law faculty of Kazan University in the autumn of 1887, he was already self-radicalized, having pieced together a new identity from the bad ideas he had found in a variety of not terribly good books, a jigsaw man assembled from pieces of mediocre yet dangerous texts. He would not last long as a student at Kazan. Expelled before the end of the year for participating in a protest, he was obliged to return to the comfort of his mother's estate in Kokushkino, where he deepened his familiarity with radical literature. In 1889 he read *Das Kapital* for the first time. That same year, the family moved to another estate even farther south, where Lenin turned his attention to translating into Russian the supreme revolutionary text of his, and, for that matter, any age—Marx and Engels's *Communist Manifesto*.

MANY OF THE twentieth century's dictator-author-murderers declared themselves Marx's intellectual disciples, and this is—understandably—a continued source of irritation for today's Marxists and Marx sympathizers. They would rather their sage be remembered for his critique of capitalism, and not for the ninety-four million corpses produced by tyrants citing his texts as inspiration.*

It is true, of course, that there is no monolithic "Marxism" but rather rival "Marxisms," in the same way that there are differing versions of Christianity, Islam, or Freudianism. And so rather than engage in a futile attempt at nailing down an official "Marxism," it is perhaps more instructive to note that perhaps the most significant difference between the nineteenth-century prophet and his twentieth-century interpreters such as Lenin, Stalin or Mao is that, unlike them, he was a titanic loser.

Consider for example that when Karl Marx died in 1883, a mere eleven people attended his funeral. A few more might have shown up had he not alienated most of the international workers' movement with his dictatorial yet inept style of leadership. He'd spent the thirty-three years preceding his death living in exile with his family in London, begging for money

---

* Death toll as estimated by the editors of *The Black Book of Communism*.

from his factory-owning patron Friedrich Engels, while failing, over the course of more than two decades, to complete his magnum opus *Das Kapital*. He never tried to get a regular job, even as his baby son died at his wife's breast. He sprouted hideous boils all over his body, impregnated the maid,* wasted vast amounts of energy on quarrels with rival socialists, and repeatedly foretold the coming revolution with all the passion and indifference to disconfirmation of an evangelical preacher giddy over the prophecies contained in the book of Revelation.

It was not always thus, however. In mid-1848, when Marx and Engels had published *The Communist Manifesto*, history briefly looked as though it was going his way. Between that year and 1851 many of Europe's monarchies were rocked by a series of uprisings and revolts. "A spectre is haunting Europe," Marx wrote, "the spectre of revolution." During this period, he indulged in wild power fantasies, dreaming of the terrible vengeance that would soon be inflicted upon the bourgeoisie—of which class he was a member, needless to say. "We are ruthless and ask no quarter from you," he wrote, addressing the Prussian government in 1849. "When our turn comes we shall not disguise our terrorism."

Engels prophesied the same year that a coming world war would "result in the disappearance from the face of the earth not only of reactionary classes and dynasties, but also of entire reactionary peoples." This genocidal fantasy of the damned receiving their final punishment in an ultraviolent apocalypse was, Engels wrote, "a step forward."

Marx, meanwhile, hoped he would be able to fulfill the exciting vision laid out in *The Communist Manifesto*, of cultivating wastelands and centralizing all communications in a government-run postal-telegraph system. Yes, he actually wrote about that, but it is very easy to forget the dull bits—and most people do—because there is also all that stirring stuff about the wresting of all capital from the bourgeoisie, the abolition of private property and of the bourgeois family, and the disappearance of differences between nations and peoples.

In fact, moments of bathos aside, *The Communist Manifesto* is quite mesmerizing: in its fevered treatment of assertion as fact, its furious demonization of the bourgeoisie, its awe at the transformative power of capitalism, its overwhelming conviction that change *is* coming, and for

---

* Thus producing a son who Marx, like any number of Victorian blackguards guilty of knocking up the help, refused to acknowledge.

the nakedness of Marx and Engels's will to power and their open endorsement of political violence, e.g.:

> The Communists disdain to conceal their views and aims. They openly declare that their ends can be attained only by the forcible overthrow of all existing social conditions. Let the ruling classes tremble at a Communistic revolution. The proletarians have nothing to lose but their chains. They have a world to win. Workers of the world unite!

The duo also echo the English mystic poet William Blake in their horror of the "dark Satanic mills," proclaiming that "[m]asses of laborers crowded into the factory . . . are daily and hourly enslaved by the machine." Perhaps most appealing of all, however, is their simplistic vision of history as a forward march through a series of crises to a state of permanent bliss on earth, where future generations will live together in harmony in a world beyond conflict and exploitation. Transparently a millenarian fantasy, Marx nevertheless insisted that his outline of history was "scientific," and thus flattered his readers into thinking they were members of an elite that had somehow gained access to a modern yet still absolute truth, providing the answer to the riddle of human existence.

Alas for Marx, the revolutions subsided and repression set in across Europe. However, he had not set a date for the arrival of future bliss; he merely implied that it was imminent. Thus, *The Communist Manifesto*, like all successful apocalyptic prophecies, remained open to reinterpretation.

Das Kapital is less mesmerizing. It emerged from long sessions Marx spent in the British Library staring very hard at government reports on the conditions in British factories thirty years earlier. By doing so, he hoped to penetrate to the essence of capital for all times and nations. He thus synthesized multiple texts into a sprawling übertext that was "scientific"—even if he disdained to do anything so empirical as to speak with an actual worker; he preferred to interact with paper and ink. In *Das Kapital*, the end-time dream of *The Communist Manifesto* acquired a dense theoretical underpinning: "scientific laws" of history replace God as the cosmic force leading a chosen elect to inevitable eternal bliss—only, now it would happen on earth rather than in heaven.

The success of Marx's ideas in Russia of all places suggested that there might be a problem with his theoretical framework. He argued in *Das Kapital* that the internal contradictions of capitalism would lead to a series of increasingly catastrophic crises, and that the conditions suffered by workers would deteriorate with each crisis, leading ineluctably to revolution, the demise of private property and the expropriation of the expropriators. This would happen, he argued, where capitalism was at its most advanced, in Britain or Germany, for instance—certainly not in backward, agrarian Russia.

And yet the very first foreign edition of *Das Kapital* (or rather, the part Marx finished in his lifetime) was published in Russia in 1872, five years after its initial German release, where it had been ignored by critics. Its translator, Nikolai Danielson, was a Populist. Ironically, the tsarist censors permitted its publication because they agreed with Marx: Russia was in a primitive state of industrial development, there was no "capitalist exploitation" to speak of, and so the book's philosophical message was not relevant there.

But as with *What Is to Be Done?* the censors had miscalculated. *Das Kapital* was a hit, selling three thousand copies in its first year, a respectable result given that only around 15 percent of the Russian population was literate. In advanced, industrialized and allegedly revolution-primed Germany by contrast, it took five years for the book to sell a third that number. But this was just the beginning: in the 1870s and '80s, Marxism flourished in Russia, and *Das Kapital* became a source of fascination, inspiration and truth for many of Russia's radicals. They had abandoned God, the tsar and the Church, but had not lost a taste for the metaphysics of apocalyptic judgment and redemption—just so long as they could be made palatable by a rationalist gloss.*

Soon Marx had acquired homegrown exegetes, such as Georgy Plekhanov, who in 1883 helped establish the first Russian Marxist revolutionary organization, the Emancipation of Labor. A lapsed Populist, he argued that Russia's salvation lay not in the peasants but in the working class, although the country was not yet ready for a proletarian revolution. Fortunately, Russia was undergoing a capitalistic transformation, which was creating the conditions for a two-stage transition to communism. In the first phase, tsarist autocracy would be overthrown and a bourgeois-

---

* Russia had a long tradition of apocalyptic belief. Since the collapse of Constantinople in 1453, tsars, bishops, and peasants had been claiming that Moscow was the Third Rome, with an eschatological mission of salvation for the entire world. A religious schism in 1666 had led to a proliferation of sects, and by the nineteenth century the country teemed with millenarian groups who believed they were living in the last days.

democratic system would replace it. During this period, the numbers of the proletariat would multiply, and under the leadership of a social-democratic (i.e., Marxist) party, a second revolution would bring about the liberation of the working class.

Lenin liked the sound of that. Plekhanov entered his pantheon, alongside Chernyshevsky, Nechaev and Marx. Fired up on texts, he was ready to transform history

THE YOUNG LENIN was the archetypal armchair radical. In fact, he sat in chairs a lot—as he read books about revolution, as he discussed books about revolution with other armchair radicals and as he wrote the articles that he hoped would establish his fame among those same armchair radicals. However, he seemed different. His comrades in these revolutionary talking shops recognized and respected his intelligence, conviction, theoretical prowess and leadership skills, referring to him as the Old Man, even though he was still in his twenties. Instead, they should have feared him: for, when given the opportunity to put his ideas into practice, he proved himself to be a merciless extremist.

For instance, in 1891, as famine ravaged the Volga region, liberals and radicals united in blaming the tsar for the food shortages and in believing they had a moral responsibility to do what they could to help the starving peasants. Not the twenty-one-year-old Lenin, however, who chided his sister for providing peasants with medical assistance. He had already sued the tenant farmers on the family property when they fell behind on their rent. Now, as they starved, he refused to lower their rates.

After all, according to Marx the suffering of the exploited classes was inevitable under capitalism, but it was also a cause for hope, as terrible crises indicated the imminent arrival of revolution. To ameliorate suffering would have meant delaying the moment of world transformation. Marx had scorned bourgeois morality as unscientific and another illusion through which the ruling class kept the workers in a state of mystification, but he also denounced capitalism using moral language. Perhaps Nechaev had put it best: moral is everything that contributes to the triumph of the revolution. And so while other radicals talked about theory but ultimately surrendered to empathy and the prompts of conscience, Lenin was willing to live by the ideas he espoused.

Thus, from his chair, he accelerated the arrival of the workers' paradise. Four hundred thousand people died. Although he could hardly claim credit for the famine's body count, he had done his bit. As Maxim Gorky (who would come to know Lenin well) later put it, "Lenin in general loved people but with abnegation, his love looked far ahead through the mists of hatred. He loved mankind not as it was but as he believed it would become."

Eventually, of course, Lenin felt obliged to leave his chair. Revolution was supposed to be the inevitable climax of human history, but he suspected it might in fact be slightly evitable, or, at least, he began to doubt it could be successful unless the proletariat were given the correct training. After all, the bourgeoisie were cunning, and they had armies and police forces at their command—they could hardly be expected to give up their diabolical ways without a fight.

In 1895, Lenin, now based in Saint Petersburg, joined the grandly named League of Struggle for the Emancipation of the Working Class. His aim was to establish direct contact with members of the proletariat and instruct them in ideology. Just as his consciousness had been remodeled through encounters with revolutionary texts, so he would perform the same service for the workers of Saint Petersburg. In November of that year, he wrote a booklet explaining the legal limits of a factory owner's authority and had three thousand copies printed. He supplied striking workers with cash. However, the secret police uncovered Lenin's subversive activities and he was arrested in December. He spent a year in detention, reading and working on a thesis on the development of Russian capitalism. Then, in January 1897, he was exiled to Siberia.

Exile under the tsars was not the brutal enslavement/death trip it would become under Stalin, however—and certainly not for a man of Lenin's social standing. His mother paid for his transport, and he was even allowed input into his place of exile. Lenin proposed two places: the city of Krasnoyarsk or the Minusinsk district of Yenisei province. He was granted his second choice, and he wound up living in Shushenskoe, a village of a thousand people in Minusinsk. I have visited the area: the landscape of taiga and snowcapped mountains is quite beautiful. The climate is dry, so even when the temperature drops to minus forty degrees Celsius, it is much more pleasant than Baltic Saint Petersburg at, say, minus twenty-five. In fact, so long as you don't mind having your flesh devoured by dense, ravenous clouds of mosquitoes in the summer, or being very far away from the center of things, Minusinsk is quite tolerable. The authorities granted Lenin's fiancée, Nadezhda Krupskaya, permission to join him. The tsar also gave exiles a stipend, and Lenin was free to read and write, and to communicate with his family and comrades.

It is true that, stranded deep in Siberia, he missed the founding congress of the Russian Social-Democratic Workers' Party in Minsk in 1898. That said, he didn't miss much: only nine socialists from around the empire showed up, and eight of them were arrested shortly afterward. Lenin meanwhile made the most of his exile, and decided not to attempt escape but to treat it as a state-subsidized writer's sabbatical. And so in between (unsuccessful) attempts at impregnating his revolutionary bride, he worked on *The Development of Capitalism in Russia*, which he hoped would be received as an earthshaking work of Marxist analysis.

Friends and family sent him books, and he plowed through over a hundred of them, including the works of Western economists, which he subjected to relentless critical analysis—Adam Smith was guilty of "fundamental error," while "utter confusion" was the norm among most contemporary economists. Although the combination of a gentleman's lifestyle and logorrhea meant that Lenin had already written quite a lot— *The Development of Capitalism in Russia* does not appear in the fifth and most expansive edition of Lenin's collected works until the third volume— it was, unquestionably, a substantial work. Certainly, it was very long. Over five hundred pages long, in fact: the first major book by the father of twentieth-century dictator literature.

In writing *The Development of Capitalism in Russia*, Lenin intended a) to establish his credentials as an unparalleled expert on the Russian economy and thus ascend to the peak of writerly fame and b) to crush the Populist view that the development of capitalism could and should be stopped and an alternative, agrarian paradise established instead, in which Russians lived in peasant-style communes, free from the tsar while making lots of crafts. Lenin's problem was that, according to the imperial census of 1897, Russia had more than 100 million peasants out of a total population of 128 million, and a mere 2 or 3 million proletarians, a third of whom were only ever employed seasonally, on railroads. Heavily agrarian and lacking a working class, Russia was a long way from meeting the conditions Marx had said were necessary for revolution.

Or so it seemed. Unwilling to accept that the social change he desired should reside in the far future, and contemptuous of any peasant utopia,

Lenin argued that Russian capitalism was not slowly and gradually emerging in piecemeal fashion, but was already in a highly developed state. The ancient and settled peasant way of life that the Populists fantasized could represent a model for Russia was no more; instead, the majority of rural workers had become farm proletarians selling their labor, while there were also smaller groups of kulaks,* who were so ruthlessly effective that they had become the primary market for Russian industrialists with knock-on effects for the rest of the economy. "The Russia of the wooden plough and the flail, of the water-mill and the hand-loom," wrote Lenin, "began rapidly to be transformed into the Russia of the iron plough and the threshing machine, of the steam-mill and the power-loom. An equally thorough transformation of technique is seen in every branch of the national economy where capitalist production predominates."

In Lenin's view, this transformation was "progressive," as capitalism was less inhumane than feudalism, but it also had revolutionary implications. If Russia was already capitalist, then according to Marxist theory, the country was ripe for the first, bourgeois stage of revolution. Once political democracy and civic rights were established in this initial phase, the second, workers' revolution and proletarian dictatorship, would soon follow. Yet Lenin resisted the impulse to deliver a full-throated demand for revolution. His tone instead was confident, but dry and scholarly. Consider for instance this brief excerpt where he explains how wealthy peasants ("kulaks") are accelerating the development of capitalism:

> The predominance of natural economy, which accounts for the scarcity
> and dearness of money in the countryside, results in the assumption of
> an importance by all these "kulaks" out of all proportion to the size of
> their capital. The dependence of the peasants on the money owners
> inevitably acquires the form of bondage. Just as one cannot conceive of
> developed capitalism without large-scale merchant's capital in the form
> of commodities or money so the pre-capitalist village is inconceivable
> without small traders and buyers-up, who are the "masters" of the small
> local markets. Capitalism draws these markets together, combines them
> into a big national market, and then into a world market, destroys the
> primitive forms of bondage and personal dependence, develops in depth

---

* Wealthy peasants (literally, "fists"), a nefarious class in Lenin's and, subsequently, Stalin's demonology.

and in breadth the contradictions which in a rudimentary form are also to be observed among the community peasantry—and thus paves the way for their resolution.

But there was a strategy behind Lenin's aggressively tedious prose. The tsarist censors had form when it came to underestimating the impact of very long, boring works on economics; they had allowed the publication of *Das Kapital*, after all. They found such texts as difficult to get through as most of us and could not imagine that anybody else would be so motivated to do so, or would get fired up by a subtext buried in hundreds of pages of statistics—if they even noticed it was there. By adopting a similarly jargon-laden scholarly approach as Marx, Lenin would get his own interminable "respectable" work of theory into print legally. He avoided rhetorical assaults on tsarism, sticking instead to expositions of theoretical analysis from which the appropriate conclusions could be drawn. He also wrote the book under a pseudonym, "Vladimir Illin," so that the state censor would not realize its author was a political exile. The ruse worked; Lenin successfully placed his magnum opus with a publishing house in Saint Petersburg in the hope that it would reach a much wider readership than it would have via the printing presses of the revolutionary underground.

The Development of Capitalism in Russia went on sale in March 1899, on the eve of the century Lenin would have such an influence over. Decades after his death, his editors at the Institute of Marxism-Leninism would claim that the book was a huge success and that the initial print run of 2,400 sold out very quickly, but in fact it was a flop.* Although in the USSR it was treated as an object of reverence, the few reviews it did receive at the time of its publication were largely negative. Even Robert Tucker's *Lenin Anthology*, a standard compilation since 1975, does not contain an excerpt. Life, after all, is short, and who wants to listen to a bourgeois radical talk himself into believing that Russian agriculture circa 1899 had already ushered in a new era of rapid industrialization? In this instance, the tsar's censors judged the text correctly: *The Development of Capitalism in Russia* was boring, irrelevant and quite harmless.

However, the book does contain the seeds of several key aspects not

---

* Although millions of copies of the book were in circulation in the USSR for the duration of its existence, needless to say.

only of Lenin's rhetorical style but also of the genre of dictator literature that was to emerge over the course of the twentieth century.

First, there is the aggressively dry, theoretical prose, engineered to awe the reader into submission before the mighty intellect on display. Whether or not a mighty intellect really is on display is of secondary importance, and would become less important as dictator literature developed.

The Development of Capitalism in Russia also demonstrates Lenin's willingness to distort reality to suit his own theoretical, political and psychological needs. His mental powers are undeniable but that was the problem: highly intelligent people are wrong all the time, and are especially good at being wrong because they have the cognitive ability to construct elaborate counterfactual arguments that appear to be backed up by judiciously selected and cleverly interpreted evidence. Lenin wanted revolution to occur in his lifetime, and via the ruthless marshaling of statistics and Marxist analysis he duly theorized reality into submission.

Of course it's not unusual for people to select facts and rationalize away discrepancies to support the things they want to be true; most of us do it all the time. But most of us do not dream of seizing power in the largest country on earth. There was something profoundly autocratic in Lenin's assumption that he had the power to overwrite the world, to author the conditions demanded by his theory into existence.

Lenin was—if you will forgive the use of a word borrowed from the arid intellectual wastelands of critical theory—profoundly logocentric.* Fundamentally, he agreed with the author of the Gospel of John: "In the beginning was the Word." His dictatorial heirs, once in power, would follow this faith to its logical conclusion, seeking to reconstruct the world no longer via argument but rather by acts of speech and written composition to utter alternate realities, wholly at odds with material conditions, into being.

IN 1900, LENIN left Siberia. Despite the failure of *The Development of Capitalism in Russia*, he was gradually making a name for himself as a writer;

---

* I use it here more in the sense that Joseph Brodsky did, i.e., referring to the privileging of the word in Russian culture, rather than in its more outré academic applications. Brodsky was talking about poetry, but Lenin and his peers mutated the tradition to place theoretical texts on an altar.

the constant flow of articles from his pen had earned him a short write-up in a prestigious encyclopedia to which many eminent Russian authors contributed entries. But he had a problem: he was banned from living in Moscow, Saint Petersburg or indeed any town with a large student or proletarian population. Preferring to live abroad over spending his days slowly decomposing in the provinces under the watchful eye of the Okhrana, he requested and received permission to leave Russia.

He traveled to Switzerland, where he swiftly found himself some new chairs to sit in, located next to some other chairs occupied by prominent Russian Marxist exiles—including his onetime idol Plekhanov, whom Lenin would soon seek to supplant as the preeminent Russian interpreter of Karl Marx. And of course, he wrote.

Indeed, now that Lenin was abroad, his only means of interacting with Russia was by writing about it and *at* it. To him, this was action, like lobbing bombs at autocrats or robbing banks to fund the cause—only *more* important. Having been personally remade by an encounter with a fictional character in Chernyshevsky's novel, he had eminent justification for believing in the power of the written word. It was time to outline the strategy and tactics for bringing about revolution.

Lenin's next step was to publish an underground revolutionary newspaper. In Russia, Marxism was starting to lose some of its glamour as other political movements coalesced in opposition to the tsar. The Socialist Revolutionary Party, which had its roots in Populist notions of a future based on an idealized vision of peasant life, was founded in 1901. Meanwhile, over in Germany, the Marxist "revisionist" Eduard Bernstein denied that capitalism was about to collapse or that a proletarian revolution would sweep away the forces of repression. Gradual reform, rather than a total overthrow of the existing order, was the way forward.

Lenin's faith was under siege: true Marxism—that is, *his* vision of Marxism—was faithful to Marx's call for violent revolution and the suppression of the bourgeoisie. Something had to be done to prevent the weakening of the idea, the decline of the theory.

In 1900, Lenin had cofounded *Iskra* (or "The Spark") with Plekhanov and several other exiles, although he soon fell out with Plekhanov, who did not want to cede authority to the rising star of Russian Marxism. Edited in Munich and printed (initially) in Leipzig, the plan was to smuggle the paper into Russia, fomenting discord and spreading the "correct" version of dialectical materialist enlightenment from afar. This mighty organ of revolutionary propaganda had only a three-figure print run, appeared sporadically, and addressed the already converted, but it was a start—and Lenin now began to think seriously about the content, practice and function of an underground newspaper. These meditations inspired him to write one of the most influential texts of the twentieth century, which he named after the book that had done more than any other to convert him to the cause of socialism: *What Is to Be Done?* (with the added subtitle *Burning Questions of Our Movement*).

At first, it can be difficult to understand what all the fuss was about. Picking up the book more than a century after its publication, the overwhelming impression is of joining a tedious and obscure argument in medias res. And that is because you are: Lenin is addressing a tiny group of radicals living underground in Russia or in exile abroad who are all reading the same books and journals, squabbling ferociously over whose vision of Marxism is legitimate. However, the style of the squabble immediately makes explicit the fervor of Lenin's belief: he may be addressing what is effectively a tiny group of cultists, but like all rabid millenarians he is convinced that the fate of the world is at stake.

Indeed, for all that he was a sedentary intellectual, the text crackles with his righteous hatreds, his joy in combat, his passion for revolution. It is alive, and his personality lives on inside it. Since *What Is to Be Done?* was published outside Russia it did not have to pass the censor, so Lenin was free to vituperate at will, although, strikingly, he reserves most of his barbs not for the tsar or capitalism, but for other Marxists. His style is awesomely belligerent, a vision of the text as warfare, but it also contains radical juxtapositions of theoretical language with sustained, repetitive, and violent abuse. He is extremely intolerant: his ideological foes, we discover, are wrong about everything, ranging from the question of "Freedom of Criticism" (Lenin is no liberal democrat) to the notion that the workers might be able to organize the revolution spontaneously (an utterly stupid idea). They are all wrong, and not just a little bit wrong or slightly wrong, but "absolutely wrong," guilty of "fundamental error," having "totally failed" to understand some critical point. Some are dismissed from on high with lofty rhetorical flourishes; others are denounced as charging toward a "marsh."

And when Lenin runs out of space for his insults in the main body of the text, he resorts to long footnotes, heaped high with opprobrium. Ah, yes, those footnotes: here, Lenin is particularly self-revealing. They leave no doubt as to what an Internet comment thread hijacked by the Father of the World Proletariat would look like, were Lenin to awake from his chemical slumber and retrieve his brain from the lab where it is stored in cross sections. Intolerant, sarcastic, correct about everything, and hell-bent on having the last word, Lenin was a master troll, king of the flame war. Here is an example of him at play in one of his many footnotes, from section V, part C:

> In his Review of Questions of Theory, Nadezhdin, by the way, made almost no contribution whatever to the discussion of questions of theory, apart, perhaps, from the following passage, a most peculiar one from the "eve-of-the-revolution point of view": "Bernsteinism, on the whole, is losing its acuteness for us at the present moment, as is the question whether Mr. Adamovich will prove that Mr. Struve has already earned a lacing, or, on the contrary, whether Mr. Struve will refute Mr. Adamovich and will refuse to resign—it really makes no difference, because the hour of revolution has struck." One can hardly imagine a more glaring illustration of Nadezhdin's infinite disregard for theory. We have proclaimed "the eve of the revolution," therefore "it really makes no difference" whether or not the orthodox will succeed in finally driving the Critics from their positions! Our wiseacre fails to see that it is precisely during the revolution that we shall stand in need of the results of our theoretical battles with the Critics in order to be able resolutely to combat their *practical* positions!

Revolution is a zero-sum game; reality must submit to a radical overhaul; there is no room for honest disagreement. How can there be? Lenin's goal is to transform the social order, not ameliorate it.

However, Lenin does not just rely on abuse to annihilate his rivals. He is a ruthlessly logical thinker, who advances systematically (section 1, then A, B, C, D, etc.), identifying weak spots and demolishing opposing arguments, although he is not above simply invoking the authority of the prophets Marx and Engels, either. Genghis Khan–like, he seeks to crush his enemies entirely, by any rhetorical means necessary, laying waste to ideological villages, setting fields of theory ablaze.

But *What Is to Be Done?* is more than a full-frontal assault on bad ideas; it also contains a plan of action for the revolutionary movement.

Here Lenin reveals the extent of his faith in the power of the written word. The term *newspaper* is misleading as a description of what Lenin has in mind. Rather, he envisions a mighty theoretical-ideological propaganda transmission machine, using writing as a tool of ideological dissemination and control, to be managed from afar by an elite cadre of professional revolutionaries. In the absence of the barely (or not yet) invented tools of radio, cinema and television, he would do what he could with ink, paper and a printing press.

Take the working class, for instance: it is largely uneducated, its members are mostly ignorant of Marxism, and they are easily seduced by promises of greater material comfort in this world. Utterly frank in his elitism, Lenin denies that the proletariat could evolve into a truly revolutionary force by itself. After all, the workers had no involvement in the development of the "theoretical doctrine of Social Democracy," which Lenin says emerged "as a natural and inevitable outcome of the development of thought among the revolutionary socialist intelligentsia." Proletarian members of the party and potential leaders in particular must thus submit to the guidance of ideologically pure radical intellectuals.

But what if the leaders are far away? They will convey their will and commands via a "newspaper." In fact, the "editorial board" is actually the ideological core of the party, which Lenin envisions as an underground central cell, issuing instructions, raising the party members' ideological consciousness, and generally steering the path of the revolution via splotches of ink on paper. A self-selecting elite, organized and ruthlessly disciplined, this core group of professional revolutionaries will make all the decisions for the party, and communicate them through the "newspaper," to be executed by the external membership. Discipline, order, and obedience to the party line are essential. Outsiders may join the elite, says Lenin, but only if invited by the secret chiefs.

Pyotr Tkachev had also argued for the necessity of a secretive, radical ideological vanguard to steer the revolution. Lenin agreed and, clearly mindful of the fate of his brother, Alexander, stressed the importance of operating deep underground, of mastering the art of conspiracy: "The more secret such an organization is, the stronger and more widespread will be the confidence of the party," he writes. Acting in darkness, its decisions were to be accepted unquestioningly by the rank and file. Indeed, Lenin ascribes awesome powers to newsprint.

The organisation, which will form round this newspaper, the organisation of its *collaborators* (in the broad sense of the word, i.e., all those working for it), will be ready *for everything*, from upholding the honour, the prestige and the continuity of the Party in periods of acute revolutionary "depression" to preparing for, appointing the time for, and carrying out the *nation-wide armed uprising.*

Marx had been vague about the revolution. The proletariat would have some agency in the suppression of the bourgeoisie but his apocalyptic scenario was largely passive: history would transform the world, bringing happiness to the chosen people. Lenin's apocalypse was active: from his chair, he wanted to write the proletariat into the position from which they would seize power and enact the narrative of world transformation.

What Is to Be Done? was published in 1902 and was an immediate sensation in Russia's Marxist underground, enraging Lenin's opponents and firing up readers inspired by his (flattering) conviction that the revolution could and should be hastened by a core group of true believers, a conviction that was expressed with such intensity, such certainty. In fact, so great was the book's success that it established its author's revolutionary identity: "Lenin" was the name on the cover, and Lenin he would remain. The seventeen-year-old boy rebuilt by texts was now a man renamed by a book. Through *What Is to Be Done?*, he had finally succeeded in writing himself the role of Major Figure in Russian Marxism.

He had also changed the course of history. Far, far away, in the mountainous Caucasus region, a young revolutionary named Iosif Dzhugashvili (who would subsequently rename himself Stalin) read it and was inspired. In Lenin, who wrote so passionately of the need for central control and secret plots, Stalin saw the ideal leader for Russian Marxism. And far, far away, in Siberia, Lev Bronstein (who would subsequently rename himself Leon Trotsky) was likewise inspired. Unlike Stalin, however, he would later temper his enthusiasm. Summarizing the book two years after its publication, and after meeting its author, he wrote, "*If anyone rebels against me, it is very bad. If I rebel, then it's good.* Such is the brief and joyous moral of a long and boring book, abounding with quotations, 'international' parallels, artificial diagrams and all the other means of mental anesthesia."

Trotsky also observed, quite accurately, that Lenin's vision of a self-selecting ruling cabal of revolutionaries would lead "to the Party organisation 'substituting' itself for the Party, the Central Committee substituting itself for the Party organisation, and finally the dictator substituting himself for the Central Committee." Thus, in 1904, Trotsky laid out the path from Lenin's pamphlet to the realities of the Stalinist regime—although that did not prevent him from teaming up with Lenin in 1917.

In 1903, Lenin attended the Second Congress of the Russian Social-Democratic Workers' Party, which was held in London to avoid the attentions of the tsar's secret police. However, as he had amply demonstrated in *What Is to Be Done?*, Lenin took less pleasure in attacking capitalism than he did in feuding with fellow Marxists, and he soon engineered a schism within the party.

The core of the dispute was a fight over membership criteria for the Social-Democrats. Lenin insisted upon a Studio 54–style door policy of the utmost strictness, in line with the conspiratorial elitism he advocated in *What Is to Be Done?* His opponents agreed with the need for tight controls—only, not quite so tight. The party split into two factions, with Lenin victorious as the leader of the Bolshevik ("majoritarian") wing, while his opponents, displaying a stunning lack of PR skills, were labeled the Menshevik ("minoritarian") wing, thus enabling their nemesis to define them forever afterward as a tribe of political pygmies. Lenin next extended the domain of struggle via textual warfare, with 1904's *One Step Forward, Two Steps Back*, in which, after spending months poring over the minutes of the meetings in London, he delivered a point-by-point assault upon the Menshevik position, all in his ruthless, scorched-earth style ("political spinelessness," "ludicrous," "fetishist worship of casuistry," etc.). The Menshevik leaders (who, after all, were members of the same party and so thought they were united against a common foe) were outraged. They did not yet know who they were dealing with.

In 1894, Nikolai II had inherited the imperial throne from his father, Tsar Alexander III. A man of mediocre intelligence and great stubbornness, Tsar Nikolai was more interested in domestic life than affairs of state, although he took his role very seriously—as the divinely appointed "father" of the Russian people, he believed it was his sacred duty to resist change and preserve the autocracy.

Events, however, were conspiring against him.

In 1904, for instance, Japan launched a surprise attack on a Russian naval base in China, after Nikolai rejected a Japanese proposal for dividing

Korea and Manchuria into mutual spheres of influence. Nikolai was shocked that the Japanese did not have the good manners to declare war first, but he and his advisers soon realized that this presented them with an opportunity for a quick, victorious conflict that would boost patriotic feeling and unite the people behind him. That was the plan, anyway. Instead, a humiliating defeat ensued when, in May 1905, the Japanese navy sank or captured much of the Russian Baltic fleet at the Battle of Tsushima, and Russia was forced to sue for peace.

Meanwhile, Nikolai faced mounting domestic unrest from an exhausted, hungry, impoverished populace. There were protests, there was terrorism; there were strikes and riots. On January 22, 1905, thousands of workers together with their wives and children marched peacefully toward the Winter Palace, the tsar's grandiose residence in Saint Petersburg, to present a petition for reform. But the tsar was away, enjoying some relaxing games of dominoes at his opulent country estate south of the capital.

The guards at the palace gates charged the protesters on horseback. Then they shot at them, killing forty and injuring hundreds, while thousands fled for their lives. Afterward, an enraged mob sixty thousand strong rampaged throughout the city, smashing, burning and looting. The authorities shot more people; by the end of "Bloody Sunday," the body count had risen to two hundred, with a further eight hundred wounded, and the tsar, in the eyes of many, was a cold-blooded butcher.

Strikes, protests, uprisings, riots and mutinies now spread across the empire—to Poland, Finland, the Baltics and Georgia. Ultranationalist, anti-Semitic "Black Hundred" groups loyal to the tsar retaliated with pogroms and ultraviolence, but the revolutionary situation continued to escalate. In October, a general strike broke out, and revolutionary governments known as "soviets" formed in Saint Petersburg, Moscow and elsewhere.

After ten months of this, even the not terribly bright Nikolai II realized that Russia was teetering on the edge of an abyss. Advisers pressured him to issue the "October Manifesto," which promised Russia her first elected parliament and civil liberties such as freedom of speech and freedom of the press. These proposals were aimed at liberals rather than revolutionaries, but promising to step away from absolutism to a form of constitutional monarchy was enough to avert catastrophe. With the tsar's more moderate critics thus mollified, the opposition split and, fragmented, lost its momentum.

And where was Lenin in this flux? Nowhere near it, in fact: he was in Switzerland, as he did not want to risk arrest by returning to Russia. What was he doing? Why, sitting in a chair and writing, of course—attempting to steer the revolution from afar, via prose.

In June and July, he wrote *Two Tactics of Social-Democracy in the Democratic Revolution*, another attack on the Mensheviks, who were willing to accept a bourgeois government of the type proposed by liberal reformers. Lenin opposed this with his usual vehemence, arguing instead that Bolsheviks should seize control of the popular insurrection and, under the guidance of the Marxist revolutionary elite, establish a "democratic dictatorship of the proletariat and the peasantry." In October, when the tsar issued his manifesto, Lenin argued for further destabilizing Russia through megaviolence. In *Tasks of Revolutionary Army Contingents*, he urged revolutionaries to arm themselves "as best they can," with actual and makeshift weapons, including "rifles, revolvers, bombs, knives, knuckledusters, sticks, rags soaked in kerosene for starting fires, ropes or rope ladders, shovels for building barricades, pyroxylin cartridges, barbed wire, nails [against cavalry], etc., etc."

Is that the best use of "etc." in the history of humanity? It might be. There is something extraordinarily casual about it, a disinterested detachment from the reality of physical violence, possible because Lenin had never participated in it himself. But he is not finished: he also talks about liberating prisoners, seizing funds, killing members of the regime, and maximizing antigovernment chaos in order to exacerbate the crisis. And although Lenin leaves it to his troops to fill in the precise details, our armchair terrorist is not entirely without imagination himself. Specifically, he suggests that pouring acid on policemen is a good idea. And then, at the end he declares:

> Revolutionary army groups must at once find out who organises the Black Hundreds and where and how they are organised, and then, without confining themselves to propaganda (which is useful, but inadequate) they must act with armed force, beat up and kill the members of the Black-Hundred gangs, blow up their headquarters, etc., etc.

Actually, *that* "etc.," so glib in its casual endorsement of killing, is the best one in the history of humanity.

Lenin returned to Russia in November 1905, once a political amnesty was in place and called for an armed uprising. Even amid the chaos, he showed remarkable focus and attention to detail, particularly when it came to texts. For instance, he saw that it was necessary to immediately define in writing the correct Marxist response to Russia's incipient press freedoms—what *should* literature written with the party imprimatur look like? In *The Party Organization and Party Literature*, published on November 13, 1905, he combined his usual tedious denunciations of ideological opponents with a demand for a unified, politically targeted approach: "Down with non-partisan writers! Down with literary super-men!" he declares. "Literature must become *part* of the common cause of the proletariat, a 'cog and a screw' of one single great Social-Democratic mechanism set in motion by the entire politically-conscious vanguard of the entire working class."

Initially, Lenin first appears to endorse freedom of the pen ("Everyone is free to write whatever he likes, without any restrictions"), but he adds the significant caveats that party literature is subordinate to party control and that anybody who writes against the party will be ejected. Then he dismisses freedom as essentially meaningless in a bourgeois society predicated upon exploitation of the masses: "The freedom of the bourgeois writer, artist or actress is simply masked (or hypocritically masked) dependence on the money-bag, on corruption, on prostitution." True freedom will exist only under socialism, and only the books of that new world will enrich "the last word in the revolutionary thought of mankind with the experience and living work of the socialist proletariat." In the meantime, every news-paper, journal and publishing house that calls itself "Social-Democratic" must integrate itself into party organizations. It is not difficult to see where this leads, of course—and it led there.

Meanwhile, Lenin continued to delight in conspiracy, even siding with the Mensheviks against his own Bolshevik faction when, following the failure of the uprising, he argued that the Russian Social-Democratic Party should put up candidates for election to the new parliament, the Duma. But the moment for the transformation of Russia had not yet come. By March 1906, Nikolai II was already reneging on his promises, and arguing that the deliberations of the Duma did not apply to him. In April he issued the "Fundamental Laws of the Russian Empire," decreeing that only he could appoint ministers, and that only he could dismiss them. Also, he could dissolve the Duma at will and hold new elections if he felt like it—and it had not even yet met. His prime minister Pyotr Stolypin cracked down on Russia's radicals and terrorists, among whom the Bolsheviks were (during this period) only ever bit players.

Lenin's "etc." notwithstanding, far more extreme revolutionary groups were responsible for most of the violence. These fanatics exulted under a selection of names as suited to black metal bands formed by Scandinavian adolescents as to political organizations, such as "Terror," "Death for Death," "Black Cloud" and "Black Ravens." These groups assassinated governors, policemen, soldiers and civil servants and blew up statues and burned churches to the ground, until newspapers stopped reporting on the atrocities out of numbness. Russia was no stranger to political violence, but whereas the nineteenth-century terror in which Lenin's brother had attempted to participate led to around one hundred deaths over a twenty-five-year period, between 1905 and 1907 alone, terrorists killed or wounded nine thousand people, nearly five thousand of whom were civilians, according to the historian Anna Geifman.

The state responded with its own violence—between 1906 and 1907, Stolypin executed more than a thousand radicals. And as it often does, violence solved the problem. Or at the very least, it took the edge off the situation. The moment of crisis passed, some limited reforms were granted, and Nikolai retained his grip on power. At the end of 1907, Lenin, fearing arrest, fled the country, returning to his chair, to his life as an author, forced to write the script for the characters in his revolutionary drama in Stockholm, in Berlin, in Geneva. But was the revolution all inside his head, or was it actually a thing that might occur in the physical world?

IN FACT, FOR many years, faith in a world-transforming cataclysmic uprising led by the Bolsheviks did indeed look a lot like a form of psychosis, as Lenin was beset by crises from within and without the party.

Lenin's insistence that the Social Democrats should participate in elections to the new parliament had led to a schism within the Bolsheviks as a rival theoretician, Alexander Bogdanov, led a faction demanding armed resistance instead. By 1908, Lenin's authority was dwindling, and only *Materialism and Empiriocriticism*—a hastily composed work of epistemology more remarkable for the savagery of its attacks on Bogdanov's theoretical output than any particular philosophical insights—prevented disaster. Lenin's rhetorical violence won the day, and Bogdanov was duly ejected from the Bolshevik Central Committee.

However, although he was back in control, Lenin still faced serious problems. The tsarist regime had reasserted itself, Mensheviks outnumbered Bolsheviks, and the situation looked so hopeless that in 1909 a new faction emerged from amid the Social Democrats—"Liquidationists" who argued that the party should abolish itself. Lenin responded with yet another paper-and-ink drubbing in his angry pamphlet *The Liquidation of Liquidationists* (1909). But the Liquidationists were right about one thing: the party was not thriving.

To put things in perspective, consider that in 1907 the Social-Democratic Party had a membership of around 150,000. The Skopts, a millenarian sect who believed that salvation would come once they had managed to castrate 144,000 people, had around 100,000 members during the same period. Even at its peak, then, Marxism was not that much more popular than crushing men's testicles between hot plates, a method of castration practiced by the sect. By 1910, it was much less popular, as membership of the Russian Social-Democrats had dropped to 10,000: it took a combination of both its squabbling factions to equal a tenth of the Skopts' total.

Still, Lenin's faith was undimmed, and just as the Skopts continued destroying genitals in the hope that they might thus realize their millenarian dream, so he kept on writing in pursuit of his own, possessed by an indestructible, absolute faith in the coming revolution. Hundreds of thousands of words flowed from his fingertips, as he wrote against rivals, as he wrote against the tsar, against imperialists, against liberals, abruptly changing his tactics whenever the historical situation demanded it, as he sought to inscribe his dream upon history.

This required immense self-belief. In 1924, Karl Radek, a participant in the 1905 revolution and later leader of the Comintern,* said that Lenin was "the first man who believed in what he wrote, not as something that would happen in a hundred years, but as a concrete thing." This was why he was able to "overcome all wavering and carry the Party into the struggle for power." Strident, staccato, charged with a throbbing, pulsating, angry energy, Lenin's prose carries along the reader willing to submit to it—like fate, like destiny. Read Lenin, and he attempts to possess you. And if that's

---

* The Communist International, an organization advocating world communism headquartered in Moscow and subject to the authority of the Kremlin.

what he can do as a paper-and-ink phantom, imagine what it was like when he was still alive, if you actually shared in his hatreds and believed in the prophecies, and surrendered as the text-Lenin reached up from the page to hand you the crack pipe of revolution for another hit of the good shit.

STUCK IN EXILE, but still leader of his dwindling Marxist sect, Lenin did not keep calm, but he carried on. In the first half of 1914, he wrote *The Right of Nations to Self-Determination* in which he advocated the breaking up of the great empires. Here he proclaimed:

> Complete equality of rights for all nations; the right of nations to self-determination; the unity of the workers of all nations—such is the national programme that Marxism, the experience of the whole world, and the experience of Russia, teach the workers.

Stirring stuff—for a middle-aged scribbler who hadn't changed his core political beliefs since he was seventeen. However, history was about to catch up with Lenin. On June 28, 1914, Gavrilo Princip shot the Austrian archduke Franz Ferdinand, setting in motion the chain of events leading to the First World War. Lenin was caught unawares, but he knew what to do: write, of course. In *Socialism and War* (1915), he argued that soldiers from different nations should stop killing each other and instead revolt against their leaders; and this when the majority of socialists in Europe and Russia were succumbing to the vice of patriotism. Lenin replied to his critics with *Imperialism, the Highest Stage of Capitalism* (written 1916, published 1917), in which he "proved" that to support a side in the war was to support capitalism, and a betrayal of Marxist principles.

Yet in spite of the carnage, and even as the old European order teetered on the brink of collapse, Lenin tentatively revised his apocalyptic timetable. In a lecture delivered in Zurich in January 1917, he expressed certainty that the war would lead to "popular uprisings under the leadership of the proletariat against the power of finance capital, against the big banks, against the capitalists," and that these upheavals could not end except with "the expropriation of the bourgeoisie, with the victory of socialism." Nevertheless, he ended with an uncharacteristic expression of doubt. Now forty-six years old, Lenin was no longer certain that this defining moment of violent upheaval was quite as imminent as he had maintained over two and a half decades of revolutionary activity; indeed, it might happen after he was dead and gone. "We of the older generation may not live to see the decisive battles of this coming revolution," he told his audience. It would be the happy lot of socialist youth to witness the transformation of the world.

But a month later, the decisive battles began. A month after that, the tsar abdicated. A month after that, Lenin caught the train to Russia. And what did he do on the journey? He wrote, of course, hammering out his *April Theses*, in which he advocated a swift move to a revolutionary dictatorship, even though the transitional phase of bourgeois democracy, allegedly essential according to theory, had only just gotten under way. Having suffered his brief moment of doubt, Lenin was intent on accelerating Russia's destiny.

Lenin had not lived in Russia since 1907, but he was convinced that he understood the revolutionary situation better than everybody else. He had barely disembarked from his cabin at Petrograd's* Finland Station when he lambasted his fellow Bolsheviks for being far too cautious. Stalin, just released from a long period of Siberian exile and now a senior Bolshevik himself, thought Lenin's talk was crazy; most of the party elite agreed. The Mensheviks declared the *April Theses* a recipe for carnage and bloodshed.

Lenin was not to be dissuaded. In a flood of articles (and the occasional speech), he denounced the Provisional Government as the worthless tool of imperialism. Marxists and proletarians, he said, must unite. High on apocalypse, Lenin succumbed to revolutionary graphomania, spewing forth no fewer than forty-eight articles for *Pravda* in May 1917. Unwilling to leave revolution to Marx's historical forces, he insisted that the Bolsheviks had to fight to bring this new world into being. This was the moment of millennial fulfillment, when the wicked would be punished and the righteous rewarded, and the workers would inherit the earth.

Yet even in this fever pitch of excitement, Lenin remained a shrewd operator, an unusual mixture of fanatic and pragmatist. He realized that ideas that had seemed so compelling on the train from Zurich might actually incur the resistance of the peasantry, whose support the Bolsheviks needed. Thus he was willing to drop the policy of immediate land nationalization outlined in his *April Theses*, as he was aware it had little

---

* The Germanic-sounding "Sankt Peterburg" (as it is pronounced in Russian) was Russified during World War I as a patriotic measure.

support from people who actually lived on the land. Apocalyptic dreamer Lenin listened to the advice of strategist Lenin.

Amid the chaos, he steered a firm course toward transformation. After all those years agitating for the revolution on paper, he now applied his ideas to actual events. He called for an immediate withdrawal from the war, which the Provisional Government was still fighting. He also spent time talking to workers, soldiers and sailors. But then things got out of hand, as the world proved to be less easy to manipulate than pen and ink.

Lenin was concerned that if the Bolsheviks staged a coup, they might peak too soon and the revolution would fail. The soldiers, sailors and workers loyal to the Bolsheviks, however, had heard Lenin's slogan "All power to the Soviets" and had assumed he meant it. And so on July 4, 1917, twenty thousand sailors left their base in search of a leader for the revolution and amassed outside Bolshevik headquarters, expecting to be told that the time had come to storm the Tauride Palace, seat of the Provisional Government. Lenin stepped out onto the balcony and reassured the horde that the revolution was coming—only, not yet. Then he disappeared, leaving the mob wondering how and when. But Lenin was a writer, not an orator. He had nothing more to say.

The crowd stormed the palace anyway, but Lenin was correct: it *was* too soon. The putsch failed, and the next day, newspapers appeared on the streets denouncing Lenin as a German spy, while the Provisional Government issued a warrant for his arrest. Stalin shaved off Lenin's goatee, and then the Father of the World Proletariat popped a wig on his head and fled across the border into Finland (in those days, a Russian territory, but not a very loyal one).

For most people, a disaster such as this, occurring as Lenin stood on the cusp of fulfilling the revolution, would have been a catastrophe or, at the very least, excellent cause to lie unmoving in a darkened room for a week or two. But Lenin, indomitable as ever, just did what he always did. He wrote.

He now resolved to do what Marx had failed to do: he would describe the postrevolutionary world—what it would look like, how it would function, how the people in it would live. He had been thinking about this since 1916, and had made a few preliminary sketches that summer. Marx had been a poor futurologist, offering little more than the grand pronouncements of the *Communist Manifesto* and, later, the phrase "the dictatorship of proletariat," which he borrowed from his friend and fellow revolutionary Joseph Weydemeyer. Friedrich Engels, for his part, had added that the state would ultimately "wither away." Lenin stepped in to fill the eschato-logical void. The result was *The State and Revolution*, a title he lifted from Tkachev, just as he had borrowed *What Is to Be Done?* from Chernyshevsky.

So what did he see coming in the future? Well, there would be violence: lots of it, in fact. Says Lenin: "[V]iolent revolution lies at the root of the entire theory of Marx and Engels." This probably would have come as a surprise to both men. Although neither of them was immune to fantasies involving the destruction of the bourgeoisie or, in Engels's case, of entire peoples, they never declared that violence was the *core* aspect of their thought. Marx's revolution was largely passive, emerging as a "natural" result of historically determined crises. The sacralization of the smiting fist was Lenin's idea, and having embraced it, he was characteristically frank in his admission that, during the transitional phase from capitalism to communism, there would be a need for "severe discipline," that is, vio-lent suppression of the class enemy, and that the entire apparatus of the bourgeois state would have to be "smashed." The third-century Christian theologian Tertullian promised his readers that, once in paradise, they would enjoy watching the torments of the damned; so too Lenin offered his readers the satisfaction of knowing that they would soon experience the exquisite delight of watching the objects of their hatred receive just punishment in the world to come.

What would replace the smashed state? Well, not a state, says Lenin. This is because, per Engels, *state* is not some neutral term describing a means for organizing society but rather the medium through which "the most powerful, economically dominant class," the bourgeoisie, "becomes the politically dominant class," thus acquiring "new means of holding down and exploiting the oppressed class." Because the proletariat would be in charge after the revolution, and exploitation would (of course) have vanished from the face of the earth, then the state, which is merely an engine of oppression, would cease to exist. Whatever organizational structures remained, they would not be a "state." Clear?

The problem, of course, was that it was difficult to imagine what a post-revolutionary world would look like, as nobody had ever lived in one—or, at least, not for very long. Lenin thus leaned very heavily on Marx and Engels's interpretation of the Paris Commune of 1871, in which for a couple of months "the people" took over the running of the city from the bosses, and only intervention by the forces of reaction prevented a new, fairer world free from exploitation from emerging. After all, a two-month-long failed experiment in radical egalitarian living is clearly the best indicator of how men and women will all live together in the future, overriding all empirical evidence of how they have lived prior to that moment. This, in fact, is the most interesting part of *The State and Revolution*, as Lenin, so good at practical tactics and the art of the attack, so cynical in his maneuverings, suddenly switches to optimist mode and attempts to delineate the positive qualities of the future world of happy proletarians. "There is no utopianism in Marx, in the sense that he made up or invented a new society," says Lenin, which is true insofar as he left out the details. Meanwhile, by referring to Paris, Lenin is able to claim that his stargazing is in fact based on evidence, and in doing so he lapses into complete absurdity.

What does it mean to say that the state will "wither away"? It is all remarkably simple:

> A beginning can and must be made at once, overnight, to replace the specific "bossing" of state officials by the simple functions of "foremen and accountants," functions which are already fully within the ability of the average town dweller and can well be performed for "workmen's wages."

Yes: in the future, pretty much anyone will be able to perform the tasks necessary for the organization of society. The will to power, the desire to dominate others and to amass wealth will vanish. Lenin continues:

> Accounting and control—that is mainly what is needed for the "smooth working," for the proper functioning, of the first phase of communist society. All citizens are transformed into hired employees of the state, which consists of the armed workers. All citizens become employees and workers of a single countrywide state "syndicate."

So long as everybody knows a bit of basic arithmetic and can read, the Bolsheviks will have this running-the-world thing sorted out in no time:

> All that is required is that they should work equally, do their proper share of work, and get equal pay; the accounting and control necessary for this have been simplified by capitalism to the utmost and reduced to the extraordinarily simple operations—which any literate person can perform—of supervising and recording, knowledge of the four rules of arithmetic, and issuing appropriate receipts.

Here we see a major drawback of putting a professional revolutionary/ writer in charge of a country. Lenin had never had a proper job: funded initially by his parents, and then by his writings and the party, he had no idea what it was actually like outside the insular world of radical politics. Later, he would come to see the need for administrators, but at this moment he is so intoxicated by the dream that he prophesies everybody will do the right thing, because . . . well, because they'll *get used to it*:

> In striving for socialism, however, we are convinced that it will develop into communism and, therefore, that the need for violence against people in general, for the subordination of one man to another, and of one section of the population to another, will vanish altogether since people will become accustomed to observing the elementary conditions of social life without violence and without subordination.

He declares, "Under socialism all will govern in turn and soon become accustomed to no-one governing." All his cynicism, violence, and ferocious critical reasoning melt away to reveal the mushiest utopianism. But who shall clean toilets? That question goes unasked.

The State and Revolution is an important book. It exposes, in stark relief, the power of a millenarian fantasy to scramble the critical faculties of a brilliant, acutely analytical mind. Lenin, a genius of revolution, who read the chaos of his times better than anyone and who successfully changed the course of history, was inspired to do so by hokum—and he used his mighty intellect to persuade himself and others of that hokum. Decades after the collapse of the USSR, *The State and Revolution* still serves as a cautionary tale regarding the capacity of highly intelligent people to deceive themselves about the most fundamental things.

Lenin had done this in a sophisticated way early in his career, with the statistical assault on reality in *The Development of Capitalism in Russia*. Now he cast aside the facts and figures in favor of wild extrapolations based on an experiment in living that had lasted for three months in a French city in 1871. Faith does not so much override reason as enslave it and then exploit it to erect fantastical pyramids constructed out of sheer desire.

After reading *The State and Revolution* it's impossible to be surprised that the USSR turned out so badly. Marx's laws of history were imaginary, and Lenin's postrevolutionary vision was an absurdity, but Lenin had invested decades of his life chasing this utopia. He believed in it with all his considerable will. What was he going to do, abandon it? Hardly. In *The State and Revolution*, he points out that Marx granted him the latitude of the transitional period during which the "dictatorship of the proletariat" would suppress resistance through just and necessary force. Before the revolution had even begun, Lenin established an excellent means for indefinitely postponing the recognition of his dream's failure, and if people had to die to preserve that state of perpetual denial, then that was okay, too. Marx had foretold that it would happen—for the future happiness of all mankind, of course.

And so you can read the classified documents Lenin wrote after the revolution, but that waited seventy years for declassification, and find him still writing about the imminence of social revolution in western Europe into the 1920s; or arguing for the formation of an army to invade Poland to help this revolution along; or talking about the need to exterminate Cossacks, to burn Baku to the ground, to shoot priests and launch the Red Terror—yes, you can read all the material that was suppressed by the Soviet regime for decades and draw the conclusion that Lenin really was a nasty bit of work. But *The State and Revolution*, by its sheer ludicrous emptiness, made it clear in advance that the violence Lenin and his successors did ultimately wreak upon their subjects in the Soviet Union was always going to happen.

And Lenin just kept on writing. After the revolution he continued to write polemics against enemies, including such texts as *The Proletarian Revolution and the Renegade Kautsky* (1918), in which he defends dictatorship in a diatribe targeted at a German Marxist he once admired; or *"Left-Wing" Communism: An Infantile Disorder* (1920), in which he inveighs against anarchists and other ultraleftists. He also added new modes of writing to his oeuvre: streams of official decrees, proclamations, and death orders.

And in power, and even after power, his faith that writing could alter reality remained overwhelming. It was so strong, in fact, that almost immediately after the revolution, he moved to establish party control over the written word.* This also required the banning of harmful words and

---

* Lenin issued his Decree on the Press two days after the October Revolution, instituting censorship as a "temporary measure." However, restrictions on the "bourgeois press" soon spread, and by the end of 1918 all non-Bolshevik papers were suppressed, while several

the very first lists of forbidden books were drawn up by his wife, Krupskaya. She was so assiduous that she included not only the Bible but also children's books among the ranks of dangerous texts.*

And it was so strong that even after he suffered two debilitating strokes, and was forced to leave his Kremlin office and retreat to a chair (with wheels) in a house in the countryside outside Moscow, he still thought that via a simple memo he could rewrite the structure of the USSR's governing bodies and neutralize the disciple he had come to perceive as a threat to all he had built, and who now occupied a seat at the heart of the party. In a document that came to be known as Lenin's Testament, he wrote:

> Stalin is too rude, and this defect becomes intolerable in a Secretary General. That is why I suggest that the comrades think about a way of removing Stalin from that post.

Rudeness, of course, was the least of Stalin's sins. But it was too late. Lenin's pen had lost its power, while Stalin, the formerly obscure activist from the Caucasus, was already consolidating his. And as the next supreme author of the Soviet Union, he would inscribe a new chapter in the revolution's history, and in the history of dictator literature.

---

agencies supervised what was permissible in the realms of literature, libraries, and education. By 1922, a "Main Press Committee" consolidated all press censorship, while the bureaucrats of "Glavlit" decided what was permissible in literature and art.

* Krupskaya was also subsequently treated as a supertheorist; an eleven-volume set of her writings on education was published in the 1960s.

2

Stalin

*Stalin, poet of pretty flowers
and moonbeams*

Lenin's body, abandoned by that apocalyptic yearning and fiery, life-giving hatred, lay in state in the House of Trade Unions in central Moscow, restfully decomposing. The crowd outside waited for hours in the ice and snow to enter the Hall of Columns, once a location for elegant balls, now repurposed as a showroom for the most eminent of the Soviet dead. The mourners shuffled past the remains in solemn tribute. What would happen next, now that the renowned author of *What Is to Be Done?* had joined Marx and Engels in the pantheon of socialist saints?

As for the future, that was unwritten, but Stalin already had plans for the corpse. Shortly after an ailing Lenin's last visit to the Kremlin in October 1923, Stalin had suggested to the members of the Politburo that to simply abandon Lenin's body would be a waste of a potent symbol. Stalin had studied in a seminary in his native Georgia and knew that the masses hungered after the sacred. They liked miracles, and revered holy relics. Why not beat the Church at its own game and preserve Lenin, putting his corpse on display?

Lev Trotsky, Lev Kamenev, and Nikolai Bukharin, three highly powerful Bolshevik leaders, were appalled by Stalin's macabre proposal, as was Lenin's widow, Krupskaya, when word about it got out. Kamenev argued that Lenin's body of work was more important than his actual *body* and proposed printing "millions of copies of his works" as a tribute instead. Preserving the actual body smacked of the "priest mongering" Lenin had despised.

But Stalin saw the value in both bodies, and when Lenin finally gave up the ghost on January 21, 1924, his argument triumphed. The Bolsheviks might not be able to defeat death, but they could at least stop the rot. Lenin's body was placed in a frozen hole in the dirt on Red Square to keep it intact while crowds shuffled past. Meanwhile, a debate raged among the members of the Committee for the Immortalization of Lenin's Memory over how best to preserve the remains of the dead leader before decomposition became too severe. Via freezing, like a mammoth in Siberia? Immersion in a chemical soup? Or some kind of embalming?

Eventually, they decided to embalm him, like the pharaoh Tutankhamun, whose tomb had recently been opened in Egypt. But this was just the first step, and a comparatively trivial one. It took only two months to find a scientist capable of preserving Lenin's body, and the USSR would have survived without its modernist mummy. It was far more important, and a lot more difficult, to assert the same authority over Lenin's vast body of work; but Stalin intended to do that also.

IOSIF DZHUGASHVILI, A.K.A. JOSEPH Stalin,* emerged squalling from his mother's womb in 1878 in the mountainous town of Gori, Georgia. This

---

* Stalin, like Lenin, had a multitude of pseudonyms throughout his life. His mother called him "Soso," his revolutionary peers called him "Koba," and he had many other names besides. For the sake of simplicity, in this book he is "Stalin" throughout.

was the periphery of the Russian Empire, the very definition of provincial obscurity. For centuries, Ottoman and Persian emperors had passed the once-mighty Christian kingdom between them until a Georgian monarch appealed to Catherine the Great for protection. Protection was granted, and then, a few decades later, the Russians installed a military governor. A process of annexation and absorption climaxed less than two decades before Stalin's birth, when the empire gobbled up the kingdom once and for all.

As for Gori, it was one of the oldest settlements in Georgia, dating back to the seventh century, but other than that, it was unexceptional. There was an old fortress, and blood feuds among clans that raged for generations. But this was ordinary violence: part of the culture, absorbed by the locals like the melodies of the local folk songs. Stalin, too, was unexceptional. Nothing suggested that the baby was destined for a career as a mass-murdering tyrant, let alone future editor of the worldwide bestseller *History of the Communist Party of the Soviet Union (Bolsheviks): Short Course.* His father, Vissarion, was a cobbler by trade and a drunk by vocation, while his mother, Ketevan, or Keke, worked as a laundrywoman and house cleaner. Both parents beat Stalin, until the day Vissarion walked out on the family; then the responsibility for Stalin's beatings lay on Keke's shoulders alone.

Had it not been for Stalin's mother, he may not have amounted to much more than a drunk like his father. Stalin's siblings had all died, and Keke's great ambition in life was that her gift from God should become a priest. Through her connections, she pulled enough strings to wangle ten-year-old Stalin into the local church school in Gori. Normally, only the children of priests could attend, and if the church had stuck to its rules then Stalin would not have learned to read or speak Russian, the medium through which he would later read Marx and Lenin and become a revolutionary.

Indeed, illiteracy is not necessarily a bad thing, as the example of Stalin demonstrates. Teaching him to read was clearly an error of world-historical proportions: in this case, we can easily revise the famous hypothetical ethical dilemma "If you had a time machine, would you kill baby Hitler?" into a scenario free from moral quandaries. Whereas many of us might hesitate to kill an infant cooing in the cradle even if it were Hitler, with Stalin, the situation is different. His lowly social origins should have prevented him from receiving an education. Therefore, a time traveler intent on preventing the deaths of millions would only need to persuade the brothers at the church school to stick to their rules. A generous donation to the local parish would probably do the trick: no books, no problem.

Alas, Stalin graduated at age fifteen with excellent marks. Keke pulled more strings and got him into the Spiritual Seminary in Georgia's capital, Tbilisi, then known as Tiflis. What she didn't know was that although the goal of the seminary was to transform their teenage charges into dedicated enforcers of religious orthodoxy throughout the land, it was actually successful at churning out atheist revolutionaries. All secular reading material was banned, so the students naturally sought it out, and were "corrupted" regardless.

Not that Stalin's early reading material seems particularly alarming to twenty-first-century eyes. He had good taste, and the books he enjoyed are still regarded as classics today. He appreciated Georgian classical poetry and Russian literature. He read Tolstoy, Pushkin, Chekhov, the grotesque satires of Nikolai Gogol and the caustic satires of Mikhail Saltykov-Shchedrin. He devoured Dostoyevsky's *The Devils*, an interesting choice for a future revolutionary, as Russia's radicals are portrayed within its pages as deranged, megalomaniacal, murderous perverts. Perhaps Stalin, the future master plotter, enjoyed the book's vivid portrayal of conspiratorial movements. Or perhaps, as a teenage boy, he simply enjoyed the carnage and death.

Also on Stalin's reading list were the great French writers/social critics Balzac, Zola, Maupassant, and Hugo, all eminently ossified classics today. Stalin was especially fond of *Ninety-Three*, Hugo's novel of revolutionary terror—again, an interesting choice. The novel features a character called Cimourdain, a priest turned revolutionary who sits on a tribunal issuing orders for his foes to be guillotined, a rather extreme case of literary foreshadowing in which the text prefigures one particular reader's personal transformation. But *Ninety-Three* may have had other lessons for the young seminarian. The book's title refers to 1793, the year in which the Jacobins launched the Terror, an eleven-month orgy of beheading and general slaughter during which tens of thousands perished in order to preserve a vaguely defined utopia.

Hugo's radical heroes are engaged in the violent suppression of a "reactionary" uprising in the rural French region of the Vendée. In Hugo's eyes, these Breton "savages" were counterrevolutionaries attempting to block mankind's glorious march toward infinite future happiness. He thus took a blood-soaked reality and transformed it via literature into an alluring myth. A third of the population died in the Vendée, roughly equivalent to Pol Pot's death toll in Cambodia. Stalin would later enlist writers to similarly recast an epoch replete with horrific acts of violence as an epic age of historical transformation; and while it does seem a bit of a stretch to imagine that, at age fifteen, Stalin was reading Victor Hugo and reflecting on how literature can be used to manipulate and conceal history, it's striking nonetheless that he was drawn to a book that demonstrates how well novels can serve the Beautiful Lie.

But Stalin's favorite book was *The Patricide*, by Alexander Kazbegi, a Georgian noble-cum-shepherd who enjoyed bothering his fellow shepherds with a bear he kept on a chain. Kazbegi wrote melodramas packed with indigenous cultural detail that sold well enough to make him Georgia's first professional author; or at least they did until the imperial censor banned them for being too critical of tsarism. Impoverished and desperate, Kazbegi died at age forty-five in 1893 of the syphilis he had contracted while studying in Moscow during his youth.

The hero of *The Patricide* is Koba, a Robin Hood–style bandit who joins a group of outlaws to fight the Russians and their local aristocrat collaborators in defense of the poor but noble mountain dwellers. This was Stalin's *What Is to Be Done?*, not a turgid ultradidactic novel—although he enjoyed Chernyshevsky's work, too—but a violent, romantic yarn of blood feuds, vigilante justice, and the forceful appropriation of other people's property. Stalin identified so strongly with Koba that he bestowed the name upon himself and used it more than any other revolutionary pseudonym prior to 1917. Later, a friend would recall, "Koba became Soso's god and gave his life meaning. He called himself 'Koba' and insisted we call him that. His face shone with pride and pleasure when we called him 'Koba.'" Thus, while Lenin's literary hero Rakhmetev embodied a vision of radicalism and modernity, Stalin's was a man of the mountains, of ancient struggles, and of eternal, transcendent justice. The future butcher was a romantic at heart.

In fact, Stalin had so much romance in his soul that he wrote poems. Here is one, entitled "Morning":

> The rose's bud had blossomed out
> Reaching out to touch the violet
> The lily was waking up
> And bending its head in the breeze

High in the clouds the lark
Was singing a chirruping hymn
While the joyful nightingale
With a gentle voice was saying—

"Be full of blossom, oh lovely land
Rejoice Iverians' country
And you oh Georgian by studying
Bring joy to your motherland."

Of course, in translation, it is difficult to tell if it is any good. All that wittering on about flowers, birds and the Motherland sounds like excruciatingly conventional nineteenth-century pabulum of the sort churned out by countless small-nation minor poets that most of us are happy to go to the grave without knowing that they ever existed, never mind reading what they wrote. Stalin at least has the excuse of youth: he was only fifteen, and so can be forgiven for leaning heavily on creaky tropes.

Still, the pubescent seminarian impressed his peers. When Stalin visited the offices of Georgia's most prestigious literary journal, *Iveria*, to show his work, the magazine's editor, Prince Ilia Chavchavadze (himself a highly esteemed poet), immediately accepted five poems for publication. *Kvali*, a socialist journal, accepted another. In fact, "Morning" was so highly regarded that before the revolution, while Stalin was an obscure revolutionary, it was selected for inclusion in a popular school textbook, *Mother Tongue*, and there it remained until the 1960s, sometimes attributed to Stalin, sometimes not.

According to Stalin's English translator Donald Rayfield, the poetry is actually good, in its fusion of the Persian and Georgian and Byzantine poetic traditions, combined with a certain facility with imagery and quality of language.* When Stalin attuned his soul to the vibrations of pretty flowers and the splendor of his native environment, his words took flight. It is nice to imagine that had he not been seduced by the apocalyptic sim-

---

* At the very least, Stalin was a much more talented poet than Lenin, whose sole contribution to the world of verse appears to have been an ode dedicated to the village where he spent his Siberian exile. It starts like this:
In Shushenskoe, in the foothills of Mount Sayan . . .
. . . And then stops. Eight words in, and the muse abandoned him.

plifications of Marx and his disciples, the boy from Gori might have been remembered as a great poet instead of a great killer. Given the globally low profile of Georgian poets, he most likely would not have been remembered at all. But that, too, would have been perfectly fine.

In the seminary, Stalin's religious faith evaporated and, as he read revolutionary texts, his eschatological impulses were channeled toward a more earthly vision of paradise. He dropped out of the seminary in May 1899 and took a job as a clerk at the Tiflis Observatory, where a light workload left him plenty of time to study the texts of Marx, Lenin, Plekhanov et al., while maintaining his regular diet of high-quality European prose and poetry. He also led two "workers' circles," where he preached Marx to the proletariat. Then, in March 1901, tsarist police rounded up his comrades, and Stalin fled the city.

Now he turned his attention from poetry to prose, contributing articles to an underground Marxist newspaper entitled *Brdzola* ("Struggle"). The first article attributed to Stalin (published in September 1901 and later included as the first article in the first volume of his *Collected Works*) is fairly dreary: there is some talk about raising the consciousness of workers, and Stalin attacks the folly of European Marxists, but there is nothing to indicate that a theoretical titan is at work, even in rudimentary form.

His next effort was more substantial. Published in the second and third issues of *Brdzola* between late 1901 and early 1902, *The Russian Social-Democratic Party and Its Immediate Tasks* sees him writing as an educator, guiding the reader through the history of socialism. Unlike Lenin, Stalin effaces himself from the text. He is a much more disciplined writer, less prone to digression, and targets his barbs at the tsar instead of fellow Marxists. Stalin serves as a guide—modest, unassuming, his central concern being to facilitate the reader's understanding of how we got from the likes of utopian socialist Robert Owen in England to the present terrible state of affairs in Russia and Europe.

In this "beginner's guide," however, Stalin the romantic lives on in purple passages such as this:

> Many storms, many torrents of blood swept over Western Europe in the struggle to end the oppression of the majority by the minority, but sorrow remained undispelled, wounds remained unhealed, and pain became more and more unendurable with every passing day.

Stalin moves from the failure of utopian socialism through the "discoveries" of Marx to the evolution of social democracy in a handful of pages. Unlike Lenin, who wrote as if he were the center from which all other Marxists deviated, Stalin is deeply provincial, describing revolutions and intellectual battles taking place far away, in more interesting places. He is also a popularizer, wearing his Marxism lightly, avoiding jargon, summarizing the work of higher authorities for a (hypothetical) mass audience.

Most striking of all, Stalin is compassionate. He strives to inspire empathy and solidarity in his readers by inviting them to identify with *all* the oppressed people in the Russian Empire, and not only the proletariat. The ex-seminarian lists an infinitude of sorrows, deploying a repetitive structure that mirrors the cadences and rhythms of sermonizing speech:

> Groaning under the yoke are the Russian peasants, wasted from constant starvation, impoverished by the unbearable burden of taxation and thrown to the mercy of the grasping bourgeois traders and the "noble" land-lords.
> Groaning under the yoke are the little people in the towns, the minor employees in government and private offices, the minor officials . . .

Etc. In fact, says Stalin, everyone is "groaning under the yoke." The list of groaners expands ever outward to include:

- The petite bourgeoisie
- The "middle bourgeoisie"
- The educated section of the bourgeoisie
- Teachers
- Physicians
- Lawyers
- University students
- High school students
- Poles
- Armenians
- Georgians
- Finns

Not to mention:

- The "eternally persecuted and humiliated" Jews

Stalin even empathizes with the Russian Empire's bizarre religious non-conformists, which included both orgiastic and self-flagellating sects among their number. At age twenty-two, it seems, Stalin loves all oppressed peoples. In fact, the empathy becomes so overwhelming he has to stop:

> Groaning are . . . but it is impossible to enumerate all the oppressed, all who are persecuted by the Russian autocracy. They are so numerous that if they were all aware of this, and were aware who their common enemy is, the despotic regime in Russia would not exist another day.

Almost never read today, *The Russian Social-Democratic Party and Its Immediate Tasks* is nevertheless a highly useful document for the student of tyranny. First, it is striking that even as Stalin is caught up in the midst of composing powerful rhetorical flourishes, he nevertheless displays an impulse to categorize and reduce large and diverse populations to manageable lists. Meanwhile, his detailed recitation of groaning demographics amounts to a convenient advance summary of the groups he himself would later oppress or annihilate in subsequent decades. He also denounces several practices (such as enforced Russification) that he would pursue with a vengeance once in power.

These early writings indicate that Stalin had not yet discovered his capacity for wickedness. In those days, he avoided direct calls to revolution, and *Brdzola*'s founder, Vano Ketskhoveli, reportedly "swore at him for being too moderate." Compare that with Lenin, who at age twenty-one did nothing to prevent the deaths of thousands of starving peasants because he believed that revolution might thereby occur sooner. Unlike Lenin, Stalin had to practice before becoming a monster.

STALIN'S CAREER AS a revolutionary writer had begun, although as an actual scion of the working class, he faced an obstacle that many prominent revolutionary theorists did not: a chronic shortage of cash. Unlike Engels, Lenin or the anarchist prince Pyotr Kropotkin, Stalin had no inheritance to fund the life of leisurely contemplation required if one is to establish a reputation as a radical thinker and champion of the proletariat. Nor, like Marx, did he have a patron from whom he could siphon funds.

Getting arrested and exiled was also disruptive to his budding literary career, especially as his lowly origins did not qualify him for the comfortable exile Lenin had received as a member of the nobility. In 1902, Stalin was rounded up with most of *Brdzola*'s staff, held in prison for a year, then dispatched to Siberia in late 1903. It was the first of many stints of imprisonment and exile as, over the next fourteen years Stalin and the tsarist authorities enacted a revolutionary farce in which the pockmarked Georgian regularly escaped his captors, who would then arrest and imprison him again.

Stalin was a keen reader of *Iskra*, the newspaper Lenin cofounded, and of Lenin's other writings, and these had persuaded him that here was a fearless "mountain eagle" leading the party along "unexplored paths of the Russian revolutionary movement." Stalin would later claim that he and the Bolshevik leader struck up a personal correspondence during this period of exile; years later, he described the "indelible impression" made upon him by a note he received from Lenin, which was filled with pungent criticisms of the party. In fact, Lenin and Stalin were not pen pals, and the leader sent no such note: he was far too busy waging textual war against the Mensheviks to write to an obscure activist from the Caucasus region stranded in Siberia. Stalin was referring to a pamphlet, one of the many Lenin churned out in an attempt to take down his foes within the party. Doubtless, Stalin, who had an excellent memory and an infinite capacity for mendacity, was conscious of his fabrication, yet this one at least contains an element of truth. So intense was his connection to Lenin's texts at the time that it may well have felt as though the leader were speaking directly to him.

As for the physical Lenin, well: the flesh paled before the word. When the 1905 revolution broke out, Stalin was back in Tiflis, and in December of that year, his comrades dispatched him to a Bolshevik conference in Finland. Here he really did meet "the mountain eagle" (this was one of Stalin's favorite metaphors for Lenin). However, the contradiction between the fire-breathing supertheorist of the texts and the physical reality proved jarring. He later recalled that he had expected to see "a great man, great not only politically, but, if you like, physically too, for Lenin had taken shape in my imagination as a giant, stately and imposing. What then was my disappointment when I saw a most ordinary man, below average height, in no way, literally in no way different from ordinary mortals." Nevertheless, when Lenin spoke, it was a different matter. Stalin was impressed by Lenin's "irresistible force of logic," although not so much that he felt cowed into supporting policies he disagreed with. In fact,

Stalin sided against Lenin over the question of Bolshevik participation in elections to the new Duma.

Lenin, in turn, was impressed by Stalin, recognizing his talents for project management and general criminality. The erstwhile poet of flowers and Motherland now channeled his inner Koba as he organized fraud, extortion, intimidation, protection rackets, bank robberies and even the occasional kidnapping to raise funds for the Bolsheviks at Lenin's behest. A knack for conspiracy was also essential, as bank robberies were officially forbidden by the Social-Democratic Party. Thus, while Stalin was in London in 1907 for the Fifth Party Congress, debating and discussing strategies for the advancement of revolution, he also took time out to discuss with Lenin a plan to have his men rob a bank in Tiflis. Ten bombs were tossed, horses and men torn to shreds, and Stalin's agents made off with 250,000 gold rubles. These were promptly spirited to Lenin in Finland.

Stalin was now recognized as the senior Bolshevik in Georgia, and had earned the epithet "the Caucasian Lenin." But there was a crucial difference: while Lenin sat in a chair and thought and wrote, Stalin concentrated on practical work, which left him comparatively little time to generate text. Indeed, his *Collected Works* for the period 1901–1913 fill a measly two volumes, whereas Lenin's for the same period fill fifteen. Still, the mere existence of those two books show that even during this period of intense underground action, Stalin continued his literary work when he could. Nineteen hundred seven was not simply a year of international revolutionary plotting, bomb tossing and theft. Stalin launched another newspaper, *Mnatobi* ("The Torch"), and as a sign of how serious he was about establishing a name for himself in imperial revolutionary circles, he switched to writing in Russian. Now his texts could be read by every leading revolutionary Marxist in the empire. Not that there were all that many of them left: Stalin's attempt to boost his career coincided with an ongoing imperial clampdown on terror and underground groups, and a drastic decline in Social-Democratic Party membership. In the spring of 1907, his potential audience was a robust 150,000, but it soon shrank to a mere fraction of that.

The clampdown also coincided with personal tragedy: in November 1907, Stalin's first wife, Kato, died, and he was arrested shortly afterward, in March 1908. Yet he persevered in his revolutionary activities, and his game of cat and mouse with the authorities now entered a vertiginous new phase of repeated arrests and escapes that went on for years, while doing nothing to hamper his revolutionary career. In 1912, he was promoted to the party's Central Committee, making Stalin one of the leading Bolsheviks in the Russian Empire, and he took on the job of launching a new daily newspaper, *Pravda*, in the capital. It was an impressive achievement: the yokel from the mountains who had learned Russian at age ten (and had never lost his guttural Georgian accent) was authorized to wield the editorial ax over a stable of well-educated native speakers, many of whom were of bourgeois origin. The first issue was published on April 22—at which point the police arrested Stalin yet again. This time he was exiled to northern Siberia, but he escaped after a mere thirty-eight days. By September he was back in Saint Petersburg and at the helm of *Pravda* once more.

Now Stalin revealed himself to be an editor of steel. At the start of the year, the Bolsheviks had formally split from the Mensheviks, but in October both parties were elected to the Imperial Duma. Stalin was much less hostile to cooperation with the Mensheviks than Lenin, a point of view that was reflected in *Pravda*'s editorial line. Lenin was furious, and wrote articles advocating an uncompromising anti-Menshevik stance. But Stalin was not to be cowed: in total, he would reject forty-seven of the Mountain Eagle's submissions to the paper. Meanwhile, *Pravda* would go on to become the most popular socialist newspaper in the empire, selling forty thousand copies per day.

Lenin got around the problem by promoting his recalcitrant editor out of harm's way, dispatching Stalin to Vienna, where he was tasked with an important theoretical matter. The rising star from the Caucasus was to write a study on the "national question," wherein he would define the correct, truly Marxist approach to the national aspirations of oppressed minorities in multinational states. For Stalin, this was a major break, given the Bolshevik reverence for the word. A decade after his debut as a provincial pamphleteer, this was his opportunity to establish those vital intellectual credentials.

And so in January 1913 he found himself staying with some wealthy Marxists in the Austrian capital. He met and befriended Nikolai Bukharin, a highly regarded theorist in the party (whom he would have killed a few decades later). He read, and wrote, and upon his return to Russia submitted the resulting article, *The National Question and Social Democracy*, to the theoretical journal *Enlightenment*. Just as Lenin had received his revolutionary rechristening courtesy of his literary breakthrough *What Is to Be*

Done?, so this essay made the erstwhile Dzhugashvili's name: it was only the second time he had used "Stalin" as a pseudonym.

The National Question and Social Democracy (or *Marxism and the National Question*, as it was retitled in its many reissues) reveals a Stalin who is a very different writer from both the adolescent poet and the young pamphleteer of Baku. If this Stalin still feels anything for mountains and flowers, he isn't going to let such frivolous nonsense distract him here. All traces of that romantic, emotive voice have been successfully purged and replaced with an austere, plodding, laboriously logical style designed to convey theoretical gravitas to its audience.

In this work, Stalin demonstrates a basic regard for the rules of narrative that often escaped the more impatient Lenin. Rather than launch into a dense theoretical discussion in medias res, he supplies the context for the coming essay: the post-1905 crisis in Marxist politics. He admits that socialism has lost its luster and that nationalism has emerged as a new radical force. He laments "the spread of Zionism among the Jews, the increase of chauvinism in Poland, Pan-Islamism among the Tatars," and "the spread of nationalism among the Armenians, Georgians and Ukrainians," not to mention "the general swing of the philistine towards anti-Semitism." This "wave of nationalism," says Stalin is "threatening to engulf the mass of the workers."

Worse, says Stalin, nationalism is even corrupting Social Democrats, who should know better. Here he singles out the Bund (a secular Jewish organization within the social democratic movement), for especially harsh criticism, accusing its members of pursuing a nationalist agenda. He also takes aim at members of the Caucasian Party for their demands of "cultural-national autonomy." These nationalisms, says Stalin, are undermining "fraternity and unity among the proletarians of all the nationalities of Russia."

In response to this accumulation of heresy and general ideological impurity, Stalin retaliates not by demanding the heads of his opponents but through a ruthless, full-on, no-holds-barred semantic assault. What, Stalin asks, does the word *nation* really mean? The answer, it turns out, is rather complex. Stalin dedicates over two thousand words to exploring all the possibilities, as he laboriously pursues the correct definition while critiquing incorrect ones. Although highly methodical and excessively thorough, his argument does not, however, represent mere pedantry. Stalin has great faith in words; like Confucius, he believes that "the beginning of wisdom is to call things by their proper name."

Given the epic levels of mendacity he later achieved as head of the USSR, it is striking that here Stalin does not seek to obfuscate, deceive, elide difficulties, or otherwise dress up logical absurdities in dense, opaque, and/or impenetrable language. He is meticulous in his clarity. He is confident in his critiques. He believes in his arguments. He dedicates enormous amounts of text to defining all his concepts, and not just *nation*. In short, he is seeking the truth.

As for *nation*, this is what he found:

> A nation is a historically constituted, stable community of people, formed on the basis of a common language, territory, economic life, and psychological make-up manifested in a common culture.

He then adds:

> It must be emphasized that none of the above characteristics taken separately is sufficient to define a nation. More than that, it is sufficient for a single one of these characteristics to be lacking and the nation ceases to be a nation.

From this point Stalin uses his definition to methodically deconstruct the viewpoints of everyone he disagrees with. Once the true meaning of the word has been pinpointed, the possibility of ambiguity vanishes; there is only correct and incorrect. His insistence on territorial integrity enables him to quickly dispatch the nationalistic aims of the Bund, arguing that because Jews do not share a single territory or language, they cannot possibly be a "nation." At great length, he also picks apart the favored concept of Austrian Marxists: cultural autonomy, regardless of whether a nation occupies a single territory. He critiques this as a bourgeois phenomenon that undermines class struggle. The "*preservation* and *development* of the national peculiarities of the peoples," he says, is retrograde nonsense that will entail preserving customs clearly in need of eradicating, such as self-flagellation among the Caucasian Tatars and the vendetta among his fellow Georgians. He instead endorses Marx's prophecy of the 1840s, that "national differences and antagonisms between peoples are daily more and more vanishing" and that "the supremacy of the proletariat will cause them to vanish still faster."

After dedicating four chapters to liquidating his foes' arguments, Stalin unveils his solution for Russia: regional autonomy for "crystallized units" such as "Poland, Lithuania, the Ukraine, the Caucasus, etc." Minorities within these territories will be guaranteed the right to use their own language, have their own schools and even be granted "religious liberty." However, regional autonomy does not mean national autonomy, and Stalin is not advocating federalism, which he argues fosters separatism while distracting workers from the class realities that transcend cultural differences. Regional autonomy can exist, but only on the "basis of internationalism," whereby a single party unites all workers in all nationalities on the basis of their class, while allowing for cultural differences. "The international type of organization," says Stalin, "serves as a school of fraternal sentiments and is a tremendous agitational factor on behalf of internationalism."

Since Stalin is against national or cultural autonomy, does this mean that no nation occupying a region may secede? Not at all, he writes. "[A] nation may arrange its life in the way it wishes. It has the right to arrange its life on the basis of autonomy. It has the right to enter into federal relations with other nations. It has the right to complete secession. Nations are sovereign, and all nations have equal rights."

If all this sounds surprisingly liberal, there is a handy built-in get-out clause that makes secession highly unlikely. Social democracy is dedicated to defending the rights of the proletariat, and if the party deems that national autonomy will hurt the interests of the working classes, it will not support it. Thus, Stalin sketched out an approach to running a multinational, multiethnic Marxist state where national interests are subjugated to class interests as defined by the party center. Many Marxist theorists were tackling the same questions; the remarkable thing about Stalin's opus is that, within ten years, this obscure ex-seminarian was putting his ideas into practice, shaping the destinies of millions.*

All that lay in the future, however. As for Stalin, although *Marxism and the National Question* was accepted as a serious contribution to theory, he soon turned out to be a literary one-hit wonder, unable to build on an early success. Rearrested shortly after the essay's publication, he was

---

* When the USSR was formed in the early 1920s, Stalin was not yet supremely powerful, and he was obliged to compromise on the question of a federal structure. He would never compromise on the supremacy of class over nation or culture, however, and the right to secede granted to union republics remained a fiction for most of the history of the Soviet Union.

sentenced to four years in exile in the remote Siberian void. Stranded at the edge of the Arctic Circle, he proved to be rather less adept at escapology than previously. So far was Stalin from the center of things that Lenin forgot his real name, and in 1915 he wrote twice to comrades asking to be reminded what that Koba fellow was actually called. Letters from this period survive in which Stalin discusses plans for composing a definitive study on the "National Question," but nothing ever materialized and the moment to capitalize on his moment of glory slipped away from him. On the subject of the Great War, raging so far away, he was also silent. His collected works break off in 1913, and Stalin the writer goes dark until 1917.

AFTER THE REVOLUTION, Lenin entrusted Stalin with numerous important positions in the new Bolshevik regime. The expertise he had demonstrated in *The National Question and Social Democracy* landed him the job of head of the Commissariat for Nationalities in the new Soviet government. Then, in May 1918, he was dispatched to Tsaritsyn, in the Russian south, to improve grain supplies as the Russian Civil War raged. He duly seized the opportunity to inflict violence, terror, and repression on the local population.

Stalin also sat on the Central Committee of the party, chaired the drafting of a constitution of the Russian Soviet Republic, and was a member of both the Politburo and Orgburo, the first and second most important bodies in the party hierarchy, responsible for policy and organizational matters. In April 1922, he was appointed general secretary, which gave him responsibility for the management and administration of the vast party apparatus. By the time Lenin died in January 1924, Stalin had accumulated so much institutional power that he was in a strong position to become the new leader.

Yet despite his influence behind the scenes, he had a much lower public profile than his rival, the charismatic Leon Trotsky, who had led the Red Army during the civil war, fighting (and ultimately winning) on sixteen different fronts. Trotsky was an excellent multitasker: as he rode around the USSR in a train ordering the killing of large numbers of people, he was still able to give speeches and churn out radical theoretical verbiage, thus maintaining his reputation as a prominent Marxist theorist. Trotsky's successes overshadowed the fact that he had been a Menshevik and had spent the ten years prior to the revolution in foreign exile, frequently at loggerheads with Lenin, joining the Bolshevik Party only in 1917. Stalin, by contrast, was no orator, and the texts he cranked out for *Pravda* during the early years of Soviet power did nothing to boost his image as a thinker of note.

Indeed, by the time of Lenin's death, Stalin's theoretical accomplishments looked embarrassingly meager, and not only in comparison with those of Trotsky but also other senior Bolsheviks such as Nikolai Bukharin and Grigory Zinoviev. *Marxism and the National Question* remained his sole major work, and it was over a decade old. Yes, Stalin was among those who carried Lenin's coffin to its resting place in the ice on Red Square, but in the word-venerating Bolshevik world of "publish or perish," this absence of public acts of Marxist deep thinking could prove problematic for his career ambitions.

But while Stalin may have lacked the flash of Trotsky, he retained his ability to communicate clearly, a skill he put to good use as the dead leader was embalmed in reverential words in addition to formaldehyde. Stalin was in the forefront of the verbal mummification process, delivering a quasi-religious eulogy that would appear in *Pravda* and subsequently be reprinted many times over:

> Before long you will see the pilgrimage of representatives of millions of working people to Comrade Lenin's tomb. You need not doubt that the representatives of millions will be followed by representatives of scores and hundreds of millions from all parts of the earth, who will come to testify that Lenin was the leader not only of the Russian proletariat, not only of the European workers, not only of the colonial East, but of all the working people of the globe.

And so on. Interspersed throughout the speech were catechistic, incantatory declarations in which Stalin pledged fealty to Lenin's epic world-transformative mission on behalf of a collective "we":

> Departing from us, Comrade Lenin enjoined us to remain faithful to the principles of the communist international. We vow to you, Comrade Lenin, that we shall not spare our lives to strengthen and extend the union of the working people of the whole world—the communist international!

But Stalin was merely at the forefront of a surge of Dead Lenin mania that swept the land. Petrograd was renamed Leningrad, Lenin's widow, Krupskaya, wrote a hagiographic biography and the Futurist poet Vladimir Mayakovsky forced his prodigious talent to submit to the requirements of propagandistic bombast. Straining furiously at a three-thousand-line poem entitled *Vladimir Ilyich Lenin*, Mayakovsky (whose work Lenin had despised) began by stressing Lenin's humanity, but very quickly lapsed into messianic hokum in which the savior did not heal the blind or the lame but instead generated magic texts:

> We're no longer timid
> As newly born lambkins
> The workers' wrath
> Condenses
> Into clouds
> Slashed by the lightning
> Of Lenin's pamphlets,
> His leaflets
> Showering
> On surging crowds.

Stalin saw that the rapidly developing posthumous cult of Lenin represented an opportunity to reestablish himself as an author. Lenin had generated unfathomable quantities of words in his lifetime: the first collected edition of his works began publication in 1920 and ultimately ran to 20 volumes in 26 books containing 1,500 documents. (By the time the fifth and final edition was completed in 1965, Lenin's "complete" works would run to 55 volumes and contain over 3,000 documents—and even then, a further 3,700 uncollected Lenin documents lay in the archives.) And of course, since Lenin had been writing in the moment, responding to rapidly changing events, switching tactics whenever necessary, the texts were complex, complicated, and contradictory. They could be dangerous in the wrong hands, without the proper context; or they might also prove useful in the right hands, as there were all those disputes with the ex-Menshevik Trotsky to highlight.

If these texts were going to serve as the holy scriptures of the state Lenin cult, then it would be necessary to impose order on the chaos, to establish a hierarchy of importance, and to steer those who read them in the correct exegetic direction. So, two months after Lenin's death, that is what Stalin did, as he delivered a series of lectures on the basics of Leninism to trainee party activists at the Sverdlov Institute in Moscow. These were subsequently published as a primer on Lenin's thought, *The Foundations of Leninism*. Despite his many day-to-day responsibilities, Stalin considered the job of ideological interpreter so important that he wrote the lectures himself; his original drafts survive in the Russian archives, typed out on yellowing paper, covered in handwritten edits.

Stalin's authorial presence is ultramodest: like Saint Paul following in the footsteps of Jesus, he presents himself as the humble servant of the text, whose goal is merely to be "useful" by laying down "some basic points of departure necessary for the successful study of Leninism." The orderly, methodical, ambiguity-annihilating exegetic approach he developed for the *National Question* proves to be highly suitable for the lecture format: over and over again, Stalin defines, elaborates, and then draws pragmatic, easy-to-digest conclusions.

The book begins with a long exploration of the concept of "Leninism" culminating with this formulation:

> Leninism is Marxism of the era of imperialism and the proletarian revolution. To be more exact, Leninism is the theory and tactics of the proletarian revolution in general, the theory and tactics of the dictatorship of the proletariat in particular.

... which is rather abstract, and replete with loaded terms. So Stalin breaks it down over the following nine chapters, placing the major themes of Lenin's thought into the following categories:

- The Historical Roots of Leninism
- Method
- Theory
- The Dictatorship of the Proletariat
- The Peasant Question
- The National Question
- Strategy and Tactics
- The Party
- Style in Work

Merely by looking at that list, I feel soothed: as if the mass of argumentative verbiage I grappled with in order to write the previous section is coalescing into something simple and coherent before my eyes. Throughout *The Foundations of Leninism*, Stalin's modest but real strengths as a writer are on display. He is clear and succinct, and good at summarizing complex ideas for a middlebrow audience: the Bill Bryson of dialectical materialism, minus the gags.

Following my first encounter with *The Foundations of Leninism*, I half-wished I had read it before the source materials. On the one hand, this would have led me to view Lenin entirely through Stalin's prism; on the other, that would have been closer to the experience of a generation of communists around the globe. In Stalin's methodical, orderly, structured world, it is always clear who is wrong, who is correct, and what things really mean, and he backs up his conclusions with quotable citations from Lenin and Marx. In a world where advancement through the party required mastery of the texts, and where ideological battles were fought by hurling citations from Marx or Lenin at each other, Stalin provided a valuable service to his readers by assembling most of the ideological material they would ever need in a single location, while providing the appropriate gloss.

The judicious selection of citations also demonstrates Stalin's skill as an editor. He appears to have read everything Lenin ever wrote, and is adept at extracting just the right passage to elucidate an idea. But Stalin does not just edit Lenin's texts; he also edits Lenin himself as he removes all the leader's long and self-indulgent tirades against ideological rivals. An indirect portrait of the recently deceased leader emerges: pithy, strong, decisive and always equipped with the right answers for this present era and those to come. Lenin the dyspeptic ranter vanishes into the dust-covered multivolume collected editions of his work, and Stalin knew that most people were never to going to plow through all of that.

In fact, with his synopsis, Stalin does not at all encourage students to go out and explore Lenin for themselves; rather he summarizes the main points and tells them what to think. Then again, as is made explicit by the book's structure, that was the plan. *The Foundations of Leninism* begins in the period of ideas and ends in the era of action. Stalin concludes the book with a description of the "Leninist style in work," which is characterized by two factors: "Russian revolutionary sweep" and "American efficiency."

If this last point seems surprising, it is clear that Stalin in 1924 was quite impressed by the United States, as he defines the nation's spirit as "that indomitable force which neither knows nor recognises obstacles; which with its business-like perseverance brushes aside all obstacles; which continues at a task once started until it is finished, even if it is a minor task; and without which serious constructive work is inconceivable." Of course, American efficiency is not wholly marvelous, as Stalin adds that it can degenerate into narrow "empiricism and unprincipled practicalism." And yet he clearly retained his admiration for the American can-do spirit, as this section remained in future editions of the book, even into the Cold War.

The Foundations of Leninism was a success, at least among its target audience of ambitious young party members. Stalin's theorist peers in the party hierarchy were less impressed. Writing in his autobiography, *My Life*, Trotsky would sniffily describe his rival's opus as a mere "work of compilation," "full of sophomoric errors" in which Stalin "made an attempt to pay tribute to the theoretical traditions of the party." He would also claim that Stalin could not possibly have written *Marxism and the National Question*, as it was insufficiently mediocre.*

But while *The Foundations of Leninism* is no masterpiece, it is more than just a work of compilation, as it also shows Stalin starting to grapple with the party's eschatological woes. Marx had prophesied that the revolution would change the entire world, and post-1917 the Bolsheviks had expected hordes of proletarians to rise up across the rest of Europe and overthrow their bourgeois masters, like early Christians in the desert awaiting the descent of the New Jerusalem from heaven. None of that happened, but the expectation that it would did not go away.

In *The Foundations of Leninism*, however, Stalin sets out to downplay that expectation of a swift transition to a "super revolutionary" period. For instance, although he cites *The State and Revolution*, he omits Lenin's embarrassing utopianism. He also combs through the works of Lenin and Marx for texts that suggest the transition from capitalism to communism might not be as fast as hitherto anticipated, citing Marx on the coming "fifteen, twenty, fifty years of civil wars and international conflicts," and

---

* All that said, Trotsky's own *Lenin*, published the year after *The Foundations of Leninism*, is itself a fairly excruciating example of hagiography.

Lenin on the "long and difficult mass struggle against the mass petty-bourgeois influences."

The problems associated with the failure of prophecy did not go away. The revolution's tenth anniversary was approaching, and global transformation still seemed distant. According to a strict application of theory, the USSR could not survive. And so it was that Stalin and the leading party theoretician, Nikolai Bukharin, revealed that, actually, it *was* possible for the USSR to survive without any revolutions in the surrounding countries. Socialism could be built in one country after all.

Stalin explored this revelation in his 1926 sequel to *The Foundations of Leninism*, entitled *Concerning Questions of Leninism*. He had been fast out of the gate with his first book codifying Leninism, but this follow-up entered a changed ideological marketplace. Two years after the leader's death the splits and struggles for power among members of the elite had deepened. Stalin's rivals had also been publishing their own deep thoughts on Leninism, as they jockeyed for power. *Concerning Questions of Leninism* is not just an elaboration on themes explored in the first book, but also a demonstration of just how seriously Stalin took the war for control of the theoretical texts. Rival interpretations were not a matter of disagreement but utterly wrong, and had to be anatomized and atomized through ruthless deconstruction. But whereas Lenin could annihilate his foes in a short pamphlet via a mixture of argument, vitriol, mockery and very long footnotes, Stalin opts for a joyless, long-winded intensification of style, a ruthless stockpiling of citations, a plodding, relentless, great heaping up of rhetoric. This time, too, he is taking names, as he heaps scorn on the false "Leninisms" of rivals such as Trotsky, Kamenev and Zinoviev, the last of whom had published his own *Leninism* in 1925, in which he defended internationalism and railed against the idea of "socialism in one country."

As Stalin slowly hammers away at his foes, he also seeks to defend his heresy, intent on proving that, all evidence to the contrary, both he and Lenin had believed this all along. Of course, it was easy enough to revise *The Foundations of Leninism* so that a passage that sounded rather skeptical suddenly vanished, giving way to an endorsement of the idea. Stalin knew Lenin's writings well, and he was a trained seminarian to boot. Like a theologian extrapolating an entire doctrine on the basis of a handful of biblical verses taken in isolation, he dug around and found some quotations that could be made to back up the new theory—so long as you ignored everything else Lenin had said and done. Stalin takes this fragment of Lenin, isolating it from its context:

> Uneven economic and political development is an absolute law of capital-ism. Hence, the victory of socialism is possible first in several or even in one capitalist country taken separately. The victorious proletariat of that country, having expropriated the capitalists and organised socialist pro-duction, would stand up against the rest of the world, the capitalist world, attracting to its cause the oppressed classes of other countries, raising revolts in those countries against the capitalists, and in the event of neces-sity coming out even with armed force against the exploiting classes and their states.

Then he zooms in on the subfragment "having . . . organised socialist production" and delivers himself of this impressive piece of exegesis:

> It means that the proletariat of the victorious country, having seized power, can and must organise socialist production. And what does to "organise socialist production" mean? It means completely building a socialist society. It scarcely needs proof that this clear and definite state-ment of Lenin's requires no further comment. Otherwise Lenin's call for the seizure of power by the proletariat in October 1917 would be incom-prehensible.

On the basis of three words, Stalin declares that the revolution stands or falls on a rather new idea he himself has only recently adopted. Social-ism could be built in one country, and if the rest of the world had to wait awhile, so be it. His revisionism had its opponents, but they were divided against each other and did not unite against the common enemy until it was too late. In fact, by the time *Concerning Questions of Leninism* was pub-lished in 1926, Stalin had already outmaneuvered his foes, exploiting Lenin's rules on party unity to prevent a debate on the idea at the Fourteenth Party Congress in December 1925.

Later, the verbal violence would turn physical, and Stalin would kill Trotsky, Zinoviev and Kamenev, all of whom he attacks in *Concerning Questions of Leninism*. Then again, he also ordered the death of his ally Bukharin, who had done so much to take the slogan "Socialism in one country" and work up some theory around it. But as we all now know (they did not, at least not yet) Stalin was like that. For now, the murders were still years away, and Stalin's faction had consolidated its grip on power. It was time for "Socialism in one country" to move from the page to physical reality.

HAVING ESTABLISHED CONTROL of Lenin's texts, Stalin now steadily built up his personal power while driving through cultural, industrial and agricultural transformation in the USSR. In order that the young Soviet state might survive, Lenin had compromised with capitalism: his New Economic Policy had permitted limited private trading. Stalin now took a different approach: he would force socialism into existence.

Of course, this required massive violence. Fortunately, it was not difficult to find passages in the Soviet sacred texts endorsing the use of the fist. No hermeneutic gymnastics were required to grasp what Lenin meant when he defined the dictatorship of the proletariat as "the supremacy of the proletariat over the bourgeoisie and unrestricted by law." And lo, socialism advanced, via the five-year plans, forced collectivization, slave labor camps, the liquidation of the kulaks as a class, the paranoid pursuit of "wreckers" and saboteurs, the executions, purges and disappearances, and an artificially induced famine that claimed the lives of millions in southern Russia, Ukraine and Kazakhstan between 1932 and 1933.

Stalin also brought the Bolshevik old guard to its knees. Whereas the mere existence of *Concerning Questions of Leninism* implies an intellectual environment in which it was possible for members of the elite to disagree with each other, by 1932 Stalin's authority was absolute. As the political ground shifted, unsuitable books were purged; librarians, either in an excess of zeal or from sheer terror, removed not only ideologically suspect works but also Marxist texts. The general tenor of fearful ambiguity is demonstrated by the fact that, in the early 1930s, terrified librarians in the Moscow region went so far as to remove Stalin's signature text, *The National Question and Social Democracy*, and Lenin's first attempt at a major work from his days in Siberian exile, *The Development of Capitalism in Russia*, from library shelves.

And as "socialism" emerged through the haze like a concrete mirage, so, too, did the cult of Stalin. He became the Vozhd, the "leader and teacher," "the true, best pupil of Lenin," the "true continuer," the "Lenin of Today" and then in 1932–1933 started to outstrip Lenin as the "great driver of the locomotive of history," the "genius of communism," the "best machinist of the world proletarian revolution," and the "gardener of human happiness." Stalin's enhanced, monumental double spread across the landscape of the USSR, manifesting itself in the form of bronze doppelgangers on plinths, colossal propaganda posters, mosaics and titanic murals. And as his cult grew, so Lenin's dwindled. On October Revolution Day in 1933, an American news correspondent took a stroll around Moscow and counted 103 portraits and busts of Stalin versus 58 of Lenin. While a poster of Stalin might enjoy a print run of 150,000, Lenin had to make do with 30,000, or appear merely as a head on a plinth in the background of a portrait of the Vozhd, or reduced to a name on the spine of a book in Stalin's study.

And, of course, as Stalin ascended to the level of man-god, his texts were revered. Writing after the collapse of the USSR, the Russian general and historian Dmitri Volkogonov recalled:

> I remember as a cadet in tank school reading from cover to cover the six hundred pages of Stalin's speeches and articles, collected under the title of his central work, *Questions of Leninism*, with all the supplementary material it included. We had to write synopses of these works, to which our instructors paid particular attention. The more extensive the synopsis, and the more key passages were underlined in coloured pencil, the better our grade.

In unofficial contexts, however, it was a different story. One joke of the 1930s revolved around an awards ceremony for Stakhanovites, overachieving workers who were praised by the state but often loathed by their comrades for the unrealistic expectations their output placed on everybody else. At the ceremony, held on a collective farm, a group of Stakhanovite milkmaids receive prizes: a radio receiver, a gramophone, and a bicycle. The fourth prize, for the leading "pig tender," is "the complete works of our beloved comrade Stalin." A profound hush descends. Finally, somebody at the back breaks the silence: "Just what the bitch deserves."

But frank assessments of Stalin's works were not conducive to a long life, and since he could publish pretty much anything he wanted there were so many reasons to stay quiet. Whereas once he had fought against other socialists in the pages of journals and books, now the most banal of his public utterances was deemed worthy of preservation for all eternity. For instance, on page 127 of volume 13 of the English edition of his collected writings, we find this work of staggering genius, culled from the pages of *Pravda*:

> To the Chief of the Harvester Combine Works Project and the Director of the Harvester Combine Works, Saratov
>
> Greetings to the working men and working women and the entire executive personnel of the works!
>   Hearty congratulations to the active of the works and, first and foremost, to the men and women shock brigaders,* on the successful completion of the building and inauguration of the works!
>   Comrades, the country needs harvester combines as much as it needs tractors and automobiles. I have no doubt that you will succeed in completely fulfilling the production programme of the works.
>   Forward to new victories!
>
> J. Stalin
> January 4, 1932

A favorite in my personal collection of dictator texts is a twenty-four-page pamphlet collecting two of Stalin's speeches from 1935, which I found in a bookshop in the Scottish town of Saint Andrews in the early 2000s. The first, "Speech at a Conference of Harvester-Combine Operators," was delivered by Stalin on December 1, 1935, while the second, "Speech at a Conference of the Foremost Collective Farmers of Tajikistan and Turkmenistan," was delivered on December 4 of the same year. In the first speech, Stalin methodically explores the reasons for the surge in demand for grain in the USSR and affirms that his audience was up to the task of producing it, to acclaim that is reproduced twice in the text as follows:

> Loud and prolonged cheers and applause. Cries of "Long live our beloved Stalin!"

This cheering occurs following the penultimate and final paragraphs of Stalin's talk. In the second speech, however, cheering erupts after the second paragraph, and is even more enthusiastic:

---

* "Shock brigades," composed of ultraproductive workers known for smashing quotas and taking on the most difficult tasks.

Loud and prolonged applause and cheers. Cries of "Long live Comrade Stalin!" Shouts of greeting to the leaders of the Party and government.

"Applause" breaks out again, halfway through the third paragraph, when Stalin reveals that all attendees at the conference will leave with a gramophone and some records, while the revelation that they will also be getting watches results in "prolonged applause." The rest of the speech fills two pages, is peppered with applause notes, and ends with a record of vociferous approval:

Tumultuous applause. All rise and greet Comrade Stalin.

The most extraordinary thing about the pamphlet is not that it is entirely vapid, or that it was deemed worthy of separate publication, but that it was also translated into English and published mere days after it was delivered. Then, berserk cultists spirited it across the waves, and read it, and found value in it, in a society where nobody was being starved to death, shot in the head or interned in a slave labor camp. And sixty years later, it found its way into my hands.

Not all these micropublications of Stalin's were quite so asinine, however. On March 2, 1930, *Pravda* published "Dizzy with Success," in which the Vozhd proposed that party bosses had gone a bit too far in their pursuit of collectivization, and that it was now time to dial back the excesses. Suddenly, terrified apparatchiks across the USSR had to reverse course and interpret for themselves what Stalin meant by concentrating on consolidating their "gains" over persecuting the kulaks. At the other end of the decade, on March 29 and April 1, 1937, *Pravda* startled its readership again when it interrupted the flow of propaganda to publish two speeches Stalin had delivered to the Central Committee weeks earlier, demanding the unmasking of enemies. The speeches were subsequently collected as a pamphlet. The man-god demanded a purge. But who? And how many? And when would it stop? The text did not specify; it lay on the page, terrifying in its implications, its ambiguity.

As paper and bronze Stalins proliferated, the flesh-and-blood variant sat in his office interacting with his empire primarily through texts. He was not one of those dictators who liked to make ceremonial visits to the showpieces of his kingdom. He did not strip down to the waist and pretend to dig holes alongside workers, or fondle tigers in stage-managed photographs, or stand on a balcony basking in adulation. Instead, he knew his realm through the vast quantities of reports, letters, telegrams and studies he digested. Stalin had graduated from author of *Marxism and the National Question* and editor of *Pravda* to supreme author and editor of the world's largest state. When Stalin shuffled his papers, the earth shook; when he took his red pen to a document, tens of thousands died. He was shaping and revising his world just as he had Lenin's texts.

Because Stalin's primary means of interacting with the physical world was through paper, it is not surprising that he continued to demonstrate a superstitious awe for the power of the written word. He was still fascinated by books, by novels and plays, and by the arts generally. He was a great balletomane and a film buff. Micromanager though he was, the archives show that he was on occasion willing to delegate the final decision making to Politburo lackeys on matters of agriculture, industry, transport, defense and security. When it came to ideology and culture, however, it was a different story: between 1930 and his death in 1953, Stalin either decided or signed off on practically every ideological question that came before the Politburo.

Sometimes, he liked to play sinister mind games with writers. Mikhail Bulgakov and Boris Pasternak famously received phone calls in the middle of the night for chats about literature or the work of their peers. Other writers might receive a critical note when they strayed too far from the path of ideological rectitude. In December 1930, for instance, Stalin terrified the "peasant poet" Demyan Bedny by accusing him of slandering socialism and the working class in a letter that would also make its way into Stalin's *Collected Works*. Bedny had known Stalin since 1912 and had ingratiated himself so successfully with the future general secretary that, between 1918 and 1933, he even lived in the Kremlin as a kind of "poet laureate" of the workers' state. A born lickspittle, Bedny had in the past found his themes in articles Stalin wrote for *Pravda*, attacking his master's enemies in verse. Now he drew inspiration from Stalin again; only, this time he dashed off a few panicked lines, furiously denouncing himself:

> Get going, Shoulder! Swing, Arm! If only a single bright line! I turn to the left, I turn to the right. That's really not good. Everywhere black lines: Vices! Vices! Vices!

Some writers sought out Stalin for literary advice. The prominent playwright Alexander Afinogenov regarded Stalin as his literary mentor and in 1930 started submitting his plays directly to him for critique. In spite of his busy schedule running a vast multiethnic totalitarian state, Stalin found time to read them and respond.

Of course, the primary goal of Stalin's literary dabbling was not aesthetic but, rather, to increase his editorial and exegetic authority. He had tamed Lenin's texts and told the Soviet people what to think; now he wanted to instruct them in how to *feel*. Such was his faith in the power of the written word that he believed he could do this by exercising control over imaginary stories and the people who wrote them.

Maxim Gorky was a Russian author who had risen from poverty to become internationally fêted for his novels describing the hard and dismal lives of the poor. Gorky had deep connections with the party. He had first met Lenin in 1907, at the Fifth Congress of the Russian Social-Democratic Party in London, where he and the Bolshevik leader bonded over Gorky's novel *Mother*. Gorky donated funds to the cause, but his relationship with Bolshevism was never smooth. Of Lenin he would observe, "He does not know the people, he has not lived among them; he has only learned from books how to stir them up." Meanwhile, almost immediately after the October Revolution, Gorky published an article in his own newspaper with the headline "Civilization in Danger." He followed it with a series of articles highly critical of the new Bolshevik leadership. Although he sided with the Bolsheviks during the civil war, he continued to criticize the party until October 1921, when Lenin suggested to Gorky's wife that it might be better if her husband left the country—for his health, of course. Settling in Sorrento, Italy, Gorky now lambasted the Bolsheviks from afar.

Gorky, then, was a principled foe of tyranny. But he was also a great Russian revolutionary writer, respected around the world, someone who could confer legitimacy upon the regime. Stalin wanted him back. But how? Demonstrating his depressingly accurate grasp of human nature in general and authorial vanity in particular, he bought him, with flattery and gifts. Secret policemen bombarded Gorky with fake fan mail, while Gosizdat, the state publishing house, paid him an astronomical $362,000 advance for "certain publication rights." And when Gorky finally returned to Russia for his sixtieth birthday celebrations in 1928, Stalin made sure that he was met at the train station by an exuberant throng. And that was just phase one. Phase two was more of the same, only more intense. Stalin wrote to Gorky personally, while a great many things were renamed in the writer's honor, including (but not restricted to) his birthplace of Nizhny Novgorod; the central street in Moscow leading to the Kremlin; the Soviet Union's most prestigious literary institute; and—why not?—a mountain in Kyrgyzstan. Thus seduced, Gorky returned to the USSR to bask in adoration three more times before Stalin invited him to settle there permanently in 1932. He accepted, and received, a beautiful Art Nouveau mansion in central Moscow. Now based in the heart of the Soviet capital, he could more easily supervise the creation of the vast series of histories he had proposed, which were to be written by teams of writers. These authoritative works on nearly everything had titles with wildly varying degrees of promise:

- History of the Civil War
- History of Factories and Plants
- History of the Two Five-Year Plans
- History of Cities and Villages
- History of the Young Person
- History of the Town
- History of Urban Culture

Stalin supported his pet literary titan in his projects. And no wonder, as he knew what he was getting: on his second visit to the USSR, Gorky had visited a gulag located in the former monastery of Solovki, and praised it in print. Once back in Moscow permanently, he headed a "writers' brigade" to produce *The History of the White Sea Canal*, wherein the marvelous corrective powers of forced labor were extolled.

But Stalin had plans beyond the corruption of a single author, and he did not wait to put them into action. Way back in 1905, in *The Party Organization and Party Literature* (1905), Lenin had cried, "[D]own with literary supermen," and declared that literature must become "a 'cog and a screw' of one single great Social-Democratic mechanism." Until April 1932, however, an assortment of creative unions, operating under a bewildering array of names and acronyms such as MAPP, RAPP, VAPP, Proletkult, LEF and "the Smithy" had advanced differing visions of what Soviet literature should be: now they were all abolished, replaced with a monolithic

Writers' Union. Then, on October 26, 1932, Stalin met with forty Soviet literary megastars at Gorky's lavish mansion. Among them were Fyodor Gladkov, whose most famous novel was the thrillingly titled *Cement*, and Valentin Kataev, whose most famous novel, *Time, Forward!*, was about pouring cement. Future Nobel Prize winner Mikhail Sholokhov was there, too, as was Stalin's playwright correspondent Alexander Afinogenov. Stalin spoke, revealing that he had an important mission for the assembled poets, dramatists and novelists: to reconstruct the inner worlds of the Soviet people.

> Our tanks are worthless if the souls who must steer them are made of clay. This is why I say: the production of souls is more important than that of tanks. Someone here has noted that writers must not sit still, that they must be familiar with the ways of life in their own country. Man is reshaped by life itself, and those of you here must assist in reshaping his soul. That is what is important, the production of human souls. And that is why I raise my glass to you, writers, to the engineers of the human soul.

Stalin's own texts were designed to shape the contents of communist heads, not hearts. For that, the Vozhd wanted literature of the sort he had read as a teenager—novels and stories and plays and poems—albeit with more concrete, tractors, hydroelectric dams and "joy in work." Despite his grasp of realpolitik, his contemptuous understanding of human weakness and general murderousness, Stalin was a naïve romantic, at least insofar as he believed in the transformative power of literature. After all, bad people read good poetry and remain evil, while good people read bad novels and remain good, and we all forget most of what we read anyway. But Stalin, the erstwhile poet of natural beauty, who had been stirred to rename himself Koba by an encounter with a potboiler, still believed.

After two years of meetings and discussions, Gorky delivered the keynote speech inaugurating this new spirit-shaping type of literature at the First Congress of the Writers' Union in 1934 (although not before submitting it to Stalin first, of course). Stalin had named the new style in art socialist realism, and it required that writers generally avoid reality and focus instead on chaste, clean, uplifting stories about Soviet construction, heroic acts of labor and noble exemplars of Soviet citizenry. The state dispatched crack teams of writers to the remote regions of the USSR to instruct minority writers in how to compose Soviet novels. Authors searched for gigantic construction projects to praise; hacks flourished; and writers who proved adept at handling politically correct material, whether industrial, historical, or war-themed, could reap great rewards, including the state's highest honor, the Stalin Prize (first class). Such was the fate of *The Rainbow*, by Wanda Wasilewska, a tale of partisan warfare and the heroic Red Army that, although now forgotten, sold out its initial print run of four hundred thousand in two days and was even snapped up for U.S. publication by Simon and Schuster.

Titanic print runs notwithstanding, socialist realism was already a creatively spent force by the time it officially launched. In fact, many of the most famous state-approved Soviet novels were published *before* Gorky delivered his keynote speech:

Chapaev, Furmanov (1923)
Cement, Gladkov (1925)
And Quiet Flows the Don, Sholokhov (1928)
Peter the Great, Tolstoy (1929–1934)
Time, Forward!, Kataev (1933)
How the Steel Was Tempered, Ostrovsky (1934)

Nor was adherence to the party line a guarantee of survival. Writers could easily fall from grace and into the grave. Of the forty writers who were in the room with Stalin when he assigned them the job of metaphysical reconstruction, eleven died in the Purges. Gorky, deceived, isolated and desperate, died in 1936, the year the gulf between the word and the world reached epic proportions, as Stalin not only announced that socialism had "basically been achieved in our country" but also unveiled a new version of the Soviet constitution, a highly enlightened document that promised citizens all manner of rights that they did not in fact have—while also launching the Great Terror.

Socialist realism itself would take a little longer to die. It colonized other art forms, was subject to reinterpretation and limped along for a few decades following Stalin's death, nevertheless leaving Soviet souls resolutely unengineered. Little wonder: who today would voluntarily read Semyon Babaevsky's epic *Cavalier of the Gold Star* (1948), in which, over the course of some six hundred–plus pages, the hero revives the local economy by organizing volunteers to collect timber?

———

WITH LENIN WRESTLED into submission and Stalin's plan for the reconstruction of the human soul via novels about hydroelectric dams well under way, the Vozhd now set his sights on the conquest of history.

He had revised and rewritten reality many times since consolidating power. Many old Bolsheviks who had once been leaders and heroes, or even close confidants of Lenin's, had been unmasked as diabolical double agents. It was one thing for the state to edit nonpersons out of official photographs, or for family members to take their old family snaps and blot out with ink the faces of relatives who had been purged, but it was another thing entirely to erase these nonpersons from memory. In private, in the theater behind the eyelids, who was to say what versions of the past persisted?

Stalin, meanwhile, was concerned about his cadres, the generation of communists that had risen to replace the older one he had wiped out. Where did this new intellectual class stand ideologically? What "facts" were in their heads? How could he control what they believed? Clearly, a text was needed: an official version of what had happened, and, by implication, what had *not* happened. This text would delineate precisely what he required his subjects to believe, or at least what they should pretend to believe: a final, Stalin-forged version of the Truth.

In fact, Stalin had been concerned about the condition of the Soviet past for some time. In 1931 he wrote a letter to the editors of the journal *Proletarian Revolution* in which he attacked a group of historians for belittling the roles of Lenin and the Communist Party in the revolution, and for devoting insufficient energy to the task of "tearing off masks" of Trotskyites. "Falsifiers of history," he had called them. What was needed, Stalin wrote, was a "scientific" and Bolshevik approach to history.

But what did the Vozhd mean by "scientific"? A series of histories appeared and disappeared in rapid succession, an unstable whirl of text generated by authors doing their best to divine what this meant. It was difficult, after all, to keep abreast of who was virtuous and who was evil, as Stalin butchered his way through many former friends and allies. In this environment, writing about the past was dangerous. Attempting to stem the tide of inadequate, ephemeral histories, Stalin had commissioned an official and ultimate party history, written by a collective of loyal professors. It was published in 1935. Two years later, however, its editor, Vilgelm Knorin, a revolutionary since 1905, was exposed as a traitor. Apparently not content to spend the prerevolutionary period as an agent of the tsar, he had also served in the Gestapo, while working his way up the ladder of official Soviet historiography. He was arrested and shot.

Undaunted, Stalin resolved to produce another absolute and final history of the Communist Party. This time he would take a more direct role: not writing it, but acting as editor, supervising the creation of a great work of fiction, in which he would restrain the disorder of memory once and for all. It was to be called *The History of the Communist Party of the Soviet Union (Bolsheviks): Short Course.*

Stalin commissioned a team of historians to work on the text, although he was the "director," providing the scholars with a chronological framework of twelve chapters and editing the completed manuscript five times before publication. He did not trust his subordinates to write the chapter dedicated to ideology—he did that himself, providing yet another précis of dialectical materialism and Marxist-Leninism for the masses. In the early days of the revolution, Stalin's peers and rivals had been dismissive of his theoretical prowess; now that they were all dead or in exile, he would have the last word on the matter.

And so Stalin's historians toiled, shaping the text to suit his requirements, revising it whenever another nonperson was created (which caused publication delays) while Stalin scrutinized their work. The drafts are preserved in his personal archive: pages and pages of typescript, some littered with Stalin's handwritten marginalia, others scored out entirely. He forced his writer-vassals not only to fit history to his demands, but even to use the conjunctions that he, the non-native Russian speaker, preferred. In addition to being a mass murderer, he was also the line editor from hell.

The *Short Course* debuted in September 1938 in serial form in *Pravda*, appearing as a book a month later. Its publication was a grand event; the party's Central Committee issued a decree declaring that the book existed to "provide unified leadership" on the history of the party, and that its publication "ends all arbitrariness and confusion" that "we have seen in numerous earlier textbooks on Party history." The critics were united in their awe. In *Bolshevik* magazine, the *Short Course* was compared to *The Communist Manifesto* for its brilliance, while the journal *Questions of History* praised it as a "model scientific work" remarkable not only for its "deep Marxist analysis" but also for its "simplicity and accessibility of presentation."

They were lying of course—except for that bit about simplicity. But it

was lie or die in those days, and perhaps, in their terror, some of those enthusiastic reviewers were even able to persuade themselves that they meant it.
Extracted from a context in which a negative review is likely to result
in death, however, and the *Short Course* is clearly not a model scientific
work but rather a sequence of truths, half-truths and untruths, a piling up of
words one after the other, smothering memory. It is a crude moral fable of
good Lenin/Stalin versus bad Trotsky/Bukharin/Mensheviks/lots of other
villains, a simplistic and reductive narrative filled with distortions, in
which (following the Lenin tradition) far more attention is paid to internal
struggles with other socialists than to the actual alleged life-or-death battle
with capitalism, imperialism or the tsar. Rendered in flat, mechanical
prose, it is the apotheosis of the Stalin style, even if he did not write most
of it: repetitive, schematic, and with lots of *a, b, c and d*. It is also curiously superficial, as if Stalin intended it for memorization and recital, not
for internalization. Each chapter comes with a handy summary at the end,
outlining precisely how the reader should interpret what he has just read.

A catechism, yes: but it is also more than that. By accident, Stalin had
rendered the history of the Communist Party into an avant-garde, almost
Oulipian* exercise in literary restrictions. He allowed, for instance, that
individuals might be able to make an impact within the correct historical
conditions, but he would not permit his underlings to attribute any significance to those individuals' personal biographies. In order to keep the
text sufficiently "Marxist" and "scientific," he had faces, bodies and subjective experience erased from its pages. As a result, the book becomes
almost purely textual, a record of the clash between good proper nouns
and evil proper nouns. The good proper nouns want to make another
noun called "the Revolution," appear, and then once it appears they have
to struggle to defend it from the bad proper nouns, who often appear to be
on the same side as the good proper nouns—until they are later revealed
to be bad proper nouns after all. The leader of the good proper nouns is
Lenin: he appears 682 times in the text (701 if you include the table of
contents). No other proper noun comes close: Trotsky, lord of the bad
proper nouns, appears 104 times; Trotskyites, the nouns that follow him,
appear 88 times. The noun "Marx" scores a paltry 76 mentions.

---

* French literary collective renowned for its clever but fairly unreadable experiments, which
involved placing restrictions upon the writing of texts, such as doing so without using any
words containing the letter *e* or, conversely, using *only* words containing the letter *e*.

As for Stalin, although the conventional critique of the *Short Course* holds that he inserted himself into history at the expense of his colleagues, making himself appear a much grander figure than he actually was, he appears only 169 times and is largely absent from the first part of the book; nor is he mentioned at all during the Bolshevik seizure of power in October 1917, while there are no references at all to "Stalinism." In fact, Stalin had a habit of scoring out references to himself in manuscripts if he considered them overly grandiose. Although his personality cult eclipsed Lenin's, he still insisted, in print at least, on presenting himself as the faithful pupil rather than the replacement messiah. In 1947, when he reedited the *Short Course*, he even reduced the official number of times he had been arrested (eight), had been exiled (seven) and had escaped (six) to seven, six and five, respectively. Whether this was a sincere attempt at reining in the personality cult or merely false modesty, or both, or neither, Stalin, whenever he does appear, is always on the correct side of history.

But the *Short Course* is not just about proper nouns; it is also about other books, some of which take on immense significance. In the early chapters, progress is measured by the appearance of Lenin's key works, which are cited forty-nine times. The appearance of his newspaper *Iskra* (fifty-nine mentions) is the climax of the first chapter and is described as the spark from which "flared up the great revolutionary conflagration in which the tsarist monarchy of the landed nobility, and the power of the bourgeoisie were reduced to ashes."

As for Lenin's writings, Stalin makes explicit their role in constructing the genesis of the proper noun, the party:

> The Bolsheviks had been working to build up such a party ever since the time of the old *Iskra*. They worked for it stubbornly, persistently, in spite of everything. A fundamental and decisive part was played in this by the writings of Lenin—*What Is to Be Done? Two Tactics*, etc. Lenin's *What Is to Be Done?* was the *ideological* preparation for such a party. Lenin's *One Step Forward, Two Steps Back* was the *organizational* preparation for such a party. Lenin's *Two Tactics of Social Democracy in the Democratic Revolution* was the political preparation for such a party. And, lastly, Lenin's *Materialism and Empiriocriticism* was the theoretical preparation for such a party.

As history unfolds, Lenin is always ready with a book or article that provides the correct response, and Stalin's editors are there to provide the correct gloss on each Lenin text, along with the appropriate citations.

Stalin's blurring of the line between word and the world is made even more explicit in the weight that the *Short Course* places on slogans, which are referred to seventy-four times. In response to events, Lenin (and subsequently Stalin) often replies with slogans, which, we learn, are significant acts of world-altering verbal magic. For instance, we learn that in the period of the Russian Revolution of 1905, in order "to guide the masses to an uprising and to turn it into an uprising of the whole people," Lenin deemed it necessary to issue these catchy lines:

a) "Mass political strikes, which may be of great importance at the beginning and in the very process of the insurrection";

b) "Immediate realization, in a revolutionary way, of the 8-hour working day and of the other immediate demands of the working class"; and

c) "Immediate organization of revolutionary peasant committees in order to carry out" in a revolutionary way "all the democratic changes," including the confiscation of the landed estates.

This elision of speech and action is further intensified by the tendency to use the same language for rhetorical struggles as for mass murder. In the *Short Course*, struggle is perpetual; the word *struggle* occurs a deadening 327 times. But when everything is a struggle then nothing is, and a weird flattening effect occurs. No distinction is made between a struggle carried out via the pen, such as Lenin's campaign against the Liquidationists, where the writing of articles is described as "smashing the resistance," and a struggle that results in piles of corpses. However, the word *smashing* is also applied to the fight against the ideological heresy of populism, the tsar's persecution of Bolsheviks, Britain's pursuit of the war against Germany, and the party's campaign against the kulaks. Verbal violence is equivalent to actual violence, but the details of the latter are never provided. Everything becomes curiously weightless, and atrocities are obscured by paper and ink.

So it goes, on and on, for over three hundred pages. Toward the end, new forms of text invade the narrative, as the *Short Course* provides the reader with long strings of statistics culled from the reports that crossed Stalin's desk:

> During the period of the Second Five-Year Plan[,] real wages of workers and office employees had more than doubled. The total payroll increased from 34,000,000,000 rubles in 1933 to 81,000,000,000 rubles in 1937. The state social insurance fund increased from 4,600,000,000 rubles to 5,600,000,000 rubles in the same period. In 1937 alone, about 10,000,000,000 rubles were expended on the state insurance of workers and employees, on improving living conditions and on meeting cultural requirements, on sanatoria, health resorts, and rest homes and on medical service.

If in the beginning of the party there was the word, and Lenin's word in particular, by the end there was Stalin, devouring reports. We have moved beyond theory to the word actualized, manifesting itself in the recitation of massaged statistics. These figures, we are promised, relate to things in the world, but actually they relate primarily to things on other pieces of paper. And outside, beyond the page: blood, terror, war.

ONCE IT WAS published, the *Short Course* took its place as a central text of the USSR, a holy book alongside Stalin's hagiographic, stupefyingly dry official biography, which he had also subjected to heavy editing. The masses studied the books in educational institutions; the elite were fawning in their praise of them. In 1939, at the Eighteenth Party Congress, Nikita Khrushchev described Stalin's ideas as "a great contribution to the treasure store of Marxism-Leninism," amounting to "a higher stage in the development of Leninism." The pupil had outstripped the master; Lenin was eclipsed.

Indeed, so great was the book that it could only be the work of one man. So in 1946, the official authorship of the *Short Course* was revised: *Pravda* announced that *The History of the Communist Party of the Soviet Union (Bolsheviks): Short Course* would henceforth be included as volume 15 of Stalin's *Collected Works*. Trees were massacred that the book might replicate and find its way across the USSR and then farther, across the waves. Between its initial publication in 1938 and 1955, a grand total of 42,816,000 copies were printed, while the section on "Dialectical and

Historical Materialism," in chapter 4, which Stalin actually had written, was extracted and published in the millions as a separate pamphlet. Some Soviet minorities had only just acquired written alphabets, and this was what they got to read. Neither were foreigners denied the delights of the *Short Course*, as it appeared in sixty-seven languages and was distributed globally. From the streets of Beijing to the avenues of Paris to the radical bookstores of San Francisco, Stalin's vision of history imposed itself upon the world. My own copy was issued in 1939, in a durable hardback format and on high-quality paper stock by International Publishers of New York. Nearly eight decades later, the pages show only a few signs of age, and unless I or one of my heirs burns it, the thing could outlast me by centuries.

As acclaim showered down upon the *Short Course*, so Europe edged ever closer to Armageddon. Stalin, as always, would emerge quite well from the ensuing carnage, standing triumphant atop the corpses of millions, extending the borders of his empire and the reach of his reality-denying texts deep into the center of Europe. The war was not long over when, in 1946, the printing presses churned out half a million copies of his collected works, and a million copies of the second edition of his official biography were in circulation by the end of the following year. Soon, colossal monuments to Stalin stood in cities of Czechoslovakia, Poland and Hungary, while his books became obligatory reading for young communists beyond the Soviet border. Not until Chairman Mao unleashed his *Little Red Book* of quotations upon the world would a communist book have so wide a reach.

But even as Stalin imposed his will on new nations, wielding greater power than ever before, he wrote less and less. Although he still read voraciously and maintained a tight grip on Soviet culture, he published no major works after the war—until 1950, when he unleashed *Marxism and Linguistics* upon the world—first as a series of letters published in *Pravda* and then as a pamphlet in its own right. Here he weighed in on the theories of Professor Nikolai Y. Marr and his disciples, who had for years dominated the discussion of linguistics in the USSR. Marr's theories were nonsensical: he claimed that he had divined that the first four syllables of human speech ever articulated were *sal*, *ber*, *yon* and *rosh*, and that language was the invention of a group of priest-magicians who had initially kept it secret from the lower classes that they might use it as a weapon in the class struggle, etc. Of this Stalin wrote, "No, it is not true"—before proceeding, in a quite sensible fashion, to dismantle Marr's theories, thus liberating the study of linguistics from a deadening dogma.*

Two years after this, Stalin published his final book, *Economic Problems of Socialism in the USSR*. It was not so much a book as a collection of notes, provoked by Stalin's reading of another set of notes on an economics textbook that did not yet exist, although it had been commissioned in 1937. A draft copy was submitted to a review panel of 250 economists and political leaders in November 1951, but was found wanting: clearly, the Vozhd needed to get involved. Stalin's metatextual jottings on the textbook and its themes were published unexpectedly three days before the start of the Nineteenth Party Congress, on October 5, 1952. Serialized in *Pravda*, and published in its own right as a pamphlet with an initial print run of 1.5 million copies, *Economic Problems of Socialism in the USSR* was met with rapturous acclaim and was the subject of much discussion in offices and factories throughout the land.

Even if *Economic Problems of Socialism in the USSR* came into existence in a somewhat ad hoc fashion, it was an authoritative text, intended by its author as a series of statements that would transcend his death, defining policies that would shape the world he had created as it moved into a future he would never see. By means of paper and ink, he would inscribe his will upon the fates of millions even as he slept for all eternity. Yet for all these grand dreams he concludes his last work on a somewhat prosaic note: not with more theoretical pronouncements on the eternal truths of Marxism, but with a demand to create yet another giant tome: the long-stalled textbook on economics. Finishing this work is, he declares, a matter of "international importance" for the benefit of both Soviet youth and "foreign comrades." There are so many lessons to be learned:

> . . . how we broke out of capitalist slavery; how we rebuilt the economy of our country on socialist lines; how we secured the friendship of the peasantry; how we managed to convert a country which was only so recently poverty-stricken and weak into a rich and mighty country; what are the collective farms; why, although the means of production are socialized, we do not abolish commodity production, money, trade, etc.

---

* Which was, of course, the reverse of the normal direction of Stalin's interventions.

That said, Stalin (as always) wants to keep things straightforward:

It must not be too bulky, because an over-bulky textbook cannot be a reference book and is difficult to assimilate, to master. But it must contain everything fundamental relating both to the economy of our country and to the economy of capitalism and the colonial system.

Stalin suggests that a book of around five hundred pages (or six hundred "at most") should do the trick. He even lays out a detailed plan for its production: there should be a committee featuring the book's authors and their more hostile critics, a statistician to verify the figures and to supply additional statistical material for the draft, and a "competent jurist to verify the accuracy of the formulations." That is not all:

The members of the committee should be temporarily relieved of all other work and should be well provided for, so that they might devote themselves entirely to the textbook.

Furthermore, it would be well to appoint an editorial committee, of say three persons, to take care of the final editing of the textbook. This is necessary also in order to achieve unity of style, which, unfortunately, the draft textbook lacks.

And finally:

Time limit for presentation of the finished textbook to the Central Committee—one year.

Stalin wrote those words on February 1, 1952. But the tyrant's time for carrying out purges and massacres while closely managing the production of publications was drawing to a close. He suffered a stroke one month after the deadline and died five days later. Soon, the books he had willed into being would start vanishing from shelves, as if they had never been there, imposing the lie, and collusion in the lie, upon millions. But that disappearance was also a lie: the books had been very real, unbearably so.

3

Mussolini

Mussolini—once upon a time, people took him very seriously indeed

We begin with the body of Benito Mussolini, hanging upside down from a lamppost outside an Esso gas station in Milan. Shot by communist partisans and abused by an enraged mob, the recently alive meat sways as if spiked on a butcher's hook in an open-air abattoir. And, by its side, the similarly desecrated remains of Claretta Petacci, Il Duce's long-term mistress.

This battered carcass had once imposed itself upon a nation. Imperious, proud, vital, it graced posters, newspapers and postcards, and flickered ghostlike in movie newsreels. It cavorted with lions and appeared half naked, stripped to the waist among workers. It posed in absurd regalia as a great military leader, and in more restrained costume as loving paterfamilias surrounded by children. It was regularly observed on the balcony of the Palazzo Venezia in Rome, where it strutted back and forth, eyes bulging, arms gesticulating, seductive words about empire and Italy raining down on the crowd gathered below.

Mussolini's body was different from the sedentary flesh of Lenin or Stalin. It was a body in constant motion, a body that fought and that was as desirable as that of any matinee idol, for Mussolini had hundreds of lovers. When he stood, it was with arms akimbo, as if he were a rocket poised to launch and strike directly at the blazing eye of the sun.

But for all his posturing as a man of action, Mussolini was also a man of inaction. That is to say, he was a writer. He was competent in multiple styles—journalism, oratory, poetry, history, fiction, drama, memoir and autobiography—and his writing was rarely, if ever, completely awful. Unlike Lenin, Stalin, Hitler or most of the other dictator-authors in this book, he wrote prose that was at times highly readable. He was also prolific: prior to his arrival at the lamppost, he cranked out enough text to fill a forty-four-volume edition of his complete works.

And sometimes, in these essays and books and plays, he prefigured the catastrophes of his own life.

A GIFTED CHILD from the provinces develops into an outsider hostile to authority. Craving power, but pursuing it in the name of freedom, justice and social transformation, he passes through the fires of exile, imprisonment and war, waiting decades for the perfect moment to strike.

Thus it was for Lenin, the minor noble from provincial Russia; so it was for Stalin, the impoverished cobbler's son in peripheral Georgia; and so it was also for Benito Mussolini, born to a blacksmith and a schoolteacher in the mountainous Romagna region of northern Italy in 1883. Unlike his Bolshevik peers, however, this boy was nurtured in the spirit of revolution; Romagna was known for its rebelliousness. Mussolini's mother, Rosa, was a churchgoer, but his father, Alessandro, hated priests and had named his son after the anticlerical Mexican president Benito Juárez. Mussolini didn't need to discover socialism in books written by faraway German theorists; he could find it in his own family, in his blood. In addition to hitting hot metal with a hammer, Alessandro Mussolini moonlighted as a radical journalist.

Revolt came naturally to the boy. So did violence: at age ten, he stabbed a classmate with a penknife. He was expelled. Unrepentant, he stabbed another classmate at his next school, and would lead local gangs on raiding expeditions against the local farms.

A hoodlum, then. But Mussolini also loved books and, occasional stabbings notwithstanding, did well in languages, literature and history at school. In February 1902 he became a teacher, but by June he was already out of work, as the school declined to renew his contract. His fondness for the local bars, propensity for quarreling with the parents of his students, and, most especially, a scandalous affair with another man's wife, cut that career short. So Mussolini emigrated, like many other Italians who were then heading abroad in pursuit of better lives. That July, with nothing (he would later claim) but a medallion of Karl Marx in his pocket, he left for Switzerland.

It didn't start out well. After making his way to Lausanne, he was soon arrested for vagrancy—the first of eleven stints he would spend behind bars before coming to power. When he got out of jail, he worked a variety of low-skill jobs but still had to sleep on park benches when he ran out of money. He also began publishing articles in a local Italian socialist paper, *L'Avvenire dei Lavoratori* ("The Workers' Future"). His first piece was on the massacres of Armenians in the Ottoman Empire. The nineteen-year-old socialist firebrand proclaimed that class struggle lay at the root of the interethnic carnage, declaring that the "tyranny" exercised by the economically privileged social class would have to disappear in order to bring an end to "race hatred and fanaticism." The editors liked his style, and Mussolini's journalistic career was off to a flying start: within months, he had published a further nine articles in *L'Avvenire dei Lavoratori*.

Mussolini embarked on a rigorous course of intellectual self-betterment, guided in his philosophical explorations by Angelica Balabanoff, a highly educated Russian-Jewish exile (and associate of Lenin and Trotsky). With her assistance, the provincial boy with a penchant for whorehouses and stabbings cut a swathe through many complicated texts he found in the Lausanne University library. Mussolini's reading list included:

- **Benedict de Spinoza** (1632–1677), Dutch lens grinder and philosopher who, despite his opposition to religious orthodoxies, held that "Knowledge of God is the mind's greatest good."
- **Immanuel Kant** (1724–1804), German philosopher who argued that

intuition rather than experience could serve as the basis for certain facts about the world, and that ethical decisions should be based on categorical imperatives, not hypothetical results.

- **G. W. F. Hegel** (1770–1831), German philosopher who claimed that his thought represented the historical culmination of all previous systems of thought, and whose teleological vision of history influenced Marx.
- **Pyotr Kropotkin** (1842 1921), Russian historian, geographer, zoologist, sociologist, prince and chief theorist of anarchist communism. Mussolini translated his *Words of a Rebel* from the French.
- **Friedrich Nietzsche** (1844–1900), German philosopher who pronounced God dead, attacked traditional morality and declared the importance of "life affirmation."
- **Georges Sorel** (1847–1922), French philosopher who denied the goodness of human nature, denounced democracy and extolled the virtues of myth, violence, class struggle and revolution.
- **Karl Kautsky** (1854–1938), German Marxist who eventually irritated Lenin to such an extent that the Bolshevik leader vituperated against him in *The Proletarian Revolution and the Renegade Kautsky* (1918). Mussolini translated Kautsky's *On the Morrow of the Social Revolution* (1902) into Italian.

Clearly, Mussolini, who could read in French, German and English as well as his native Italian, was intellectually curious. However, his capacity for consuming large amounts of complex text was not matched by an equal ability to synthesize any of this information in original ways or to articulate any complex ideas of his own, a fact made abundantly clear in his first "major" work, *Man and Divinity: God Does Not Exist.*

This forty-seven-page pamphlet was published in 1904 by the grandly named "International Library of Rationalist Propaganda."* Mussolini wrote it after attending a meeting in Lausanne led by an Italian Protestant evangelist named Alfredo Taglialatela. The event climaxed with Mussolini climbing on a table and giving God five minutes to strike him dead if He existed. Apparently dissatisfied with this argument, Mussolini felt compelled to generate text to further combat Taglialatela's arguments by writing an essay.

---

* In fact, this grand-sounding organization consisted of Mussolini and a friend.

Mussolini's "thesis" is a cheerful profanation of all that is sacred. He advances his viewpoint via mockery, assertion, appeals to authority and hyperbolic but utterly familiar atheist tropes:

How can the idea of a creator be reconciled with the existence of dwarfed and atrophied organs, with anomalies and monstrosities, with the existence of pain, perpetual and universal, with the struggle and the inequalities among human beings?

If the arguments are not novel, Mussolini's pleasure in language is nevertheless infectious. There is an exuberance to the play of insults, a delight in mockery, a joy in blasphemy. It is much less personal than Lenin's vituperations, and consequently less tedious. Mussolini is not engaged in a life-and-death battle over doctrine: he is having fun annoying people, like a proto–Richard Dawkins throwing rhetorical firecrackers at a series of straw men, declaring that religion "is the certain cause of epidemic diseases of the mind which require the care of alienists."

Mussolini most enjoys himself when he discusses Jesus. Next to the Buddha, who spent "forty-five years of his life in India, preaching fraternity, benevolence and love of one's neighbor," the Christian Messiah is "small and insignificant." His disciples are even worse: "a dozen ignorant vagabonds—the scum of the plebe of Palestine!"

Mussolini declares it an "inconceivable absurdity" to make Christ "the originator and propagator of any morality whatsoever." The Sermon on the Mount is a work of plagiarism, while "the few precepts of morality that would constitute a Christian ethic" are nothing but "counsels of subjection, of resignation, of cowardice." Finally, he inverts Christianity with his own blasphemous revolutionary preaching. Forget the kingdom of heaven, he declares, for "Wretched are those poor who do not know how to gain their kingdom on earth!" As for turning the other cheek, Mussolini instead proclaims, "Repay in kind the provokers; oppose force with force, violence with violence."

Simplistic, ignorant, but also utterly confident in his opinions, here Mussolini demonstrates precisely the skill set required for a career as a political journalist and provocateur. And so, although he also published poetry during this early phase of his literary career ("On the Day of the Dead" in 1902 and another poem dedicated to the French revolutionary journalist Baboeuf in 1903), it was as a strident opinion-generating machine that he would make his name. By the end of his stay in Switzerland, Mussolini—following spells in prison, expulsions from cantons, and shifting professions—was already known as a fire-breathing socialist, journalist, propagandist, trade unionist and public speaker. God was only one of the authority figures he subjected to vitriolic abuse: he also attacked kings, the Russian tsar, priests and capitalists. He demanded strikes and praised violence; like Lenin, he enjoyed verbal battles with fellow socialists and dreamed of a day of reckoning. There would be expropriations; there would be blood. The advent of socialism, he declared, would require an "insurrectional tempest."

Mussolini's gift for inflammatory rhetoric won him attention outside the expat circles of Switzerland. He wrote for socialist papers as far afield as New York, and also closer to home in Milan. His reputation grew. In 1904, a Roman newspaper published a story on one of his run-ins with the Swiss authorities, referring to him as the "grand duce" of a socialist organization in Switzerland. He was still only twenty years old.

IN LATE 1904, Mussolini returned to Italy. His mother was sick; she died. For a couple of years, he attempted to lead a life less marginal. He served in the military. He briefly, and disastrously, resumed his career as a teacher. But even during this period he still wrote and made speeches, and eventually he abandoned any effort at being a "normal" person with a "normal" job. Meanwhile, he experimented with more ambitious literary forms.

For instance, he dabbled in the long essay format, publishing a piece marking the twenty-fifth anniversary of the death of Karl Marx. Marx was not the only nineteenth-century thinker Mussolini praised that year. In an essay entitled "The Philosophy of Force," he extolled the virtues of Nietzsche's thought, despite the fact that the German philosopher had described socialism as "the tyranny of the meanest and most baseless." Never mind that: according to Mussolini, Nietzsche was "the most extraordinary mind of the last quarter of the last century." He appealed directly to Mussolini's iconoclastic, church-baiting, anti-Christian side, but Mussolini also liked the idea of "new men" who would live beyond good and evil, and was effusive toward the concept of the superman:

The "superman" is the great Nietzschean creation . . . Nietzsche has rung the bell of an imminent return to the ideal. But it is an ideal fundamentally different from those in which past generations believed. To understand it, there will come "free spirits" of a new kind fortified by war, by solitude, by great danger, spirits who will have experienced the wind, the ice, the snows of mountains and will know how to measure with a serene eye the depth of the abysses—spirits equipped with a kind of sublime wickedness— spirits who will liberate us from the love of our neighbor, from the desire of the void (*nulla*) giving back to the earth its purpose and to men their hope—new, free spirits who will triumph over God and over the Void!

It's an inspired piece of writing that reads as though it were written in a state of word intoxication. Mussolini's encomium to Nietzsche is poetic, romantic, energetic, fueled by its own infectious vitality: prose like this can get by without logic. It is very far from the doctrinally obsessed dogmatism of Lenin or Stalin, who insisted on framing everything in pseudoscientific terms. Il Duce doesn't do that. Borne aloft on the backs of "spirits," he raves about victory over cosmic nothingness.

Mussolini continued trying to establish himself as an intellectual. He wrote short stories and composed an essay on Friedrich Klopstock, a German poet celebrated for an epic religious poem entitled *The Messiah*. According to Mussolini's first official biographer Margherita Sarfatti, the twenty-six-year-old genius also wrote an entire history of philosophy in which "all the philosophical systems were dealt with . . . critically and analytically, and all new methods were subjected to Nietzsche-like examination." Alas, this masterpiece was incinerated by a young woman who, Sarfatti tells us, mistook the names of the philosophers for love rivals.

The most enduring work from this period (in the sense that it can easily be purchased secondhand over the Internet) is Mussolini's first and only novel, *The Cardinal's Mistress*, which was serialized in the socialist newspaper *Il Popolo* in 1910. Mussolini had until recently worked for the paper, which was published in Trent, a city with a large Italian-speaking population that was under Austro-Hungarian rule. However, a stream of offensive articles from his pen on themes as varied as the Church, democracy and Freemasons had resulted in his deportation to Italy, and he was forced to send the novel's fifty-six installments over the border by post.

Given its origins—as a potboiler Mussolini cranked out late at night for desperately needed cash—*The Cardinal's Mistress* should be awful. However, although it is by no means good, at times it at least borders on the readable. The plot, derived from a true story, is exceedingly convoluted. I summarize it below.

It is the seventeenth century, and Carl Emanuel Madruzzo, cardinal and archbishop (and secular prince) of Trent, is passionately in love with his much younger mistress, Claudia Particella, whose body has a "provocative outline" beneath her clothes and whose eyes understand "the sorcery of poisonous passions." He has squandered his wealth. He wants to marry Claudia. Everybody else hates her, including the rest of the ecclesiastic hierarchy and the masses, who are oppressed, overtaxed, hungry and poor.

Madruzzo's niece Filiberta is sole heir to the family fortune; Madruzzo wants her to marry Claudia's brother, but she wants to marry Count Antonio di Castelnuovo. So Madruzzo imprisons Filiberta in a convent. The mob blames Claudia, "of the dark and devilish eyes." Filiberta dies; the count, rather upset, digs up her reeking corpse.

The prelate Don Benizio now aligns with Count Antonio to bring down his enemy Madruzzo. However, he is less inspired by a love of the Church than by sexual jealousy: he, too, yearns for the exquisite flesh of the cardinal's mistress, Claudia.

At this point, things get very complicated. Plots proliferate, clerics behave badly, and the pope refuses to let Madruzzo marry Claudia. Madruzzo succumbs to grief, and Claudia informs him that it's over. Some more stuff happens. Finally, somebody stabs Claudia. She dies.

Often described as a "bodice ripper" by people who have almost certainly not read it, *The Cardinal's Mistress* actually contains very little in the way of bodice ripping and much in the way of Church bashing, including a catalogue of wicked popes ranging from Clement VII, who "maintained a troupe of lascivious women, among them a celebrated African, to solace him in the Vatican"; to Julius III, who "practiced Greek love." It is, in addition, admirably perverse. The novel has a sadistic, undisciplined physicality: in contrast to the sterile, bodiless world of Bolshevik prose, *The Cardinal's Mistress* wriggles and writhes with exuberant fleshiness.

There is Poe-esque body horror:

> . . . the acrid odor of decomposing human flesh compelled us to draw
> back a few paces . . . There Antonio wished to see the woman whom he so

loved, so desired. The body was recognizable by the golden hair which fell over the pure forehead, and by the eyes not yet contaminated. But from the lips, decomposed into a ferocious grin, oozed a dense, whitish liquid.

. . . lurid fantasies of rape and revenge:

I shall let the common brutes of the market place satiate their idle lusts on your sinful body. You shall be the mockery of the unreasoning mob. Your corpse shall not have the rites of Christian burial.

. . . the beating of a horse out of sexual frustration:

The whip continued to hiss while flagellating the skin. The horse had recognized its master and did not kick. It only stamped furiously as though begging mercy.

. . . self-flagellation:

. . . at the beginning he had sought to forget, abandoning himself to all the privations of a fierce novitiate. He had scourged his flesh with lead-knotted whips. He had fasted to the point of danger if not death from starvation. He had slept upon the bare ground, his slumber haunted by perverse visions. He had followed the minutest prescriptions of the spiritual exercises of expiation.

. . . and masturbatory fantasies:

Useless! After the flagellation, while his livid flesh was swelling under the bloody lashes, the image of Claudia would leap before his eyes. Claudia nude, quivering, seductive, offering the mortal caresses of Cleopatra!

But *The Cardinal's Mistress* is not only about quivering meat. It shows that Mussolini, although a Marxist, could allow for the significance of the inner, subjective world in human action. Now, admittedly, these inner worlds are attached to two-dimensional fictional characters, but at least they have desires and hatreds—in stark contrast to the proper nouns who serve as the protagonists of Stalin's *Short Course*. Mussolini's fictional people, motivated almost entirely by superstition, greed, lust and hatred, have more substance than Stalin's "real" people.

That said, Mussolini's vision of humanity is dark, and like both Lenin and Stalin he places no faith in the poor he claims to support. He depicts "the masses" as unreasoning beasts, easily moved by rumors, ready to erupt in an orgy of violence. It is not the noble proletariat we see, but the stupid, volatile, uneducated mob. Lenin expressed his contempt in coded form as a loathing of "spontaneity"; Mussolini is more honest. He understands the passions and fears of the poor, but he also despises them; perhaps this cynicism is why he was so good at manipulating the millions.

Yet in *The Cardinal's Mistress*, Mussolini the novelist also intuits the limits of how far that manipulation could be pushed. Writing in the third person, knocking out this throwaway piece of pulp trash late at night, he already knew truths that his future self would have to relearn, at the cost of his life: that the mob's patience is finite, and it does not forgive failure. Lose control, and you will lose everything. Thus the mob's hatred of Madruzzo and its visceral loathing of his mistress, Claudia, foreshadow the blame and hatred directed toward Mussolini and his own, much younger mistress, Claretta Petacci, in the later stages of his regime. Both narratives end in failure and in murder.

Mussolini's career as a successful man of the (offensive) pen flourished. In 1912, after a stint in the city of Forlì editing a new socialist weekly entitled *La Lotta di Classe* (followed by a five-month prison sentence for political provocations), he reached the apex of his journalistic career: the hoodlum from Predappio and onetime sleeper on Swiss park benches was appointed editor of *Avanti!*, the Italian Socialist Party's daily newspaper, published in the metropolis of Milan.

Mussolini knew what his audience liked: antinationalist, anti-imperialist, anticapitalist, anticlerical content, expressed in a radical, dynamic, violent, humorous and abusive style that broke completely with Italian traditions of the elegant and sophisticated sentence. Mussolini despised the dominant verbose style and vowed to strip away "all that is decoration, frippery, superficiality, annulling all the flotsam of fifteenth centuryisms, all vain chit-chat." His editorial strategy worked: *Avanti!*'s daily circulation more than tripled from twenty-eight thousand copies to ninety-four thousand while Mussolini also sat on the executive committee of the Italian Socialist Party. In the span of a decade, his skills as an orator and hack adept at generating copious streams of revolutionary rhetoric and colorful abuse had transformed him into a leading figure in radical politics.

Yet Mussolini was chafing under intellectual constraints. He was much less interested in "theory" than Lenin and the Bolsheviks, and although he was a socialist he did not revere Marx as a prophet. On the contrary, he was consistent in his iconoclasm. In 1911 he had even written that Karl Marx was "not necessary" for socialism. "We are not Theologians, nor priests nor bigots of literal Marxism . . . It is not necessary to interpret Marxist theories to the letter."

Mussolini had developed an interest in Jan Hus, a fifteenth-century religious rebel from Bohemia (in today's Czech Republic) who was burned at the stake by the Catholic Church for heresy. So fascinated was he by Hus that in 1912 he wrote a biography of the heretic/martyr in spite of the fact that (as he admitted in the foreword):

> The Latin works of the Bohemian heretic are unattainable in our libraries, the Czech works or those translated into Czech have not yet been translated into Italian; nor does he who writes these lines have the good fortune to belong to that small group of Italians who are able to read Czech easily.

These minor obstacles aside, the story of Hus was ideal subject matter for Mussolini. Here was a man who had criticized clerical corruption and advocated reform, an intellectual forerunner of the Reformation who was incinerated even though Church authorities had promised that he would not be harmed. Hus's biography thus provided ample opportunities for both body horror and attacks on the Church, which Mussolini exploited to the full:

> After the first blaze, only the lower part of the body was burned, the half-carbonized trunk remained fastened to the stake. Then the stake fell down into the ashes, and the fire flared up again, while a new wagon-load of wood was thrown on. The executioner's assistants raked out the bones and broke them up so that they might burn better. Thus the head was broken in two and thrown back into the flames, together with the heart, which had not been touched by fire.

Mussolini was able to indulge his love of violence further, as after the immolation of their leader, Hus's followers formed berserk apocalyptic armies that cut a swathe of destruction across Bohemia for decades. One sect, the Adamites, forswore clothes and rampaged across the countryside thieving and participating in orgies before they were massacred by a one-eyed general named Žižka. For a commercial writer like Mussolini, who understood the power of shock and sensation, this was great material, ideally suited to his target audience.

Even so, he strikes a different note than in his earlier assault on God and Christ. He is not so much antireligious as anti-Catholic. Ten years earlier, he had denounced Christ and his apostles as backward yokels and labeled the religious mentally ill. In Hus's heresies, however, he finds "a somewhat social, at times even socialistic, content." There is value in the preacher's writings and, not only that, but in the Bible also: Mussolini approves of Hus's insistence on "a return to the Gospel" and "a return to the poverty and solidarity of the early Christian communities."

Mussolini notes that Hus's followers were exceedingly violent, and that their desire to return to simplicity was "frequently accompanied by a call to revolt and to war." However, this is less an issue if a heretic is responsible for the killing, it would seem. When Mussolini describes the atrocities of the Taborites, an apocalyptic army of Husites, it is without the tone of moral condemnation he uses for the Catholic Church whenever it tortures or kills its opponents. The Taborites, he notes, "were determined to live, politically, without a sovereign; perhaps they wished to found a republic or to extend their community to all Bohemia. They were nationalists."

In fact, says Mussolini, Europe is deeply indebted to these religious extremists. Hus initiated a "heretical storm" that revitalized European civilization. "All the heretical movements of central Europe work toward the Reformation," he writes. "Thus, the history of the progressive liberation of the human race from the shackles of dogmatic beliefs knows no interruption as it proceeds from century to century." This is a broad endorsement of heresy in principle. The Taborites were a bit socialist, Mussolini says, but they were also a bit nationalist and, actually, very religious: they blended ideas together. Mussolini had already declared that Marx was not off-limits, and in the introduction he states that his little book is to be read broadly: "I cherish the hope that it may arouse in the minds of its readers a hatred of every form of spiritual and secular tyranny whether it be theocratic or Jacobine."

Jan Hus was published in 1913, when Mussolini was a leader of the Italian socialists. A year later, he himself took the leap into heresy. Having spent the buildup to World War I maintaining a hard-line, anti-imperialist, antiwar stance similar to Lenin's, he suddenly changed his mind. On September 25, 1914, the conflict suddenly ceased to be a "crisis of capitalist society," and he published an article calling for Italy to intervene on the side of France and Belgium and "to drown the war in its own blood."

He swiftly founded his own rabidly pro-interventionist paper *Il Popolo d'Italia*, which first appeared in Milan on November 15, 1914, bearing a quotation from Napoleon on the front page: "Revolution is an idea which has obtained bayonets." Mussolini's comrades were enraged by this act of betrayal. If they could not burn him as a heretic, they could at least kick him out of the party and anathematize him in public. Although he was officially still a socialist when he founded *Il Popolo*, nine days later he was expelled from the party and excommunicated from the creed into which he had been born. Within a few months, he had even fought two sword duels with former comrades, both of which he survived (more or less) intact.*

Mussolini's erstwhile comrades accused him of treachery and opportunism. Yet given his volatile temperament and open identification with morality-transcending Nietzschean supermen and heretics such as Jan Hus, it is not, in hindsight, all that surprising that he felt disinclined to submit to something so trivial as ideological consistency.

In *Jan Hus*, as with *The Cardinal's Mistress*, he had once again foreshadowed an aspect of his own future. This time it was the theme of the radical thinker who tries to change the world, but who is captured by his enemies and killed. Anticlericalism notwithstanding, perhaps Mussolini owed more to Catholicism's traditions of martyr veneration than he realized. After all, he could have chosen a different heretic, Martin Luther, say, who emerged victorious in his battles with sacred and secular authorities. Or perhaps his sense of history and of fate was fundamentally tragic. Written in a moment of personal triumph, Mussolini's book is about a man who rebels but loses his life. He was attracted to great, doomed figures. It is a self-aggrandizing fateful vision, and one he would return to again before he arrived at the lamppost.

---

* Mussolini was wounded in the second duel, but his opponent came out worse.

PRIOR TO THE war, Italy had been part of the "Triple Alliance" with Germany and Austria-Hungary and was theoretically obliged to fight with those nations against the "Triple Entente" of Britain, France and Russia. However, the Italian government preferred to wait several months to see how the conflict was going, and on May 23, 1915, it declared war on its erstwhile allies instead, having been (secretly) promised large chunks of Austria-Hungary if victorious. That September, Mussolini, now thirty-two and a father, was conscripted and sent to the front, which, in his case, was not the muddy charnel fields of Belgium or France, but the mountainous region between Italy and the Habsburg Empire.

He started writing immediately, jotting down notes in a diary the moment he departed for the front lines and later publishing them as *My Diary 1915–1917*, a book long out of print and little discussed today. This is an error, for *My Diary* is no mere work of propagandistic bluster. It is one of the few texts written by a twentieth-century tyrant that confronts experience honestly, minus all the apparatus of political theory, and which at times even crosses into genuinely literary territory. In its pages, Mussolini the poet of violence, the bard of mangled bodies, gazes upon the carnage of war and discovers that actually it can get deeply unpleasant.

Not immediately, however. At first, *My Diary* demands some patience of the reader, as it is an unconsidered, spontaneously generated text written in Mussolini's free moments as he headed out toward the front. The first part, which covers three months from September to November 1915, is fragmentary and filled with boring minutiae, as Mussolini the war tourist sits on a train and notes the changing landscape, or jots down the first time he sees an antiaircraft gun take a potshot at an airplane, or has a brief conversation with a child, or observes that his rations are "a trifle frugal, but excellent." At one point, he even tells us as he sits down to write an entry that he is sitting down to write an entry. It is vivid enough, but inconsequential, although Mussolini writes like a man who has found his destiny, declaring, "I like this active life which is full of trivial and great things."

During this sunny period of war love, the threat of annihilation means nothing to him. It does not even disturb his sleep:

Evening. We are stretched out, leaning against the trees, on the bare ground. Rockets and a deluge of bombs.

. . . while a little shooting only adds to the delights of the day after:

Calm. A little cannonading, and some shots from the outposts. A marvelous, sunny morning.

Here we encounter a Mussolini who sounds a lot like the posturing buffoon of old newsreels: chin out, arms akimbo, fez on his head, a Hemingwayesque parody of machismo.* In fact, "diary" or no, Mussolini remains a professional writer, painfully alert to the possibility that one day he will publish some kind of instant book based on his war experiences. In the early entries in particular, the diary is a sustained work of public performance and political positioning.

Having destroyed his career as a socialist, Mussolini the newly minted nationalist is keen to display his patriotic credentials, and repeatedly boasts of his close bond with "the people." Practically every soldier he meets has a) heard of him and is b) delighted to make his acquaintance. Grown men embrace him, or ask him to write letters for them, or ask him to be their leader. Mussolini reciprocates by praising the noble, brave Italian soldiery. His superiors, too, are perpetually impressed, he tells us—and yet, curiously, the Italian military authorities passed him over for training as an officer.

However, as early as chapter 2, a different tone enters the narrative. In the entry for September 20, 1915—the diary begins on September 9— Mussolini spots the moldering remains of the enemy. He pauses to jot down this imagistic micro-story:

A little farther away an Austrian corpse—abandoned. The dead man still gripped in his teeth a part of his uniform which, strangely enough, was still intact. But beneath it his flesh was decomposing, and I could see his bones. His shoes were missing. That was easy to understand. The Austrian shoes are much better than ours.

---

* In fact, Mussolini beat Hemingway to the punch. *A Farewell to Arms*, also set during the Italian campaign, was not published until 1929, four years after the English edition of the dictator's similarly terse war diary. Hemingway interviewed Mussolini in 1923.

Erupting amid the ebullient, high-on-war boosterism, it is a startling shift. Indeed, as I sat reading *My Diary* over catfish in a restaurant in rural Texas one winter evening, I stopped and reread the passage several times: Wait, was that . . . good? I asked myself. What happened to the poseur, the provocateur, the propagandist? Up until this point, I had enjoyed Mussolini's texts insofar as, after Lenin and Stalin, they offered something akin to light relief. Ideologically insubstantial and written in airy, amusing prose, they were more or less entertaining, although of historical interest only. There is no reason to read *The Cardinal's Mistress* or *Jan Hus* unless you are for some reason obsessed with dictator prose or writing a biography of Il Duce. But this . . . this sounded like *real* writing, something reflective of deeper experience that might have value in and of itself.

Of course, Mussolini the public performer soon returns. Little over a month later, he describes how Italians die like so:

> . . . the superb silence of these humble sons of Italy, when their flesh is torn and tortured by the ruthless steel, is a proof of the magnificent sturdiness of our race.

But Mussolini also talks about the men in the trenches alongside him using a different tone. He listens to their stories and records some of them. When they express religious faith, he tones down his atheism so as not to cause offense. Then, as the conflict drags on, the misery of the war compels him to write with increasing truthfulness. In the second part, which covers February–May 1916, he is frequently bored, cold and hungry; in the third part, which covers November 1916–February 1917, he is appalled and in despair: drunk soldiers collapse in front of him while on the march, and death, when it comes, is arbitrary and meaningless. One moment, a soldier is walking in front of him; the next, he is lying in the dirt, cut down by an enemy bullet. Mussolini keeps track of the steadily increasing quantity of Italian corpses in the local cemetery, and on December 6, 1916, he meditates on an Italian corpse that has not yet made it under the soil, in the same stark, imagistic style he used for the dead Austrian a year earlier:

> There is one of our men missing, a *Bersagliere* of the motorcycle corps. He lies with his head still stretched forward as if he was going to attack. Near him is his musket with the bayonet raised. He lies there alone. Why

does no one bury him? In order to allow his family to keep the illusion that he is "missing"? Perhaps.

Whereas once Mussolini happily slept in the open as bombs rained down, now he complains about the lice crawling over his skin and reflects upon the importance (and shortage) of sterilized underwear. He observes that the Austrians have nicer gas masks. He also loses his passion for violence: "Today the Austrian guns fired their usual harmless shots here and there. We yawn—either because we are hungry or because we are bored. This is the war of immobility." Finally, even his desire to write collapses in on itself: words (very nearly) escape him. His entry for January 27–28, 1917, is a short, unintentional poem of complete disillusionment, a requiem for a thoroughly shitty war:

Snow, cold, infinite boredom.
Orders, counterorders. Disorder.

Just as the English poet Wilfred Owen started the war writing upbeat letters home but ended it expressing the most profound despair, so Mussolini traces a similar arc in *My Diary*. The problem with his text is that all of the nonsense comes at the beginning, and readers have to plow their way through it to get to the quality bitterness expressed at the end, whereas with Owen you can simply ignore his correspondence with his mother and concentrate on the later works.

Actually that is not the only problem with Mussolini's book. The other problem is that its author later became a fascist dictator who fought on the side of Hitler in World War II. Outside the Italian far right and admirers of punctual trains, few people today are inclined to look for "good things" in anything Mussolini might have done. Regardless, *My Diary 1915–1917* is a well-written work in which, despite the self-mythologizing, Mussolini reveals himself to be an insightful and even poetic observer of the miserable awfulness of war.

Once again, Mussolini the writer was wiser than the head of state he would become. Would the Mussolini of 1917 have leapt as eagerly into war as the Mussolini of the 1930s? It seems unlikely.

And then, during mortar practice, one of those bombs he had once been so blasé about exploded a little too close to him, spraying his body with hot shrapnel. Mussolini's war was over, but his destiny was about to resume.

———

ITALY FINISHED WORLD War I technically victorious, but the attitude of the French, English and Americans to their southern ally was dismissive. Little had changed since the nineteenth century, when Bismarck observed, "As to Italy, she does not count."

Indeed, the leaders of the "Big Three" believed that the Italians had not pulled their weight during the war. The Italian army had never managed to progress farther than ten miles into enemy territory; then, in November 1917, it suffered a disastrous rout at the Battle of Caporetto, which climaxed with an ignominious retreat to Venice. Along the way, eleven thousand soldiers were killed, while a further twenty-nine thousand were wounded. German forces took three hundred thousand Italian troops prisoner, while an additional three hundred thousand ran for the hills. Having entered the war in the hope of gaining Austro-Hungarian territory, at the end of it the Italians were instead "rewarded" with a few meager parcels of dirt, while the lion's share of Dalmatia (their most coveted prize) went to Yugoslavia. All that suffering, death and economic devastation had been for nothing.

The ensuing postwar vortex of poverty, political instability, revolutionary politics, strikes, hunger, rage, nationalism and chaos provided ideal conditions for a priapic warrior poet known as Il Duce to seize his moment, which he did in September 1919. Backed by a nationalist militia dressed in black shirts, he occupied Fiume and enough of the surrounding territory to link it to Italy. The postwar redrawing of borders had left this ancient city of the Roman Empire inside Croatia; now Il Duce declared it a free state. Relishing his moment of glory, he addressed crowds from the balcony of the city hall, saluted them Roman style, held mass rallies, led sing-alongs of the Fascist anthem "Giovinezza," and exulted in the Fascist war cry "Eia, eia, eia, alalà!" He also oversaw the development of a corporatist constitution that guaranteed civil rights and equality of the sexes—all very unexpected for a Fascist, at least from a twenty-first-century reader's perspective.

The confusing thing is that this was not Mussolini but rather a *different* writer-leader who was also known as Il Duce: the scandalous poet Gabriele D'Annunzio, an aristocratic debauchee and advocate of incest (but only when practiced in the cause of "beauty").

D'Annunzio is an interesting case in that he demonstrates the crucial difference between a writer who attempts to commit an act of politics, and a politician who attempts to commit an act of writing. D'Annunzio freely admitted that he had no interest in economics, and although he maintained his grip on the city for a year, the Free State of Fiume swiftly degenerated into an orgy of cocaine-fueled, end-of-the-world sex and violence. With apocalyptic style, D'Annunzio dubbed Fiume the "Holocaust City," and even if he was no good at running an administration, he did have a keen eye for aesthetics.

Later, Mussolini would steal much of D'Annunzio's style, but in 1919, the ex-socialist turned would-be nationalist leader cut a rather flaccid figure by contrast. In March, he had formed the embryonic Fascist organization Fascio Italiani di Combattimento out of several smaller organizations. About 120 people, a motley crew of ex-soldiers, nationalists, republicans and Futurists, turned up for this historic meeting. The poet Filippo Tommaso Marinetti, author of the Futurist Manifesto, was a founding Fascist, while the celebrated conductor Arturo Toscanini joined shortly afterward,* so Il Duce could at least count on support from some of Italy's most celebrated artistic figures. But Mussolini had no city-state over which to govern, and he was still ideologically flexible. In the pages of *Il Popolo*, he raged against the "shameful victory" and attacked Bolshevism, but in fact the new organization's first political program, published in the paper in June 1919, had much in common with tenets of the radical left. Fascism at this stage was republican, anticlerical and against the rich: Mussolini called for mass land appropriations from both the Church and landowners and high taxes on the wealthy. He also called for an eight-hour workday, proportional representation in elections and universal suffrage. The fire-breathing man of the people from before the war still lived.

This was not a winning platform, however. In November 1919, the Fascists fielded nineteen candidates for elections; only one of them entered Parliament. Mussolini lost, and a group of socialists paraded gleefully past his window in Milan wielding a coffin to represent his political death. But his enemies had celebrated too soon. Italy plunged yet deeper into the postwar vortex, and by the middle of 1920, the government had demonstrated that it was unable to cope with waves of strikes and mutinies and factory seizures, while socialist victories in local elections later that

---

* The influence of Futurism on Fascism is obvious from article 9 of Marinetti's manifesto, which was written in 1909. "We will glorify war—the world's only hygiene—militarism, patriotism, the destructive gesture of freedom-bringers, beautiful ideas worth dying for, and scorn for woman." As for Toscanini, he would grow disillusioned and leave the Fascists before Mussolini rose to power.

year fueled fears of Russian-style revolution. Industrialists, landowners, members of the upper and middle classes, not to mention the many members of the working classes who desired stability and work, were deeply alarmed.

Now Mussolini found the role he had been searching for—not as foe of the landowners and factory bosses, but as their defender, and, more than that, as the fist of retribution, the bringer of order to a land that had suffered from turmoil for too long. Seizing the moment, he unleashed his Fascist paramilitary units upon socialists throughout northern and central Italy. "Punitive expeditions," the Fascists called them, although Mussolini's violence was very different from the cold-eyed sociopathic butchery of the Bolsheviks. Thuggish and puerile, the Fascist squads preferred beatings and humiliation to murder. Forcing the targets of their wrath to drink castor oil was one particularly popular tactic. Il Duce may well have studied Marx and Nietzsche and learned how to speak three foreign languages, but he was still a country boy at heart, who thought it was pretty hilarious when a grown man shat his pants.

Now that the Fascists were Italy's bulwark against communism, membership exploded. By May 1921, the party had nearly two hundred thousand members, making it the largest political organization in the country—and that same month, Mussolini was finally elected to the Italian Parliament, an impressive resurrection. Still, Il Duce was impatient and did not conceal his desire for greater order, and more power. In August 1922 he declared, "Democracy has done its work. The century of democracy is over. Democratic ideologies have been liquidated." Two months later, he mobilized his "Blackshirts" for the famous March on Rome, having calculated that the government and the Italian king, Vittorio Emanuele, would sooner hand over power than risk civil war. Weapon-wielding Fascists entered the city on October 30, and the king duly offered Mussolini the post of prime minister, which Mussolini accepted, although he was not yet a dictator. This was soon to change, as he proved adept at exploiting the ongoing chaos and turning it to his advantage. By January 1925, he had imposed a Fascist dictatorship, and *Il Popolo*, the journal of dissent he had founded in 1914, became the regime's mouthpiece.

Mussolini moved quickly to install the apparatus of the totalitarian state, and pioneered many of its now familiar forms: the youth groups; the monumental propaganda; the crushing of dissent; the secret police; the colossal construction projects; the after-work adult education programs;

the creation of theaters, museums and libraries; control over the arts; the sporting groups; and the Balilla, a Boy Scout–like Fascist organization that enjoyed "rigid but gay discipline." The Fascist regime even declared that its ascent to power represented the dawn of an entirely new historical epoch and restarted the calendar in 1926, with October 1922 defined as the zero hour of the new era.

In fact, the very term *totalitarian* was first coined by critics of Mussolini's regime in 1923, before he had even assumed the dictatorship. What is unusual is that the Fascists embraced the word, and openly referred to themselves and their system as totalitarian. In this, Mussolini was very different from the Bolsheviks, who spoke of democracy and justice even as they waged bloody campaigns of terror and repression. Mussolini openly scorned Western pieties with the same passion with which he had once ridiculed God or described mangled corpses—and it all started before he was even dictator. In 1923, for instance, he had published an article entitled "Fascism: 'Reactionary,' 'Anti-Liberal,'" in which he dismissed liberalism as a hopelessly dated nineteenth-century ideology, adding that Fascism, which knew "neither idol nor faith," would, "if needful . . . pass again over the more or less decomposed body of the goddess of liberty." On October 28 of that year, Mussolini produced one of his many definitions of Fascism: "all is for the state, nothing is outside the state, nothing and no one are against the state." He did not deign to hide his intentions. Perhaps uniquely of twentieth-century political ideologies, Fascism—antidemocratic, totalitarian and pro-violence—did exactly what it said on the tin.

Fascism was different from Soviet communism in other ways. Whereas Bolsheviks existed in conditions of severe cognitive dissonance as they denied their patently millenarian goals, Fascism openly announced its mystical aspect: in 1926, for instance, Mussolini declared, "Fascism is not only a party, it is a regime, it is not only a regime, but a faith, it is not only a faith, but a religion that is conquering the laboring masses of the Italian people." It was nationalist rather than internationalist; its vision of the state was as an adjudicator and conciliator between classes, rather than as an instrument of violence to be used by one against the other; and of course it was not hostile to religion. Mussolini found a sufficient amount of God to marry his wife in a religious ceremony in December 1925, and he successfully negotiated the 1929 Lateran Accords, which ended decades of hostility between the Church and the state following the seizure of Rome that had completed the unification of Italy in 1870. Mussolini was also far less violent than Lenin or Stalin. Within a year of seizing power, Lenin had launched a campaign of mass killings, torture and repression known as the Red Terror. By contrast, Italian public opinion was scandalized in 1924 when some Fascists murdered *a single person*, socialist politician Giacomo Matteoti, an outspoken critic of Mussolini.

Fascism was also a work in progress, unmoored from any quasi-sacred founding texts, even though Mussolini was by now a highly experienced writer with two decades of professional work behind him. Unlike the Bolshevik leaders, he was averse to tying himself to any definitive statements of "scientific" truth. In his days as a socialist, he had criticized slavish adherence to Marx. Now, although there were plenty of precursors to Fascism and the corporate state, he felt no eagerness to invoke the authority of a prophet; his own authority was enough. Mussolini gave speeches and published articles and produced aphorisms, but there was no "Bible" of Fascism. He appreciated a state of flux; he liked to improvise, to change his mind.

In fact, he had no choice. The inconvenient truth was that when he became dictator, much of his bibliography supported and promoted ideas he now opposed. Lenin and Stalin had switched tactics often enough in their careers, but it was relatively simple for them to edit or suppress certain works that exposed ideologically embarrassing positions since they had remained largely consistent in their core beliefs. With Il Duce, it was a different story: the godless, anti-authoritarian young Mussolini was the patriotic, Church-defending Mussolini's worst critic.

Mussolini's autobiography, *My Life* (which remains in print today), might seem like an ideal candidate for a core text, but it was actually a work of PR for the American market, initiated at the suggestion of Richard Washburn Child, the U.S. ambassador to Italy and a slavish admirer of Il Duce. In a fawning fifteen-page introduction, Child explains that he was so impressed by Mussolini's insistence on "work and discipline" that he felt the dictator had to write a book to explain to outsiders the "spiritual ecstasy" he had inculcated in Italians. "In our time it may be shrewdly forecast that no man will exhibit dimensions of permanent greatness equal to those of Mussolini," Child declared, and who better to explain this than Il Duce himself?

Who better indeed? In reality, Mussolini's involvement appears to have been minimal. Child worked on the "autobiography" with Mussolini's brother, Arnaldo, and a journalist named Luigi Barzini,* providing a summary of the dictator's rise to power and an explanation of his worldview, effacing contradictions and playing down scandals for an external audience. Nonetheless, the text is striking for the vitality of Mussolini's disembodied "I," which acquires a life of its own even when other people are largely responsible for it. Consider the opening passage, for instance:

> My childhood, now in the mists of distance, still yields those flashes of memory that come back with a familiar scene, an aroma which the nose associates with damp earth after a rain in the springtime, or the sound of footsteps in the corridor. A roll of thunder may bring back the recollection of the stone steps where a little child who seems no longer any part of oneself used to play in the afternoon.

Terse, economical, poignant—it successfully evokes the kind of sense memory fragments that link us all to our earliest years. Thus "Mussolini" summons forth the images and sounds of "his" developing consciousness, transporting us backward in time with "him." And so Child/Arnaldo/Barzini/Il Duce continues, as "Mussolini" sketches out in vigorous prose a brief history of his hometown of Predappio (full of rebels, like him), the Mussolini clan since the Middle Ages (headstrong leader types, like him), and the personal qualities of his devout, loving mother and strong, rabble-rousing blacksmith father: "Alessandro the neighbours called him. His heart and mind were always filled and pulsing with socialistic theories." The autobiography was published in the United States in 1928, following serialization in *Saturday Evening Post*. However, Italian readers would have to wait until the 1970s for an edition to appear on their shores.

When Mussolini did allow Fascism to be written down, he treated it as something mutable—like an opinion journalist blithely revising his assessments and positions from column to column, assuming that nobody is paying that much attention as he does so, and blithely carrying on before somebody does notice. This of course was the school of writing at which Mussolini had excelled, and he never abandoned the belief that

---

* In 1911–1912, Mussolini himself had sketched out an autobiography of his early years while sitting in prison, but it would not see print until after his death.

internal coherence, consistency and logic mattered less than timeliness, speed and a catchy turn of phrase.

Even the "Fascist Decalogue," the Ten Commandments meant to encapsulate the core aspects of the regime, was subject to revision as it was published and republished over the years. An injunction, "Mussolini is always right," might remain on the list, but despite its obvious centrality to the Fascist project, its status was not so certain that it would stay in the same place in the decalogue. Instead, it moved around, shifting from number eight in the 1934 edition to number ten in the 1938 revision. There were no tablets of stone; all was flux.

THROUGHOUT THE 1920s, whenever Mussolini expatiated upon his "philosophy," he stressed that Fascism was an Italian phenomenon. This was in stark contrast to the universalizing pretentions of Marxism, or even to Stalin's "socialism in one country," which was nevertheless predicated on the belief that socialism would ultimately triumph everywhere.

Then Mussolini changed his mind. Partly he was motivated by the spread of Fascist parties around the world that had been inspired by his own, and partly by the Marxist texts he had once studied. The Wall Street crash of 1929 was a critical moment in history, yes, the terminal crisis of democracy and capitalism, even—only, it would lead not to the dictatorship of the proletariat but to the era of Fascism. On October 27, 1930, Mussolini addressed a crowd from the balcony of the Palazzo Venezia and reversed his previous stance that Fascism was for Italy alone:

> The phrase that Fascism is not an article for exportation is not mine. It is too banal. It was adopted for the readers of newspapers who in order to understand anything need to have it translated into terms of commercial jargon. In any case it must now be amended.
>
> Today I affirm that the idea, doctrine and spirit of Fascism are universal. It is Italian in its particular institutions, but it is universal in spirit; nor could it be otherwise, for the spirit is universal by its very nature. It is therefore possible to foresee a Fascist Europe which will model its institutions on Fascist doctrine and practice . . .

The same year, a "School of Fascist Mysticism" opened in Milan—a swift and grand transformation for the earthy band of thugs who, a mere eight years earlier, had been running around northern Italy forcing their foes to drink laxatives. Mussolini was becoming ever more grandiose, yet remained resolutely opaque. In this fertile compost of quasi-religious mumbo-jumbo, his conception of fascism grew more ambitious still, and in 1932, in a speech delivered in Milan to mark the tenth anniversary of Fascism, he declared that "within ten years, Europe will be *fascista* or *fascistizzata!*" (i.e., "fascist or fascistized").

That same year, Mussolini finally produced an official, formal, written definition of Fascism. Even then, he hedged his bets. It was very short, fitting neatly inside a new national encyclopedia as the entry on "Fascism: Its Theory and Philosophy." When extracted as a pamphlet, it is fewer than fifty pages long, and thus shorter than either of Stalin's primers on Marxism-Leninism. Furthermore, Mussolini did not even write it by himself but enlisted as coauthor Giovanni Gentile, an idealist philosopher who was unpersuaded that individual minds actually existed, while also holding that the divisions between past and present or subject and object were artificial constructs with no bearing on the nature of reality.

The signs were ominous for fans of clarity, and sure enough, the most admirable quality of *Fascism: Its Theory and Philosophy* is that it can be read very quickly. Mussolini was well read in modern thought, but unlike, say, *The State and Revolution*, the text does not have the virtue of sounding like the work of a brilliant man persuading himself to believe in nonsense. Rather, it sounds like the work of a clever autodidact, way out of his depth, drowning in his own pretension.

So what is this Fascism, this astonishing idea spawned from the bullet-shaped head of the man who so impressed Gandhi that he declared him the "Saviour of the new Italy"?

> Like all sound political concepts, Fascism is both practice and thought, action in which one doctrine is inherent, and a doctrine which, rising from a given system of historical forces, remains bound with it, and works from the inside of this system. There is no concept of the State which is not fundamentally a concept of life: philosophy or intuition, a system of ideas that moves within a logical construction, or is gathered in a vision or in a faith, whatever it is, it is always, at least virtually always, an organic conception of the world.

Hmm: Fascism is both thought and action, and is inside and outside, and is also philosophy and intuition and numerous other things? Clearly it contains multitudes—and this is only the first paragraph. From this point, it only gets more all-inclusive as Mussolini and his coauthor expound at length in cosmic fashion, rambling on about the moral law, a world beyond the material one, and the importance of self-abnegation and sacrifice and death in enabling man to go beyond the limits of time and space and to thus live a "totally spiritual existence."

Or, as Mussolini puts it:

It is an interior form and norm and discipline of the whole person; it permeates the will like the intelligence. Its principle, a central inspiration of the human personality living in the civic community, descends deeply and lodges in the heart of the man of action as well as the thinker, of the artist as well as the scientist: it is the soul of the soul.

And so on, ad (or so it feels) infinitum. Yet three years earlier, Mussolini had also started work on a dramatic text, cowritten with the playwright Giovacchino Forzano, that represented a much less metaphysical meditation on power, and instead highlighted its ultimate transience, even in the hands of the greatest of rulers.

Just as Stalin had enjoined the USSR's writers to create ideologically sound novels, plays and films, so Mussolini likewise attempted to harness the creative classes in Italy to produce Fascist art. However, as he lacked the will or the desire to use terror to enforce his ideological demands, many writers accepted subsidies while failing to produce anything that met his standards when it came to promoting his ideology. For instance, Luigi Pirandello joined the Fascist Party and gladly accepted state subsidies for his Teatro d'Arte in Rome, but references to the glory of Fascism in the works he staged, or in his own plays and novels, are scant to the point of nonexistence. Another artist Mussolini admired, the Futurist Anton Bragaglia, also took Fascist coin—only to put on productions of plays by socialists such as Bertolt Brecht and George Bernard Shaw, as well as Dadaists, Surrealists, and Expressionists. With the new Fascist art proving slow to emerge, Mussolini decided to intervene directly and created some dramas of his own.

Giovacchino Forzano was well known in Italy as the author of popular historical plays. In 1929, Il Duce proposed a collaboration on the theme of Napoleon's last days in power. Two years later, the play, consisting of a single act divided into eleven scenes, was published as *Campo di maggio*. In its English translation, it was known as *Napoleon: The Hundred Days*. There was another difference: in Italy, Il Duce was modest and the play went out under Forzano's name. In England, France and Germany, Mussolini was explicitly identified as the coauthor.

In *Napoleon: The Hundred Days*, the dictator writes about a dictator. Napoleon was obviously appealing subject matter: like Mussolini, he was a rude provincial who rose from obscurity to lead an ancient nation. He was also everything Il Duce wanted to be: a great leader, a master of violence, a brilliant military tactician, a passionate lover, a gifted writer. As a work of drama, however, *Napoleon: The Hundred Days* falls short. It lacks action and consists largely of very long speeches and dialogues given by Napoleon, his allies and enemies. It also contains some fairly obvious attacks on the weakness of parliamentary democracy, which Mussolini had long since dispensed with in Italy. What *is* interesting is that Mussolini's Napoleon is not the conqueror who advanced through Europe, winning victories and changing the face of the continent by replacing a patchwork of feudal laws with one universal civil code. He is the defeated titan who stands betrayed and isolated by all those who once pledged allegiance to him.

Once again, Mussolini foreshadowed his own downfall in a literary work. Once again, he did so in a moment of personal triumph: Il Duce had concluded the Lateran Accords with the Vatican and was basking in global acclaim and international fascination with his "new conception" of the state. He thrived in the spotlight, but while officially he spoke of a new era in the history of humanity, and a new type of government that would long outlast his death, once untethered from the persona of Il Duce, he wrote about the possibility of an alternative, more tragic ending—just as he had in *Jan Hus* and *The Cardinal's Mistress*. Indeed, *Napoleon: The Hundred Days* seems to be a product of anxiety and contempt, as Mussolini writes of a great man dedicated to the people, but who overreaches and is subsequently betrayed by cynical former allies.

Mussolini collaborated with Forzano on two more plays, *Giulio Cesare* and *Villafranca*, and the playwright benefited greatly from his association with the dictator. But it was *Napoleon: The Hundred Days* that attracted the most attention on an international scale. Its 1932 staging at London's

New Theatre was written up in the American and Australian press, while the Hungarian production was especially well received, according to Mussolini's biographer R. J. B. Bosworth. In 1936, a movie adaptation was released, starring Werner Krauss in the title role. (Krauss played Dr. Caligari in the legendary German expressionist film *The Cabinet of Dr. Caligari.*) A critic at the *New York Times* wrote this terse but complimentary review:

> Collaboration of German and Italian film companies, backed by the powers-that-be in Berlin and Rome, has resulted in the production of a historical picture which can stand comparison with the best things in that line ever turned out in Hollywood or anywhere else.

Viewed in that light, the film version of *Napoleon: The Hundred Days* was an ominous harbinger of a far worse collaboration to come between the Fascist and Nazi regimes.*

As LATE AS 1934, the future was still going Mussolini's way—or at least you could have been forgiven for thinking that, looking in from the outside. That year, a state organization dedicated to the dissemination of Mussolini's doctrine claimed that thirty-nine countries now had Fascist parties. Il Duce was accustomed to basking in praise from prominent global figures, ranging from the Chinese Nationalist leader Chiang Kai-shek to Franklin Delano Roosevelt to Churchill. The legendary and notorious press baron William Randolph Hearst admired Mussolini so much that he tried to sign him to a contributor's contract in 1927, but instead had to settle for purchasing his articles from the United Press syndicate. This changed in 1932, when Hearst started paying Mussolini the princely sum of $1,500

---

* Despite the success it enjoyed in its day, the play appears to have succumbed to oblivion more readily than any other text by Il Duce, at least in its translated editions. For while it is relatively easy to find Mussolini's other books in research libraries, and some are even still in print, I had to have my own moldering copy of *Napoleon: The Hundred Days* shipped to the United States from Ireland. A sticker on the bottom inside cover reveals that it was originally purchased in Foyle's bookshop, on London's Charing Cross Road. A certain "Christopher Willard," or perhaps "Williams," took sufficient pride in ownership that he signed his name to the frontispiece in 1939, the year Mussolini took his decisive step toward that lamppost. Yet even this surviving copy arrived speckled with mold, creased, torn, and disintegrating, as if in a hurry to exit this world.

per (ghosted) article for publication in his papers. While not universally beloved in the United States (he was opposed by the left), Mussolini was widely regarded as a great leader who had transformed a backward, broken-down country by sheer willpower. He was even the honorary head of the International Mark Twain Society.

In reality, Il Duce's situation was not that rosy. He remained personally popular in Italy, but other members of the Fascist elite were not. Mussolini had stamped out all opposition and brought the state under his control, but the Catholic Church remained autonomous and a source of spiritual authority with its own rival institutions and organizations. After he issued the constitution for the corporate state in April 1926, it took a further eight years for Mussolini to get around to issuing the decree that worked out the details, formally establishing twenty-two corporations, each for a field of economic activity. Corruption abounded, the state bureaucracy remained bloated and inefficient and, worse still, since the 1929 stock market crash, there just hadn't been that much cash to splash on dams, opera houses or social entitlements. The New Fascist Man was not emerging; the old, Italian Man persisted. The gap between reality and illusion grew ever greater. Il Duce bemoaned that he had become a captive of his own propaganda, with little room to maneuver.

Had Mussolini's sense of timing been better—that is to say, had he managed to drop dead in the first half of the 1930s—history would have been much kinder to him. Responsibility for the collapse of his system would have fallen on the heads of his less charismatic lackeys. Despite his rhetoric, Mussolini was extremely restrained in comparison to his dictatorial peers. Although there was a Fascist secret police force, the Organization for the Vigilance and Repression of Anti-Fascism (OVRA), there were neither concentration camps nor gulags in Italy, and of the five thousand political prisoners rounded up between 1927 and 1940, only nine were executed. Even a minor dictator such as Fidel Castro killed many more of his own people.*

Alas, Mussolini did not die. Instead, he tried to become great, like a Roman conqueror, the builder of an empire. It all started to go seriously wrong when he dispatched Italian forces to invade Ethiopia in October

---

* Castro is estimated to have killed between fifteen thousand and seventeen thousand Cubans during his reign, although this did not prevent him from meeting Pope John Paul II in 1996, or Benedict XVI in 2012, or, indeed, Sean Penn in 2008.

1935. After overwhelming the poorly armed Ethiopian army with bullets, bombs and poison gas, triumphant Fascist forces entered Addis Ababa seven months later. According to Mussolini, it was a great and noble war of conquest; however, pacifying the population proved difficult, and savage reprisals were inflicted upon civilians (soldiers practiced their marksmanship by shooting Ethiopian men in the testicles). And while the war was popular within Italy, the unprovoked Fascist aggression turned Western opinion hostile. Accustomed to fawning treatment from the foreign press and dignitaries, Mussolini now found himself regularly vilified as a tyrant and a monster. He thought this sudden change in attitude hypocritical: after all, Britain and France had not acquired their empires by tickling indigenous peoples into submission, while King Leopold of Belgium (officially in the club of civilized countries) had managed to kill ten million Congolese during his stint as imperial overlord of that unhappy land. The United States had enjoyed its own colonial war in the Philippines in the early 1900s, and was still massacring Native Americans during Mussolini's childhood in the 1890s. Who were these imperialists to criticize *him*?

Buoyed by his victory in Africa, Mussolini next intervened on the Nationalist side in the Spanish Civil War, hoping to expand his influence still further. But Fascist armies proved to be less effective at fighting opponents armed with modern weaponry, and they suffered a crushing and humiliating defeat at the Battle of Guadalajara in 1937. By this point, however, it was too late. The increasing success of a mustachioed homunculus from Austria would provoke in the aging Il Duce an envious desire that would inspire the most disastrous decision of his life.

In 1939, Mussolini's ghosted autobiography was reissued with updated material justifying his invasion of Ethiopia. It also included explicitly racist and anti-Semitic passages that had not appeared in the original edition. Also new was a sense of kinship with Germany:

> There is a great deal of similarity . . . between Fascism and National Socialism, differences between the two movements being due to the innate differences between the two nations, their history, their traditions. The similarity of ends and means to achieve them, the policy of treaty-revision to which both Heads of the government were pledged, were sufficient however for both countries to march together since 1934. Political and ideological reasons brought the two countries together, and started a

cooperation in the international field which was as inevitable as the Triple Alliance of forty years ago.

In fact, Mussolini had treated Hitler with barely concealed contempt for many years. In 1927, the Führer, who kept a bust of Il Duce on his desk, had written asking for a signed photograph; Mussolini declined. The Führer had to wait another four years for his wish to be granted. While Hitler worked hard to emulate Mussolini's style, and had his men salute like Fascists and parade around in shirts only a shade less dark than those of the Fascists, Mussolini saw huge differences. In particular, he poured scorn on Nazi racism and laws on sterilization, publicly declaring that he regarded "certain doctrines from the other side of the Alps" with "utter disdain." He was no anti-Semite; not only were there Jews among the founding members of the Fascist Party, but 25 percent of Italy's forty-eight thousand Jews had subsequently *joined* the party. His longtime mistress (and ghostwriter) Margherita Sarfatti was Jewish.

Indeed, in August and September of 1934 he wrote a series of pseudonymous articles for *Il Popolo* in which he scorned Nazism and Hitler's claims of Germanic racial supremacy. As for *Mein Kampf*, he mockingly labeled it Hitler's "New Testament" and complained that when he first met Hitler the Nazi leader, "[i]nstead of speaking to me about current problems[,] . . . recited to me from memory his *Mein Kampf,* that enormous brick which I have never been able to read."

But as Hitler ceased to look like a crumpled janitor and started to look like an aggressive leader capable of defeating the imperial powers, Mussolini's old habit of emulating the style of more successful leaders came into play. Whereas once he had lifted from D'Annunzio, he now ordered his soldiers to goose-step like Nazis—forgetting that in his war diary of 1915 he had observed that "[t]he 'made in Germany' form of militarism has no foothold in Italy." In the revised edition of his autobiography, he retroactively designated 1934 the start of the Nazi–Fascist collaboration. He also introduced explicitly anti-Semitic "racial laws" in 1938, albeit with significant exceptions. Mussolini reserved the right to magically "Aryanize" anyone he pleased, indicating that his sudden turn toward anti-Semitism was more a step undertaken to keep up with Hitler than a sign of a sudden conversion to Nazi-style pseudoscience.

The Nazi Germany–Fascist Italy geopolitical romance reached its apex when Mussolini and Hitler signed the "Pact of Steel" in 1939. The two dictatorships were now officially an axis, and yet there was a degree of unrequited passion on Il Duce's side. Hitler treated his former hero as a junior partner from the start, and did not even bother to consult with him before invading Poland. In a fit of pique, Mussolini invaded Albania, and then Greece. However, the Italian armies performed with their customary lack of success, and Hitler was forced to dispatch German troops to do Mussolini's fighting for him. Corpses multiplied and the regime unraveled. Then, in 1943, a majority of his closest advisers in the Fascist Grand Council voted to remove the fifty-nine-year-old dictator from power.

The sequence of events had essentially been laid out by Mussolini thirteen years earlier, in his play on Napoleon. In the following passage, the substitution of "Bonaparte" with "Mussolini" and references to "France" with "Italy" results in a fairly accurate summary of Il Duce's position four years into the war.

> Bonaparte, the days of autocracy are over. You were a success so long as France could give you armies unexampled in numbers, courage and discipline, these you destroyed. So long as the enemies of France quarreled amongst themselves, employed antiquated weapons, obsolete strategies, you, without a drop of French blood in you, could fulfill the ideas, the work of a true Frenchman—Lazare Carnot. When you had dried up every spring of French enthusiasm, drenched the whole soil of Europe with French blood, you found the world united against you, hating you as no man was ever hated before, crying desperately for peace.

As King Victor Emmanuel put it when he informed Mussolini that he no longer required his services, Il Duce had become "the most hated man in Italy." He was arrested, and almost overnight, two decades of Fascism vanished like smoke through a keyhole. The public celebrated, although an enfeebled successor regime would stagger on for another forty-five days.

But it was not yet the end. Mussolini did not have the tragic dignity of his fictional Napoleon, who knew when he was defeated. He had been declared a political corpse before and had resurrected himself. He still dreamed of a comeback, an opportunity he was afforded when Nazi forces rescued him from his imprisonment and Hitler installed him as the puppet leader of the "Italian Social Republic."

Compared to the standard of his own literary ideal, Mussolini failed miserably in this last act. In *Napoleon: The Hundred Days*, he had written: "Downfall is nothing, if one falls with greatness. It is everything, if one falls basely." Yet whereas the fictional Napoleon had accepted his exile, declaring:

> I will not be King of a new September massacre. I came back from Elba expressly to avoid it. Gentlemen, the dream of ruling a prosperous Europe in peace might well justify even such an expense of blood as I have seen. For that dream I have allowed a generation to perish. But I am not a petty king, sending men to death to save his petty crown, or to vindicate his quarrel with an Assembly of childish demagogues.

Mussolini distinguished himself by deporting seven thousand Jews to the death camps and executing his own son-in-law.

The voyage to the lamppost was almost complete, but not before Mussolini returned to his literary roots, publishing a series of newspaper columns in *Corriere della Sera* in the spring of 1944. Writing under the byline "The Globetrotter," he reflected upon his fall from grace and apparent resurrection, and the texts were swiftly collected as his final bestseller, *The Story of a Year*.

The Story of a Year represents a missed opportunity. Mussolini was a skilled writer, and had he been capable of honest self-assessment, this could have been a great book, an opportunity to explore an epic fall from grace through hubris, pride and bad decisions. Of course, to do that would have required a wholesale dismantling of both cherished illusions and his very self, and entering that abyss was a task beyond Mussolini, as it is beyond most of us. Instead, he composed a work of titanic self-justification, a cry of outrage at the erstwhile close associates and ordinary Italians who had failed him. Italy, he declares, is "not even a nation," and he wages bitter rhetorical war on the "traitors" who deposed and then imprisoned him. It is a sad and strange text, filled with self-justification, self-delusion and repeated yelps of wounded megalomaniacal pride.

Yet Mussolini comes close to that abyss. The most interesting aspect of *The Story of a Year* is his habit of referring to himself in the third person throughout, as if in tacit admission that the "I" of the great Mussolini no longer exists. This "I" had once been so powerful that it existed autonomously, in ghostwritten articles and in his autobiography, immediately identifiable as the voice of the dictator even when somebody else was speaking it. It was a strong, confident, self-assured voice that went all the way back to his earliest texts, denouncing God and capitalists. It had filled thousands and thousands of pages, promising fire, violence and rebirth. And then, suddenly, it was gone. The third-person voice that replaced it was wooden, flat, without style. *The Story of a Year* is a work that screams exhaustion, and is possibly the least vibrant thing Mussolini ever wrote. It persuades nobody; if anything, its function is to persuade its own author.

Thus, Mussolini lists all the assassination attempts on Mussolini, asserting that Mussolini is a hard man to kill, with a "bulletproof skull." Mussolini also reports on Mussolini speaking to Germans about Hitler's loyalty:

> The Duce answered: "I knew all along that the Führer would give me this proof of his friendship."

When Mussolini is voted out by the Grand Council, the breakdown of the self becomes so extreme that even Mussolini does not know what Mussolini is thinking, and stares at himself from the outside, as if contemplating an alien entity:

> Mussolini did not seem to enjoy this occasion, since he had a longstanding aversion to meetings with no program planned in advance.

Still, there are moments when Mussolini confronts his fate with something approaching honesty. While he denounces the Italian people for their fickleness:

> Within half an hour a whole people changed its thoughts and feelings and the course of history . . . What are we to make of a people that makes a spectacle of itself before the rest of the world, by such a sudden and almost hysterical change of heart?

. . . he subsequently half-admits that his personality cult was artificial and unsustainable:

> It is not surprising that the people should destroy the idols of their own creation. Perhaps this is the only way to restore them to human proportions.

There are also moments when he reflects on what is perhaps the plight of all dictators who bask in the love of the people and yet are always fundamentally alone. Indeed, for Mussolini, this is an essential existential fact, and he records the third-person Mussolini reflecting upon this while in prison:

> All his life he never had any friends. Was this a good thing or a bad one? He gave considerable thought to this problem when he was at La Madalena, where he wrote: Good or bad, it doesn't matter, for him it is now too late. Someone in the Bible said, "Woe unto the lonely!" But there was a saying during the Renaissance, "Be alone and you will be your master."

A conundrum indeed; Mussolini does not resolve it:

> If I had any friends now would be the time for them to sympathize, literally to "suffer with" me. But since I have none my misfortunes remain within the closed circle of my own life.

But had he not reported himself saying that the Führer was his friend? Yes, he had—seventeen pages earlier, in fact. That statement seems to have been superseded by this later statement of utter aloneness. By the end of the book, however, Mussolini starts to write as though he is not a German puppet but a master of war whose star is on the rise again. His imaginative muscle kicks in, and Il Duce fantasizes that a revival of his political fortunes is at hand—"Let us set out again on our way, with our eyes on the road before us"—only to lapse, at the very end, into grandiose, mystical philosophizing, as if to suggest that this is the end but not really the end. Is he hinting that a grand reassessment will come?

> History is a sequence of eternal returns. The phases in the lives of nations are measured in terms of decades. Sometimes of centuries.

Italian communist partisans captured and executed Mussolini on April 28, 1945, as he was attempting to escape to Switzerland en route to Spain. An ecstatic mob vented its fury on his blubbery remains, and then his corpse was hung upside down outside an Esso gas station in Milan.

Had he not confused his gift for words with a superhuman ability to transform the course of history, thus misidentifying his true vocation as dictator instead of writer, the world would most likely have been a less awful place in the twentieth century. Alas, as a writer, Mussolini was subject to the same vanity and delusions of grandeur that afflict many born to the calling—and in particularly extreme form: instead of merely hurting his own family and loved ones and seething against critics, he managed to wreak havoc upon two continents.

Hitler

"It is truly miserable to behold how our youth even now is subjected to a fashion madness which helps to reverse the sense of the old saying: 'Clothes make the man' into something truly catastrophic."—A. Hitler

In 1889 a babe was born to Alois and Klara Hitler in Braunau am Inn, a town in the Austro-Hungarian Empire, close to the Bavarian border. Bright but unruly, young Adolf received copious beatings at the hands of his father, a ferocious disciplinarian with a much bigger mustache than his son would ever grow. Alois aspired for young Adolf to become a frustrated, rage-fueled civil servant, just as he had been. Klara coddled her darling boy.

Beatings notwithstanding, Hitler had difficulty submitting to anybody else's discipline. His teachers thought him lazy, and unlike his fellow future dictators in Russia, Georgia and Italy, he did not do well in school, although he was a keen reader and remained one his whole life—when he died at age fifty-six, he owned around sixteen thousand books. However, Hitler had no transformative encounter with a radical pamphlet or stodgy activist novel. Instead, he enjoyed nationalistic works on German history and devoured the pulp fiction of Karl May, a German author of Westerns featuring an Indian brave called Old Shatterhand. May had not yet been to the United States when he wrote his yarns, so his vision of the West and Native American culture was conjured entirely out of things he had found in other books. However, he was an innovator in that he inverted the standard trope of the good, civilizing cowboy versus the wild, savage Indian. May's decidedly pale Teutonic readership was encouraged to identify with the "noble savage" Red Man in his struggle against white settlers, many of whom, of course, were ethnic Germans. Young Adolf lapped it up and viewed Old Shatterhand as a model of bravery.

Hitler may have embraced these tales of a heroic underdog, but he did not react to them by generating any substantial texts of his own, other than the usual brief dabbling in adolescent poetics. After his father died in 1903, Hitler dropped out of high school to dedicate himself to art, opera, the theater, the study of Nordic mythology and the general nurturing of his own genius. At last, there was nobody to prevent him from pursuing his dreams—except, that is, for the admissions tutors at the art institutes he attempted to enter. In October 1907, the Vienna Academy of Fine Arts turned him down—the rector suggested he study architecture instead, but Hitler lacked the necessary qualifications. A few months later, his mother died and then, in 1908, the academy rejected him a second time. Maybe he should have become a civil servant after all.

Hitler stayed in Vienna, still intent on becoming a great artist. Instead, he found poverty, miserable nights on park benches, and grotty meals in soup kitchens. In 1909, aged twenty, he wrote "Writer" as his profession when registering a new address with the authorities in Vienna, but this was a fantasy. He eked out a precarious existence, subsisting through menial jobs and by selling landscape paintings and postcards of famous landmarks he had drawn. He was not entirely without talent: for instance, a picture entitled *Standesamt und Altes Rathaus Muenchen* (*Civil Registry Office and Old Town Hall of Munich*), which was sold at auction in Nuremberg in 2014 for $161,000, is a perfectly acceptable example of the mediocre tourist watercolor school. The sky is blue, the building looks old, the lines are straight, there are no obviously wrong elements: it does not offend.

Meanwhile, as Hitler daubed and starved, and starved and daubed, he read about Jews in virulently anti-Semitic newspapers and pamphlets. After laws restricting migration to the capital were lifted in the mid-nineteenth century, Vienna's Jewish population had leapt from around 2.0 percent in 1857 to 8.6 percent in 1910. In 1909 a quarter of the students enrolled at the university were Jewish. Jews were successful in business and finance and the arts, and were accused of "controlling the media." This was the epoch of Sigmund Freud, Gustav Mahler, Franz Kafka and Arnold Schoenberg, but it was also the epoch of debates in Austria-Hungary's Imperial Council over whether sex between Christians and Jews should be punished under the same laws as bestiality.

Although Hitler would later claim that he became an anti-Semite during his Viennese years, he certainly did not become an activist; nor was he even particularly politicized. On the contrary, eyewitnesses attest that the future leader of Nazism had numerous Jewish friends, freely mingled with Jews at the hostels he inhabited, praised Jewish composers such as Mendelssohn, and sold many of his paintings to Jewish art dealers. Friends (and enemies) from his Vienna days were later amazed when he emerged as the most prominent anti-Semite on the planet.

Hitler, in short, was still drifting, without a purpose. He drifted for years. Prior to the outbreak of the First World War, he was the most aimless, the hungriest, the most doomed of all the twentieth century's future despots, the one who could most easily have vanished, leaving behind no testament to his existence. Consider this. In January 1913, Trotsky and Stalin were also in Vienna, in close physical proximity to Hitler. Bolshevism was at a low ebb, but Stalin was researching his breakthrough work, *Marxism and the National Question*, while Trotsky was writing pamphlets, drinking coffee and editing a Viennese *Pravda* that predated (and was hostile to) Lenin's Saint Petersburg version. Meanwhile, Josip Broz, the future Marshal Tito, president of Yugoslavia, was living a few miles south in a town called Wiener Neustadt. He was working in the Daimler automobile plant but was already politically engaged: he had been a social democrat for six years.

As for Hitler? Nothingness.

———

To MANY, THE demise of 80 percent of your regiment in the first weeks of a war might be a catastrophe or, at the very least, a sign that things were not off to a very good start. Not so for Hitler, who found in the mound of bullet-riddled, bomb-shredded corpses evidence of the noble, self-sacrificing, valorous German fighting spirit. As he wrote to his landlord in Munich:

> ... with pride I can say our regiment handled itself heroically from the very first day on—we lost almost all our officers and our company has only two sergeants now. On the fourth day only 611 were left out of the 3600 men of our regiment.

Hitler had moved to Munich in 1913 to avoid military service in the Austro-Hungarian army. However, when the war broke out a year later, he was willing to fight for Germany and joined the Royal Bavarian Army's Sixteenth Bavarian Reserve Infantry Regiment (List Regiment, for short). According to the traditional narrative, he was a dispatch runner, responsible for carrying messages from HQ to the fighting units on the front lines, dodging bullets, mines and shells. As the bodies piled up around him, he repeatedly evaded death, whether by listening to a mysterious voice telling him to step away from an area mere moments before a shell landed or when he emerged the only survivor on the German side from a duel to the death with British forces. A little thing like shrapnel in the leg kept him away from the action only temporarily. No wonder he won two Iron Crosses, one of which was the rare "First Class," awarded only to soldiers who demonstrated exceptional courage. The apocalypse of war had brought dignity, meaning and purpose to Hitler's life: the deracinated Austrian dauber had become a Teutonic super-warrior.

Even amid the carnage, though, Hitler retained his cultural enthusiasms. In quieter moments, he would whip out his watercolors and paint the battle-scarred landscape, or dip into books on German history and architecture, or perhaps participate in anti-Semitic bonding sessions with his brothers-in-arms. In the trenches, the bohemian wastrel Hitler was one of the boys, sharing in the joys, sorrows and Jew hatred of the rank and file.

When the Armistice was declared on November 11, 1918, Hitler was convalescing in a military hospital, recovering from a British mustard gas attack that had left him temporarily blind. He was so enraged at this "betrayal" that he lost his sight again. Germany's leaders were traitors, criminals, saps of the international Jewish conspiracy. To make matters worse, two days earlier—on the first anniversary of Lenin's putsch—a revolution in Bavaria had terminated the eight-hundred-year reign of the House of Wittelsbach, culminating with the declaration of a Socialist Republic.

In Hitler's eyes, Marxism was a front for the Jewish desire for world dominance. Appalled, he resolved to go into politics—a decision that was only strengthened when representatives of the Fatherland signed the Treaty of Versailles seven months later. With a few strokes of a pen, Germany submitted to catastrophic humiliation, surrendering huge swathes of territory, accepting all responsibility for civilian damage caused during the war, and meekly submitting to the Allies' demand for the permanent decimation of the German armed forces. Cue hyperinflation, wheelbarrows of valueless money, political chaos, cabaret music, right-wing Freikorps militias, the scapegoating of the Jews, swastikas, goose-stepping, lots of speeches, sex with his underage niece* and, lo, a Führer was born—not out of books, but from the fiery crucible of war, death and societal collapse.

For decades, this version of Hitler's rise to power stood more or less intact. The problem is that it is based on Hitler's own account of the war as relayed in *Mein Kampf* as well as official Nazi propaganda in school textbooks, newspapers and magazines.[†] Yet if Hitler was so astounding, then it is exceeding strange that he was never promoted, nor given any authority over men, nor ever rose higher than the equivalent rank of U.S. private first class, which is the closest translation of his military rank, *Gefreiter.* Strange, too, that if (as he claimed) he embraced virulent anti-Semitism with his band of Jew-hating brothers in the trenches, and was already showing signs of impending Führerhood, he would be nominated for the Iron Cross (First Class) by one Hugo Guttmann, a Jewish officer.

Documents unearthed in the early twenty-first century by historian Thomas Weber reveal a different picture. It turns out that Hitler's job as a dispatch runner for regimental HQ was one of the less deadly careers open to military men during World War I, which is demonstrated by the fact that although there were hundreds of thousands of casualties on both

---

* Allegedly.
† Except for the sex with his niece part.

sides in 1915, there were precisely zero among the dispatch runners with whom Hitler served. Little wonder that frontline soldiers referred to the likes of Hitler as *Etappenschwein,* a "rear-area pig."

Hitler's anti-Semitic bonding sessions were also mythical. Indeed, he attended only one reunion of his regiment, in 1922, and did so while canvassing (with little success) for his brothers-in-arms to join the Nazi Party. By 1933, when his star was ascendant, a mere 2 percent of them had signed up.

Perhaps most bizarrely of all, Hitler actually worked *for* the Bavarian Soviet Republic, as a representative of his battalion. This is all very remote from the image of the sworn enemy of Bolshevism and world Jewry born in the mud and fire and blood of the trenches. Rather, it seems that Hitler's ideas were fluctuating, and that as late as 1919 he was interested in pursuing career opportunities other than crazed ultranationalist anti-Semitic genocidal tyrant.

Hitler does not appear to have set foot on that path until that autumn. He was still employed by the military and had been assigned the task of monitoring extremist political groups, a job that involved infiltrating gatherings of monomaniacal racists, paranoid anti-Semites, communists, ultranationalists, conspiracy theorists and general inadequates. One evening, he attended a meeting of the microscopically small German Workers' Party, which had been cofounded earlier in 1919 by one such inadequate: a railroad worker named Anton Drexler. Drexler blamed Jews and trade unions for his many failures and disappointments and had evolved a political ideology that married Jew hatred with socialism and nationalism. Hitler left the meeting with a copy of Drexler's autobiography and read it that night during a bout of insomnia. And if this sorry pamphlet did not make him into Der Führer immediately—indeed, he claims to have promptly forgotten about it—it nevertheless primed his consciousness for a shift.

A few days later, Hitler received a membership card in the mail, and although he viewed the group, quite accurately, as a collection of marginal freaks, he attended another meeting and found his destiny there, amid the losers and inadequates. The German Workers' Party would mutate into the National Socialist German Workers' Party, a.k.a. the Nazi Party.

It was now, via his membership in this trilobitic group, that Hitler began to move in literary circles. One of his new writer friends was actually talented: Dietrich Eckart was the scion of a courtly family (his father had been a counselor to the Bavarian king) and his version of Ibsen's *Peer Gynt* was hugely popular in Germany; the kaiser himself attended two performances, and the play was translated into Czech, Dutch and Hungarian. However, Eckart was also a drug addict, a drunk, a nationalist and a raging anti-Semite who published his own weekly newspaper, *In Plain German*. Although he was twenty-one years older than Hitler, the two were united by their bohemian backgrounds and shared hatred of Jews. Eckart discussed books, ideas and history with Hitler—including works by Houston Stewart Chamberlain* and Paul de Lagarde.† Eckart even helped Hitler with his grammar, which was never the Führer's strong suit.

Salubrious company indeed. Meanwhile, Hitler met another writer, Alfred Rosenberg, a refugee of German descent from the collapsed Russian Empire. Like Hitler, he had a flair for the arts; he had even studied architecture in Riga and Moscow before the revolution. Rosenberg served as the Russia expert for Eckart's newspaper, and contributed articles on the "Jewish" Bolshevik Revolution. In 1923 he wrote a gloss on *The Protocols of the Elders of Zion*, the notorious text alleged to be the record of a meeting between a cabal of Jews living in Basel who were plotting to start terrible wars and generally foment chaos in order to take over the world. In fact, the *Protocols* had already been exposed as a fake: in 1921 the *London Times* had published a report demonstrating that much of the text had been plagiarized from a French polemic targeted at Napoleon III, titled *The Dialogue in Hell Between Machiavelli and Montesquieu*. The tsarist secret police had in fact produced the *Protocols*, although this detail has never stopped those who seek to be deceived from deceiving themselves.‡

Yet even now Hitler did not suddenly start generating hundreds of texts to compete with these theorists of emerging Nazism. For logocentric Bolsheviks, the written word was a gladiatorial arena in which they had to assert dominance; and Mussolini was a prose generator by trade. But writing does not appear to have been a means by which Hitler fed his ego or sought to advance his political career. As he rose through the party, he was dis-

---

* Son-in-law of Richard Wagner and a racist.
† Biblical scholar and racist.
‡ Among them Henry Ford, who in 1922 published his own take on the *Protocols*, entitled *The International Jew*, in which he revealed that the Jews were also to blame for jazz and had taken control of the U.S. liquor business. Hitler owned a copy.

covering instead that his métier was *talking* rubbish, not scribbling it on paper. Hitler could hold a hall in the palm of his hand whenever he opened his mouth to spout toxic gibberish about Jews, Bolsheviks, how the Soviet star was actually the Star of David and that communist stars were gold because the Jews love gold and what more proof do you need? For Hitler, speech was enough.

In fact, although Hitler had considered writing a book about the history of the Jews, he successfully resisted any impulse he may have felt to inflict a volume of his musings upon humanity until he suffered an unexpected period of forced idleness in 1923. The year before, his idol Mussolini had marched on Rome and become prime minister of Italy. Hitler wanted to duplicate that success in Germany by marching on Berlin, but his revolution got only as far as downtown Munich before the authorities opened fire on his assembled rabble of two thousand support-ers. *Etappenschwein* that he was, the Führer hit the ground at the first sound of gunshot. He was unharmed. Not everyone was so lucky: sixteen loyal Nazis died.

Hitler was arrested and put on trial for treason, for which he would normally have been executed, had the presiding judge not sympathized with his views. Thus, although he was found guilty, he was sentenced to a mere five years with time served and the possibility of early release for good behavior—so he anticipated serving much less than that.

Now resident in Cell No. 7 of the faux-medieval Landsberg Prison in southwestern Bavaria, he soon won over both the warden and the guards, who greeted him with a "Heil." The prison was extraordinarily comfort-able: Hitler had a cell with a window, received many visitors, and took plenty of strolls around the gardens. He even enjoyed visits from his pet Alsatian. The one drawback was that it was difficult to run the party from inside a cell, so he handed over the reins to Rosenberg. However, Hitler realized, like Lenin in Siberia, that the state had provided him with the perfect conditions for a writer's sabbatical; furthermore, he had scores to settle and lawyers' bills to pay. His friend Eckart had paid off eleven thou-sand marks in debt after publishing *Peer Gynt*, and the royalties had con-tinued rolling in until his death the year before. Maybe if Hitler also wrote a bestseller . . . ? Indeed, in 1942 he would admit to a group of veteran Nazis who had been with him since the 1920s, "Had I not been in prison, *Mein Kampf* would never have been written."

The warden supplied the typewriter, while Winifred Wagner, the English-born daughter-in-law of noted anti-Semite and composer Richard Wagner, provided Hitler with some beautiful paper. What else did he need? Well, talent, for a start. But he was willing to give it a go regardless.

INITIALLY HITLER TRIED to sit in a chair, Lenin-style, and physically write *Mein Kampf,* or, as it was originally titled, *Viereinhalb Jahre Kampf gegen Lüge, Dummheit und Feigheit* ("A Four-and-a-Half-Year Battle Against Lies, Stupidity and Cowardice").

However, as he scribbled on paper or bashed away two-fingered at the typewriter, his vision and his ambition expanded. Instead of just writing a trenchant attack on Jews, Bolsheviks and his other hate objects, he began weaving his own life story into the narrative. It thus became a titanic *David Copperfield*–style epic, beginning with Hitler's birth and following his personal, philosophical and political development through his schooling, bohemian years, war years, all the way into the ongoing Weimar-era chaos. He became so rapt in recollecting emotion in tranquility, so absorbed in the exploration of his own ideas, that he cut back drastically on visitors so as to dedicate himself more fully to the generation of his masterpiece.

Of course, ambition outstripped ability. Like *David Copperfield, Mein Kampf* is far too long. Unlike *David Copperfield,* however, it is exceedingly badly written. It wasn't just that Hitler had no idea how to structure a text, nor that he was a self-aggrandizing propagandist: no—his inadequacy reveals itself in the prose at a molecular level.

After all, no matter how dull Dickens gets, he was a professional. But Hitler—he was not a professional. Here is the verdict of Thomas Ryback, a scholar who has scrutinized Hitler's prose in its purest, prepublication manuscript form: "At age thirty-five, Hitler had mastered neither basic spelling nor common grammar. His raw texts are riddled with lexical and syntactical errors. His punctuation, like his capitalization, is as faulty as it is inconsistent."

Nevertheless, the surviving fragments of the manuscript reveal that Hitler was trying, that he was striving, even. He actually wanted this book to be *good.* The initial paragraphs were revised multiple times as he struggled to come up with a striking opening, *just like a real author.* In the end, he settled for this:

Today it seems to me providential that Fate should have chosen Braunau on the Inn as my birthplace. For this little town lies on the boundary between two German states which we of the younger generation at least have made it our life work to reunite by every means at our disposal.

. . . which is not entirely terrible, as it connects his birth with the destiny of Germany and excuses his own non-Germanness in two sentences. The major themes, minus the Jew hatred, are thus revealed.

However, as Hitler continued, he found that typing the entire thing out himself was far too difficult, so once his better-educated acolyte Rudolf Hess joined him in the fortress, he switched to doing what he was good at: conjuring words in the air, while Hess committed them to paper, in the process demonstrating that Hitler's speechifying gifts required an audience of more than one to work properly. For while the structure of *Mein Kampf* is "oral" in that it is full of rhythmic repetitions and reemphases of favorite ideas, whatever rhetorical magic Hitler used to captivate huge audiences does not translate to the page. Even reading it aloud to the docile fan club imprisoned with him could not capture any of that rhetorical "magic."

Although the finished text gives few signs that Hess did much to restrain any of the Führer's excesses, Hess's wife later recalled struggles with Hitler over suggested revisions to the manuscript. In fact, over the years, around ten of Hitler's associates, ranging from his driver to his publisher to a Nazi music critic, either claimed credit for or were blamed for playing a role in shaping the text before it finally went to print. Did they all fail? Or did they prevent an even greater literary catastrophe from being birthed upon an unsuspecting world? Who knows what *Mein Kampf* we would have ended up with if Hitler had continued to toil away on it alone. However bad things may appear, never let us assume that we live in the worst of all possible realities.

As for what is actually in the damn thing, well—like all politicians who crank out unreadable fat volumes mythologizing their lives, Hitler desired to seduce his readers, to present himself as a child of destiny, the logical choice for national savior. He projects attitudes he developed later in life backward in time, and reveals that even as a child he was a leader of men, while it was during his hungry years in Vienna that he discovered the "spiritual pestilence, worse than the Black Death" of Jewish involvement in the press, art, literature and the theater.

Hitler also piles on self-aggrandizing tales of his valor in war and his imaginary close bond with the valiant warriors in the trenches. According to *Mein Kampf*, by the end of the war, he was already philosophically and politically fully formed, and there is, of course, no mention of his brief career working for the Bavarian Soviet Republic. Much of this mythologization became Truth, accepted by serious historians. For all its awfulness, then, *Mein Kampf* was highly successful as an exercise in mendacity.

What is most striking is the book's willful brutality. Although Hitler poses as a deep thinker—using words such as *intrinsically* and *cognizance* while invoking spurious racial science, and indulging in grandiose historical theorizing—he nevertheless disdains to dress up his millenarian beliefs with a quasi-scientistic style à la Marx, Lenin or Stalin; Mussolini's poetic invocations of "sacred" violence seem thoroughly meek in comparison to Hitler's toxic verbiage.

Thus, early on in the text, he asks:

> Was there any form of filth or profligacy, particularly in cultural life, without at least one Jew involved in it?
>   If you cut even cautiously into such an abscess, you found, like a maggot in a rotting body, often dazzled by the sudden light—a kike!

Hitler's text has a visceral, crude, almost aggressively stupid quality, which fits neatly with his worldview: Jews are evil; Aryans are good. Bolshevism is a Jewish plot for world domination. The world teeters on the brink of disaster. WE MUST SAVE THE WORLD.

Like Lenin, like Mussolini, Hitler believes he is living at the cusp of transformation, only, for him, the horrors of the abyss loom closer than the promised utopia. Socialism was an optimistic metaphysics—according to Marx, the transformation was inevitable; Mussolini claimed he had ushered in a golden age. Hitler, on the other hand, stressed the possibility of apocalypse without salvation, doom at the hands of the Jew. He was living in a world where everything was collapsing, and fast.

In the book he lays out the cosmic stakes:

> If with the help of his Marxist creed, the Jew is victorious over the other peoples of the world, his crown will be the funeral wreath of humanity

and this planet will, as it did thousands of years ago,* move through the ether devoid of men.

Then, toward the end, having led us on his personal voyage to manhood amid war and strife, he explores the root causes of the looming collapse in wearying detail. His vision is curiously circumscribed, however: ever the bohemian, he focuses on syphilis and art. The "syphilization of our people" is so acute that Hitler dedicates eleven pages to discussing the plague, neatly segueing into the "syphilization" of cultural life. Not only is the theater "hastening toward the abyss," but in the art world, the likes of Cubism and Dadaism reflect "the morbid excrescences of degenerate men."

Hitler's vision of the end-time is balanced by a belief in a rather vaguely defined mythical golden age. "Culture," he says, first arose "in places where the Aryan, in his encounters with lower peoples, subjugated them and bent them to his will. They then became the first technical instruments in the service of developing a culture." According to Hitler, to be subjugated by an Aryan "conqueror" was "perhaps" a gift, "a fate that was better than their previous so-called 'freedom.'"

Hitler the high school dropout is not particularly bothered by the intellectual capacities of the master race. Whereas aggressive displays of intellect were obligatory for Bolsheviks tormented by status anxiety, Hitler appears to be at ease with his brains and is happy to admit that the *Volk* just aren't that bright: "[T]he Aryan is not greatest in his mental qualities as such." No, what sets him apart is "the extent of his willingness to put all his abilities in the service of the community."

Hitler is so intensely relaxed about the relative unimportance of cerebral mightiness that he returns to his point two pages later, by stressing that "not in his intellectual gifts lies the source of the Aryan's capacity for creating and building culture." Again, it is thanks to his capacity for self-sacrifice on behalf of the entire community that "the Aryan owes his position in the world, and to it the world owes man." (Although he subsequently contradicts himself, adding that it was via a "unique pairing of

---

* Whether this was a result of Hitler's lack of education or a slip in the fever of dictation faithfully transcribed by Hess is impossible to know. Hitler was not immune to embarrassment, however: in the second edition that "thousands" would be changed to "millions."

the brutal fist and intellectual genius" that the Aryans "created the monuments of human culture.")

And so, through the wonders of projection, Hitler was able to look back on his mediocre life and sufferings and come to the conclusion that, like some twentieth-century Christ, it had all been necessary for the greater good of Germany. And did he secretly believe that some of those daubings he had knocked out in Vienna might not themselves be hidden "monuments"?

Of course a metaphysic that posits the existence of a master race must explain why said race is riddled with syphilis and teetering at the verge of extinction. Hitler keeps it simple with a Nazified myth of the Fall: "The Aryan gave up the purity of his blood and, therefore, his sojourn in the paradise ended." Indeed, he stresses, increasing the asininity of his simplification, "Blood mixture and the resultant drop in the racial level is the sole cause of the dying out of old cultures; for men do not perish as a result of lost wars, but by the loss of that force of resistance which is contained only in pure blood."

He then proceeds to explain, again, why the Aryan's "mightiest counterpart," the Jew, is so bad, only in much more detail. In the Jew, says Hitler, "the will to self-sacrifice does not go beyond the individual's naked instinct of self-preservation."

But that is not all: in my edition of *Mein Kampf* every other page comes with a heading. These running heads, many of which are repeated as Hitler pursues his thought ad nauseam, should be enough to give a sense of the exhausting relentlessness of this section:

Consequences of Jewish Egotism
Sham Culture of the Jew
The Jew a Parasite
Jewish Religious Doctrine
Development of Jewry
Development of Jewry
Development of Jewry
Development of Jewry
The Factory Worker
Jewish Tactics
Organization of Marxist World Doctrine
Organization of Marxist World Doctrine

Dictatorship of the Proletariat
Bastardized Peoples

And on, and on. And then on some more. In Hitler's apocalyptic vision, the distinction between anti-Semitism and racism is clear. The Führer does not regard the Jews as an inferior subrace, as he does the Slavs. Rather, the Jews are a diabolical force, a parasitic superintelligence moving from culture to culture, creating nothing but instead absorbing, synthesizing, in order to more fully achieve its sinister goals of complete domination. This, of course, was the only way Hitler and other anti-Semites could (and can) force their hatreds to make any sense whatsoever: there were very few Jews in the world; they had no country; yet nevertheless, they were secretly manipulating history, had instigated World War I and the Russian Revolution, and were on the point of dominating the planet. The Jews had to be supermen—albeit of a very different sort.

Hitler refers to *The Protocols of the Elders of Zion* to support his conspiratorial vision of history, one of the very few external sources he refers to in the text. He conceals his influences, preferring to present himself as largely sui generis. For instance, Mussolini, who had directly inspired his attempted march on Berlin, and from whose Fascist government Hitler's representative, Hermann Göring, was trying to extract a loan while Hitler was in prison, is conspicuous by his absence from volume 1, and would score only the briefest of mentions in volume 2. However, the *Protocols* are an exception: they clearly fascinate Hitler, even if he appears to admit that the text is a forgery. But, he says, this does not matter. That the critics of the *Protocols* denounce them as a forgery is "the best proof that they are authentic."

Aware that even by his standards this is a weak argument, Hitler continues:

What many Jews may do unconsciously is here conspicuously exposed. And that is what matters. It is completely indifferent from what Jewish brain these disclosures originate; the important thing is that with positively terrifying certainty they reveal the nature and activity of the Jewish people and expose their inner contexts as well as their ultimate final aims.

Whether some of the *Protocols* is true or not does not matter. Like his own biography, it can serve the cause equally well as a myth, expressing a higher truth. What does it matter if the story is not true when it is in fact true? Such was Hitler's dangerous "logic."

ON SEPTEMBER 18, 1924, the warden at Landsberg Prison recommended Hitler's release on the grounds that he had grown more "mature" and "thoughtful" and "does not contemplate acting against existing authority." However, Hitler was to be disappointed; he did not leave prison for another two months. Still, he made the best use of his prolonged period of incarceration, and continued dictating his book to Hess.

Hitler got out just in time for Christmas—slightly plumper following his restful spell inside, and now with a complete manuscript in his hands, which he was ready to unleash upon the world. All in all, prison had been an intellectually stimulating experience. Hitler described his stint in Landsberg as "higher education at state expense," while one associate claimed that he had used the time not only to write *Mein Kampf* but also to delve into the works of such significant thinkers as Schopenhauer, Nietzsche, Marx and Otto von Bismarck. If this is true, then Hitler cannot have delved very deeply, as generating almost four hundred pages of gibberish takes a lot of time, and those thinkers did not exactly optimize their texts for easy assimilation.

As for *Mein Kampf,* Hitler had tried to find a respectable, mainstream publisher for it before it was finished, but without success. So, on July 18, 1925, the official Nazi press, Franz Eher Verlag, issued the book in Munich in a large format (nine by twelve inches) at twelve marks a copy. The subtitle at least was excellent: *A Reckoning,* but the reviews were terrible. The *Frankfurter Zeitung* titled its review "Hitler's End," while even as senior a Nazi as Alfred Rosenberg could offer the at best ambiguous response that the book appeared to have been "quickly written." As for sales, they were mediocre. Hitler's publisher, Max Amann (who had served in the same Bavarian regiment as the Führer), claimed he shifted 23,000 copies during that first year. In fact, the book sold fewer than 10,000 copies, a less spectacular result for sure—yet one that nevertheless accounted for most of the first print run. A second edition of 18,000 copies was issued on December 2, of which under 7,000 were sold in 1926, even though Hitler had a built-in audience of 17,000 party members. The number of card-carrying Nazis rose to 40,000 the following year, yet sales figures dropped still further, to 5,600. With those kinds of numbers, Hitler might have been able to scratch together the cash to splash out on a few stuffed baby pigeons,* but he certainly wasn't going to do much damage to his lawyer's bills.

However, even before volume 1 was published, he was already working on volume 2, this time in a relaxing Alpine setting, barking away at a secretary while Amann, who had prevented the first book from going out under Hitler's original, disastrous title, assisted with edits. Once again, enforced idleness played a part in the genesis of the text, as Hitler had been banned from public speaking following a particularly incendiary public rant he spewed forth on February 27, a mere two months after his release from prison. Prevented from unleashing his oratorical superpowers on the masses, he had returned to the idea that he might in fact have some literary talent and so embarked upon a sequel that rejoices in all the flaws of part 1 while deepening the tedium.

With *Mein Kampf* volume 2, Hitler faced the obstacle many memoirists must overcome with their second book: now that the life story is out of the way, what else is there to write about? To make matters worse (from a content-generation point of view, at least), Hitler had also already expounded at length upon his racial theories, and had explained in detail why Jews were *übel*[†] but Aryans were *Übermenschen*. *Mein Kampf episode eins* had been his big book, his shot at reaching a mass audience. He had already used up all the juicy stuff. What next?

Well, there was always repetition; and so Hitler elaborates upon themes of Jewish and Marxist wickedness already expatiated upon in volume 1. There is also plenty of "fan service," that is, material that could only ever be of interest to the true believer, such as Hitler's account of his discovery of his oratorical superpowers and his detailed description of how the party, under the benign and wise guidance of himself (with the help of an unnamed dentist), chose its striking flag. Hitler was either abandoning his hope of writing a bestseller for a mass audience or, more likely, had no clue what else he could do other than preach to the choir.

However, as Hitler's sense of his audience narrows he is liberated to write in much more detail about specific *policies* of the future Nazi state, so crafting a National Socialist answer to *The State and Revolution*. Unlike Lenin's text, though, Hitler's is inordinately detailed, as he rejects vague

---

* One of his favorite meals, according to Victoria Clark and Melissa Scott, authors of *Dictators' Dinners: A Bad Taste Guide to Entertaining Tyrants*.
† "Evil."

utopianism, theoretical blather and copious citation in favor of lengthy discussions of propaganda, party organization and foreign policy, and includes forceful declarations of intent as regards the need to expand to the east.

Hitler grapples with how the future state will protect the "holiest human right" of keeping the blood pure. Gleefully antidemocratic, he states frankly that the government must become involved in the lives of its citizens to an extraordinary degree. It is an "absurdity" that "with the end of the school period, the state's right to supervise its young citizens suddenly ceases, but returns at the military age." On the contrary, says Hitler, "This right is a duty and as such is equally present at all times."

Precisely what this entails is as bizarre as it is chilling—or possibly *more* bizarre than it is chilling. For instance, Hitler is greatly irritated by the sartorial choices of "the youth" and rails against "[t]he boy who in summer runs around in long stovepipe trousers, and covered up to his neck, loses through his clothing alone a stimulus for his physical training." With uncharacteristic coyness, he rambles on about the need to "exploit ambition and, we may as well calmly admit it, vanity as well." However, it is not vanity about clothes that he wants to encourage, but rather vanity "about a beautiful, well-formed body which everyone can help to build."

Having railed against syphilis, whores, and general sexual degeneracy for page after page in volume 1, Hitler now advocates the transformation of *das Vaterland* into a vast open-air meat market, where boys and girls display their physical attributes to one another. By wearing more revealing clothes, the Führer explains, the finest Aryan flesh will naturally gravitate toward other fine specimens of Aryan flesh. He then effortlessly segues from disdain for "foppish fashions" into an apocalyptic rant: were it not for all those high collars and stovepipe trousers, he says, "the seduction of hundreds of thousands of girls by bow-legged, repulsive Jewish bastards would not be possible."

Indeed.

Hitler clearly spent a lot of time fantasizing about his future state while in prison as, in addition to his reflections on fashion, he also uses *Mein Kampf II* to unveil a detailed philosophy of education, where he develops his doubts about the significance of the intellect into something resembling full-blown contempt. Perhaps all that Marx he read in the fortress had hurt his head; or perhaps he stopped reading Schopenhauer's *On Education* after this bit: "A man sees a great many things when he looks at the world for himself, and he sees them from many sides; but this method of learning is not nearly so short or so quick as the method which employs abstract ideas and makes hasty generalizations about everything."

Or perhaps Hitler was still bitter about his miserable childhood experiences in the classroom—a conclusion that becomes difficult to resist once he starts bleating that "the youthful brain should in general not be burdened with things ninety-five percent of which it cannot use and hence forgets again." Continuing under the almost unbearably poignant heading "NO OVERLOADING OF THE BRAIN," Hitler also calls for the "shortening of the curriculum" that there might be enough room for the all-important "training of the body, of the character, of the will power and determination."

According to Hitler, since "a healthy, forceful spirit will be found only in a healthy and forceful body," the future state must "not adjust its entire educational work primarily to the inoculation of mere knowledge, but to the breeding of absolutely healthy bodies." That "mere" is telling, and Hitler also stresses that scientific education should come in "last place" after the development of character. As for Latin, it will be reduced to a set of "general outlines," while in history, "an abridgement of the material must be undertaken" and the emphasis placed upon lessons useful for "the continued existence of our own nationality." Roman history is acceptable in outline, while Greek history is good for "exemplary beauty." Although Hitler grudgingly admits that "practical subjects" are necessary, the half-talented painter, amateur historian and opera buff insists that the "humanistic subjects" are higher. In short, everything Hitler was bad at should be limited or proscribed, and everything he enjoyed should be boosted: the dream of bored schoolkids everywhere.*

Having dispatched science and "practical subjects" in summary fashion, Hitler also launches an attack on the written word that is as surprising as it is scathing, given that he was engaged in writing a foundational work of dictator literature.

This marks a sharp change in attitude from volume 1, where Hitler argues for the primacy of political speech but also waxes lyrical about his

---

* Of course, once a reality, the Nazi state still placed a strong emphasis on "practical subjects"—otherwise, Hitler's scientists would not have developed all those rockets, and the U.S. government would not have been so keen to forget about their crimes in exchange for exploiting their expertise in the postwar era. No ex-Nazis, no man on the moon.

love of reading and expresses an almost Bolshevik awe of the press, declaring that "its power really is immense" and "cannot be overestimated" as it "really continues education in adulthood." The problem, says Hitler, is that most readers are "simple-minded" and "believe everything they read."

In volume 2, Hitler has changed his position. Writing less than a year after he finished the first book, he now reveals that writers are in fact inadequates who write only because they "lack the power" to move masses with the spoken word. Writing is effete, a compensatory act, and those who dedicate themselves to "purely literary activity" do so because they have lost influence over the crowds. Laboring the point in classic Hitlerian style, the Führer mocks "the bourgeois scribbler who comes out of his study to confront the great masses" only to be "nauseated by their very fumes" and who "faces them helplessly with the written word." Compare this loser with the orator, who, says Hitler, can interact with his audience in real time, who knows them intimately, who studies their faces and responses and works upon their emotions, changing his words in the moment that they might have the right effect.

The writer, by contrast, "does not know his readers at all," and the result is a loss of "psychological subtlety and in consequence suppleness." The good news (for Hitler) is that the speaker's skill with words is transferable to written prose, and so, "a brilliant speaker will be able to write better than a brilliant writer can speak, unless he continuously practices this art."

Never one to make a point without beating it to death and then dragging the corpse for several exhausting miles through the mud, Hitler continues with his denunciation of the text, declaring it inferior to any sort of media with pictures in it, including movies, which are better than books because "[h]ere a man needs to use his brains even less." Indeed, says Hitler, "the whole newspaper flood and all the books that are turned out every year by the intellectuals slide off the millions of the lower classes like water from oiled leather."

This can prove only two things: "either the unsoundness of the content of this whole literary production of our bourgeois world or the impossibility of reaching the heart of the broad masses by written matter."

Ah, but what of the texts of Marx, or Lenin? Hitler remains unconvinced, declaring that the "illiterate common people" did not develop enthusiasm for revolution due to a "theoretical reading of Karl Marx, but solely by the glittering heaven which thousands of agitators, themselves, to be sure, all in the service of an idea, talked into the people." Nor was the Russian Revolution a consequence of Lenin's writings; it was "the hate-fomenting oratorical activity of countless of the greatest and the smallest apostles of agitation" who brought about the events of 1917. The same goes for the French Revolution: speakers, not writers, turned the world upside down.

Hitler, of course, was correct to state that the masses did not rush to spend their leisure hours devouring the works of Marx and Lenin in, say, *Harry Potter* quantities, and the vast majority did not read them at all unless required to by force. Yet he is savaging a straw man: neither of those writers considered the "illiterate common people" to be their audience in the first place, not least because, pace Hitler, it is exceedingly difficult for illiterate people to read books. Those revolutionary texts were not intended for mass consumption (except, perhaps, *The Communist Manifesto*), and Lenin was almost as contemptuous of the masses as Hitler. He did not believe that they could lead a revolution on their own, and he wrote for an educated audience of professional radicals, instructing them on how to prepare for and seize power. Hitler's approach was different: he wanted to breathe lunacy into the people. Rather than accept that there were different approaches to bringing about radical political change, he was suddenly denying that the written word had any efficacy whatsoever.

But why? Well, as with his attitudes toward education, it was personal. By the time he wrote his attack on the written word, the first volume of *Mein Kampf* had been published to no acclaim, and Hitler now realized that his book had few admirers outside his own circle. In volume 2, he refers to "a lengthy discussion in a part of the press" in which "bourgeois wiseacres" derided his claim "that all great, world-shaking events have been brought about, not by written matter, but by the spoken word." He carps about one newspaper critic in particular, who argued that "the writer must necessarily be mentally superior to the speaker" and who stung Hitler with his comment that "one is so often disappointed to see the speech of a recognized great orator in print."

For all his efforts to downgrade the importance of the intellect, Hitler was clearly deeply wounded. Cut to the quick, he responds with a scorched-earth attack on the written word and, as if to demonstrate his point, proceeds in the rest of part 2 to illustrate with merciless efficiency just how ineffectual, impenetrable and hopeless it can be.

———

AND THEN, TO the printer's. *Mein Kampf II* was published just in time for Christmas, on December 11, 1926, with a dedication to the (now-deceased) Dietrich Eckart, "who devoted his life to the awakening of his, our people in his writings and his thoughts and finally in his deeds."

Whatever disappointment Hitler had felt with the reception given to volume 1 was compounded with the sequel. In his review of the 1939 British translation, George Orwell observed that the book revealed the seductive power of Hitler's assault on the "hedonistic attitude to life" and his knowledge that "human beings don't only want comfort, safety, short working-hours, hygiene, birth-control and, in general, common sense; they also, at least intermittently, want struggle and self-sacrifice, not to mention drums, flags and loyalty-parades." However, if that seductive power existed, then it was lost on its intended audience in 1927. Nobody could be bothered even to mock the book, and *Mein Kampf II* went largely ignored in the marketplace. Sales were correspondingly sluggish: after a year, it had sold a dismal 1,200 copies out of an initial print run of 18,000, and it was downhill from there. Sales of the first book were also on a downward slide; it sold fewer than 6,000 copies in 1927.

Even before the sequel hit the shelves, however, Hitler had been in talks with a bigger, non-Nazi publisher about writing a memoir dedicated to his wartime experiences, but this project never came to fruition, as in 1927 the speaking ban was lifted in most German states, and Hitler promptly lost interest in the written word. He briefly dabbled in prose again in 1928, but once more it was as a result of external forces. Conditions in Germany were stabilizing, and the Nazis had suffered a catastrophic setback in that year's elections, winning a mere 3 percent of the vote. The party stood on the brink of extinction and, increasingly few people were willing to listen to Hitler ramble on about the Jews, the *Volk* and stovepipe trousers. Over the course of six weeks in June and July, he spewed forth a 234-page manuscript filled with repetitions of things he had already said, plus far fewer narrative passages than ever before, and a triumphantly ludicrous passage in which he revealed that Russia was "anything but an anti-capitalist state" but had "destroyed its own national economy . . . only in order to give international finance capital the possibility of absolute control." In the end, the text was locked away in a safe and forgotten about for years, seeing print only decades later, in the 1960s. Since it is unlikely that Amann nixed the book due to its exceedingly low quality—he had, after all, published Hitler's first two volumes without blinking—it seems possible that disappointment over the sales of *Mein Kampf* may have played a role in deciding the book's fate.

In his introduction to my copy of *Mein Kampf*, Konrad Heiden, a German-Jewish journalist and historian who had identified Hitler as a dangerous demagogue as early as 1923, describes the book as "proof of the blindness and complacency of the world . . . in its pages Hitler announced—long before he came to power a program of blood and terror in a self-revelation of such overwhelming frankness that few among its readers had the courage to believe it."

It is unlikely that an absence of courage was the issue, however. The Nazis were a tiny party, and Hitler was regarded by most as a political corpse. Likewise, Lenin and Stalin had spelled out exactly what they were going to do in books for years, but since they, too, represented a minuscule sect of extremists, nobody cared. But whereas in *The State and Revolution* Lenin reveals himself as a brilliant man who has persuaded himself to believe in nonsense, in *Mein Kampf* Hitler exposes himself as a posturing autodidact who seems to have no difficulty believing the utmost drivel.

Mein Kampf is staggeringly incompetent. Without the benefit of hindsight, why would anyone have received this literary atrocity as a warning? This is the danger of dictator books: they hide in plain sight, and their sheer awfulness makes it impossible to believe in their power to infiltrate and transform brains until it is much too late.

But a change was coming. In 1929 the stock market collapsed, and Germany tumbled once more into the abyss. Hitler rose from the political dead as Mussolini had before him, and Franz Eher Verlag reissued *Mein Kampf* in a smaller, single-volume edition that retailed for eight marks— a third of the total cost of both editions in their original format. Amann also took the opportunity to ameliorate the reader's suffering, and an astounding 2,294 corrections were made to *Mein Kampf* between the appearance of the first edition in 1925 and the combined volume in 1930, the overwhelming majority of which focused on correcting Hitler's appalling style rather than factual errors.* In the new climate of apocalyptic crisis,

---

* The publisher continued trying to make the text less awful via further corrections, although not quite so many, until the end of the 1930s.

incoherent screeds scapegoating the Jews found a wider audience, and the book's sales picked up. Between 1930 and January 1933, Eher Verlag shifted a more than respectable 287,000 copies. After Hitler became chancellor in February 1933, sales exploded, and 1.5 million copies were sold by the end of the year. Hitler's change of career from the leader of an extreme political party to dictator of Nazi Germany turned out to be very good for business, and *Mein Kampf* was transformed into a compulsory bestseller. Starting in 1934, quotations from the Führer's *meisterwerk* appeared in school textbooks, while in April 1936 the minister of the interior recommended that the book be given to newly married couples as a gift, which led to the creation of the legendary *Hochzeitsausgabe*, a.k.a. "Wedding Edition." The blind were lucky enough to receive a Braille version in 1936, and in 1940 a special edition printed on rice paper was issued for the troops. In 1938, booksellers were instructed that only new copies should be put on display, as the book was obviously too marvelous to be sold secondhand. Meanwhile, in 1939, a luxury edition was issued in honor of Hitler's fiftieth birthday, for the delight and edification of the party elite. By the end of 1945, ten million copies were in circulation in Germany, and the Führer had collected around eight million marks in royalties, since, like Scientologists today, the Nazis sold rather than gave away their holy book.

Foreign editions also proliferated throughout the 1930s, and the venerable American publisher Houghton Mifflin was first to get some skin in the game with the publication of the somewhat clumsily titled *My Battle* in 1933, which was followed by a different English translation in the United Kingdom later that year. The Danes, Finns, Swedes, Norwegians, Brazilians, Bulgarians, Iraqis, Spaniards, Hungarians, Chinese, Czechs and French all enjoyed full translations, while émigré Russians and Japanese speakers could read extracts. Fascist Italy was a comparatively late participant in the *Mein Kampf* translation party, and a local edition did not appear until 1938. Mussolini of course considered himself the supreme Fascist and had always been dismissive of both Hitler's book and his anti-Semitism. It did not appear in Italy until Il Duce felt the need to ingratiate himself into Hitler's favor.

And yet, and yet . . . how many of these millions actually read it? While Joseph Goebbels was no doubt sincere when, after reading part 1, he wrote in his diary, "Absolutely fascinating! Who is this man? Half plebeian, half god," even committed Nazis had their doubts as to its quality. One senior party leader would later claim that his ability to recite passages from memory was a source of amazement for his colleagues; when he admitted that he had learned only a few select parts for effect, they confessed that they, too, had not been able to make it all the way through.

Even Hitler admitted that the book was not much good. Having studiously avoided all mention of his idol Mussolini until the very end of volume 2, he compared himself in 1938 unfavorably to Il Duce while talking to his lawyer Hans Frank: "What beautiful Italian Mussolini speaks and writes. I can't do that in German. I lose my train of thought when I write." Hitler is also said to have told Frank that he would never have written the book if he had known in 1924 that he would become chancellor. And who would disagree with Hitler's ultimate assessment of his skills? "Ich bin kein Schriftsteller" (I am not a writer).

It is striking that although Hitler, like Stalin and Mussolini, luxuriated in a personality cult, he was nevertheless quite willing to share the limelight as an author with his fellow Nazis. *Mein Kampf* was the holiest of holies, but Goebbels also published *From the Kaiser to the Reich Chancellery*, a collection of excerpts from diaries he kept between 1932 and 1933 as the Nazis ascended to power. In 1934, Hermann Göring published *Germany Reborn*, while Alfred Rosenberg's titanically unreadable magnum opus, *The Myth of the Twentieth Century*, swiftly attained bestseller status under the Nazi regime.

Rosenberg, in fact, was supposed to be the ideological heavyweight of the Nazi Party. Over the course of seven hundred merciless pages dedicated to such themes as "racial hygiene," "the coming reich" (he did not think it had arrived yet), and "religion" (he wished for the extinction of Christianity), he attempted to place the party's nonsensical beliefs on a solid philosophical basis. However, *The Myth of the Twentieth Century* was so turgid and unreadable that, in 1938, a helpful author published an entire book dedicated to defining Rosenberg's neologisms, entitled *850 Words of the Myth of the Twentieth Century*.

Hitler occasionally spoke in disparaging terms of Rosenberg's text, as Mussolini had of *Mein Kampf* ("that thing nobody can understand"), but he also praised it as a "tremendous achievement." Ultimately, however, he did nothing to prevent it from taking root in Nazi culture. By 1936, half a million copies were in circulation, a figure that rose to one million six years later. The book joined *Mein Kampf* on the syllabi, and in 1943, in Hitler's presence, Rosenberg was awarded the first German National Prize, receiving the following eulogy from Goebbels:

> Alfred Rosenberg has with his works most excellently helped in intuitively founding and strengthening the scientific ideology of National Socialism. By his indefatigable battle for the purity of National Socialist ideology he has earned outstanding and special merits. Only a later age will fully appreciate how deep the influence of this man has been upon the spiritual and ideological foundation of the National Socialist state.

Thus Hitler, true to his word that the intellect was not as important as other aspects of the Aryan man, was willing to share the glory with other, even worse writers than himself. And yet, when the Third Reich collapsed, Rosenberg's book vanished, while Hitler's went on to enjoy an eerie afterlife. Not only that, but in spite of its rank awfulness, only Hitler's book has outlived the specific political context that spawned it, and *Mein Kampf* enjoys a genuine popularity far in excess of any text written by any of his dictatorial peers. Unencumbered by the theoretical and stylistic obligations of nineteenth-century economic "science," and secure in its anti-intellectualism, *Mein Kampf* rejects both class war and searching for the "soul of the soul" in favor of a berserk hatred that is far more visceral, enduring, and alluring to the great darkness of the human heart. Homeric in its crudity, in its liberating simplicity, it transcends epochs and borders, attaining a perverse immortality by its sheer, unrelenting evil. Let us not delude ourselves into thinking that it is only the masterful expression of great truths that grants a book access to the pantheon of the immortals; the violent and shameless expression of hatred also endures. As J. G. Ballard put it, "The psychopath never dates."

5

Mao

Best book evah

With Hitler and Mussolini both dead, Stalin now ascended to ever greater heights. The years following World War II were pretty good to him: Roosevelt and Churchill gave the nod to his continued dominion over the nations the Red Army had liberated from Nazi occupation, enabling the man of steel to impose his grim vision of utopia on millions more victims. But it wasn't just that he now stood unchallenged as the supreme leader of the USSR *and* imperial overlord of a string of emerging satellite states, no—he was also the dictator-author nonpareil.

Who else combined so much military and political power with complete control over the printing presses? Which other leader had such reach and so many distribution channels for his works? There was no other.

And so Stalin's lackeys set to work, vigorously imposing the Vozhd's strand of Marxism-Leninism, historical fabrications and blocky prose upon his new possessions in Eastern Europe, covering these freshly "liberated" nations in a smothering blanket of turgid "theory" and bold mendacity. Oceans of ink flooded forests of trees in a Gutenbergian literary apocalypse, as the ink was corralled and coerced into assuming alphabetic shapes, arranged and rearranged in a Babel of tongues that, once decoded, nevertheless amounted to variations on the same old tripe. From East Berlin to Vladivostok, the lies were now the same, and translated copies of the *Short Course* instructed the newly captive populaces in the mythology they were to live by. An accelerating crisis of tedium engulfed and conquered an immense geography.

Yet this triumph was short-lived; in fact, it barely lasted a decade. Stalin died in March 1953, and following a short power struggle among his bloodstained henchmen at the top of the party, his erstwhile lackey Nikita Khrushchev emerged victorious as the new leader of the Soviet Union. Khrushchev, a jovial fat man of peasant stock, was keen to maintain continuity and at first displayed respect for his predecessor and his texts. This did not last: having just spent two decades wading through gore on behalf of a capricious master who had murdered many of his close colleagues, Khrushchev no longer wished to live by lies—or at least not by those lies. Three years passed, and on February 25, 1956, he stood at the podium at a closed session of the Twentieth Party Congress, the first since Stalin's death, and delivered the (secret) speech of his life.

In *On the Cult of Personality and Its Consequences* Khrushchev denounced the man-god before an elite audience of 1,500 delegates from across the Soviet Union and its Eastern European satellites. He stared out at the hall full of professed Stalinists, men who had spent decades applauding the great leader and citing his books, and railed against his cruelty. To bolster his case, he quoted from Lenin's long-suppressed "Last Testament," in which the Father of the World Proletariat had warned against Stalin. Having invoked the authority of the USSR's founder, Khrushchev then gave examples of why Lenin had been correct as he denounced Stalin for crimes ranging from the Great Terror of the 1930s in which many party members died,* to the mass deportations of entire ethnic groups, to

---

* Khrushchev was considerably less interested in denouncing Stalin for his use of terror against the general population.

the purges of the Red Army, to Stalin's early mishandling of the war, which had almost ended in disaster.

He didn't just attack Stalin the man. So powerful were the leader's texts that he felt compelled to denounce those also. Of Stalin's official biography, Khrushchev declared:

> This book is an expression of the most dissolute flattery, an example of making a man into a godhead, of transforming him into an infallible sage, "the greatest leader, sublime strategist of all times and nations." Finally, no other words could be found with which to lift Stalin up to the heavens.

Khrushchev railed against the "loathsome adulation" filling the book, which he said Stalin himself had approved and edited, adding self-praise in his own handwriting into the manuscript copy of the text. He poured scorn on Stalin for rewriting history to transform himself into the author of the *Short Course*, and then revealed his true attitude toward the book, upon which he had once poured so much unctuous praise:

> Did this book properly reflect the efforts of the Party in the socialist trans-
> formation of the country, in the construction of socialist society, in the industrialization and collectivization of the country, and also other steps taken by the Party which undeviatingly traveled the path outlined by Lenin? This book speaks principally about Stalin, about his speeches, about his reports. Everything without the smallest exception is tied to his name.
>
> And when Stalin himself asserts that he himself wrote the *Short Course*, this calls at least for amazement. Can a Marxist-Leninist thus write about himself, praising his own person to the heavens?

It was not enough to attack the man; Khrushchev also had to destroy the reputation of the holy texts. So violent was the shock to some delegates that it is said they suffered heart attacks right there in the hall.

Following Khrushchev's delivery of the speech, officials traveled the country reading it aloud to closed sessions of the party; it was considered so explosive that the text itself was not published in the USSR until 1989. And it was explosive: Stalin's reputation never recovered, and soon his books began to vanish from shelves around the Soviet Union and its satel-lites, leaving large gaps where once had been epic compendiums of lies.

Literary glory proved transient: without the repressive power of the state behind them, Stalin's works went the way of the books of so many best-selling authors whose success tapers off after their deaths. It was time for Lenin to rise again, as the printing presses geared up to start churning out a greatly expanded edition (already the fifth) of his collected works.*

But the era of the giants of dictator literature was not over. Far from it: in the East, a new rough beast was slouching toward Beijing to be born. The billion-selling *Quotations from Chairman Mao* was coming. In comparison, the text worship of the Lenin, Stalin, Hitler and Mussolini regimes was tame, a prelude to a madness unprecedented in its scale or passion.

MAO ZEDONG WAS born in 1893 in the village of Shaoshan located in Hunan province in southern China. The son of a wealthy farmer, he was, like every other dictator-author in this book, a baby of no obvious significance. He should have grown up, lived, died and been forgotten like the rest of us—and had his father succeeded at limiting his son's education to basic literacy and numeracy for the purposes of a career in bookkeeping, that is exactly what would have happened. Alas, Mao discovered the creative and destructive power of literacy.

At first, the texts Mao was exposed to caused no harm. In school, he studied the Confucian canon and swiftly developed a hatred for the sage, whose message of respect for parents, authority, tradition and virtue had been a favorite of the ruling classes for over two millennia. Like Stalin, he smuggled banned books into class. Mao's *Koba* was *The Water Margin*, the tale of 108 bandit brothers who defend the poor against unjust officials; but he also lost himself in the historical epic *The Romance of the Three Kingdoms*, and loved *Journey to the West*, which features among its protagonists the mischievous, irrepressible Monkey King, who pisses on the Buddha's finger when he mistakes it for a pillar at the end of the world—and this is but one of his many deeds regarded as outrageous in the eyes of heaven. Mao also developed a love of poetry and classical Chinese literature that in later life would enable him to make his texts,

---

* In addition to hardbound collections of Khrushchev's own speeches and pamphlets, which ran to a total of twenty-three volumes by 1964, the year he was removed from office.

through which he scattered literary references, feel slightly less hermetic (if not necessarily less boring) than those of most other communists.

At age sixteen, Mao left the farm to study in a school with a modern, Western curriculum. An encounter with a book called *Words of Warning in an Age of Prosperity* had persuaded him that the answers to China's many problems lay overseas, and he now learned about the Enlightenment, nationalism, science and the lives of "great men" including Napoleon, Peter the Great and George Washington. It turned out that Mao's intuition was correct: China's future was coming from the West, albeit not in the form expected. In 1911 Sun Yat-sen, a former resident of Honolulu and onetime regular visitor to the British Library in London, led a revolution that toppled the Qing dynasty, which had been rotting for a long time. Mao served in Sun Yat-sen's victorious army, but the declaration of a republic in 1912 was followed not by national rebirth but rather by an extended period of chaos as dueling warlords fought amid the wreckage of the collapsed empire.

Meanwhile, Mao kept reading. He attended teacher training college, completing his studies in 1918, and then moved to Beijing, now the epicenter of the radical "New Culture," or "May Fourth," movement, which demanded a cultural revolution that would overthrow the old Confucian order and usher in a new era of science, democracy, intellectual rebirth, individual freedom and even a new style of writing, *baihua*, which was much closer to the vernacular than classical Chinese. By now Mao was reading Darwin, John Stuart Mill, Rousseau and Adam Smith and was taking his first tentative steps as a writer. His emphasis, however, was physical rather than cerebral. In the April 1917 issue of *New Youth*, the journal of the New Culture movement, he argued that China was *literally* weak, as people didn't do enough exercise and needed to develop willpower. Mao was not a revolutionary yet, but slowly, slowly, he was getting there. In October 1918 he landed a job in a library, the ideal location for a cash-strapped nascent megalomaniac in need of easy access to inspirational bad ideas. Today you can go to the Internet for that, but in the nineteenth and twentieth centuries, libraries were the only option for those lacking the means to build up extensive private collections of theoretical and revolutionary works.

That there was a thing called "Marxism" had been known in China since the end of the nineteenth century, but it was not until 1903 that a fragment of the vast and unwieldy corpus first appeared in translation, in a book entitled *Contemporary Socialism*. Like some clay inscription found in the sands of Mesopotamia, it was a microscopic particle, a single quotation from *The Communist Manifesto* in a work translated from the Japanese on the history and development of socialism (where Marx was singled out for praise for his "profound scholarship"). More books and articles about "Marxism" started to appear, but access to the source texts remained elusive. It was not until 1908 that Engels's preface to the 1888 edition of *The Communist Manifesto* appeared in a journal with the title *Heaven's Justice*—and the preface was all that was published. It was impossible on the basis of these fragments to grasp what "Marxism" entailed, and by this point the prophet's followers had already split into warring subtribes anyway. Mao himself would say years later that in those days the Chinese "knew nothing about the existence in the world of imperialism or any kind of Marxism." However, his boss at the Peking University library was Li Dazhao, an enthusiast for the Bolshevik strain of Marxism, right down to the Trotsky-style circular wire-frame glasses perched on his nose. According to Li, the Russian Revolution represented not only "the light of a new civilization" but also "the victory of a new spirit based on the general awakening of mankind in the twentieth century." Mao now began to learn about the tentacles of capitalism, the horror of the bourgeoisie, the scientific power of the historical dialectic, and the inevitability of world revolution. Although he had read many, much better books by other Western authors, it was his encounter with Marx via Li Dazhao that transformed his life, and China's destiny. Within three years, he would declare that China's only option was "extreme communism" with its "methods of class dictatorship."

Mao had finally discovered the texts that would for decades to come provide a theoretical basis and ideological fig leaf for his tumescent will to power. In 1920 he opened a "Cultural Bookstore" in the city of Hunan, where he sold leftist publications. He eventually expanded this successful little enterprise to seven branches, where the stock was comprised of books and pamphlets on such assorted left-wing themes as socialism, Marx and the USSR. A year later, he joined the Chinese Communist Party as a founder member. Mao was now pushing thirty. It had been a leisurely, even bohemian stroll toward radicalism, but at last he had arrived.

EVERY DICTATOR IN this book led an eventful life, but Mao managed to cram more than most into his regrettably numerous orbits around the sun. Having come to the Marxist light later in life than the likes of Lenin or Stalin, he wasted no time getting down to business, spending the next three decades or so fighting civil wars, surviving Stalin's paranoia, recovering from catastrophic setbacks, outwitting his rivals in the party, battling with the Japanese, and running rogue communist ministates before finally emerging victorious in the struggle for control over China.

And that is only the first phase of his career. Once ensconced in power, Mao spent the next twenty-seven years attempting to realize an absurd utopian fantasy that led to the deaths of many millions, while simultaneously achieving literary notoriety as author of the best-selling book in history, after the Bible. Alas, as fascinating as Mao's biography is, there is no room here to explore it in detail. Nevertheless, some context is essential to make sense of Mao's writings. Here is a brief outline of his life en route to power, during which he wrote his most influential works.

1921: Mao joins the Chinese Communist Party (CCP) as a founder member.

1923: At the CCP's Third Congress, Mao is elected to the Central Executive Committee. He marks the occasion by insisting on the revolutionary potential of the peasantry. However, reliance on the peasantry raises a theoretical problem. The Moscow-based Comintern adheres strictly to the orthodox Marxist line that revolutions happen in capitalist countries with a proletarian class, which China lacks. Since China is not ready for a workers' revolution, the Comintern instructs the CCP leadership to join with the Nationalists, or Kuomintang, to form a "United Front." The CCP will support the Kuomintang and fight for a Nationalist-bourgeois revolution as a stepping-stone to the proletarian version, where the working class will be triumphant. The CCP, almost completely dependent on the Comintern for money and other forms of support, submits to the will of Moscow.

1927: The dream of a two-stage revolution doesn't quite work out as hoped. After defeating the warlords of northern China, Kuomintang leader Chiang Kai-shek marches on Shanghai, where he promptly aligns himself with powerful vested interests in banking and industry, then starts killing communists, launching a civil war that will last more than two decades. Resistance from the CCP ends badly: the party loses 84 percent of its membership, and of what remains, a mere 10 percent can claim to be actual proletarians. Within fifteen months, that number drops to 3 percent. Mao escapes and establishes a "peasant soviet" out of a handful of villages in the Jinggang Mountains. To celebrate, he composes some verse:

> The foe encircles us thousands strong,
> Steadfastly we stand our ground.
> Already our defense is iron-clad,
> Now our wills unite like a fortress.

Mao and his allies recruit from the peasantry to build up the Red Army and start developing the guerrilla warfare tactics he would use for the next twenty years. However, powerful forces within the CCP remain fixated on the idea of a workers' revolution based in cities, and when communism ultimately fails to take root in the Jinggang base Mao will be obliged to move again.

1929: Mao moves south to the town of Ruijin where he starts to establish a communist government modeled along his ideas. A faction of Moscow-educated Chinese communists known as the "28 Bolsheviks" returns to China. Over the next few years, its members will take control over the CCP, bringing the party closely in line with the will of Stalin as conveyed through the Comintern. Their leader is Wang Ming, who emerges as a major rival to Mao for influence within the party, and who bitterly criticizes Mao for his focus on the peasantry. According to Wang Ming, Mao is guilty of "Nationalist" deviations from "pure" Marxism, for the revolution must come from the cities. Mao, on the other hand, is contemptuous of "experts" and theorists who lack experience on the ground. Although he agrees that the working class must be in the vanguard of the revolution, he is convinced that the peasantry will play a leading role.

1930: In February, Mao establishes the Southwest Jiangxi Provincial Soviet Government. He continues to develop the Red Army, and as political commissar alongside General Zhu De, he boosts troop numbers from five thousand to two hundred thousand by 1933. However, the Central Committee remains convinced that the revolution will be urban and orders the Red Army to occupy cities in South China in support of a workers' uprising. When this strategy fails, Mao returns to Jiangxi in defiance of Zhu's orders. His wife is less lucky: she is captured and beheaded. Mao survives an attempted coup in Jiangxi (he is considered "too moderate") and ruthlessly suppresses those who rose up against him.

1931: The Southwest Jiangxi Provincial Soviet Government is rebranded as the Soviet Republic of China, and Mao is elected chairman, effectively making him the leader of a state, if not the CCP itself. The same year, the Japanese invade Manchuria and rename it Manchuko. Mao pursues moderate land policies so as not to alienate the peasants, and develops his skills in guerrilla warfare, successfully resisting three attempts made by Chiang Kai-shek to surround the republic. However, the 28 Bolsheviks are in the ascendant, and they oppose his policies. Mao's influence steadily diminishes despite the high office he holds on paper; in 1932 he even loses control of the Red Army. In 1933 the CCP leadership relocates from its base in Shanghai to Jiangxi, and Mao is sidelined further.

1934: Worried about the state of public morals, Kuomintang leader Chiang Kai-shek launches the "New Life" movement, a blend of Confucianism, nationalism and a few borrowings from the West. It does little to improve public morals, but Chiang Kai-shek does succeed at encircling the communist foe in Jiangxi. Once again, Mao survives: on October 16, he breaks through enemy lines to lead a force of eighty-five thousand Red Army troops on an epic six-thousand-mile retreat, later celebrated as the "Long March." Once again, Mao celebrates his continued presence on the earth by writing a poem:

The Red Army fears not the trials of the March,
Holding light ten thousand crags and torrents.
The Five Ridges wind like gentle ripples
And the majestic Wumeng roll by, globules of clay.

1935: Slightly more than a year after it begins, the Long March reaches its end, although more than a few soldiers short. On October 20, 1935, a mere eight thousand of the original eighty-five thousand troops arrive in the northern Shaanxi province. The city of Yanan becomes the new communist capital. Close ties to Stalin and the Comintern notwithstanding, the 28 Bolsheviks no longer look like the strong horse in the struggle for control over the party. Mao's star is on the rise.

1937: U.S. journalist Edgar Snow publishes *Red Star over China*, based on four months spent among the communist guerrillas the year before. His admiring portrait of Mao and stirring account of the Long March establishes the Chairman as a heroic freedom fighter to many Western readers—an image that will endure even in the face of famine and the madness of the Cultural Revolution. Meanwhile, Japan launches a full-scale invasion of China, with the intent of toppling Chiang Kai-shek.

1937–43: Mao strengthens his position as supreme political leader and top theoretician of the CCP. A leader cult emerges. Stalin's *Short Course* appears in Chinese translation in Yanan, and Mao adopts its guiding principle that "History sometimes demands that it be corrected." Party history is revised so that Mao appears as the crucial prophetic figure throughout. In 1942, Mao declares that the study of Marx, Engels, Lenin and Stalin, and *The History of the Communist Party of the Soviet Union* in particular, should "constitute the heart of our studies." A "Rectification Campaign," carried out over the next two years, purges the party of all those insufficiently loyal to Mao, and his own writings feature prominently in the reeducation program. The result is the "Sinification" of Marxism by adapting it to Chinese conditions rather than blindly following the example of the USSR. Theory wars break out: in March 1943, Chiang Kai-shek publishes a book, *China's Destiny*, which sells a million copies. The CCP responds by further elevating Mao as leader and master of theory, coining the term "Mao Zedong Thought" to refer to the Chinese strand of Marxism-Leninism.

1945: Mao's ascent continues. His comrades elect him chairman of the Central Committee, of the Politburo, of the Secretariat, and of the Military Council of the Central Committee. All power is now in his hands; only Stalin stands above him.

1946: The Japanese are defeated. Civil war resumes between the Kuomintang and the communists.

1949: The communists are finally victorious. In April they seize Nanjing, the former imperial capital. Once again, Mao celebrates via verse:

> Over Chungshan swept a storm, headlong,
> Our mighty army, a million strong, has crossed the Great River.

The City, a tiger crouching, a dragon curling, outshines its ancient
    glories;
In heroic triumph heaven and earth have been overturned.
With power and to spare we must pursue the tottering foe
And not ape Hsiang Yu the conqueror seeking idle fame.
Were Nature sentient, she too would pass from youth to age,
But Man's world is mutable, seas become mulberry fields.

From this point, Kuomintang-controlled towns fall into communist hands one after another. The People's Republic of China is founded on October 1, and Mao addresses the reborn nation from Tiananmen Square, declaring, "The Chinese people have stood up!"

A new era requires new books of course, and Mao's *Selected Works* are published in Harbin and then promptly published in Moscow in Russian. And it is to Mao's works that we now turn, as I must report on my own Long March through some choice selections from the Chairman's (for the most part) rather excruciating canon.

Report on an Investigation of the Peasant Movement in Hunan (1927)

Mao wrote this long essay in early 1927, shortly before Chiang Kai-shek began his purge of the communists within Kuomintang ranks. Violent uprisings were rocking the countryside, and Mao saw an opportunity to use the peasantry as a means of hastening the revolution. His was a lonely voice, as the Comintern maintained that the conditions in China were not right for a proletarian revolt, while many Chinese Marxists scorned the peasantry as a class relic doomed to obsolescence. The future would come from the cities.

In *Report on an Investigation of the Peasant Movement in Hunan*, Mao presents the case for the countryside. He describes his experiences in Hunan province, where he spent thirty-two days studying the situation up close. The result is a semi-gripping read, at least by the (admittedly low) standards of Marxist texts. It is certainly not a neutral, dispassionate analysis, as the subtitle makes clear: *Down with the Local Tyrants and Evil Gentry! All Power to the Peasant Associations!*

Mao does not bother much with theory; at this stage in his career he had not read much of it. Thus, rather than reinterpret the peasantry as somehow actually proletarian, or suggest that China might vault over several stages of historical development so long as the USSR built a few factories and railways (a fudge that would be adopted to explain away the emergence of a communist state in hitherto theocratic Mongolia), he urges the CCP to embrace the peasantry. This is the force that will not only overthrow feudal landlords, but also destroy the authority of ancestors, temples, husbands, clan elders, village gods, etc.

Mao describes the humiliations heaped upon the ruling classes with a loving, evocative detail rarely encountered in the hermetic world of communist prose. The smashing of sedan chairs, the tossing of landowners in prison, the banging of gongs, the thrusting of humiliating dunce caps on the heads of former masters: Mao describes it all, conjuring up the noise and the chaos, clearly enjoying himself immensely. Not only does he reject the party leadership's criticism that the peasants have "gone too far" and the accusation that the peasants are mere "riffraff," but he does so with a few tossed-off lines that are far better than anything Stalin ever wrote—or anything *most* authors ever write, for that matter:

> A revolution is not a dinner party, or writing an essay, or painting a picture, or doing embroidery; it cannot be so refined, so leisurely and gentle, so temperate, kind, courteous, restrained and magnanimous. A revolution is an insurrection, an act of violence by which one class overthrows another.

It is easy to advocate violence, of course. It is not so easy to do so with such insouciance, while also coming up with a smart one-liner that revolutionaries will be citing as justification for their own acts of terror decades later—as happened with the simple declaration "A revolution is not a dinner party." But Mao was a master of slogans, adept at selecting the Chinese characters that resonated with the most meaning. That said, his report is no mere encomium to the pleasures of class warfare and destruction punctuated by the occasional snappy phrase. It is also an act of divination: Mao can already see a new, more moral society emerging, as the peasants have already banned gambling, opium and "vulgar performances."

Pungent though his prose may occasionally be, it is clear that Mao has not yet learned the significance of theoretical posturing in Marxist-Leninist rhetoric. The text contains no references to Lenin, while the word *Marxist* appears but once, toward the end. In fact, Mao's dismissive attitude toward the significance of the proletariat was so heretical that it was edited out of the official editions of his works once he was in power: "to give credit where credit is due, if we allot ten points to the accomplishments of the democratic revolution, then the achievements of the city dwellers and the military rate only three points, while the remaining seven points should go to the peasants in their rural revolution."

Despite its failings from the perspective of "theory," *Report on an Investigation of the Peasant Movement in Hunan* was a success nonetheless. Here, timing was key, as the communists were much more open to collaboration with the peasantry after Chiang Kai-shek had cracked down on the CCP. Praise for Mao spread to Moscow, where Nikolai Bukharin, the theorist behind Stalin's idea of "socialism in one country," gave his *Report* a positive review. An English translation then appeared in the May–June 1927 edition of *Communist International* magazine. Mao's career as a writer was off to a strong start.

A Single Spark Can Start a Prairie Fire (1930)

This text originated as a letter from Mao to a young communist named Lin Biao. Three decades later, Lin would rise to the heights as minister of defense and chief sycophant in Mao's court, playing a major role in the rise of Mao's personality cult and the publication of the infamous *Quotations from Chairman Mao*. At the time of *A Single Spark*, however, Lin was merely an officer in the Red Army, conducting "roving guerrilla actions" in the hope that the people would eventually rise up. Mao criticized these actions as poor strategy: far better to take the time to establish a base first, and then build toward the revolution.

In *A Single Spark Can Start a Prairie Fire*, Mao's prose is still more or less readable, if not quite as lively as in *Report on the Peasant Movement*. This time he is arguing against despair and fantasy, as Lenin had done so often during the Bolsheviks' slow rise to power. Specifically, Mao seeks to blast away that pessimism while also tackling the threat of "revolutionary impetuosity." Three years after the Shanghai catastrophe, Mao looks around and sees that many of his comrades in the Red Army are lost in a world of delusion, living in the hope that the CCP will somehow eventually unite all the masses countrywide via "roving guerrilla actions." After that they will lead the masses in a nationwide revolt that will bring about the (currently delayed) revolution.

Mao dismisses this view as insufficiently concrete, arguing that conditions in China do not indicate that a unified mass uprising is likely as revolutionary forces are weak. But so are the opposing reactionary forces; he therefore advocates a policy of gradually building up bases, developing the army, deepening connections with the peasants, and advancing the revolution steadily and methodically.

This time, however, he decides to toss in a bit of "theory," pointing to the multitude of "contradictions" that exist between the imperialists and the Chinese nation, and also within the imperialist camp itself. These, he says, indicate that the revolution not only is coming but will arrive in China sooner than in Europe, where reactionary forces are stronger.

The text's most resonant aspect is its brief outline of how to conduct an effective guerrilla struggle, ideas that Mao would follow and expound upon throughout the course of his revolutionary career.

Here are his four basic principles:

1. "Divide our forces to arouse the masses, concentrate our forces to deal with the enemy."
2. "The enemy advances, we retreat; the enemy camps, we harass; the enemy tires, we attack; the enemy retreats, we pursue."
3. "To extend stable base areas, employ the policy of advancing in waves; when pursued by a powerful enemy, employ the policy of circling around."
4. "Arouse the largest numbers of the masses in the shortest possible time and by the best possible methods."

Rather than fret about how to create a proletariat out of nothing, or wait for Marx's impersonal historical forces to finally kick in, Mao gets down to the basics of fighting a long guerrilla war against superior forces, and building up centers of communist power with the ultimate goal of seizing control. The strategy not only worked for him but has influenced revolutionary groups in Asia, Africa and Latin America, making him a "living" author in a way most dictators are not.

From a less utilitarian standpoint, *A Single Spark Can Start a Prairie Fire* is also notable for its occasional flourishes of poetry. Unlike most communists who conflated tedium with virtue, Mao throughout his career sprinkled allusions and citations from classical literature into his texts. But while the title may be borrowed from an old Chinese saying, the best words come from Mao's own pen. After dispensing advice and critiques, and generating numbered lists, another voice erupts—lyrical and filled with power and hope and the fire of belief:

> Marxists are not fortune tellers . . . But when I say that there will soon be a high tide of revolution in China, I am emphatically not speaking of something which in the words of some people is "possibly coming," something illusory, unattainable and devoid of significance for action. It is like a ship far out at sea whose masthead can be seen from the shore; it is like the morning sun in the east whose shimmering rays are visible from a high mountain top; it is like a child about to be born moving restlessly in its mother's womb.

Oppose Book Worship! (1930)

Following the publication of A Single Spark, the Comintern announced that Mao had succumbed to tuberculosis, and an obituary was published. He was very much alive, however, and still busy writing. Perhaps it was wishful thinking on the part of the authorities in Moscow: Mao had not studied in the USSR, and did not speak Russian (let alone German), so his exposure to the sacred texts of Marxism was limited. Meanwhile, Moscow was pumping out better-educated young Chinese communists who were not only more familiar with the texts but had much closer ties to the Comintern. It was during this period that the 28 Bolsheviks arrived in China to take control of the party.

For these Moscow-educated communists, Marxism was a kind of cargo cult focused on the USSR, and they were similarly unsubtle in their attacks on Mao. For instance, in 1929 a young man named Liu Angong returned to China having spent a year at the Infantry School in Moscow. He immediately injected himself into a dispute between Mao and Zhu De, the commander of the Red Army. Liu labeled Mao a factionalist, a particularly deadly term in the lexicon of Marxist insults. Factionalism (that is, disagreeing with the party line) had been banned in the USSR in 1921, and Stalin had used the law to force Trotsky's expulsion from the party in 1927. Liu died that October, but he was merely the tip of a very long spear arriving from Moscow. Mao was bitter about Soviet-educated communists who presumed to know more about the revolution in China than him, yet were wholly ignorant of conditions on the ground.

In *Oppose Book Worship!* Mao again insists upon the position that communists should investigate empirical reality and find out the facts before leaping to conclusions. Strikingly obvious? Perhaps, but the fact that he had to keep insisting on the point demonstrates how wedded communists were to dogma and castles of theory. Indeed, Mao not only defends the primacy of evidence, research and investigation, but expresses a desire to shut down everybody who hasn't done the work:

> Unless you have investigated a problem, you will be deprived of the right to speak on it. Isn't that too harsh? Not in the least.

Mao criticizes communists for their habit of "invariably" drawing conclusions before an investigation (a habit that is hardly restricted to Marxists, it must be said) and also launches an attack on party logocentrism:

> Whatever is written in a book is right—such is still the mentality of culturally backward peasants. Strangely enough, within the Communist Party there are also people who always say in a discussion "Show me where it is written in the book."

Later, Mao would take book worship to world-historical levels, but for now he urges restraint. "Of course we need Marxist books," he concedes, "but this study must be integrated with the country's actual conditions." And so he challenged not only the arrogance of "Moscow communists" but also the extreme Marxist fetish for the word. This was not the kind of thing that went down well with Stalin or the Comintern, and Mao's broadside was unsuccessful. Moscow-educated communists continued to dominate the party leadership.

On Practice (July 1937)

So far, Mao's work has been more or less readable, even occasionally displaying flashes of stylistic excellence in a handful of passages. The early Mao texts are pragmatic, focused on identifying ways to advance the revolution based on the actual "concrete conditions" he observed in China. In the communist world, however, ostentatious displays of theorizing were central to establishing authority, and here Mao was sorely lacking.

Lenin had generated a vast edifice of commentary as he and his foes battled to out-Marx each other in the prerevolutionary period, while Stalin had leaned heavily on his work *Marxism and the National Question* to pose as a deep thinker once in power and was adept at spraying citations all over even the flimsiest texts. Other communist leaders in central and eastern Europe also generated turgid works of "theory" to demonstrate their suitability to lead.

Mao was more a *Short Course*-style of communist than a deep thinker, and it was not until after the Long March that he enjoyed a period of stability that allowed him time to study at least some of the Marxist works he had hitherto neglected. And now, after railing against the book worshipers, he felt confident enough to generate a spot of "theory" himself, to buttress his authority as the preeminent revolutionary in China. The Mao "classics" *On Practice* and its follow-up, *On Contradiction*, were written during this period.

Within China, careers and ancillary bibliographies would be built upon demand for "interpreters" of Mao thought. During the 1960s and '70s, the Chairman's "theoretical" works also enjoyed a certain cachet among non-Chinese-speaking philosophers in the West. The French proved particularly susceptible, as the likes of Jean-Paul Sartre, Michel Foucault, Julia Kristeva and Louis Althusser all demonstrated their immense intellectual sophistication via their enthusiasm for the ideas of a totalitarian despot. Of course, only exceptionally clever people can be so stupid, and I approached these famed "theoretical" works with a degree of dread, certain that only monumentally tedious and opaque prose could be so appealing to titans of French critical theory. Indeed, so reluctant was I to read *On Practice* that I waited until I was suffering from a violent fever in the hope that engaging with Mao's "philosophy" through a hallucinatory fog would make the experience somehow more tolerable. It didn't, and nor did the text improve when I reread it in a lucid state.

The grandiose subtitle *On the Relation Between Knowledge and Practice, Between Knowing and Doing* certainly suggests that the reader is in store for some very deep thinking, and Mao is keen to establish his debt to Marx at the start:

Before Marx, materialism examined the problem of knowledge apart from the social nature of man and apart from his historical development, and was therefore incapable of understanding the dependence of knowledge on social practice, that is, the dependence of knowledge on production and the class struggle.

However, as he proceeds, fumbling with the theory of knowledge with all the confidence of somebody who has read somebody who has read somebody who has read a bit of Hegel, it becomes difficult to understand precisely why *On Practice* was ever brandished by anyone as a totem of Mao's significance as a thinker. The enthusiast for peasant violence outlines what he assures us are the two stages of cognition: "perceptual knowledge," which grasps only external appearances, and "logical knowledge," which seeks to arrive "at the comprehension of the internal contradictions of objective things, of their laws and of the internal relations between one process and another, that is, to arrive at logical knowledge." Mao then delves into the history of class struggle, where we learn that cognition is crucial. When trapped in the perceptual stage of cognition, the proletariat participated in violent uprisings that achieved little, since they didn't understand anything. Only once the proletariat advanced to the "period of conscious and organized economic and political struggles" did the situation improve, as Marx and Engels "scientifically summed up [the proletariat's experience of prolonged struggle] to create the theory of Marxism for the education of the proletariat."

Mao's immersion in the radioactive wasteland of Marxist theory has clearly had a disastrous effect upon his prose style. Words pile upon words and it is difficult to unpick his arguments, such as they are. Rather than sing the praises of peasant violence or ridicule egghead readers, Mao now delivers himself of grandiose banalities such as "All knowledge originates in perception of the objective external world through man's physical sense organs," and "The sum total of innumerable relative truths constitutes absolute truth," or "Marxism-Leninism has in no way exhausted truth but ceaselessly opens up roads to the knowledge of truth in the course of practice."

To describe Mao's convoluted cod-philosophical cogitations in detail requires the generation of unforgivable amounts of verbiage, at least as awful as his own, which is in itself a highly successful form of defense against criticism. Yet in spite of all his stylistic and theoretical contortions, Mao is starting from what Lenin described as the "living soul" of

Marxism—the analysis of concrete conditions, albeit now couching his arguments in "theoretical" language: "Start from perceptual knowledge and actively develop it into rational knowledge; then start from rational knowledge and actively guide revolutionary practice to change both the subjective and the objective world."

The bibliography for *On Practice* is suspiciously slight, however. Mao cites only one book by Marx, Stalin's student primer *The Foundations of Leninism* and three works of Lenin. In fact, Lenin is cited much more often than Marx, and the most frequently cited of his texts is *Materialism and Empiriocriticism*, the slapdash work of pseudophilosophy he cobbled together in the British Library in order to wage textual war against Alexander Bogdanov in 1908. Little wonder that *On Practice* is tedious, prolix, and unpersuasive. Some critics have argued that Mao wrote it much later than 1937 and subsequently "rectified" the historical record to make it seem as though he had emerged as a major theorist much earlier. Others disagree. Either way, only those with an urgent need to believe, or pretend to believe, that Mao was a theorist of note could ever be taken in by it.

On Contradiction (August 1937)

Mao continued to wax philosophical throughout 1937, following up *On Practice* with *On Contradiction*, in which he delivered himself of a lengthy exposition on the law of materialist dialectics. Mao begins by citing Lenin on the contrast between the "metaphysical" and "dialectical" world outlooks. Apparently, "metaphysicians" "hold that all the different kinds of things in the universe and all their characteristics have been the same ever since they came into being." Since this means that capitalism will endure forever, they must be wrong. Dialectics—which allows for developments to arise as a result of contradictions inside a thing—is correct. Or something like that.

As evidence, Mao points the reader toward plants and animals whose growth, he assures us, is "the result of internal contradictions." Social development, too, is a result of internal contradictions and not external causes. Even so, he is quick to stress that a materialist dialectic does not exclude external causes. After all, "external causes are the condition of change and internal causes are the basis of change and that external causes become operative through internal causes." For instance, says Mao, "in a suitable temperature an egg changes into a chicken, but no temperature can change a stone into a chicken because each has a different basis." And as Engels pointed out, "one of the basic principles of the higher mathematics is the contradiction that in certain circumstances straight lines and curves may be the same." Quite.

On Contradiction contains no wisdom, and were it to somehow vanish from time and space, the history of the printed word would be enriched by its absence. Yet from its own contradictions, a certain, limited fascination may arise. Intricate and useless, reading it is like staring at a detailed model of a ship inside a bottle: you wonder how its creator got it in there, while also thinking that the energy would have been much better spent doing something else.

Assorted Poems

If Mao's philosophy leaves much to be desired, then what about his poetry? Unlike Stalin, he never abandoned the practice of writing verse, and like "real" poets, he used it as a medium of self-expression. He wrote following defeats and personal tragedies; he wrote after miraculous escapes; he wrote after titanic victories over his foes. He was, in truth, much more of a poet than he was a theoretician.

Some critics would have us believe that Mao's efforts have a value beyond the curio factor. My own edition of Mao's poetry comes with fulsome praise on the dust jacket. According to the *Los Angeles Times*, Mao is "a poet of sensibility and power," while the *Hudson Review* refers to him as "a master." The translator Willis Barnstone describes Mao as "a major poet." It is remarkable indeed that a man responsible for the deaths of so many should have received so much praise.

A bad man need not be a bad poet of course, although given the scope and scale of Mao's crimes, it is hard not to view some of these claims as the intellectual equivalent of what economists would describe as a "positional good"—that is to say, an opinion held primarily to signal the high status of the person holding it (in this case, a judgment so perverse and unpopular that it requires great intellectual dexterity to prove it, and so demonstrates membership of an elite class).

It is difficult for a non-Chinese speaker to assess the quality of Mao's poetry. That said, it is clear that although a revolutionary when it came to politics, Mao was a reactionary when it came to aesthetics, much like Lenin and Stalin. He uses conventional patterns and structures, and regularly alludes to or borrows lines from poets of the classical tradition. The judicious use of the right quotation is in itself a poetic skill, and Mao had long put this ability to good use in his articles and speeches. In fact, even in English it is clear that Mao is at least *competent*. The poems read like exercises, with recurring imagery of mountains, heaven, armies, clouds and nature, making them a bit boring in a nonoffensive manner: the literary equivalent of those scrolls that Chinese artisans paint for tourists. One Chinese translator described it in pretty much those terms: "not as bad as Hitler's painting, but not as good as Churchill's."

However, whether Mao's poetry is the work of a master or merely "pedantic and pedestrian," its most problematic aspect is in fact something that emerges unscathed by the vagaries of translation: the relentlessly grandiose, pompous, "god's-eye view" of the author.

Consider this effort, for instance:

Against the First Encirclement Campaign

Forests blaze red beneath the frosty sky,
The wrath of Heaven's armies soars to the clouds.
Mist veils Lungkang, its thousand peaks blurred.
All cry out in unison:
Our van has taken Chang Hui-tsan!
The enemy returns to Kiangsi two hundred thousand strong,
Fumes billowing in the wind in mid-sky.
Workers and peasants are wakened in their millions
To fight as one man,
Under the riot of red flags round the foot of Puchou!

After starting as an uninspired but acceptable bit of verse, the poem ends on a standard propaganda trope staggering only in its banality. That said, it is better than the following poem, which begins with a propaganda trope and ends the same way.

The Long March

The Red Army fears not the trials of the March,
Holding light ten thousand crags and torrents.

The Five Ridges wind like gentle ripples
And the majestic Wumeng roll by, globules of clay.
Warm the steep cliffs lapped by the waters of Golden Sand,
Cold the iron chains spanning the Tatu River.
Minshan's thousand li* of snow joyously crossed,
The three Armies march on, each face glowing.

Although artfully done, Mao once again assumes a god's-eye view, building up to his concluding image of a majestic assortment of bold communists defying nature, blah blah blah. This may be poetry, but it is also propaganda.

This small effort is less inhuman, but nevertheless hagiographic in its own quiet way:

On Militia Women

How bright and brave they look, shouldering five-foot rifles
On the parade ground lit up by the first gleams of day.
China's daughters have high-aspiring minds,
They love their battle array, not silks and satins.

The god's-eye view even seems to be reflected in Mao's leisurely publishing schedule for his verse. He had written poetry for most of his life, but it was not published in collected form until 1965, when he was on the verge of launching the Cultural Revolution. Chinese emperors also wrote poetry, and Mao officially outed himself as a practitioner of the art shortly before he emerged as the central focus of the most extreme personality cult of the twentieth century.

That said, Mao could work in a less bombastic mode. In "I Lost My Proud Poplar," he writes mournfully about the death of his second wife. This may be a genuinely good poem, although as I don't speak Chinese it is impossible for me to judge. It does at least have a more personal tone. Even so, the existence of a few tolerable lines does not constitute compelling evidence of greatness. Life is short and there are many, far better poets out there.† Let us read them instead.

---

* Chinese unit of distance.
† Among them, Mao's revolutionary comrade Ho Chi Minh. Although his revolutionary writings are held in less regard than those of Mao, the Vietnamese leader's poetry is much

Chairman Mao's Guide to Fighting and Killing People

Mao's reputation is less tarnished than seems reasonable for a man responsible for the unnecessary deaths of tens of millions. His crimes receive far less attention than those of other twentieth-century dictators, and it is not uncommon to find academic historians arguing for a more "nuanced" understanding of Mao's achievements in their biographies of him, as if sixty million or so dead is a perfectly acceptable level of collateral damage to incur while building a state. In 2002 the U.S. publisher Citadel even inflicted upon the world a book titled *The Wisdom of Mao*; other entries in the series focused on the likes of Carl Jung, Abraham Lincoln and the Buddha.

Mao was sharp and cunning and shrewd, but did he have wisdom? That seems like a bit of a stretch. Yes, some of Mao's slogans were catchy, and they have even entered the English lexicon, but so has "Just Do It." And while Mao's dabbling in philosophy may have helped establish his brand as a communist supergenius, he was, of course, a fraud.

Mao's real strength was in his pragmatism. He early on grasped the importance of the peasantry to revolution, and in a work such as *On the New Democracy* he provides an outline of a single-party state. Perhaps where he really excelled, though, and certainly where he outdid all other dictators, was in his understanding of how to fight a guerrilla war. If you're not a deracinated Western thinker looking for a few cheap intellectual thrills, but rather a radical from the developing world planning to run an insurgency for decades, then Mao is your man.

In *Strategic Problems of China's Revolutionary War* (1936) and *On Protracted War* (1938) and in his other military writings, Mao writes clearly, expanding upon the principles outlined in *A Single Spark*. Thus his insistence on adapting Marxism to Chinese conditions paradoxically

---

better, even in translation. Between August 1942 and September 1943, he was a prisoner of Chiang Kai-shek in South China, and during that time he wrote 115 verses about the experience. Like Mao, he wrote in Chinese and used classical Chinese forms, but unlike Mao, he did not write as a god standing above history. Instead, his poems are detailed, humane, and compassionate. In all his years, Mao never wrote anything as simple and affecting as Ho's "Goodbye to a Tooth":

> You are hard and proud, my friend,
> Not soft and long like the tongue:
> Together we have shared all kinds of bitterness and sweetness,
> But now you must go west while I go east.

resulted in international appeal. Radicals in other "colonial, semicolonial or feudal" countries could learn from China how to enlist the peasants in a war that lasted forever, or near enough.

Mao outlines in detail how to fight and win. He offers no promises of a quick victory: he admits that the revolution will take a long time. The revolutionary army will have to retreat to the countryside, and rely on rural dwellers for supplies and manpower, waging a long campaign of guerrilla warfare against the enemy. With little territory to defend, it becomes much easier to harass those who do. He argues for building up bases and provides a structure for the resistance, broken down by three stages: strategic defensive, strategic stalemate and strategic counteroffensive, the last culminating in victory. Eventually the peasants will grow in strength, and with the cities surrounded, they will choke the bourgeois imperialists to death. Through guerrilla warfare, the weak can confuse and disperse and eat away at the enemy until he is weak—and then destroy him through regular warfare.

Every now and then, Mao attempts to layer a theoretical gloss over his guide to conquest and power, for instance, "War is the highest form of struggle for resolving contradictions, when they have developed to a certain stage, between classes, nations, and states of political groups." But as with all his best writings, his military texts are based on Lenin's principle of the concrete analysis of concrete conditions. It is this that has enabled Maoism to flourish in poor countries with large peasant populations. Mao may not offer "wisdom," but he can show the weak how to fight the strong and not worry about waiting for an urban proletariat to emerge. Through his own example, he gives hope. And so Mao's most faithful readers are to be found not in China, where the revolutionary struggle was abandoned decades ago, but rather in places such as the Karala region of India, where a Maoist group has fought an insurgency against the central government since 1967; and in Peru, where Abimael Guzmán's Shining Path caused havoc for decades; or in Nepal, where Maoists first fought against the government before entering and then leading it.

As USUAL, THE new happiness foretold by Marx and Engels had to be consolidated by means of terror and violence, through assaults by the newly liberated Chinese peasantry on landlords, through the repression of "counterrevolutionaries" and those deemed too religious, through forced labor and the herding of peasants onto collectivized farms, and, at least to begin with, through the deaths of between two and three million people. But Mao also kept a close eye on the purity of the party. In 1951, a mere two years after the dawn of the new era, he launched the "Three-Antis" campaign, which targeted corruption, waste and bureaucracy. This, it turned out, was an insufficient quantity of "Antis." A few months later, a second, Five-Antis campaign was launched to fight bribery, tax evasion, theft of state property, corruption in the allocation of government contracts and the pilfering of economic information. Pummeling reactionaries and corrupt bureaucrats was a popular policy, and party membership swelled.

Meanwhile, Mao set to work reengineering souls. The party had been using propaganda texts in literacy campaigns for peasants and soldiers since the mid-1930s, but now it was possible to operate on a far larger scale, and to create hundreds of millions of new readers, rearing them all on a diet of Marxist-Leninist classics. By the 1950s there were five decades' worth of prose by Stalin to digest, as well as the works of Lenin, Marx, Engels, and a horde of Soviet authors, whose words now flowed across the border of the USSR into China. Over a six-year period commencing in October 1949, some 2,300 Soviet and Russian literary works were translated into Chinese. Some of it was even good, such as classic books by Mayakovsky and Chekhov, and some was useful, such as the science and technology textbooks. But all of it came from Moscow, reinforcing the Soviet capital's status as the epicenter of the new world. Mao's works and those of his high-ranking party colleagues were also available but, even so, "Mao Zedong Thought" was not regarded as a systematic ideology but rather a refining of the core truths of the Marxist-Leninist canon, adapted to Chinese conditions.

Mao was always careful to demonstrate the necessary reverence toward Stalin, even though the Vozhd distrusted the Chinese leader, who had often ignored his orders during the civil war with the Kuomintang. Mao's distance from Moscow and popular support gave him much more latitude than the leaders of Stalin's Eastern European satellites, who were establishing repressive regimes under the watchful eye of the boss. At the same time, Mao understood the balance of power and accepted Stalin's seniority as the "father" of communism with a Confucian sense of duty. A mere two months after declaring that the Chinese people had stood up, Mao made the pilgrimage to Moscow to attend Stalin's seventieth birthday celebrations. It was his first visit to the Soviet capital, and he was seated at the right hand of the master. During the celebrations, Mao delivered himself of an unctuous speech worthy of the most dependent supplicant, in which he described Stalin as "a teacher and friend of the people of the world as well as a teacher and friend of the Chinese people," who was responsible for "extremely outstanding and extensive contributions to the cause of the world Communist movement."

This was hardly Mao's first encomium to the supreme author of world communism, yet due to his habit of quietly ignoring Stalin's orders whenever he felt he could get away with it, the encounter between the two giants of dictator literature was somewhat tense. Only the year before, Stalin had ordered the CCP to sit down for talks with Chiang Kai-shek's Kuomintang; instead, Mao had pressed his advantage home and defeated them. This may have led to the victory of communism, but even so, disobedience was disobedience. To make matters worse, the Yugoslav dictator Marshal Tito had broken with Moscow the year before, and Stalin was on the hunt for enemies and traitors. Chinese communism was "nationalistic," he observed, and Mao "inclined toward nationalism."

As a three-decade veteran of perilous ideological struggles, Mao recognized immediately that this was an ominous utterance. To defend himself he turned to his texts, requesting that a Soviet expert on Marxism-Leninism be dispatched to China to analyze his publication record and to "review and edit" his works. The gambit worked. In early 1950 the new Soviet ambassador, Pavel Yudin, arrived in Beijing. An academic and expert on the "science" of Marxism, he closely scrutinized Mao's works for signs of heresy. He officially pronounced them ideologically sound at a meeting of the Soviet Politburo two years later, by which time they certainly were: a revised edition of Mao's *Selected Works*, purged of awkward ideological lapses and Mao's occasionally spicy language, had begun publication in 1951 and was up to three volumes by 1953. It sold in the millions, but then Stalin died and the point was moot.

Even so, when Khrushchev denounced Stalin at the Twentieth Party Congress in February 1956, Mao was displeased. It wasn't just that the new Soviet leader had treated Mao as a junior partner. (Khrushchev never let Mao know the speech was coming; nor was the Chinese leader even provided with a copy.)* Mao regarded the Secret Speech as an act of disrespect to a great predecessor, who, for all their disagreements, had been a giant among communists. In China, parades always ended with the slogan "Long live the great leader of the people of the world, Stalin!" As for Khrushchev's criticism of the "personality cult," well, Mao had one of his own. In fact, Mao Zedong Thought had been enshrined in the constitution of the CCP since 1945. Khrushchev's position, in Mao's eyes, lacked nuance: "The question is not whether or not there should be a cult of the individual, but rather whether or not the individual concerned represents the truth. If he does, then he should be worshipped." When Mao and the rest of the CCP leadership published their official verdict in the *People's Daily*, it was mathematically precise: Stalin was 70 percent Marxist, 30 percent not Marxist. That was a pretty good ratio. His books remained in print, his portrait still hung in official buildings, and his collected works lined the shelves of bookshops—even as he vanished from the bookshelves and walls of the USSR and its satellites.† Yet the party was apparently rattled enough by Khrushchev's criticism of Stalin's cult that Mao Zedong Thought was removed from the constitution and replaced with a more general emphasis on Marxism-Leninism and "collective leadership."

A slow drift now set in, further separating China from its Soviet ally. Although Khrushchev revered Lenin and placed his texts at the center of the state, his vision of a socialist paradise was less austere than that of his predecessors. He loosened censorship, opened Stalin's gulags, and, even as the Institute of Marxism-Leninism set to work on a fifty-five-volume edition of Lenin's works that would occupy the space liberated by the sudden disappearance of Stalin's oeuvre, Khrushchev dreamed of a future communism that was less abstract and involved a lot more sausage. Khrushchev's ambition was to ascend to a standard of living higher than that of the United States. Mao scorned Khrushchev's materialist conception of communism. Although now in his early sixties, he had not grown less radical. His concern was that life was too easy, that the party was growing fat and complacent and alienated from the people.

---

* Mao had to read about it in a Chinese translation of a *New York Times* article.
† Not until 1989 did the party resolve that it was no longer necessary to display portraits of Stalin on major holidays.

Intellectuals in particular were disaffected, and Mao wanted to harness their energies to the cause of revolution.

In 1956 Mao plucked a slogan from the Chinese classics that he hoped would herald a new era in the life of the country: "Let a hundred flowers bloom, and a hundred schools of thought contend." From now on, he said, China's intellectuals would be free to express themselves—even to criticize. Given that hundreds of thousands of their peers had perished in Mao's repressions a few years earlier, they were slow to take him up on his offer. But Mao insisted, and in his February 1957 speech, "On the Correct Handling of Contradictions," he declared that there was no need to worry. Whereas Stalin had failed to distinguish between helpful criticism and the treacheries of real enemies, this would not happen in China; the time for violent class struggle was over. Even the party could make errors, and only through openly debating those mistakes could the correct path be reached. However, when free thought did begin to bloom, it turned out that this was not what Mao wanted after all. Attacks on corruption and party arrogance were acceptable, but once the intellectuals started criticizing such sacred cows as the one-party state, collectivization, the country's reliance on Moscow and the leader cult, Mao quickly changed his mind. The labor camps and fields filled up with intellectuals in need of "rectification."

Let down by the educated elite, Mao now turned his attention to the masses. In his earliest pre-Marxist writings, he had argued that the cultivation of willpower and large muscles were central to China's development; now he returned to that theme. The historical dialectic was all well and good, but Marx's impersonal forces took a backseat to Mao's faith that immense acts of exertion and self-sacrifice could propel the country into the future. In 1958 he started calling for "permanent revolution," urging the people to produce "more, faster, better and more economically." "Dare to think, dare to act," he declared; it was time for a "Great Leap Forward." When "More/Faster" was adopted as an official slogan at the CCP's Eighth Congress that May, it turned out that it entailed merging smaller agricultural cooperatives into mega-collective farms known as "People's Communes." The masses formed Study Chairman Mao's Works reading groups so that they could derive spiritual sustenance and direct guidance from the words of the leader as they set about the business of building new factories, roads, and bridges. They also composed poetry, and state employees roamed China collecting this new, mass-produced literature that had arisen as a result of the sudden release of the people's creative energies. Since time was short (Mao demanded that China overtake the United Kingdom in fifteen years) peasants rushed with their wedding rings and tools and kitchen utensils to "backyard furnaces" to provide the state with the steel it needed.

Perhaps it was in the Great Leap Forward, and not in his actual poetry, that Mao was at his most poetic—in the sense of poetry as an act of lyrical, impassioned, transcendent utterance, at least. His sloganeering during the Great Leap shared the same god's-eye view that makes his poetry so bombastic and unpersuasive. Viewing "the people" from on high, as an extraneous mass swept forward in response to the great historical moment, Mao did not care what this meant for the individuals caught up in the onward rush. Worse, he substituted verbal magic for strategy, as if mistaking Stalin's cynical efficacy at overwriting empirical reality on paper for a revelation about the ability of the word to just as easily revise the world of actual physical bodies and objects. It was logocentrism gone wild. So inspired was Mao that he began to dream not only of a new China but of a new earth, which would be unified under a single planning system organized in Beijing, leading to "an era of perpetual happiness."

Things didn't work out quite as planned. Having tossed their metal into the smelters' flames, the peasants were left with low-quality pig iron and nothing to cook, eat, or work with. But it was when Mao's verbal magic was aimed at the animal kingdom that matters really got out of hand. Convinced that mosquitoes, flies, rats, and sparrows ("the four pests") were restraining China's advance into the future, he declared that the entire nation, including "five-year-old children," had to be mobilized to exterminate them. But while few would disagree that the first three pests can be unpleasant and unhygienic, the threat posed by sparrows is less obvious. According to Mao, these tiny birds were eating grain that could otherwise have been used to feed humans. Thus began a bizarre war on sparrows, during which peasants charged into the fields clattering the pots and pans and gongs they hadn't already melted down to scare sparrows away, as children clambered up trees to demolish their nests. The campaign was a success: sparrows circled in the air until they dropped dead of exhaustion, which they did in their millions. The fourth pest was on the verge of extinction—the only problem being that the sparrows had actually not been eating the *grain* but in fact the *insects that ate the grain*.

In the absence of sparrows, these other pests were now free to ravage China's crops almost unimpeded, resulting in famine. The victors over the sparrows were reduced to eating mud, insects and, on occasion, each other. The additional plagues of drought and state-mandated production quotas resulted in the entirely avoidable deaths of as many as forty-five million people. That's a greater body count than either Stalin's or Hitler's.

Undaunted, Mao maintained the god's-eye view expressed in his poetry. "When there is not enough to eat, people starve to death," he told his colleagues. "It is better to let half of the people die so that the other half can eat their fill." And as millions duly starved, the party offered extra helpings of propaganda. Via slogans, posters and patriotic songs, the Chinese were reminded that, present sufferings notwithstanding, their leader was an unparalleled supergenius, guiding them toward history's triumphant denouement. By 1960, however, even Mao recognized that the Great Leap Forward more closely resembled a suicidal plummet to the bottom of an abyss. Shaken, the great slayer of sparrows now retreated to the "second line" of China's leadership, resigning as head of state and handing over responsibility for cleaning up the mess to President Liu Sha-oqi and party general secretary Deng Xiaoping (who had handled the "rec-tification" of the intellectuals after the debacle of the Hundred Flowers Campaign). That same year, the tensions that had been building between the USSR and China since Khrushchev's Secret Speech finally erupted into the open as the Soviets, having reneged on a promise to supply China with nuclear technology,* withdrew all their advisers from the country as a result of the ensuing dispute. Disaster followed disaster, but at least there was some good news: volume 4 of Mao's *Selected Works* finally hit the shelves.

THE SINO-SOVIET SPLIT was both a challenge and a liberation. China had lost its massive subsidies, but the CCP was now free to compete against its former hegemon for leadership of the global communist movement. That said, the fight got off to a feeble start: of all the communist countries in the world, only tiny Albania sided with China.

---

* Mao once dismissed the bomb as a "paper tiger" but this is more expressive of his insou-ciant attitude toward the death of his subjects than doubt in its efficacy as a weapon of mass slaughter. In 1957 he told a Yugoslav visitor to Beijing that since China had "a very large territory and a big population," the atom bomb did not pose a real threat. "What if they killed three hundred million of us? We would still have many people left."

In Mao's eyes, Khrushchev's heresies had only multiplied since his 1956 denunciation of Stalin. The Soviet leader didn't seem to have much appetite for the violent overthrow of the bourgeoisie and the establishment of the dictatorship of the proletariat. He now proclaimed that capitalism and communism could abide together in a state of "peaceful coexistence," that war was not an essential prelude to the establishment of socialism, and that it might even be possible for communist countries to ally themselves with noncommunists. To Mao, this was not a sign that the USSR was getting soft in its middle age, or that Khrushchev was revising Marxism-Leninism's more apocalyptic aspects to explain away the repeated disconfirmation of prophecy. Instead, it was indisputable evidence of something much more sinister: that the bourgeoisie was staging a comeback in the USSR. Like some ancient, malign spirit, this evil force had lurked patiently on the threshold, awaiting its moment—and then struck.

If it had struck in the birthplace of the revolution, then it could strike anywhere, including in China. And so, from his position of self-imposed exile in the "second line," Mao grew increasingly suspicious of his comrades who were attempting to rebuild the nation following the catastrophic failure of the Great Leap Forward. Initially, he had sat back as the new leadership pursued a series of pragmatic economic reforms and "adjustments," and even delivered a "self-criticism" at a conference in Beijing in June 1961. However, he resented their eagerness to act without consulting him, and soon came to regard their more earthly pragmatism in a different light: clearly the bourgeoisie was staging a comeback in China, too. It was time to return to the "front line." Mao now began to intone ominously in his speeches of the threat posed by "revisionism," the need to renew the class struggle, and the necessity of staging a revolution within the revolution to stamp out the resurgent feudal and bourgeois values he saw around him.

As the 1960s progressed, Mao continued to pursue the theme. "The thought, culture, and customs which brought China to where we found her must disappear," he told the visiting French author (and minister of cultural affairs) André Malraux in 1965, "and the thought, customs, and culture of proletarian China, which does not yet exist, must appear." He was also quite keen for his rival, president Liu Shaoqi, to disappear, along with his book *How to Be a Good Communist*, which had shifted fifteen million units between 1962 and 1966, outselling anything attributed to

Mao during the same period. Worse, a *Selected Works* of Liu's was in the planning stages. That should be made to disappear before it had even appeared. But how? To a text-obsessed communist with boundless faith in the power of the written word, the answer was obvious: via the publication of a scathing review of a play by somebody else, of course.

The Dismissal of Hai Rui from Office was the work of a scholar of the Ming dynasty named Wu Han. During the Great Leap Forward, Mao had cited the titular Hai Rui as a fine example of an honest official who wasn't afraid to tell a tyrannical emperor some inconvenient truths. Wu Han dashed off a piece of propaganda on the theme, which received its first performance in 1961. Mao enjoyed the play so much that he invited the lead actor to dinner, and presented Wu Han with a signed copy of the fourth volume of his *Selected Works*.

By 1965, however, Wu Han was deputy mayor of Beijing, and he was associated with the "revisionist" leadership that Mao now believed was intent on restoring the rule of the bourgeoisie in China. Mao's (fourth) wife, an ex-actress named Jiang Qing, insisted that *The Dismissal of Hai Rui from Office* was a covert attack on the Chairman himself. Seeing an opportunity to strike against the resurgent bourgeoisie, but either too busy or too lazy to write anything himself, Mao commissioned a work of literary criticism from a journalist in Shanghai, to be supervised by Jiang. The deployment of a bad review in ideological battles was a favorite tactic of Stalin's, and Mao took his foray into the form very seriously. After more than half a year and ten drafts, he finally had a satisfactory critique, which was published in November 1965 in the Shanghai paper *Literary Reports*. (Mao feared that the "revisionists" in Beijing would block its publication.) The line of attack? That Wu Han was guilty of a grievous ideological error: he claimed that it was possible for a man of Hai Rui's elevated class background to overcome the limitations imposed upon him by his social origins. Wu's play, in short, was a "poisonous weed."

Unaware that Mao was behind the attack on Wu Han, the playwright's allies attempted to prevent republication of the review in the capital. When Mao threatened to organize its publication as a pamphlet they backed down, and the citizens of Beijing were soon able to read all about the deputy mayor's antiparty, anti-China heresies in their copies of the *People's Daily*. Pleased, Mao celebrated the success of this first salvo in the culture wars by writing a poem about a bird excited by a coming storm. It scorns another sparrow cowering in a bush as a clown who's "farted quite enough."

Emboldened, Mao launched a series of attacks on all those agents of the bourgeoisie who were undermining the Chinese revolution from within. In his speeches and publications, he criticized the intelligentsia, artists, writers and members of the party elite for their "revisionism," comparing them to Khrushchev. In fact, Khrushchev had by this point fallen from power, but the march of the enemy continued and Mao derided the new Soviet leadership as "new Khrushchevs." He also vituperated against teachers, and called for class struggle in universities, high schools and primary schools, where, he declared, students should "overthrow the professors." On a roll, Mao denounced the propaganda department of the Central Committee as the "Palace of the King of Hell," and in a meeting of the Politburo he declared that nefarious forces had infiltrated the government, the army and the cultural bureaucracy in order to establish their own dictatorship. China had its own Khrushchevs, and it was time to launch a "mass campaign" against them. The stage was set for a titanic battle between good and evil, which Mao, content as he was in his own revolutionary virtue, was certain would leave him unscathed. Something was about to happen, but what?

On May 29, 1966, a group of radical middle school students at an elite school attached to Tsinghua University in Beijing christened themselves "Red Guards." They were, like the vast majority of radical egalitarians, vehemently opposed to the privilege of others, if not their own. At first it was all just words, albeit violent ones. Somebody stuck up a poster at the university that read, "Beat to a pulp any and all persons who go against Mao Zedong Thought—no matter who they are, what banner they fly, or how exalted their positions may be." When the Red Guards contacted Mao to ask what he thought of their agitprop, he was delighted. The seventy-two-year-old Chairman publicly praised the pubescent radicals, declaring that it was "right to rebel against reactionaries." Following Mao's endorsement, the Red Guard movement spread rapidly, with bands of pimply teenagers rejecting the authority of grown-ups and rising up against their teachers. "To rebel is justified," they proclaimed. The slogan, ironically enough, came from a 1939 speech Mao entitled "Stalin Is Our Commander," in which the Chairman had striven to demonstrate his acceptance of and loyalty to communist hierarchy rather than any spirit of disobedience.

Buoyed by the support he was receiving from the youth, Mao continued his rhetorical assaults on the party elite. He denounced his comrades
as "monsters and freaks" at a party conference, and shortly afterward
published a short article entitled "Bombard the Headquarters—My Big
Character Poster," followed by an outline of "Sixteen Points" essential for
a successful Cultural Revolution in China. The words were flowing and
the revolutionary sap of the Red Guard was rising. When Chen Boda, the
party's chief ideologue, called upon China's youth to come to the capital
to show their support for the leader, they turned up en masse. At a rally
on August 18, 1966, Mao stepped out from behind the shelves of his
Selected Works and the propaganda photos of his tubby form bobbing
along the Yangtze River to display his living body to tens of thousands of
teenage fans, in a great spectacle that provided the missing link between
Nuremberg and Beatlemania.*

Wearing a military tunic and a red armband, Mao did not move very
much, nor did he speak at all. Merely being there was enough. He presented his moving meat to the seething, hormonal throng and let them
stare at it and yell and scream in acclamation. Occasionally he might lift
an arm, to acknowledge their presence—but what an arm! That was the
arm at the end of which was the hand that had held the pen that wrote
On Practice and so many other masterpieces that were so, so precious to
the Red Guards! They wept and cheered and danced; they sang revolutionary songs and waved Mao's portrait and held aloft banners that read,
"I Love Chairman Mao's Books Best of All." And of all those books, the
one they loved the most, and the one they waved in the air, was the pocket-
size *Quotations from Chairman Mao*, the already legendary anthology
of the Chairman's "greatest hits."

Seven more mass rallies were held through November, by which point
twelve million Red Guards had been in the presence of their idol. Mao
thought that one reason for the failure of the USSR's revolution was that
Lenin had died before enough people could see him in the flesh; he had
solved that problem as far as China was concerned. More than that, his
support meant that China's youth now had a heroic struggle of their own.
Their parents' revolution had gone wrong; only the young people could
help the Chairman save it by carrying out a revolution within the revolu-

---

* Coincidentally, the Beatles also performed before a screaming crowd the same day, albeit
in Boston.

tion, a purifying rebirth. The kids *were* alright, and they would act as the fist of the Great Helmsman, striking down the "Four Olds": old ideas, old culture, old customs and old habits.

The purification began shortly after that first August encounter with the smiling, waving Mao, when Red Guards raided and ransacked more than one hundred thousand homes in Beijing, destroying books, paintings, sculptures, religious texts and other symbols of the old culture wherever they found them. In September the revolution spread across the nation, as the right to free travel, board and accommodation was bestowed upon the Red Guards. Bands of kids, teenagers and young adults embarked upon a thrilling cross-country fun ride, toppling monuments, burning down temples, incinerating or stealing the contents of libraries, ransacking museums and exhibitions, destroying artifacts, and desecrating the graves of ancient philosophers (including that of Confucius). They also destroyed less sacrosanct artifacts, such as Soviet books, chess sets (deemed to be too Soviet), goldfish and songbirds—all of which were apparently barriers to China's happiness. Red Guards set up checkpoints where they subjected passersby to tests designed to reveal whether or not they knew Mao's words, and imposed a puritanical revolutionary morality, attacking women with excessively bourgeois hairstyles, or who wore too much perfume, or who favored fancy shoes. Nor was the culture of the street exempt from the scourge of Mao's youthful attack dogs: from pubs to puppet shows, many pleasures of the poor were eradicated in a ruthless purge.

Mao, the connoisseur of violence, exulted in the chaos. "The babies want to rebel," he said; "we must support them." At first rebellion was restricted to the privileged student class, but it proved to be an impossible task to deny workers and peasants the delights of iconoclastic orgies of destruction. In Shanghai, groups of workers teamed up with students to form the Scarlet Guards and went on strikes. On December 25 a group of protesters shut down the Ministry of Labor in Beijing. A day later, Mao celebrated his seventy-third birthday, toasting the "unfolding of a nation-wide all-round civil war." Meanwhile, the Red Guards continued their pursuit of his "revisionist" enemies, exposing as "capitalist roaders" the onetime heroes of the revolution, and their wives and their children, too.

Things quickly started to spiral out of control. The cult of Mao fragmented into a multitude of competing sects. The provinces of Hubei, Hunan and Guangxi and the cities of Beijing, Canton and Shanghai served as bases for no fewer than 1,417 distinct groups of passionate "justified rebels." Rival factions fought each other, while local bosses set up their own bands of Red Guards for self-protection, as "conservatives" battled "radicals" in orgies of torture, murder and public humiliation. When the government of Shanghai was overthrown in early 1967 and replaced with a radical Shanghai Commune, an excited Mao initially endorsed the uprising. However, he soon came to regard the commune as too extreme and demanded the creation of "revolutionary committees," composed of Red Guards, party members and military men, to govern the provinces instead. Nevertheless, by midsummer, he felt that "conservative" forces were in the ascendant, and so proposed "arming the left"—with the entirely predictable result that the carnage grew still worse. The kids were not alright after all: they started shooting and stabbing each other with weapons hitherto reserved for those trained in how to use them. At funerals, Red Guards held aloft the severed limbs of fallen comrades. Spinal meningitis swept through the provinces, probably spread by revolutionary youth from the cities. The peasantry went on a rampage. According to official records, some 1.5 million died in the carnage.

"Youth is easily deceived because it is quick to hope," said Aristotle. Thanks to baby boomer nostalgia for the civil rights battles of their youth, two generations have grown up in the West reared on the myth that revolt by young adults is always and everywhere a benign force. Yet Aristotle was being a tad too generous: youth is also easily deceived because it is ignorant and suffers from an almost total lack of perspective, while being boundlessly confident in its own judgment. And let us not forget the words of Aldous Huxley, either:

> The surest way to work up a crusade in favor of some good cause is to promise people they will have a chance of maltreating someone. To be able to destroy with good conscience, to be able to behave badly and call your bad behavior "righteous indignation"—this is the height of psychological luxury, the most delicious of moral treats.

THE CULTURAL REVOLUTION wasn't all about destruction, however. In his 1965 meeting with André Malraux, Mao had spoken of a new culture that needed to appear, and it was not a new theme for the Great Helmsman even then. Two years before that, in an address to a party conference in the city of Hangzhou, he had essentially reaffirmed his metaphysical belief in the power of words to define and control reality: "one single [correct] formulation, and the whole nation will flourish; one single [incorrect] formulation, and the whole nation will decline. What is referred to here is the transformation of the spiritual into the material."

Language purification crusades occur in our own society, of course. But in China the Red Guards went a little further in their faith that through acts of ritual incantation and vigorous renaming campaigns, old things might be consecrated anew and reborn for the revolutionary era. Shops, schools, towns, streets, newspapers—all received new titles more in tune with the times. Thus the "Blue Sky" tailoring shop in Beijing became "Guard the East" tailoring shop, and "Peking Union Medical College" (a name bestowed by imperialist U.S. aggressors) became "Anti-Imperialist Hospital." Sometimes the renaming had a rather heavy-handed, satirical aspect: for instance, the Soviet embassy suddenly found itself located on Anti-Revisionist Street. Nor was it only inanimate objects that received revolutionary titles; newborn babies likewise rejoiced in names such as "Red Hero," "Learn from the Peasants," "Protect Red" and "Cultural Revolution."

Renaming was a relatively simple matter. In 1963, Mao had complained that Chinese stages were too full of "emperors, kings, generals, chancellors, maidens and beauties," and his wife Jiang Qing had taken on a far grander project: to create new, revolutionary Chinese art that would replace the outmoded culture of the past. Jiang was an ex-actress and so understood the arts from the perspective of a practitioner as well as a political figure—and, perhaps better still, this preserved domestic peace: Mao could more easily pursue his interest in the bodies of his nubile female staffers if his wife was occupied with an important revolutionary task. Jiang supervised a squad of ideologically pure creators, who eventually emerged from their cultural laboratories to unveil "eight model works," which were formally recognized as such in November 1966. Five operas, two ballets, and a symphony were now available to the masses as a replacement for five thousand years of culture. Well, it was a start at least. But it was a slow start, and it didn't get much faster as Jiang and her comrades suffered from an embarrassing paucity of ideas. Even within the limited scope of eight works, the only symphony, *Shajia Village*, was based on the same source novel as one of the operas, also called *Shajia Village*. This strikingly thin canon of works was performed around the country ad nauseam, and also adapted as films that were broadcast around the country ad nauseam, too. Eventually some more model works were added to the canon, but not many.

As for literature, the Red Guards burned old books, and the state more or less stopped printing new ones that didn't have the name "Mao" on the cover. That is an exaggeration, but not a very great one as most of the oxygen was sucked out of literary life during the Cultural Revolution. In total, around one hundred novels appeared, although readers at least had a reprint of the classic *The Water Margin* and Mao's own poetry to enjoy: censorship becomes a much easier task if you have only a handful of works to keep an eye on. The great bibliophile Mao was never personally deprived, of course: his own collection of classic editions was not incinerated, and he not only worked in an office surrounded by books but also slept in a room where books filled the shelves and spilled onto his bed. Sublimely confident in his revolutionary purity, the Chairman did not fear that the wrong words might harm him.

But even those one hundred novels published during the Cultural Revolution were in the end mere shadows of the brilliance on offer from Mao, who was now dominant among his colleagues once again. Although his were not the only works in existence, they were the only ones that truly mattered—and of those books, one was revered above all the others.

In 1959, China's minister of defense, Peng Dehuai, had criticized the excesses of the Great Leap Forward. Even though he avoided directly criticizing Mao, the Chairman was enraged. Peng did not last much longer in his post, and he would ultimately die in prison in 1974. He was replaced by Lin Biao, who long ago had received from Mao the letter that became *A Single Spark Can Start a Prairie Fire*.

Lin Biao was a Mao loyalist with no interest in generating theory of his own. His ideal of wisdom was that it be brief and easy to remember, and preferably delivered in prechewed, easily digestible form (he liked to write down wise sayings on index cards). Averse as he was to reading long books containing complex arguments, Lin empathized with the common soldier, who could hardly be expected to master the entire Mao canon yet still needed to develop familiarity with both the lexicon of the revolution and its core principles. Taking inspiration from his index cards, in 1961 he instructed the army newspaper *PLA Daily* to start publishing a daily quotation from Mao. These small, bite-size chunks of ideology (helpfully printed in red ink to distinguish them from more ordinary utterances) could be memorized and then put into practice, all under the watchful guidance of the army's political instructors.

It turned out that Lin Biao had a good grasp of the army's ideological needs. Soldiers began cutting out the Chairman's words from the *PLA Daily* and pasting them into scrapbooks, creating homemade compilations of Mao's wisdom. In January 1964 the political department of the People's Liberation Army centralized the process and produced an official selection of the Chairman's most sagacious words. This edition was brief: it contained 200 short excerpts from Mao's works organized into 23 sections. Then wisdom inflation kicked in, and by May an expanded edition was in print, now featuring 326 quotations spread across 30 chapters, also intended for military use. There were two versions: one with white paper covers for the lower ranks and another with red covers for the elite. In August 1965 a third edition appeared, resized to fit in the pocket of a military uniform. Now every copy came covered with a red vinyl dust jacket that would soon become iconic but which had a purely practical function: it was there to protect the precious words of the leader from water damage.

Expanded to 427 quotations arranged in 33 chapters, this "ultimate" edition of Mao's greatest hits was a huge success with both a military and a civilian readership. Lin Biao had tapped into a deep demand not only from the military but from the populace at large for a quick guide to the onslaught of words that had engulfed them since 1949, but which had hitherto been scattered across Mao's *Selected Works* and countless pamphlets. The Ministry of Culture decreed in June 1966 that two hundred million copies should be in print by the end of the year, and the country experienced paper shortages as the Word of the Chairman devoured most of the resources available to China's publishing industry. At last, everything essential had been gathered together in one place. These were the words that mattered. Thus was born *Quotations from Chairman Mao*, a.k.a. *The Little Red Book* or (as it was known in China) *The Red Treasure Book*.

The foreword, attributed to Lin Biao, makes grand claims:

Once Mao Tse-tung's thought is grasped by the broad masses, it becomes an inexhaustible source of strength and a spiritual atom bomb of infinite power. The large-scale publication of *Quotations from Chairman Mao Tse-tung* is a vital measure for enabling the broad masses to grasp Mao Tse-tung's thought and for promoting the revolutionization of our people's thinking.

The description of the book as a "spiritual atom bomb" was of course a ludicrously over-the-top metaphor in classic totalitarian style. But it was not only that: in late 1964 the Chinese had successfully detonated a nuclear weapon of their own in the country's northwestern Xinjiang region. Developed without Soviet assistance, this homegrown mushroom cloud had risen above the desert sky just as Khrushchev was falling from power in Moscow. The atom bomb was an emblem of national pride, saturated with symbolic resonance, evidence that China could challenge the USSR for leadership of the communist world. *Quotations from Chairman Mao* was its ideological equivalent, a textual weapon that would likewise transform the balance of power in the world.

Mao—who by this stage had green teeth and had entered the decadent orgiast phase of his dictatorship*—was pleased with this third edition, comparing it to the epochal, civilization-shaping works of Confucius and Lao-tzu. However, while its table of contents is certainly very long, the book is not especially comprehensive. Rather, the hierarchy of interests clearly reflects its origins as a manual for soldiers. After a few chapters dedicated to the basics of communism, the book dedicates many pages to military and party issues before finally addressing (at the very end) such trifling afterthoughts as "Youth," "Women," "Culture and Art," and "Study."

These limitations become even more obvious upon turning the page. Whereas Stalin was careful to impose his interpretation of the USSR's official ideology by filling *The Foundations of Leninism* with not only copious citations from Lenin but also explicatory context, there is no such careful framing of the ideological material in *Quotations from Chairman Mao*. This is because the book was designed for use by people who had full-time ideological professionals at hand to drill them in the official party line. They were never far from an expert who could tell them exactly

---

* According to his doctor, he spent his days lying around the pool in his robe and his evenings cavorting with young women on his staff and spreading venereal disease to young ballroom dancers who were also expected to service him sexually.

how to interpret what they were reading. Once removed from the barracks, however, *Quotations from Chairman Mao* becomes precisely what it proclaims itself to be: a pile of quotations stripped of context, disjointed, repetitive, tedious and banal.

That said, the book is not entirely without redeeming features. It contains some of Mao's greatest lines, including the one about the dinner party from *Report on an Investigation of the Peasant Movement in Hunan.* Brief highlights aside, however, much of *Quotations from Chairman Mao* is strikingly flat. Based as it is on the sanitized version of Mao's publication record, the anthology contains no colorful evocations of demons, farting birds, or the "Palace of the King of Hell," nor any of his poetry, which, however mediocre, is less excruciating than his overtly propagandistic or theoretical works. The mummified hand of Marxism-Leninism lies heavy upon the style as the reader is subjected to rote pap that any communist dictator after 1917 could have produced:

> People of the world, unite and defeat the U.S. aggressors and all their running dogs! People of the world, be courageous, and dare to fight, defy difficulties and advance wave upon wave. Then the whole world will belong to the people. Monsters of all kinds shall be destroyed.

Wooden rhetoric such as that alternates with bland nostrums such as this:

> Thrift should be the guiding principle in our government expenditure. It should be made clear to all government workers that corruption and waste are very great crimes. Our campaigns against corruption and waste have already achieved some results, but further efforts are required. Our system of accounting must be guided by the principle of saving every copper for the war effort, for the revolutionary cause and for our economic construction.

Conclusions of speeches are cut and pasted into the book wholesale, alongside long key passages from "major" works. Thus, for instance, the reader is presented with the six-point conclusion to *The Present Situation and Our Tasks* without having read any of the supporting arguments leading up to it. The point is not to engage with Mao's thought but to learn how to produce the correct words and ideas on command.

Meanwhile, many of the "wisdom" quotes are excerpted from different bits of the same essays. *On Contradiction* and *On Practice* feature heavily; barely readable when endured in their complete form, they are not improved once broken up into fragments and stripped of context. It is difficult to imagine that a soldier or collective farm worker returning from a hard day's labor in service of the state ever got much out of this raw, unappetizing gobbet of text ripped from the word carcass of *On Contradiction*:

> Qualitatively different contradictions can only be resolved by qualitatively different methods. For instance, the contradiction between the proletariat and the bourgeoisie is resolved by the method of socialist revolution; the contradiction between the great masses of the people and the feudal system is resolved by the method of democratic revolution; the contradiction between the colonies and imperialism is resolved by the method of national revolutionary war; the contradiction between the working class and the peasant class in socialist society is resolved by the method of collectivization and mechanization in agriculture; contradiction within the Communist Party is resolved by the method of criticism and self-criticism; the contradiction between society and nature is resolved by the method of developing the productive forces.... The principle of using different methods to resolve different contradictions is one that Marxist-Leninists must strictly observe.

The achievement of *Quotations from Chairman Mao* is that it reduces Mao Zedong Thought to a herky-jerky series of riffs on hard work, self-sacrifice, hating imperialists, the importance of frugality, stoicism, obedience and loyalty to Mao and the party. Stupefyingly dull from a content perspective, the book is also extremely conventional in its form. In China, anthologies of quotes intended to provide moral or religious guidance were known as *yulu* and went all the way back to Confucius and his *Analects*. Thus, *Quotations from Chairman Mao* had many antecedents in classical and modern Chinese letters, and in no way represented an improvement on the form.* Despite this, market conditions

---

* Mao wasn't even the first tyrant to inflict a *yulu* on the Chinese people. Centuries earlier, the founder of the Ming dynasty had produced a compilation of his own deep thoughts. Titled *Ming ta kao* ("Great Ming Edict"), all families were obliged to own a copy and, because

were exceedingly favorable for Mao's text, and not just because of his dominance of political power. With the help of his pimply teenage allies, Mao had laid waste to Chinese culture and successfully liquidated all his rivals, creating that which nature most abhors. By unleashing the transcendentally ignorant Red Guards upon the nation, its history and its institutions, Mao had opened up a vacuum that only his divine image and word could fill.

And so huge vats of ink, immense warehouses of paper and great lakes of red vinyl were dedicated to the worship of the radiant Mao-god. By the end of the decade, over 1 billion copies of *Quotations from Chairman Mao* were in circulation, adding to the 783 million copies of his other books and pamphlets that had been printed between 1949 and 1965. Given that China's population during the Cultural Revolution was in the area of 750 million, a number that includes babies, preschoolers and small children unable to read anything more complex than a propaganda cartoon about the Sino-Japanese War, it is clear that supply considerably outpaced demand. Even had the many dead of the Great Leap Forward suddenly returned from the grave filled with an irresistible urge to read Mao's prose, there would still have been a few hundred million copies left over.

Mao's quotations leapt from between the confines of their red vinyl covers to infiltrate the world via other media, metastasizing across the physical landscape. They appeared as writing on the walls of private homes in the form of quotation posters, or pasted to quotation boards in streets and parks, while some particularly enthusiastic Red Guards also proposed attaching quotation plates to cars, trains and bicycles. In disembodied form, and to the accompaniment of jaunty music, Mao's quotations invaded the airwaves as songs blasted from radios across the country. The first ten were released on September 30, 1966, while Mao's mass receptions were still under way. As the rebellious youth of the West were irritating their parents by listening to "Let's Spend the Night Together" so their counterparts in Red China were getting down to "The Force at the Core Leading Our Cause Forward Is the Chinese Communist Party" and "Ensure That Literature and Art Operate as Powerful Weapons for Exterminating the Enemy." In total, 365 of Mao's quotes were rendered in

---

China had a population of eighty million, this meant that the book enjoyed an extremely high circulation for the period.

musical form, one for each day of the year. Some of the Chairman's verses also received the song-and-dance treatment.

These were official manifestations of Mao's word. However, there were hundreds of local, unofficial editions of *Quotations of Chairman Mao*, and foreign editions, too, as the Chinese state unleashed its "spiritual atom bomb" on the planet earth, in the hope that it might blast out of existence the USSR's influence on world revolution. China commenced the launch of the *Quotations* at overseas targets in 1966. By May of the following year, over 800,000 copies in fourteen languages were in print; those numbers would rise to 110 million copies and thirty-six languages by 1971. The versions of *Quotations* that appeared overseas appealed not only to revolutionaries in the developing world and youthful campus radicals in Paris and Berkeley but also to older people who should have known better, such as Jean-Paul Sartre, Michel Foucault and, er, Shirley MacLaine.* In the process, Mao became very wealthy. Like Hitler, he collected royalties on the sales of his books: according to a 2007 article published in the magazine *Literary World of Party History*, by 1967 Mao had earned 5.7 million yuan ($780,000) from the sale of Chinese, English, Russian, French, Spanish and Japanese editions of his books.

But there was a problem. As his young disciples turned to the sacred book for guidance, they had no political commissars with the exegetic authority to instruct them in the correct understanding of the master's word. They found not a single truth but multiple truths, and interpretive chaos reigned as warring factions of Red Guards lobbed quotations at each other in bitter ideological battles. Mao's words were now free-floating fragments that could be used to justify opposing arguments.

The Chairman was displeased, and he was again displeased when Red Guards began publishing editions of his suppressed texts, which they had discovered when raiding the homes of the "revisionist" party elite who had access to the unsanitized Mao. These "lost gospels" revealed other Maos: the earthy Mao, the radical Mao, the not very Marxist Mao. The revelation of these hidden sayings of the man-god had the potential to destabilize the official canon and the carefully constructed image of the Chairman himself. And it was not only control over the sacred texts that

---

* Sartre made a fool of himself in his latter days by hawking copies of Maoist newspapers on the streets of Paris, while Shirley MacLaine published a memoir, *You Can Get There from Here*, in which she elaborated on a "life-changing" tour of China she undertook in 1972.

was slipping out of Mao's control; the official party proscription on graven images representing the still living collapsed as Red Guards began raising up monuments to the Chairman. In 1967, students at Qinghua erected a large Mao effigy, an act that led to a monumental arms race as rival factions competed to erect statues of their idol, frequently with elaborate number symbolism encoded in their dimensions.

One by one the "revisionists" had fallen, among them Mao's nemesis Liu Shaoqi, who was placed under house arrest in 1967. Although Liu was not dead yet (the Grim Reaper would not come for him until 1969, following a prolonged period of torture in prison), he was unquestionably a political corpse—and yet the Red Guards continued to rage. Mao knew that the carnage could not continue indefinitely: it was embarrassing when corpses floated to the British territory of Hong Kong, and even more embarrassing when a group of fervent Mao worshipers attacked the British consulate in Beijing. In October 1967, he decided to restore some order, and the nation's youth received instructions to return to class, following a recess dedicated to fomenting revolution that had by this point lasted over a year.* Mao also repeated his call to form "revolutionary committees" to govern the provinces in place of the old (and now devastated) bureaucratic structures. Crack squads of ideological workers were mobilized across the nation, organizing Mao Zedong Thought study classes to ensure that the people were properly instructed in the correct handling of the Chairman's ideas.

Despite these efforts to rein in the chaos, Mao's little brothers and sisters still insisted on maiming and killing each other. Battles between Red Guard factions raged on into 1968. Having been told to fight, they continued to fight, not realizing that it was Mao himself, and not the forces of "black reaction," who now wanted them to stop. So intent was radical youth on continuing its revolt that when the Chairman dispatched Mao Zedong Thought Worker Propaganda Teams from Beijing's factories to the city's campuses in July 1968, the Red Guards responded to these would-be conciliators and ideological educators with violence. At one school, they threw stones and shot at these officially designated exegetes, killing five of them. Enraged, Mao summoned the leaders of the Red Guards for a personal encounter in which he revealed that his was the "black hand" that had dispatched the teams they had attacked. The army

---

* A similar call had gone out earlier in February, but evidently very few Red Guards heeded it.

moved onto campuses to restore order, while millions of Red Guards were sent far away to do agricultural work or to toil in factories as part of the "Up to the Mountains, Down to the Villages" movement. Many were never to return to their home cities, although there were fates worse than permanent exile. Mao's clampdown included a "cleansing of the class ranks," which led to further violence, maimings, persecution and mass death, while in some parts of the countryside the class struggle had evolved to such a point that the politically righteous ate the flesh, liver or even genitalia of their counterrevolutionary nemeses.

Repression and exile alone were not enough to resolve the contradictions unleashed by Mao's top-down youth revolution. When the Great Leap Forward went awry, the party had dialed up the volume on the Mao cult to drown out the cognitive dissonance. Now they resorted to the same tactic, only in an even more extreme form. Not only did the army impose order, but it reasserted its authority over its "spiritual atom bomb." *Quotations of Chairman Mao* was to be retrieved from its state of interpretive chaos, and a single unified understanding was imposed upon the fragmented nation. The People's Liberation Army was to serve as "the great school" for Chinese society and teach the people the true meaning of Mao. For millions, this meant daily, intense, organized study of his word. The goal was not to advance the theoretical consciousness of the people but rather to deepen the degree of their submission to the man-god. In 1968, the party launched the Three Loyalties Campaign:

1. Loyalty to Chairman Mao;
2. Loyalty to Mao's thought; and
3. Loyalty to Mao's proletarian revolutionary line.

And, for good measure, added Four Boundless Loves:

1. Boundless love;
2. Boundless loyalty;
3. Boundless faith; and
4. Boundless adoration for Chairman Mao.

After two years of purported Cultural Revolution, Mao immediately fell back on numbered categories that came straight from the sacred books of old China to reestablish order. And in fact he was about to elevate another old tradition—veneration for the philosopher/sage/emperor and his word—to unprecedented levels of absurdity.

IN 1965, THE great Californian science fiction writer Philip K. Dick published *The Three Stigmata of Palmer Eldritch*. In this novel, a group of colonists who have been drafted to construct a new society on Mars find the environment so harsh and their lives so full of drudgery that they regularly escape into alternative realities. Initially they take the drug Can-D, which enables them to participate in a communal hallucination centered on a Ken and Barbie–style play set. Together, they cruise around in a car, living the ideal life of 1950s consumerism, the kind of thing Khrushchev thought was a suitable goal for the USSR, so long as it was even better than the U.S. version. The problem is, the colonists tend to squabble inside the hallucination as to what course it should take, which ruins the experience. Besides that, the trip is all too brief. So when a mysterious industrialist named Palmer Eldritch returns from a ten-year voyage among the stars with a new, more potent hallucinogen, Chew-Z, they abandon Can-D almost immediately. Users of Eldritch's drug can create their own alternative realities, which they can remold at will, like gods, so transcending the unbearable awfulness of their lives.

Unfortunately for the colonists, Eldritch is more devil than savior. Identifiable by his three "stigmata"—a mechanical arm, stainless-steel teeth and robot eyes—he manifests himself in the hallucinatory worlds created by Chew-Z's users, even imposing himself upon the bodies of those who have taken it. Palmer Eldritch is everywhere, an evil demiurge who has trapped his victims in a reality he controls: "it's all him, the creator," says Barney Mayerson, the novel's protagonist. "That's who and what he is, the owner of these worlds. The rest of us just inhabit them and when he wants to he can inhabit them, too. Can kick over the scenery, manifest himself, push things in any direction he chooses."

Although Dick cranked out *The Three Stigmata of Palmer Eldritch* while high on astronomical quantities of amphetamines (and inspired by a vision of an evil face he had seen in the sky), it is a model of restrained realism compared to the events that actually unfolded in China shortly after *Quotations of Chairman Mao* was published. Without the aid of a cosmic drug discovered in another galaxy, Mao invaded reality to an extent undreamt of by the fictional Palmer Eldritch.

His own stigmata—the receding hairline, the rays of sunshine ema-nating from behind his head, the chubby cheeks, the beatific smile—were ubiquitous throughout China. Mao was in the landscape, beaming down upon the masses from millions of posters affixed to walls, while his body replicated itself in gold on town squares, on university campuses, and on the streets of cities. In button form, billions* of Mao faces were pressed to the bodies of the masses, separated from hearts only by an inch or so of fabric, skin, flesh and bone: some even glowed in the dark. Mao's image was to be found in red plastic hearts, or embroidered on cloth, or carved into billiard balls, or surrounded by polished seashells and fake ostrich feathers. Bigger Maos dangled from the necks of the faithful in large framed portraits, or ejected older gods from their altars in rural homes.

It wasn't just Mao's image that proliferated. So, too, did his word. It was carved into the sides of mountains and etched onto rice grains; it was reproduced on posters and inscribed on monuments. It covered the walls of the "quotation pagodas" and "loyalty halls" erected in his honor. But Mao's divine invasion was not just an assault on the eyes: it was some-thing intimate, and visceral, that seized hold of the tongue and jerked the limbs. Increasingly, when the denizens of Mao's China spoke, it was to utter the words of the Chairman and not their own, as the nation was gripped by a bizarre, revolutionary glossolalia. Via the mouths of millions Mao spoke, repeating himself over and over again, testing the limits of the meanings of his quotations to destruction in a vast, stifling, ideological echo chamber.

The Beijing General Knitting Mill was a "model factory" renowned for its nylon stockings, but during the Red Guard madness it had descended into two camps bitterly divided over questions of textual exegesis. In late 1967, Mao dispatched ideological experts from his Central Bureau of Guards to the Knitting Mill to instruct its two thousand staff members in the correct way to read his works. The results delighted him: not only did workers attain unprecedented levels of unity through the intense study of his word, but they were pioneering new rituals of worship, centered on his image and holy writ. Each day began with the workers gazing upon Mao's portrait and "asking for instructions," as if the Great Helmsman, or his spirit, were present in the room. And thanks to the medium of his

---

* Estimates range from 2.5 billion to 5 billion.

word, Mao was always close at hand. Throughout the day, the workers of the Knitting Mill were able to stay inspired in their tasks by turning to the quotation boards that surrounded them, boosting their "working enthusiasm" by dwelling on the wisdom of Mao. At the end of each shift, the Chairman was also present as workers transmitted inspirational power to their replacements through the utterance of the leader's word. Nor did Mao abandon his children at the end of the working day, for his photograph was still hanging on the wall, listening as they "reported back" on their achievements and struggles. But there were still further rites of communion to be performed, as the workers met in the evenings to discuss their experiences in light of the Chairman's quotations. What lessons could be learned? What wisdom applied next time? Mao intruded upon every waking moment.

Mao scribbled a quick endorsement of the goings-on at the Knitting Mill on the report he received ("very good"), and this became the next bit of paper with ink on it to scramble the senses of the earth's most populous nation. Rebellion was out; reverence was in. And lo, the supercharged logocentrism of the Beijing General Knitting Mill metastasized and spread across the nation. China began to resemble a giant Maoist monastery in which hundreds of millions of novitiates were obliged to participate in the rigorous new rites of the state cult. If Stalinism's religious aspects were obvious beneath the communist dress, Mao's were not even covered by so much as a diaphanous nightgown. There was the ubiquitous holy red book, the collective morning prayer before the icon, regular breaks for readings of scripture throughout the working day, public recitations of the sacred works, the confession of sins, and the blessing of food by pronouncing "Long Live Chairman Mao" or still longer recitations of good wishes for the Great Helmsman. It was not enough to work and pay lip service; the godhead had to be constantly invoked, his word constantly consulted, his majesty constantly praised. This left little time for reflection, but that was the point.

Like a sinister ventriloquist with more than 775 million arms, Mao caused the jaws of the masses to clatter up and down, parroting his words. In schools, students participated in "quote exchanges," batting the Chairman's wisdom at each other as if engaged in a game of ideological Ping-Pong. In shops in Nanjing, staff and customers were united in song and salutes to the Chairman, and also periodically forgot about trade that they might study his works more closely instead. When they finally engaged in the exchange of goods, they did so with apposite quotes from the Chairman: handbooks survive in which guidance is given as to which sayings fit which contexts, right down to the social category of your interlocutor. Perhaps the most remarkable instance of Mao's invasion of language comes from the Chinese literary critic Huang Ziping, who recalls a friend's attempt to inveigle his way into a female comrade's affections exclusively through the use of Mao quotations, resulting in this exceedingly stiff "found poem":

1. Hailing from the five lakes and the four seas, for a common revolutionary aim, we come together.
2. We must share information.
3. We must first have a firm grasp, and secondly be attentive to politics.

Mao's word also seized direct control of bodies via "quotation gymnastics," in which fitness-conscious comrades—the Great Helmsman had stressed the importance of physical training even in his prerevolutionary works, you will recall—acted out a revolutionary story line via a sequence of nine exercises derived from Maoist themes. To a recently arrived alien or foreign visitor, what would have looked like a mildly strenuous sequence of stretches was actually an evocation of Mao's "Three Constantly Read Articles" while there was also a series of exercises based on Mao's famous observation that "Political power grows out of the barrel of a gun." The exercises climaxed with a declaration of intent to read more Mao.

More widespread still were the loyalty dances through which the worshipers attempted to demonstrate "boundless hot love" for the Chairman. Although these had less narrative coherence than the quotation gymnastics, one variant did require twisting the body into the shape of the Chinese character for "loyalty." So it was that Mao Zedong Thought grew ever further removed not only from Marxism but also from thought itself. Instead, it was about ritual, catechisms, and public demonstrations of loyalty: only thus could the people be saved. Of course, where there are believers, there must also be blasphemers, and they were treated with all the ruthlessness of religious inquisitors. Even accidental transgressions against the Word, such as mistaking a bit of paper with Mao's texts on it for toilet paper (easy enough to do amid paper shortages), or uttering a Mao phrase with the wrong intonation, might result in imprisonment or death.

But these were lesser manifestations of Mao's majestic word. Astonishing stories began to appear in the Chinese press that made it clear that uttering the right Mao quotation in the right place at the right time could cause miracles to happen. These miracle stories tended to follow a simple formula: there was a problem; doubters said it could not be overcome; then one of the faithful looked to Mao's written corpus and discovered a quote (or quotes) of great power. In this Mao went one better than Jesus: whereas the Son of God generally had to be physically present to raise the dead or make the blind see, Mao streamlined the process and performed his miracles remotely, without even knowing they were taking place. He outsourced the work to anyone who read his words with sufficient faith.

At first the miracles were relatively minor. A report published by the New China News Agency in August 1966, before the Cultural Revolution went completely berserk, began with a profound question:

> What is the secret behind the rapid progress of the Chinese table tennis team and its winning brilliant victories in international tournaments? The answer, members of the team say, is the great thought of Mao Tse-tung.

It turns out that Mao's essays *On Contradiction* and *On Practice* were the first to have a deep impact on the team's Ping-Pong skills. Seven years earlier, the team had found some crucial strategic insights (not specified) amid the "philosophy." But that was only the beginning. Since then, the Chinese team had developed a deep familiarity with many of Mao's writings, and now they found them so useful that on a recent tour of Japan, Cambodia and Syria they had snatched "every bit of available time" to study them. In fact, exposure to the leader's prose, and not athletic training, was the team's "primary need." After all:

> At a recent discussion, the Chinese players agreed that "armed with Mao Tse-tung's thought, we shall have the greatest unity, the clearest sight, the greatest courage and the highest morale. We shall fear neither monsters and demons in the class struggle, nor strong opponents in playing."

By 1968, however, Mao's word had acquired so much power that it could do much more than win a few games of table tennis. It now cured cancer. One particularly detailed miracle story, that of Chiang Chu-chu, a woman afflicted with a ninety-nine-pound tumor, appeared in the *Peking Review* in

August 1968. When the story begins, Chiang's original doctors, corrupted as they have been by exposure to bourgeois imperialist Western science, have no faith in her survival. It is only when she meets doctors who have read a lot of Mao that she receives hope. These doctors not only abandon their egos but they also leave behind any idea that they should rely on medical expertise to guide their decisions. Instead, they surrender to the Chairman as he manifests his will in assorted quotations. During the initial diagnosis, for instance, Chiang's doctors draw upon this profound thought: "You can't solve a problem? Well, get down and investigate the present facts and its past history."

Grasping the significance of the Chairman's insight, the "investigation group" next takes the remarkable step of asking the hospital where the patient previously received treatment for copies of her records. Until this moment, it seems, nobody had thought of doing this. That's not to say that reading Mao suddenly solves all problems. The battle against cancer remains a dramatic struggle. Fortunately, obstacles can always be overcome through faithfulness to the Chairman and the act of locating an inspirational quote, regardless of the original context. This is particularly helpful when it comes time to remove Chiang's tumor. Now the doctors turn to the Chairman's *military* writings, where they find these words: "Attack dispersed, isolated enemy forces first; attack concentrated, strong enemy forces later." And also: "Encircle the enemy forces completely, strive to wipe them out thoroughly."

Duly inspired, they remove the stupendous tumor from Chiang Chuchu, who recovers from the surgery, thanking not the doctors who saved her but the Great Helmsman himself. "Long live Chairman Mao! Chairman Mao has saved me!" she cries. And on the eighth day following surgery, she rises and walks.

Mao quotes were also revealed to be very effective against inclement weather, rescuing sailors from choppy seas in the fashion of Jesus. Peking Radio informed its listeners on February 23, 1969, that when a terrible storm threatened to send a boatful of prawn fishermen to watery graves, squadron leader Chen Chao drew strength from this quote:

The party organization should be composed of the advanced elements of the proletariat; it should be a vigorous vanguard organization capable of leading the proletariat and the revolutionary masses in the fight against the class enemy.

He and his fellow prawn fishermen then recontextualized the elements as the class enemy and, with additional support from a few lines of Mao's poetry, made it safely to shore.

And so the miracles proliferated in the Chinese press. When two girls were trapped in an icy gully, they overcame frostbite thanks to the words of the Chairman. When eight comrades were thirsty, they recited the word of Mao and "two or three mouthfuls" of water became enough for all of them—and there was still water left over. Mao's word also helped a husband overcome the grief he felt following his wife's death, made reluctant wives fall in line, resurrected the dead, restored sight, and enabled deaf-mutes to sing the communist hymn "The East Is Red."

I could keep going, but let's stop here. Mao, it turned out, had been quite correct about the persistence of old ways of thinking and seeing, only not in the way he imagined. A belief system that began as a linguistically complex pseudoscience had devolved into a faith considerably less sophisticated than that of snake handlers in West Virginia. And at the center of it all was a book that was little and red and that had been written by a man with the blood of millions on his hands.

TYRANNY AND
MUTATION

Small Demons

Lin Biao's description of *Quotations from Chairman Mao* as a "spiritual atom bomb of infinite power" was apposite not only in light of the book's devastating impact upon Chinese culture but also in terms of the position it holds in the history of dictator literature. To extend the metaphor further: if Marx and Engels represent the "big bang" at the dawn of time, and Lenin and his rivals the formation of the stars and planets following that inaugural blast, then the advent of Mao represents a swift acceleration to the age of Einstein and Oppenheimer, when it became possible to harness that textual power to engineer a massively destructive word weapon that could wreak havoc upon all that had been created.

In fact, it was a spiritual atom bomb in another sense: as ephemeral and elusive as the spirit, it exploded but then faded from memory quite quickly. In 1969 it was all looking so final: Lin Biao was officially named Mao's successor, the victory of the Cultural Revolution was declared, and "Mao Zedong Thought" was restored to the constitution after a thirteen-year absence. But Lin Biao turned against his master and "died in a plane crash" while attempting to defect with his family to the USSR in 1971. Then, in 1976, Mao himself became yet another dead thing in a glass box at the heart of a communist country, despite the fact that he and his fellow CCP leaders had signed an anti-embalming pact decades earlier. Now that he was dead, he could be tamed, and his words brought to heel.

And so although dead Mao, like Lenin, enjoyed and continues to enjoy the status of a fetish object, the status of his writings was not so enduring. The fifth volume of his *Selected Works* covering the years 1949 through 1976 was withdrawn as "too revolutionary," with the result that the official canon stopped in 1949, before the Hundred Flowers Campaign, the Great Leap Forward, and the Cultural Revolution. In 1979 the *Little Red Book* was denounced for distorting Mao's thought, withdrawn from the shelves and pulped. Two years later, Mao's successor Deng Xiaoping echoed the party's earlier verdict on Stalin, declaring that Mao was 70 percent correct and 30 percent wrong. The party, in short, went out of its way to pretend the Mao bomb had never gone off, and before too long it was chasing investment and opening up trade, and the country's elite was getting fantastically wealthy.

Meanwhile, for all the destruction that Mao's bomb had wrought upon China, and although it had its adherents in the jungles of Latin America, and in Nepal and India, and among overeducated imbeciles on the campuses of Western universities, many other dictators carried on as if it had never detonated. Some came after Mao, some were his peers. For many, it was enough that in their own realms they were supreme, although even then, some of them were subjugated to more powerful dictators.

In this section we take a look at small demons: dictators who never attained or even desired to attain the global impact of a Hitler or a Mao, but whose regimes and works nevertheless achieved chronic and stultifying longevity and were often virulently awful in their own way.

How did they do it? To quote one of the greatest poets of the twentieth century, who was himself an admirer of the first dictator we shall study in the next section,

Oh, do not ask, "What is it?"
Let us go and make our visit.

2

Catholic Action

"I say, I've just published a really boring
book with the word 'doctrine' in the title."
"Oh, really? Me too."

Although the spectacle of European Union officials lecturing other countries on democracy and human rights is certainly a familiar one, it is worth remembering just how recently arrived democracy and human rights are to so many countries on the old continent. For while it is still not unusual to hear journalists and commentators referring condescendingly to the "new democracies" of Poland, Romania, Hungary et al. more than twenty-five years after they emerged from under the rubble of communism in the 1990s, the truth is that even in many western European countries, liberal democracy is only a generation or two deep. It is approximately seventy years old in Germany and Italy, and while the ancient Athenians may have invented democratic forms of government, their modern descendants were living under a military dictatorship as recently as 1974.

As for the democracies of the Iberian peninsula, they are younger than the Muppets, Johnny Depp and disco. For much of the twentieth century, both countries were ruled by dictators: Dr. António de Oliveira Salazar in Portugal and the extravagantly named Francisco Paulino Hermenegildo Teódulo Franco Bahamonde in Spain. The two men had very different temperaments, but both were authoritarian Catholic nationalists who had at one time or another expressed admiration for Mussolini. They were also united in their complete lack of interest in testing the popularity of their rule by plebiscite, and of course they both produced books. Salazar, the older of the two, was the first to rise to power and the first to send copy to the printing presses. Born in 1889, he was a mere nine days younger than Hitler, and although little remembered outside Portugal today,* his regime not only predated those of both Hitler and Mao, it also outlasted Stalin's and Mussolini's by decades.

Like much of Europe, Portugal in the early twentieth century provided solid conditions for the emergence of a dictator. Long, long ago there had been Vasco da Gama, a sea route from Europe to Asia, and the establishment of many colonies around the globe, ruled from afar by a succession of absolute monarchs ensconced in elaborate chairs in Lisbon. But absolutism gave way to a constitutional monarchy in the nineteenth century and then—following a spot of regicide in 1908—revolution and the foundation of an avowedly secular republic in 1910. The republic's first president, Teófilo Braga, was yet another man of the pen, a poet and collector of Portuguese folklore, stridently anticlerical, carried away by his own cleverness and his ability to create worlds with words. He didn't last. Over the next sixteen years, Portugal had forty-five governments, and the nation endured civil war, insurrection, violence and heavy losses in conflicts fought in its African colonies and on the Western Front. If something cannot continue then it will not, and so it stopped. There was a military coup, and Salazar appeared soon afterward to usher in a new way of doing things.

---

* The first English biography of Salazar was not published until November 2009, a year after the autobiography of Cheeta, the chimpanzee companion of Johnny Weissmuller's Tarzan. Cheeta's book was more widely reviewed, and sold more copies.

What was this new way? Like many intellectuals of his generation, Salazar was underwhelmed by democracy and liberalism, but he was not seduced by the words of Marx or Lenin; he was appalled by Bolshevism. Nor was he some marginalized autodidact from the provinces nor a petit bourgeois poet-cum-revolutionary journalist; rather he was a professor at the University of Coimbra, one of the oldest institutes of higher learning in the world, and he could speak English, French and German. Unlike Lenin, Salazar finished his law degree, and, unlike Stalin, he never repudiated his seminary education. His holy book was still the Bible. Meanwhile, his area of expertise was economics, but he had a decidedly different take on the subject than the author of *Das Kapital*.

Salazar's political career got off to a false start: he was elected to the Portuguese parliament in 1921 but soon returned to his teaching post. However, in 1928, two years after the military coup, he agreed to serve as the finance minister of the military dictatorship before becoming prime minister in 1932.

Salazar proved to be a quick study in the ways of power. The next year, he published a new constitution, declaring the birth of the "New State" that would blend corporatism, Catholicism, nationalism and unremitting hostility to communism. The fusion proved to be enduring: he ruled the country with a firm grip for the next thirty-six years, stopping only when a stroke rendered him incapable of doing so.

Salazar's regime was authoritarian, repressive and undemocratic, yet by the standards of his dictatorial peers it stands out for its singular restraint. Although he kept a signed photograph of Il Duce on his desk, he rejected the Italian dictator's "pagan Caesarism" and criticized the Fascist state for failing to recognize the "limitations of legal or moral order." In fact, Salazar not only outlawed Marxist organizations but clamped down on extreme Fascist ones, too—while in his 1937 book, *How to Raise a State*, he criticized Hitler's Nuremberg Laws, which placed the weight of the German state behind Nazi anti-Semitism. His New State had all the usual trappings of a dictatorship: censorship, torture and even a secret police force identified by a sinister acronym, PIDE. However, while thousands were convicted for political reasons, there were no mass extrajudicial killings of dissidents. Salazar also proved immune to the midcentury expansionist delusions that scrambled the wits of Hitler and Mussolini, and so he kept Portugal out of World War II. He fought wars to defend its imperial territories, but this is hardly a feature unique to dictatorial regimes: in the 1950s and '60s, Britain and France shot and hanged people in Kenya and Algeria in the name of civilization, while the high-minded interventions of Western powers in the early twenty-first century have likewise led to immense carnage.

Salazar, then, was not a poet, or a dreamer, or a fanatic. The allure of the balcony and the adoring throng was alien to him; nor did he believe that by exterminating nations or social classes he might usher in heaven on earth. As a devout believer in a supernatural deity, he could more easily perceive the follies of materialist utopias. What Salazar wanted was order, tradition, religion and . . . things that excite economists. Entering government, he declared that he would end Portugal's deficits and build up a budget surplus to fund development. He succeeded. Yet even though he was a modest sort of dictator, with no interest in imposing a universalizing ideology upon the world, and while he could resist the urge to invade his neighbors, open gulags, return the calendar to year zero and plaster his face on everything, there was one area where even this quietest of dictators could not restrain himself: he wrote.

That said, aside from the fact that they exist at all, Salazar's books otherwise demonstrate his characteristic restraint and caution. *Doctrine and Action* (1939) certainly sounds fascist, like something Mussolini in his pomp might have (ghost)written, but the words *doctrine* and even *action* are derived from Catholic rather than fascist rhetoric. The implications of the title are clear: these are truths to be believed in and acted upon, rather than "theoretical" performances conveying a spurious scientism on socialist or racist phantasmagoria. But Salazar begins his magnum opus with a strikingly hesitant tone, expressing doubt about the value of the book and declaring, "I have hesitated for some time in publishing these speeches, as I felt there were already far too many books in existence for their number to be thoughtlessly increased by people who, having nothing new to say, have on the other hand important duties to perform."

This implied criticism of the vogue for the dictator book is of course belied by the fact that Salazar himself has produced one. Yet the book's understated opening suggests that he might be telling the truth rather than indulging in a typical display of dictatorial false modesty. Rather than declare the historical greatness of the New State or the inherent superiority of Portuguese blood, Salazar quietly commends himself for keeping orderly accounts and disavows violence. He then launches into a discussion of his financial reforms, which are (he assures us) common sense anyway. For example:

> To say that in spite of the crisis which has devastated the world our budget has been balanced during the last eight years, and that these years have been crowned by a substantial credit balance, is to boast of a matter which seems almost ludicrous, since such should always be the case.

Stability is Salazar's primary concern, and while he insists that the New State does have an ideology, the mere fact that he has to stress that one exists at all indicates that its defining characteristics are not immediately obvious in the way that, say, the core beliefs of Nazism are hard to miss. When Salazar does start to outline his ideology, he defines it as admitting the "verity of certain principles." However, this does not mean he is about to write "a treatise on jurisprudence." Rather, these principles "are the outcome of those social and political experiences latent in the conscience of the nation and capable of becoming a reality."

Thus he avoids committing himself to anything too systematic, and what follows are lots of unremarkable musings on the importance of family, traditional gender roles, national unity, spiritual values, religious belief and self-control. The Salazar who emerges from the text attains radicalism via paradox. He is the dictator as antivisionary, standing out among his peers for his explicit rejection of every half-assed utopian theme of the twentieth century.

> [W]e are against all forms of internationalism, communism, socialism, syndicalism, and everything which may minimize or divide or break up the family. We are against class warfare, irreligion, and disloyalty to one's country; against serfdom, a materialistic conception of life, and might over right.

Forget the grand dreams of the political messiahs, says Salazar. Forget the quasi-religion of Fascism or Marxism. This is what Portugal needs: electrification, better schools, a national airline, improved education, good roads, women in the home, bread on the table and families in church. He seems determined to dampen popular enthusiasm and frenzy with his texts. After decades of instability, an economist has taken command to put things in order, and things are as boring as you'd expect. Leave the running of state to him and everything will be not exceptional but, well, okay.

This vision of an unrevolutionary regime persists in Salazar's 1939 opus, *Salazar Prime Minister of Portugal Says*. A collection of quotations predating *Quotations from Chairman Mao* by a quarter century, it is the Portuguese dictator's entry into the competitive field of authoritarian aphorisms and slogans. However, unlike the *Little Red Book*, it contains no vacuities dressed up in jargon or pretentious theorizing. Even at its most radical, it reads at best like Mussolini lite, and if Salazar is going to be banal he will do so in straightforward language. Thus he mixes pabulum:

We live our life on earth and it is our duty to give it a meaning and a value.

. . . with metaphysical subfascist waffle derived from Catholicism:

Truth, like authority, partakes of the nature of the absolute.

. . . with vaguely Nietzschean aphorisms:

There are no insoluble problems for a nation which knows how to will.

Salazar is repeatedly critical of the creation of new moralities, of revolutionary fantasies. Instead, he stresses the importance of restraints even on the powerful:

The state must be strong, but it must be limited by the demands of morality, by the principles of men's rights, by individual guarantees, which are the first and foremost condition of social solidarity.

Salazar's works, then, represent a modest entry in the dictator canon, and are interesting primarily for how hard the author strives *not* to generate excitement. He maintained his dedication to not frightening the horses for decades. For as long as he was in power, books and pamphlets kept appearing with his name on them, from *At the Crossroads* in 1946 to *Portugal and the Anti-colonial Campaign* in 1961 to *The Decision to Stay; the Prime Minister's Reply to the Tribute Paid to Him by the Province of Angola on 13 April 1966*. He also dabbled in poetry, composing religious and patriotic odes to inspire the people. Strikingly, Salazar never left Portugal, and yet he sent his texts into the world to act as emissaries for his thought, translating them into English and distributing them overseas. In 1968, a stroke brought his long career as both dictator and author to a halt. He died two years later.

None of Salazar's books are read today. But they still exist, on slowly disintegrating paper: mementos of the dictator who wrote without having anything particularly interesting to say, yet never attained the transcendent levels of superboredom attained by leftist dictators. If not quite a victory, this at least represents a peculiar strain of mercy.

MERCY, HOWEVER, IS not a quality usually associated with Spain's Nationalist general Franco, who, by the time Salazar was writing about his success at balancing the budget in next-door Portugal, had already embarked on a twentieth-century-style total war against leftist Republican forces. The events that led to this career military man assuming the role of "El Caudillo" were not dissimilar to those that had led Salazar to power—up to a point. Spain, like Portugal, was an ex-Catholic monarchy, formerly absolute, once possessed of a globe-spanning empire but that had entered a prolonged twilight, complete with political and economic instability, anticlericalism and, in 1931, the declaration of a republic some two decades after Portugal did the same.

Whereas in Portugal it took about fifteen years for the military to stage a coup against the Republican government, in Spain it took five years and ended in failure. What followed was a vicious civil war that divided the nation against itself, along lines of left and right, nationalist and socialist, fascist and communist, city and country, worker and bourgeois, Catholic and atheist. Franco emerged as the leader of the Nationalist forces, backed by Mussolini, Hitler and Spain's own homegrown fascist party, the Falange. The leaders of the leftist Popular Front had a tyrant of their own in their corner: Stalin. The Vozhd dispatched NKVD veteran Alexander Orlov to advise the Republican government, and also instructed the Comintern to organize International Brigades, which supplied the Spanish government with fifty thousand armed antifascist volunteers dedicated to defeating Franco. In terms of aesthetics, the Republicans were victorious: George Orwell and Ernest Hemingway both fought as volunteers and wrote *Homage to Catalonia* and *For Whom the*

Bell Tolls on the basis of their experiences, while Picasso painted his masterpiece *Guernica*. However, aside from the production of some artistic classics, the war was otherwise a complete defeat for the left. After nearly three years of fighting, Franco declared victory on April 1, 1939. And he promptly executed some twenty thousand Republicans.

Unlike Salazar, Mussolini or Hitler, Franco had risen to power not through a coup or by gaming a parliamentary system, but via an act of conquest in a civil war. And since (unlike Salazar) he was also the head of a party founded by enthusiasts for Italian Fascism, it seems reasonable to assume he might then have gotten carried away and embarked on imperialist wars, or at the very least have spat out some pretentious, quasi-philosophical prose extolling the joys of violence, the ineffable sublimity of the Spanish soul, and the superiority of Latin blood. But when Hitler invaded Poland five months after the end of the Spanish Civil War, Franco declined to commit the forces of his exhausted, war-weary, famine-stricken country to the assistance of the Third Reich. For while Der Führer certainly anticipated payback for his contribution to El Caudillo's victory over Republican forces, Franco had other ideas. He would concentrate his efforts on consolidating his regime, rebuilding the country, and—why not?—writing a book while he was at it. He was a dictator now, and that probably meant he should write something.

Franco wrote *Raza* at the end of 1940 and the start of 1941, and published it a year later under the pseudonym Jaime de Andrade, a noble surname found in his own genealogy. *Raza* is an unusual work for a dictator in several ways, but perhaps most notably in that it is explicitly a work of fiction rather than an assemblage of lies passed off as truth, in the fashion of Franco's peers. Indeed, until the appearance of *Raza* in bookstores in 1942, Mussolini was the only dictator who had worked in the form, and even then *The Cardinal's Mistress* dated to his days as a radical journalist on the make. Franco produced his novel while he was already running a country. When asked how it was possible, he replied, "Time management." This attentiveness to time may have led to another unusual aspect of the book: its form. *Raza* is a novel-screenplay hybrid, heavy on talk and short on descriptive passages. It is much easier to write piles of dialogue than long sections of expository prose that require a lot of revision—the perfect form for a busy dictator, then.

The novel is also pretty minimal when it comes to pseudoscientific expatiations on quack twentieth-century ideology. While the title, meaning

"Race," may sound ominous and is precisely what you'd expect from a Hitler-allied military dictator leading a party whose full name was the Spanish Phalanx, Franco, if not quite as aggressively dull as Salazar, is decidedly restrained once his dedication to the youth of Spain, "whose blood opened the way to our resurgence," is out the way. Rather than leap into crazed ramblings that blend Spain's pre-Christian past with nineteenth-century racial theories, he ambles into a schematic melodrama about a noble Spanish family divided against itself during the civil war.

The plot is simple and not wholly incompetent. The family is based on Franco's own, albeit idealized and upgraded to a higher social strata, a choice that expresses the same status anxiety evinced by the dictator's reaching into his family's past for an illustrious pseudonym. One brother, José (an analogue for Franco himself), fights for the Nationalists, while another brother, Pedro (an analogue for Franco's real-life brother Ramón), joins the Republican side. Pedro is torturing a bird when he is introduced to the reader and this is but a sign of things to come. The Republicans are very bad and do very bad things. They are even cruel to nuns. The Nationalists on the other hand are very noble and do noble things. They do not hurt nuns. They have a strong sense of duty, they fight for God and family and country, and they embrace martyrdom if the cause demands it. That said, bad brother Pedro is not entirely evil. By the end of the novel, he has repented of his Republican ways and crossed over to the National-ist side, which suggests that forgiveness and reconciliation can exist in the new world. That said, Pedro dies, which suggests that it comes at a high cost. A whiff of fascism does enter the novel in its closing scene at the Vic-tory Parade of 1939. This, the reader is told, represents the "Spirit of the Race." However, arriving as late in the book as it does, it is more of a slightly malodorous puff than a full-blown flatus. More striking is Franco's sudden digression into postmodernist metatextual play, as his analogue, José, pledges allegiance to "our Caudillo." Thus Franco appears both as ego and alter ego in his own book, an innovation decades ahead of its time.* That it was probably entirely accidental rather than the result of

---

* Autobiographical doubling is still uncommon in fiction, and it took the literary world several decades to catch up with Franco. The science fiction authors Kurt Vonnegut and Philip K. Dick staged interactions between themselves and differently named fictional ana-logues in *Breakfast of Champions* (1973) and *Valis* (1981), respectively, while the technique entered the literary mainstream with Philip Roth's *Operation Shylock: A Confession* (1993), in which "Philip Roth" interacts with another "Philip Roth."

a ludic approach to literary creation is insignificant: after all, the discovery of penicillin was also unplanned, was it not?

This incandescent moment of the avant-garde aside, *Raza* is otherwise a deeply conservative work. If Franco's novel shares anything at all with a radical text such as *Mein Kampf*, it is only the fact that its author dictated it to a typist while pacing back and forth in a room. There is none of Hitler's *nostalgie de la boue*, none of his spite or resentment, none of his racial theorizing. Nor, for instance, does Franco indulge in Mussolini-style body horror, despite the fact that *Raza*'s civil war setting provided him with ample opportunity to do so. Instead, he pushes a conservative Catholic-nationalist agenda that has much in common with Salazar's restrained approach and little in common with the utopianism of the left or right. In some ways Franco is even more restrained than Salazar, who, for all his reserve and caution, nevertheless shared with his dictatorial peers the view that long-form narratives were best reserved for tedious ideological expatiations demonstrating the leader's wisdom and suitability to rule. Franco instead tells what is effectively a very long bedtime story that neatly resolves all the tensions and conflicts of the civil war, without asking the reader to think too hard (or at all). The wicked are vanquished and the good are victorious, and in the end Church and nation are restored. Franco wants to connect with and inspire the masses, not awe them into submission; his monopoly upon violence took care of that.

Raza was swiftly adapted into a film so that even people who couldn't read (around 23 percent of Spain's population) could benefit from its message. Alfredo Mayo, a tall, handsome actor with a line in noble military types, played the part of José/Franco. And while it is hard to trust movie reviews published in a 1940s dictatorship, one viewer in particular was profoundly impressed when the film was released in 1942: Franco was so overcome with emotion when he saw his imaginary world realized on the big screen that he watched the film with tears streaming down his otherwise manly cheeks. He subsequently watched *Raza: The Movie* many times over, and it was even modified to keep pace with the changing times. In 1950 it was rereleased minus all the fascist salutes and references to the Falange.

Unlike those other dictators who viewed their works as tools for the promotion of their regimes abroad, Franco did not translate *Raza* into English; nor did he distribute it in the United States or the United Kingdom through a state agency. This was probably an error, as El Caudillo missed an opportunity to demonstrate to his foreign critics that he was a dull, unimaginative military type and not a demented fascist ideologue. In the postwar years, Franco was widely reviled as Europe's "last surviving fascist dictator," and while Stalin's ultrarepressive USSR was welcome at the top table at the founding congress of the United Nations in December 1946, Franco's less despotic Spain was shunned. UN member states were encouraged to withdraw their ambassadors from Spain, while the General Assembly asked the Security Council to consider "measures" if Spain did not transition to an elected government. Undaunted, Franco had himself appointed head of state for life in July 1947.

In his collection *Essays on Political Doctrine: Words and Writings 1945–1950*, Franco advances a primarily Catholic, reactionary, nationalist, authoritarian agenda. Cobbled together out of speeches, articles and even letters to newspapers, this book is certainly an imposing volume—in the sense that it is physically very large, very heavy and unwieldy—but in terms of content it is relatively light, less philosophical and gnomic than Salazar's works and much less strewn with jargon than communist texts. Its twelve chapters cover such themes as "Politics of Spain," "International Politics," "Religious Politics," "Military Politics," and "Politics of the Spirit." Franco casts his regime as the force defending Spain from the vicissitudes of a chaotic and godless postwar world, seeking to build the future. Stability will emerge from continuity, from the Church, the monarchy, the historic greatness of Spain. As with Salazar's works, this is doctrine, not theory: these are things to believe, not to reason your way toward.

That said, Franco was not entirely dedicated to a policy of respectable boredom. Had World War II ended with a victory for Hitler, it is easy to imagine an alternative reality where Franco's writings would have become more and not less racist, and in which the vague mumblings about blood in *Raza* would have reached epic proportions. It is not even necessary to do much imagining. For Franco knew the fiery passion of hatred, only his spite and paranoia were focused on a different hidden hand of history: he really, *really* hated Freemasons.

In *Raza* this hatred is muted. Although Franco writes that the Republicans received arms from this sinister global network, he holds back from delivering a full-scale paranoid denunciation. In 1952, however, he published a compilation of newspaper articles titled *Masonry* in which (writing as "Jakim Boor") he assails Masons relentlessly. At last, one of the Iberian dictators had produced a genuinely extreme text, a true and pure eruption of hatred, fear and magical thinking. In this lunatic opus, a frothing-at-the-mouth Franco reveals that worldwide Freemasonry lies at the root of many of Spain's problems, including the country's exclusion from the United Nations. According to Franco, Masonry is a "cancer corroding our society," and its members are "murderers and thieves." Chapter titles such as "Masonry and Communism," "The Grand Secret," and "The Great Hatred" effectively convey a strong sense of the conspiratorial mentality on display within, while alongside vitriolic attacks on liberals, democrats, communists and the United Nations, Franco also reveals that Eleanor Roosevelt is "an extremely well-known mason" and party to the plot to destroy Spain, which (needless to say) stretches back centuries and also involves the British Empire. Here at last is that Hitlerian awe and terror before the diabolical Jew, that Marxist-Leninist hatred for the many-tentacled bourgeoisie, the irrational rage of the monomaniac, worthy of a grubby mimeographed pamphlet passed around in beer halls a century ago, or metastasizing on the Internet today. Finally, Franco had used the pen to reveal the truth, if not about the world, then about himself. He had torn off the mask and exposed his inner loon.

And yet . . . not quite. There was still an awareness there, which was lacking in his Fascist, Nazi and Marxist-Leninist peers. Franco, after all, did not sign his own name to this assemblage of ravings. Even in the darkest, sweatiest, most febrile part of his brain, he knew that this was not the type of thing you wanted associated with the grand title of "El Caudillo," especially not if you hoped to be welcomed into the club of "civilized nations" ever again. Franco never forgot that the paranoid crackpot within should not be allowed to overwhelm the repressive authoritarian without, an act of self-control that was impossible for his former allies Hitler and Mussolini.

This self-awareness bore fruit, and Franco maintained a steady drift toward "respectability" into the 1950s. In fact, by the time he published *Masonry*, Spain had been a UN member state for two years and would join NATO within three, as those who had once denounced Franco as a brutal dictator now fêted him as an ally in the fight against communism. No longer a pariah even as he refused to countenance running for election, he would for the rest of his long rule periodically release volumes of his speeches and thoughts, such as *Words of the Caudillo* in four volumes and *Speeches and Messages of the Head of State* in five volumes, while even managing to issue the two-volume *Political Thought of Franco* in 1975, the year he finally shuffled off this mortal coil. Long gone were the stirring if clunky melodramatics of *Raza*; now Franco filled pages with tedious speeches. Even brief telegrams were preserved for posterity, whether it be one sent to congratulate Lyndon B. Johnson on a successful space launch, or another fired off to express condolences over the death of a cardinal in Toledo.

As with *Raza*, Franco never bothered to have any of it translated into English, and he seemingly never attracted the attention of a commercial publisher looking to make a quick buck from controversy, as happened with Mussolini, Hitler, Stalin, Mao, Ho Chi Minh, Muammar Gaddafi and Saddam Hussein. Or perhaps he did, but rejected these approaches. Was this modesty on the part of the general? It seems unlikely; he was El Caudillo, after all. But it may be a sign of robust self-confidence. Franco's publishing strategy exposes him as one of the most self-assured dictator-authors ever, a true nationalist, content to bore his local readership exclusively, while leaving the rest of the world alone.

3

Disembraining Machines

In the mid-1920s the USSR stood almost alone in the world, and the failure of every single attempt at exporting revolution to Europe had made it abundantly clear that intellectuals intoxicated by the words of Marx made for exceedingly poor heralds of the dictatorship of the proletariat. In the aftermath of 1917, revolutionaries in Berlin, Bavaria, Budapest and beyond had attempted to establish workers' states in their homelands. Yet each time one of these bespectacled readers of the German prophet lifted his (or occasionally her) nose out of a book to stoke the fires of a popular uprising, he invariably wound up dead, in prison, or on the run, sometimes as a result of the proletariat itself violently rejecting the leadership of the self-proclaimed revolutionary vanguard. Like many people who spend rather too much time reading, writing and cogitating, these Marxist intellectuals mistook their ability to shape words and ideas into forms that they found pleasing on the page for an ability to impose the same coherence upon the chaotic, physical world. While the word provided inspiration, it was not in itself enough to hasten the advent of the new era unless supported by tanks, cannon and airplanes. Thus Lenin and Trotsky, for all their fluency in theoretical matters, perhaps owed more of their success to their willingness to inflict extreme violence on their foes than to their grip on Marx's labor theory of value.

Violence, too, was essential to the emergence and survival of the regime in Mongolia, which for almost three decades was the only country in the world besides the USSR with a communist government. A landlocked moonscape with a population of around 647,000 monks and nomads ruled over by a (hard-drinking) living Buddha, Mongolia lacked both industry and a proletariat, and was about as likely a location for a Marxist revolution as the ocean floor. Yet following the disastrous pattern of failure in the advanced capitalist countries of Europe, Lenin would take what he could get. If history would not obey the prescripts of the books, then the books would be reinterpreted—again. Projecting his revolutionary fantasies eastward, Lenin revealed as early as 1920 that it was now possible for "backward countries" to proceed to communism while "bypassing the capitalist stage of development." However, this could happen only so long as these countries were assisted by the proletariat of "more advanced countries."

Lenin had long been willing to reinterpret Marx, but this was a new level of mutation, a radical unmooring of theory in service of political desire. This new text—because of course nothing could be done without a theoretical justification—established the ideological grounds for spreading whatever "communism" was becoming to wherever it would take. When the Russian Civil War spilled over the borders of Mongolia in 1921, Lenin accepted the "revolution" that followed on the heels of victory over tsarist forces there. Soviet agents had long been active behind Mongolian borders, and the USSR was ready to "assist" the new government. This assistance proved to be rather substantial: the ruling Mongolian People's Revolutionary Party even received its name from Soviet experts and formally joined the Moscow-led Communist International in 1924.

Although Mongolia was granted permission by Lenin to skip a key developmental stage, communism was relatively slow to arrive. To smooth the transition to the new era, the living Buddha was left on his throne as a figurehead until his death in 1925, and the golden age of the workers' paradise did not really get under way until a Moscow-trained communist named Khorloogiin Choibalsan consolidated power in the early 1930s. Choibalsan, like Stalin, was the son of an impoverished single mother, and again like Stalin he had attained literacy by means of a religious education before discovering the doctrines of Marx and Lenin (in his case, at a school for Russian-Mongolian interpreters in Irkutsk, Siberia). Inspired by these pamphlets, Choibalsan began a career in communism that culminated in his being appointed regional manager for the USSR's first Stalinist franchise. Yet reliant as he was upon the master in the Kremlin for his preeminent position, he was not so much an autonomous tyrant as a Stalinoid homunculus, an artificial creature bedecked with medals and titles, able to operate only within the parameters set for him by his creator.

Aggressive literacy campaigns were launched, and thousands of copies of Stalin's *Short Course* were imported to provide the party leadership with the correct understanding of Mongolia's ideological parent. These literacy campaigns were aimed not only at the masses: in 1934, 55 percent of the party was illiterate, and thus unable to read the "truths" upon which their authority was purportedly based. Meanwhile, the lived experience of purges, five-year plans, collectivization and industrialization provided party leaders and their subjects with an intimate understanding of the details concealed by official propaganda. Stalin's cult of personality was imported wholesale, but also localized and used as a template for Choibalsan's subsidiary cult. The Mongolian leader added a flair for archery to his Stalinesque revolutionary virtue and godlike genius, in much the same way a McDonald's in Istanbul might add a "McTurco" kebab to the franchise's otherwise Western menu. Soviet literary forms were imported wholesale, and the communist word became central and sacred in Mongolia.

Choibalsan himself was keen to stress the superiority of Stalin's cult and, specifically, Stalin's texts. In comments reported in *Unen*, the party newspaper, on December 11, 1947, he declared that "the most important event in the ideological life of the party" during the preceding decade was "the appearance in translation and the publication of the books of Comrade Stalin *Questions of Leninism* and the first volume of the collected works of Comrade Stalin and his other works."

But Choibalsan was also obliged by socialist tradition to perform public acts of "theory" on paper and felt pressure to create his own work. As a homunculus, however, he was in a tricky position. Stalin was the pope of communism and had closed the gates of interpretation. Nothing new or substantial could be said about Marx or Lenin for as long as the Vozhd was in power. How, then, was Choibalsan to write as a great genius while never saying anything of substance?

Fortunately for the Mongolian dictator there were precedents. As early as 1926 a disillusioned ex-Comintern executive, Boris Souvarine, had observed the hollowness and flexibility of Soviet language.

> Not one fact, not one quotation, not one idea, not one argument: only impudent affirmations with a half-dozen interchangeable words come from the "heights" (for even that is decided in the higher reaches) . . . Take the phrase "for the Bolshevik unity of the Leninist Party"; if you invert the order of the adjectives you get "for the Leninist unity of the Bolshevik Party," if you invert the order of the nouns, you get "for the Bolshevik Party and Leninist unity," and so on. Isn't that marvelous?

Stalin himself had provided a practical demonstration on how to escape the theoretical cul-de-sac. He, too, had lacked a substantial theoretical bibliography when he came to power, but the editors of his *Collected Works* expanded their master's meager output by treating almost every utterance of the man-god as holy writ, just as the companions of Muhammad had collected the sayings and doings of the prophet, greatly expanding what would otherwise have been a very brief set of scriptures (the Quran is only four-fifths the length of the New Testament). Even as fundamental a work as *The Foundations of Leninism* had originated as a series of spoken lectures, but it was as a book that it had its greatest impact. In fact, the flat, artless nature of Stalin's speeches proved to be an asset once they were printed and bound and presented as texts. A Stalin speech was not an exercise in demagoguery intended to inflame passions à la Hitler or Mussolini; it was instead a series of instructions, or perhaps a dry report containing statistics easier to ingest on paper than as vocalizations vanishing in the air. The speeches were boring, they did not attempt to engage; this gave them the appearance of weight.

Following the example set by his master, Choibalsan managed to fill four volumes of *Reports and Speeches* with words he had delivered at party congresses. A "greatest hits" was subsequently published in Moscow; a glance at a few of the titles on the table of contents gives a sense of the excitement contained within:

Letter to Mongolian Youth About the Soviet Lands 7 November 1923
The Eleventh Anniversary of the Death of Lenin and National Indepen-
dence of Mongolia
The Great Celebration of the Revelation and the Politics of the New
Course
Speech at a meeting of workers in the city of Ulan Bator 23 June 1941

The speeches themselves contain mechanical death language such as
this:

We shall unite ourselves and devote our lives and property to the work of
uniting the minds of the people and officials of the Mongolian Banners
and the Shav* to guard the lives of the Mongols and the territory of
Mongolia. After establishing the Mongol People's Party, we shall declare
the aim of the Party to the Mongol People. The aim is more rights and
privileges for the common people. After eliminating the sufferings of the
people, they should be allowed to live in peace, and like any other nation
the Mongol people should develop their strength and talents. Then they
would be able to happily live an enlightened and just life.

It wasn't all stifling propaganda, however. Choibalsan also mastered
Stalinist virulence. His speeches from the late 1930s contain many denunciations of comrades from the dawn of the Mongolian Revolution, similar
to the attacks the Vozhd and his lapdogs launched against Trotsky and
other erstwhile leading Bolsheviks in the *Short Course* and innumerable
public utterances besides. In a speech on the eighteenth anniversary of the
Mongolian Revolution, Choibalsan vituperates against comrades he has
known for twenty years:

Damba, Naidan and Dovchin, remnants of the Gendung-Demid organization, and likewise other insidious enemies have meanwhile been
exposed. And since then, Amor who went under the name of premier of
this country, and who in his whole person was a feudal noble, imbued
with the reactionary doctrines of the old feudality, the Buddhists and the
Manchus, has, together with other devils, been arrested. Even now we are
utterly rooting out the enemies who have tried to obstruct the people's

---

* Members of the "commoner" class.

freedom and the warm friendship of the USSR and Mongolia (*Thunderous applause: shouts of "Hurrah"*).

Following another Stalinist precedent, Choibalsan generated works of history, including a biography of the Mongolian war hero Khatan Bator Maksarjab (who had fought against the Chinese before turning his attention to the tsarist armies) and a history of the Mongolian People's Revolution, in which he was always careful to pay homage to his mighty neighbor.

FOR THE FIRST three decades of the USSR's existence, Mongolia was Moscow's sole satellite, and Choibalsan's solitary homunculization the only observable instance of the phenomenon by which a local strongman subservient to Stalin disappeared behind a largely fictional persona closely modeled on that of the Vozhd. Following World War II, however, a cluster of new satellites appeared on the USSR's western border as the tanks and guns of the Red Army brought socialism to Europe. In East Germany, Hungary, Romania, Albania, Yugoslavia, Czechoslovakia and Bulgaria, Stalinist homunculi assumed power, while the Baltic states of Latvia, Lithuania and Estonia were absorbed wholesale into the USSR. Only in Czechoslovakia did the communists win a mandate to govern through an election, while only in Yugoslavia did local forces rather than the Red Army liberate their own country. However, even in these instances, the local party leaders, Klement Gottwald and Josip Broz Tito, respectively, were long-term recipients of Stalin's patronage who had spent years living in Moscow.* Nor was the Communist Party of Czechoslovakia's dedication to elections anything more than opportunistic: faced with the prospect of losing the popular vote in 1948, the party staged a coup to guarantee that the working masses could continue to enjoy the benefits of socialism—even if they preferred not to.

None of these new states had appeared as a result of a proletarian revolution. Once again, actual historical events did not fit the "scientific laws" inscribed in the sacred texts. But that Rubicon had long since been

---

* So closely bound together were the future dictator-authors of Europe that most of them had at one time or another lived under the same roof, at the Hotel Lux on Gorky Street, fifteen minutes' walk from the Kremlin. Ho Chi Minh, the future communist leader of Vietnam, was also a resident.

crossed, and the theoreticians in Moscow were by now adept at reinter-preting inconvenient aspects of doctrine. After all, if socialism was possi-ble in one country (as Stalin had said), and Mongolia could bypass the capitalist stage entirely (as Lenin had implied), then surely the creed could easily be modified to accommodate the existence of the USSR's European satellites? And so it was revealed that in relatively "advanced" European countries, neither revolution nor the dictatorship of the proletariat was absolutely necessary. Countries could advance toward socialism in "People's Democracies," where communists might even collaborate with non-Marxists in local parliaments. Perhaps, even, it was possible for these satellites to find their own roads to socialism: the Soviet model was not the only path!

But as the Cold War intensified, Stalin changed his mind. It turned out that the new way forward looked a lot like the old way forward, and it involved five-year plans, purges, collectivization, secret police, socialist realism, statues of Lenin, statues of Stalin, and the celebration of Stalin's birthday on December 21 each year.* Like Choibalsan in Mongolia, the local franchise holders now disappeared behind localized variants of Stalin's personality cult. Hungary's Mátyás Rákosi smiled as he fondled a stalk of wheat in propaganda photographs; Polish leader Bolesław Bierut, a charisma-free life support system for a bureaucrat's mustache, basked in the glory of the poems composed in honor of his birthday; and Lenin-style mummification was de rigueur (mortis) for homunculi who died during the period of high Stalinism, such as Bulgaria's Georgi Dimitrov and Czechoslovakia's Klement Gottwald.

And of course there were the texts, so many texts. In addition to masterpieces such as the *Short Course* and *The Foundations of Lenin-ism*, turgid Soviet socialist-realist novels rolled off the presses. But the inhabitants of the new Soviet satellites were subject to a special, addi-tional suffering. Living in countries with much higher rates of literacy than Mongolia, they had to actually *read* the millions of additional otiose words generated in their own homelands, such as the following hymn to the Czechoslovakian Communist Party by Vítěslav Nezval, a

---

* The balance of power is neatly illustrated by the fact that although every Communist Party leader in Eastern Europe had a direct telephone link with the Kremlin, none of them could call Stalin without submitting a formal request first. The Vozhd, on the other hand, could call up the homunculus of his choosing whenever he damn well pleased.

gifted Surrealist poet whose talent withered up and died the instant he started shilling for the new era:

> Salute our most beloved party,
> Long live Stalin, our shining ideal . . .
> Long live Klement Gottwald our leader,
> In that is your strength, in that is your celebrity!

As for the homunculi, they found themselves in the same tricky position as Choibalsan: how to write as a great genius while never, ever saying anything meaningful? They had to produce text, but they could not innovate. Unlike Mao, they owed their elevation entirely to Stalin. They were dependent upon Stalin; they were subjugated to Stalin. None would dare insist on the importance of the peasantry, or aggressively talk about local conditions as Mao had—and he, too, had been subject to limitations on how far he could go.

Instead, they followed the model pioneered by Choibalsan during his lonely years as commander of the Soviet Union's first satellite: compiling speeches, reports, denunciations of imperialists and updates on the staggering progress toward socialism in multivolume editions that adhered strictly to Stalin's line. And lo, communist prose billowed forth like a toxic word smog across the world, as the foreign language departments of the state publishing houses in Hungary, Romania, Poland, East Germany, Czechoslovakia and Bulgaria made certain that the wise words of their leaders were available in English, German, Spanish and many other tongues besides.

What unreadable dross it all was! Like so many academic papers in the arts and humanities, only perhaps even more so, these texts are almost entirely unread today. And no wonder: suffering through but a few fragments reveals an epic conformity and interchangeability that is truly remarkable given the diverse ethnic and cultural backgrounds of the authors.

The Hungarian Jew Rákosi praised Stalin:

> . . . the great majority of party members are not familiar with Stalin's latest elaboration of Marxist-Leninism. He has truly enriched it day by day over the last twenty-five years: consequently our action program should not be pure Marxism or Leninism but Marxism-Leninism in its Stalinist form.

As did the Pole Bolesław Bierut:

In building socialism in Poland we stand together with the great legion of builders of socialism and fighters for socialism which grows today in all the countries of the world. Our leader and guide is Stalin, and thus our idea and our ranks are invincible.

Faithful to the ideas of Marx, Engels, Lenin and Stalin, we shall spare no effort for the fulfilment of the Six-Year Plan, our contribution to the cause of the defence of peace and the full victory of socialism!

As did the Bulgarian Georgi Dimitrov:

Strong in the gigantic scope of its socialist construction, in the high fighting capacity of its Red Army, in its moral and political unity, the Soviet people—rallied around the Communist Party, the Soviet Government and Comrade Stalin, leader of the working people—is a powerful support for the workers of the whole world.

By subtracting a handful of phrases, a speech delivered by a leader in one country can easily be turned into a template for another to be delivered by a different leader in another socialist utopia. Consider this passage from a 1949 speech delivered by the German leader Walter Ulbricht. By removing three words, *Bitterfeld*, *Germany*, and *two*, the text is rendered fit for purpose in almost any of the USSR's satellite states, or in the USSR itself.

The plan of reconstruction confronts the technical intelligentsia with a great and honourable task. After the introduction of the____year plan, I spoke at a meeting in_____ to chemists, engineers and technicians. I must say that the ____year plan met with the approval of the majority of those present. This was no coincidence. The____year plan offers longer term opportunities to the technical intelligentsia. They have a goal before them as specialists. Hitherto they had rebuilt factories, often with great effort and literally out of ruins. Now that considerable sums have been allocate to investments within the framework of the plan, these sums will have to be rationally used; the quality of production will have to be improved by means of technical innovations, and output must be increased with the aid of a better organization of work and an improvement of the means of production.

Having spent years submitting themselves to Stalin's changing whims, the dictators of Eastern Europe had acquired a formidable capacity to live with cognitive dissonance, in the process developing a style of writing and speech that was malleable, solipsistic, opaque, sentimental, empty, interchangeable and riddled with jargon. If the language revealed anything, it was their state of mental slavery. In his influential 1971 essay "The Anxiety of Influence" literary critic Harold Bloom described "Influenza," an "astral disease" afflicting poets, who, since they are inspired by other poets, are perpetually at risk of producing derivative verse. If poets are to achieve originality and produce work that survives into posterity, Bloom argues that they must intentionally misread the work of their precursors. Perhaps the most striking aspect of the works of the homunculi is their desperate fight to achieve the opposite: for them, influence was something to be explicitly stated, lest Stalin suspect them of disloyalty. Their anxiety was to *demonstrate* that influence, and to be constantly seen and heard and read demonstrating it. Hardly authors of their own destinies (and most likely not of their own works, either), they were subject to a terrible gravity from which they could never escape. As the Polish communist leader Władysław Gomułka later put it, their glory "could be called only a reflected brilliance, a borrowed light. It shone as the moon does."

4

Eastern Approaches

"Freedom of expression is the right of every natural person, even if a person chooses to behave irrationally, to express his or her insanity."

As the twentieth century advanced and globe-spanning empires of old crumbled, collapsed or simply abolished themselves, new states emerged in Asia and Africa, creating fresh possibilities for the formation of identities and ideologies. Rather than submit blindly to the rigid dogmas of the era's totalitarianisms, the frequently Western-educated elites of these newly independent lands experimented with a panoply of -isms, resulting in the emergence of their own hybrid ideologies. One idea from the former colonial powers that they did not reject was that super-wise leaders should demonstrate their wisdom by writing books.

So it was that in Haiti, François "Papa Doc" Duvalier, a physician turned black nationalist, took a break from murdering his opponents to wag an anti-imperialist finger at the United States in *A Tribute to the Martyred Leader of Non-violence Reverend Dr. Martin Luther King Jr.* (1968). In Zaire, the newspaper editor turned mega thief Mobutu Sese Seko* squeezed ten years' worth of inspirational speeches into two volumes in 1975, while also publishing a collection of interviews in France entitled (with breathtaking cynicism) *Dignity for Africa*. Over in Uganda, Idi Amin issued several books. *The First 366 Days*, it must be said, was rather light on words, consisting as it did mostly of photographs of the leader himself. *The Middle East Crisis: His Excellency the President Al-Hajji General Idi Amin Dada's Contribution to the Solution of the Middle East Crisis During the Third Year of the Second Republic of Uganda* (1974) was a more substantial effort, although Amin's enthusiasm for Hitler's Final Solution undoubtedly lost him some credibility as a peacemaker in some quarters. Perhaps his greatest contribution to dictator literature, however, was *Telegrams by and to President Amin* (1975), which pretty much does what it says on the tin. Meanwhile, in Zimbabwe, the Jesuit-educated African nationalist Robert Gabriel Mugabe took a break from declaring that he would build socialism while not actually building it to issue such classics as *Prime Minister Addresses State Banquet in North Korea, October 6 1980* (1980); *Our War of Liberation* (1983); *The Construction of Socialism in Africa* (1984); and *War, Peace and Development in Contemporary Africa* (1987). The last publication, although in hardcover, is a mere twenty-five pages, if you exclude the introduction—which is not Mugabe's work.

And yet as much as these books (and others) certainly came into existence, occupied physical space on shelves, gathered dust, and were subject to raids by silverfish and the effects of oxidation, it would be an exaggeration to state that they contained any serious or systematic attempts at building ideologies. They were even more ephemeral than the books of the homunculi, although like those works they sought to appropriate the cultural authority of "the book" to give their regimes a patina

---

* Or, to give him his full title, Mobutu Sese Seko Koko Ngbendu Wa Za Banga ("the all-powerful warrior who, because of his endurance and inflexible will to win, will go from conquest to conquest, leaving fire in his wake").

of respectability. Liberationist rhetoric aside, the works of Mobutu et al.—like enormous marble-clad palaces with golden toilets or chests festooned with medals—were for show.

Elsewhere, there were rather more serious attempts at building new ideological systems to inspire and guide countries as they emerged from the ruins of empire.

THE ELITES IN Turkey, Egypt and Iran were, like those of Europe and China, the inheritors of a profoundly logocentric culture. Although Islam emerged during the era of quill, parchment, and codex, tradition holds that Muhammad was illiterate. Muslims believe he received the text of the Quran in Arabic by means of direct dictation from the angel Gabriel, who was reciting from the "Mother of the Book," which is located by Allah's side in paradise.

The very word *Quran* is derived from the Arabic *qara'a*, meaning "to recite" or "to read," and only when the book is read in Arabic is the experience of interacting with God's word regarded as fully authentic. Indeed, so powerful is this text that learning it by heart is said to guarantee entrance to paradise.* In Islamic tradition, the Quran as a physical object is also sacred, and complex rules govern its handling. For instance, it should always be placed higher than other books, and should the exigencies of earthly existence render a copy unusable, it must be disposed of very carefully.†

In addition to the Quran, there were the hadith (collections of the prophet's sayings) and centuries of commentaries to contend with—a vast accumulation of text piling up over generations. A traditional Islamic education places a strong emphasis on the memorization of scripture, while at universities such as Al-Azhar in Cairo, the study of grammar has for centuries been central to an imam's education. Yet in the early twentieth century, many members of the educated elites in Muslim-majority countries disdained what they perceived as the retrograde influence of Islam on their cultures. New leaders emerged who were interested less in

---

* "Such a person as recites the Quran and masters it by heart will be with the noble righteous scribes in heaven. And such a person as exerts himself to learn the Quran by heart and recites it with great difficulty will have a double reward" (Bukhari, Book 6, Volume 60, Hadith 459).
† The Ayatollah Khomeini recommended that if a page from the Quran fell into a toilet, it was to be retrieved immediately "regardless of expense." If rescue proved impossible, the toilet should remain unused until the decomposition of the page was complete.

the sacred words of the Quran than in the new Western creeds of nationalism and secularism.

The first and most influential of these leaders was Mustafa Kemal, a.k.a. Atatürk ("Father of the Turks"), who founded the Turkish Republic in 1923, the year after Benito Mussolini's successful March on Rome. As a military officer with a solid track record of defeating European armies in both World War I and the subsequent Greco-Turkish War, Atatürk had earned immense prestige in the final days of the Ottoman Empire. Although not a totalitarian despot in the mold of Il Duce, he was nevertheless immensely comfortable with authority, and stood at the head of a single-party regime until his death in 1938. Such was the aura of power that attached itself to Atatürk that after his death even his undergarments acquired the status of "relics" worthy of preservation—as I discovered in 2012, on a visit to a museum of industry and transport in Istanbul. There I beheld a shrine to the leader that included among the objects on display his lovingly preserved long johns.

Atatürk was a voracious reader and rigorous thinker. While fighting wars, establishing and running a state, and mastering the art of ballroom dancing, he also managed (it is claimed) to read around four thousand books during his lifetime, mostly in Turkish and French. Whether he was a full-blown atheist or more of an Enlightenment-style deist, it is clear that Islam had limited appeal for him. He was far more interested in the modern ideas he found in European books and launched a radical campaign to eliminate Islam from the public sphere.

He abolished the office of the caliphate, transforming the Hagia Sophia from a mosque into a very big museum dedicated to no religion in particular. He abolished Sharia law, replacing it with a secular legal code along European lines, and removed the line from the constitution that made Islam the religion of the state. He was intensely relaxed about breaking the Islamic taboo against alcohol, and not only allowed himself to be photographed drinking raki (alcohol content: 45 percent) but even managed to die from cirrhosis of the liver. He also launched a not-so-covert assault on the texts of the Islamic past. By abolishing the Arabic script and replacing it with a Latin-derived alphabet, he at a stroke rendered even the inscriptions on the tombs of their ancestors unreadable to most Turks, meanwhile aggressively furthering the culture's reorientation toward the West. Not only was the Turkish language purged of Arabic and Persian loan words, but Atatürk also supported the translation of the Quran into "inauthentic" Turkish, despite the fact that had Allah wanted Gabriel to communicate his final revelation in that language, he probably would have found somebody other than Muhammad to whom to address it.

And of course, Atatürk generated text—lots of it in fact, on a wide variety of themes. Like Mussolini (only, with victories), he published an account of his military campaigns, gathering together his journals and notes in an anthology. He was an early adopter of the strategy of establishing a bibliography built on the notes, speeches and other documents he produced in the course of running the country. His *Nutuk* was originally a mammoth speech delivered to the Turkish parliament in 1927 that took six days to deliver and which was subsequently published as a book: it established the official way to think about the foundation and future of the new republic. Many more volumes of speeches and documents were published under the title *The Complete Works of Atatürk*. More unusually, he also authored school textbooks, including a work on geometry in which he dethroned Arabic as the language of science and mathematics. Instead, he sought out Turkish (or Turkic) terms to describe geometric concepts, for instance replacing *zaviye* with *Açı* for "degrees."

Unlike his communist or Nazi peers, however, Atatürk had no grand, simplifying theory of everything. Instead he had "six points" (republicanism, statism, populism, secularism, nationalism, and reformism), and since the unifying factor was that they were all things he approved of, this ideology was ultimately branded "Kemalism."

ATATÜRK WAS NOT the only leader in the Islamic world intent on banishing religion to the private sphere. Following his example, both King Amanullah of Afghanistan (1892–1960) and Reza Shah Pahlavi of Iran (1878–1944) embarked on top-down campaigns of modernization, albeit without ever generating any books of note. In Egypt, home to Al-Azhar, the most important seat of learning in Sunni Islam, attitudes toward the faith were more mixed. Some regarded it as the answer to the crises of modernity—in 1928 a schoolteacher by the name of Hassan al-Banna founded the Muslim Brotherhood, a politico-religious organization with the express aim of forging a new society based on Islamic law;* however,

---

* In 2012 the Brotherhood's political party, Freedom and Justice, finally won the Egyptian presidency. Needless to say, things didn't quite work out as planned.

there were plenty of intellectuals much more interested in delving into Western books and exploring the possibilities inherent in nationalism and socialism. The future president of Egypt Gamal Abdel Nasser was born into this complicated environment in 1918.

Although hardly a scion of privilege—he was the son of a postmaster—Nasser nevertheless received a good education, and during his teenage years he lived in close proximity to the National Library in Cairo, which enabled him to indulge his appetite for books to the full. He shared with the young Mao a taste for stories about "great men" such as Napoleon, Alexander the Great and Garibaldi, but he also read a biography of Atatürk titled *Grey Wolf*, billed as "An Intimate Study of a Dictator," and several books about the colonial history of North Africa. Nasser appears to have been particularly interested in Muhammed Ahmad, a Sudanese sheikh who declared himself the Mahdi (the Islamic messiah) and then led an uprising against the British Empire, which just so happened to be the occupying power in Egypt as well.

One account of the conflict, *The River War*, was the work of Winston Churchill, who as a young soldier had fought against the Mahdi. Churchill pronounced some notoriously harsh judgments upon Islam in the book, but Nasser was not some Atatürk-in-waiting, intent on casting aside tradition. He was instead inspired by a hybrid cultural product, a novel titled *Return of the Spirit*, in which the author, Tawfiq al-Hakim, deployed a Western literary form in service of a nationalist narrative about a youth caught up in Egypt's 1919 revolution against the English. "Wretched though they are today," wrote al-Hakim, the Egyptian people might produce "another miracle besides the pyramids" should the right leader come along. If Nasser had a *What Is to Be Done?* then this was it: he never forgot al-Hakim's words.

Nasser took part in street protests against the British while still a schoolboy, but still managed to pursue an education. Following his graduation from the military academy in 1938, he rose swiftly through the ranks, while carrying on a sideline as a journalist commentating on the ideological battles of the day. After Egypt's humiliation in the 1948 war with Israel he grew disillusioned with the government, and in July 1952 participated in a military coup that removed the king from power. By 1954 he was prime minister, and it was during this year that he wrote his magnum opus, *The Philosophy of the Revolution*.

Grandiose title aside, *The Philosophy of the Revolution* is more pamphlet than book, and what it lacks in analytical rigor it also lacks in any kind of pretentious theoretical apparatus that could be used to disguise that first, fundamental lack. Instead, Nasser commits to paper a set of rambling personal ruminations on deep questions facing himself, Egypt, the Arabs and the continent of Africa. Aggressively metatextual, Nasser even begins by warning the reader that this work of philosophy is not really a work of philosophy—besides, what does the word *philosophy* mean, exactly? Surprisingly for a military strongman with the confidence to stage a coup, ban all opposition and implement one-party rule, Nasser doesn't appear to know precisely what it is that he stands for, or even why he is writing the book; by this point in the twentieth century it was just something that "Great Leaders" did. So Nasser writes about trying to write, and grasps for themes, and grapples with mysteries, and in the process produces torturously nocturnal passages such as this one:

> I firmly believe that nothing can live in a vacuum. The truth that is latent in our depths is this: whatever we imagine to be the truth is, in fact, the truth plus the contents of our souls; our souls are but the vessels wherein everything lives in us, and the shape of this vessel gives form to whatever is introduced into it, even facts.

Now gazing into the navel, now telescoping through time to ponder the pharaohs, Rome, the Arab migrations, the Crusades, the uprising of the Mamluk slave army and Egypt's struggle for self-government, Nasser searches for his theme, producing words, sentences, and paragraphs as he does so. As a book of sorts begins, grudgingly, to emerge from the trails of ink on paper, Nasser eventually finds the most apt metaphor for whatever it is that he is writing about in European high modernism. That said, he still seems perplexed:

> I see no reason, as I sit alone in my study with my thoughts wandering away, why I should recall, at this stage of my thinking, a well-known story by the Italian poet Luigi Pirandello which he called, "Six Personalities in Search of Actors."*

---

* Usually translated as *Six Characters in Search of an Author.*

Pirandello was a card-carrying Fascist who, shortly after the murder of one of Mussolini's most outspoken critics in 1924, had dispatched a telegram to Mussolini asking if he could join the party. But it is not Pirandello's shady politics that attract Nasser. Although he claims that he "sees no reason" for why he suddenly thought of the play, the Egyptian leader soon makes clear why it resonates so strongly for him. It is about a group of characters from an undeveloped drama who crash the rehearsal of another to demand that the author turn his attention to *their* story. As Nasser explains (in characteristically rambling fashion):

> The annals of history are full of heroes who carved for themselves great and heroic roles and played them on momentous occasions on the stage. History is also charged with great heroic roles for which we do not find actors. I do not know why I always imagine that in this region in which we live there is a role wandering aimlessly about seeking an actor to play it. I do not know why this role, tired of roaming about in this vast region which extends to every place around us, should at last settle down, weary and worn out, on our frontiers beckoning us to move, to dress up for it and to perform it since there is nobody else who can do so.

Having spent a long time "wandering aimlessly in search of a hero," the moment has come for the Arabs to play a "positive role in the construction of the future of humanity." No longer a colonial backwater, Egypt stands revealed as a critical center of civilization, located at the heart of three overlapping circles: Arab, African and Islamic. The Arab aspect is weak, but it is potentially the greatest due to factors including its cultural heritage, monotheistic traditions and access to oil, which, says Nasser, is the "nervous system of civilization." Through the African aspect, Egypt participates in the global fight against colonialism. Islam offers the prospect of unity—Nasser proposes that the annual pilgrimage to Mecca might become more than a religious rite and also acquire a political aspect. The holy city could host a political congress wherein "Moslem states, their public men, their pioneers in every field of knowledge, their writers, their leading industrialists, merchants and youth meet to draw up in this universal Islamic Parliament the main lines of policy for their countries and their cooperation together until they meet again."

And so, after a slow and rambling start followed by a slow and excruciating crawl to the point, Nasser climaxes his book with a declaration of grandiose ambition. The Egyptian revolution shall spread beyond the country and not only unite the Arabs but also bring together Africa—only, maybe not quite yet. Suddenly, Nasser picks up the Pirandello theme again:

> I now revert to the wandering role that seeks an actor to perform it. Such is the role, such are its features and such is its stage.
>
>   We, and only we, are impelled by our environment and are capable of performing this role.

According to one account, *The Philosophy of the Revolution* exists at all only because Nasser's wife retrieved it from the trash into which its author had tossed it. The book is sufficiently half-baked that this may be true. Nasser's ambiguity and tentativeness could also be explained by the fact that he wrote the manuscript in 1954, when he was a powerful figure behind the scenes but two years away from assuming the mantle of president. Nasser was still a character awaiting that lead role in the drama, but he was about to storm the stage.

In 1955, however, while in the antechamber of destiny, he published his *Memoirs of the First Palestine War*. That year, Israel staged a raid on the Gaza Strip, which at the time was under Cairo's control, and Nasser was inspired to write about his earlier experience fighting against Egypt's new and unwanted neighbor. He didn't even manage to get to the end of that one, although in contrast to his rambling work of "philosophy" he does provide a lot of concrete detail. The text is strikingly personal, and Nasser successfully evokes the life of a professional soldier during a disastrous conflict, in a manner very different from Mussolini's mode of war-tourism-followed-by-despair. Nasser writes like a real soldier accustomed to risking his life for his country. The highlight of *Memoirs* arrives when he gets shot in the chest, which he describes as a "most curious sensation," one that leaves him "neither sorry for myself nor sad." This sanguine attitude continues once he is in the hospital, where he attains levels of unfazed toughness in the face of adversity that would be unmatched until Chuck Norris memes started circulating on the Internet some sixty years later:

> I lay on the operating table while he fished in my chest. Within ten minutes he was handing to me bits and pieces of twisted metal saying: "Take these and keep them."

Finally, in 1956, the role Nasser had been waiting for since reading *Return of the Spirit* in his teenage years arrived. In January he unveiled before the Egyptian parliament a draft constitution through which Egypt would became a one-party socialist, Arab nationalist state, with Islam as the official religion. Following a referendum in June, it was law—and he was president. As the sole candidate in the election, he won a remarkable 99.948 percent of the vote—only 0.052 percent less than Kim Jong-un's result in North Korea's 2014 "election."

Only death or disaster could prise the power out of his hands now, and Nasser, with years to go before he met his maker, moved swiftly to seize his place in history. A month after his election he nationalized the Suez Canal. France, Britain and Israel promptly invaded, but soon withdrew, leaving Nasser in place. It helped, of course, that the United States declined to back its allies, instead condemning them and supporting a cease-fire resolution at the United Nations. Nasser may not have won a military victory, yet it mattered little: he had outmaneuvered and humiliated his opponents and emerged as a hero of the Arabs, global champion of anticolonialism and committed foe of the state of Israel.

As he ascended the ranks of the era's "great men," Nasser also ceased writing introspective essays referencing Italian modernists. Now he took to the airwaves to preach a message of nationalism, socialism and Arab unity via the Voice of the Arabs radio station. That doesn't mean that books with his name on the spine ceased to appear, mind you. On the contrary, speaking proved to be a lot easier for Nasser than writing, and he was able to quickly generate an instant bibliography. A seven-volume set of speeches appeared in 1959, and many more were to follow, so many that he resorted to filling pages not only with inspirational utterances aimed at the Arab nation but also with such generic dictator fodder as addresses delivered at missile launches and factory openings: the kind of thing that a Choibalsan or a Klement Gottwald might have produced. And so while Nasser is unquestionably a historical figure of great significance, it is hard to resist the conclusion that he is nonetheless a relatively minor author in the dictatorial canon.

LIBYA IS NOT, like Turkey, the inheritor state of a hitherto vast multiethnic empire run by Muslim sultans. Nor is it, like Egypt, an ancient center of civilization turned cultural heart of the Arab world. Rather, it is a sparsely populated colonial patchwork, stitched together by Italians from scraps of the Ottoman Empire, which would not become independent until after World War II. Indeed, when Muammar Gaddafi was born, oil was yet to be discovered, Mussolini had not yet completed his journey to the lamp-post, and Libya was still part of his Fascist empire.

As for Libya's future "Brother Leader," he was from the margins of the margins, having entered the world as the son of an illiterate Bedouin goat herder in 1942. His trajectory from tent to heavily armed compound with fairground rides, a private zoo and an elite team of female bodyguards has more in common with the rise of provincial autodidacts such as Stalin or Mao than that of a well-educated radical bourgeois such as Lenin. Yet Gaddafi was much less well read than either the Soviet or the Chinese tyrant. He learned to recite scripture by heart as a child, then graduated from the Benghazi Royal Military Academy, before traveling to the United Kingdom in 1966 to complete his training during a five-month stay at an army school in Beaconsfield, near London. Mao's Cultural Revolution was getting under way in China, and a different type of cultural revolution was unfolding in Britain, but Gaddafi showed no interest in the experimental culture of Swinging London. He did not drop acid nor did he attend any gigs by the Jimi Hendrix Experience. Instead, he walked around Piccadilly Circus in Arab robes and enjoyed visiting villages in the prosperous counties near London.

It was Nasser's anticolonial revolution that gave Gaddafi's life a point and purpose. As a teenager he had listened to the Egyptian president's radio broadcasts, drinking deep of the message of Arab unity, repeating Nasser's speeches to classmates from memory as he had the word of God for his teachers in his childhood Quran school. Libya's own leadership was much less inspiring. After the discovery of oil in 1959, King Idris had adopted a pro-Western foreign policy, and had declined to back Nasser during the Six-Day War of 1967, during which Israel inflicted a humiliating defeat upon Egypt (then known as the United Arab Republic), Jordan and Syria. Gaddafi viewed the Libyan king's refusal to join in the struggle against Israel as a betrayal of the Arab nation, and within two years he had staged a successful coup, Nasser-style. The boy from the desert became head of state, aged only twenty-seven. To celebrate, he promoted himself from captain to colonel, in emulation of his hero.

This was just the start of Gaddafi's borrowings from Nasser's playbook.

In line with his mentor's message of anti-imperialism, the new colonel evicted the Americans and the British from their bases and seized back control of his country's resources from the foreign exploiters. In line with his mentor's anti-Semitism, he also expelled Libya's ancient Jewish population.* In line with his mentor's pan-Arabism, he sought to merge Libya into a political union with Egypt and Sudan, although this North African superstate failed to materialize following Nasser's death in September 1970.†

But Gaddafi was no mere Nasserite homunculus. Like a prophet of old, he had emerged from the desert to change the course of history, and young as he was, things started going to his head almost immediately. The very first communiqué issued by Libya's Revolutionary Command Council stated that the Libyan revolution was related to "the unity of the Third World and to all efforts directed toward the overcoming of social and economic underdevelopment." Clearly, this was not just another instance of political upheaval in a dusty land of which most people knew little, but an event of earthshaking significance. Gaddafi's own public utterances received full dictator reverence almost immediately, as they were collected, bound and published in a series entitled *The National Record*, the first volume of which appeared on September 1, 1969. Within two years of the revolution, he had extended his authority into the spiritual domain: in 1971 he led prayers in Tripoli's main mosque for the first time, much to the alarm of Libya's religious establishment. This was not a rite to be performed by twenty-nine-year-old colonels.

In early 1973, in true prophetic style, Gaddafi withdrew to the desert. Apparently disillusioned with his revolution, he offered to stand down as leader, only to quickly change his mind. Instead, on April 16—the birthday of the prophet Muhammad, no less—Gaddafi, Mao-style, delivered a speech announcing the beginning of a revolution within the revolution. Something was coming—but what? All was revealed at a conference for youth from Arab and European countries where he unveiled the fruit of his meditations in the wilderness: the "Third Universal Theory." This, the

---

* A mass exodus of Egypt's ancient Jewish population began in 1956. Some were expelled directly as a result of alleged "Zionist" sympathies, while many others "opted" to leave.
† Another plan to unite Egypt, Libya and Syria into one country was voted on in September 1971 but never actually implemented, while a 1974 "Arab Islamic Republic" uniting Libya and Tunisia also failed to cross the Rubicon between dream and reality. Gaddafi signed a treaty of union with Hassan II of Morocco in 1984, but that possible country likewise failed to rise to the challenge of existing.

colonel revealed, was "a universal truth" and an alternative to the rival ideologies of communism and capitalism. The Third Universal Theory, Gaddafi proclaimed, would "serve all humanity." Only four years into his reign, and the colonel had gone full messiah.

Gaddafi preached the word in Libya, Egypt and Sudan, but confusion as to exactly what his Third Universal Theory entailed was widespread. In the West, he attracted attention if not converts. When he took his road show to Paris in 1973, his exoticism won him comparisons to de Gaulle and Marx, while over in California, David Berg, leader of the Children of God cult, grew convinced that the colonel had a role to play in the looming end-time, and praised the Third Universal Theory in sermons and songs.* It was only a matter of time before Gaddafi declared himself "leader of the world," which in fact he did, following a trip to Pakistan in 1974. California cult leaders aside, however, the prophet was with honor only in his homeland, and perhaps not even there. In 1975, Gaddafi survived a coup attempt. The usual purges followed, as did something else: a new text for the world to live by.

In *The Green Book*, Gaddafi produced a political, economic and social blueprint for a new society. Although its title shows the influence of Mao and implies a desire to cash in on an era of student unrest and global radicalism, the change in hue was significant for other reasons: green is rich in symbolic resonance in Islam—Muhammad, it is said, wore a green cloak and turban—but symbolic resonance was about as far as Gaddafi was willing to go; he does not refer to Islam or even the Arab nationalism of Nasser. It really was supposed to be something new, this Third Universal Theory.

The problem is that the book is exceedingly awful, even by the supremely low standards of dictator literature. My copy of *The Green Book* is a mere 137 pages long, and Gaddafi achieves that length only by using a very big font. There are no citations or any indications that Gaddafi himself had ever read a book (although he might have read some newspaper articles).† It is not merely boring, or banal, or repetitive, or nonsensical, although it is certainly all those things. It is, quite simply, stupid, and as

---

* For a while, Gaddafi saw potential in Berg's global following; here was a way to spread his ideas to a wide audience. Berg had a worldwide network of followers dedicated to promulgating his ideas—even through acts of self-prostitution, if necessary.
† That said, in the 1970s a journalist claimed to have seen a copy of something or other by Heinrich von Kleist in the vicinity of Gaddafi.

such, it is perhaps more difficult to engage with than any dictator book besides *Mein Kampf.* Yet for more than four decades, Gaddafi forced it upon his nation and spread it around the world through an institute dedicated to its propagation. If he did not quite achieve Mao levels of ubiquity, it was not for want of trying. But what was in it?

PART 1 OF *The Green Book,* "The Solution of the Problem of Democracy: The Authority of the People," appeared in 1976. Gaddafi begins by addressing a "prime political problem which faces human communities," that is to say, the "Instrument of Governing." For this, he assures us, *The Green Book* is "the final solution."

Democracy according to Gaddafi is a zero-sum game. Since, as it is currently practiced, the winning 51 percent will always dominate the losing 49 percent, it is in fact dictatorship and not "genuine democracy," the nature of which he shall reveal. Gaddafi continues in this vein, delivering a long discourse on the failings of parliaments and plebiscites. Representation is a fraud, voting is a fraud, the poor always lose, and parties are an instrument of tyranny, as anybody who forms one only ever wants to exercise power over others. Indeed, says Gaddafi, "The most tyrannical dictatorships the world has known have existed under the shadow of parliaments"—which may in fact be true, as Stalin's USSR had a parliament, albeit not a very democratic one. It is doubtful, however, that this is the example Gaddafi has in mind.

Instead, Gaddafi advocates a style of direct democracy, which, he reassures us, represents "the end of the journey in the masses' movement in its quest for democracy." His vision of democracy is superior because it is not a product of the imagination but in fact the culmination of all experience expressed via thought. And lo, "the problem of democracy is finally solved."

The next step is easy. All that the masses need do now is struggle to put an end to all forms of dictatorial rule, to all forms of what is falsely called democracy—from parliaments to the sect, the tribe, the class and the one-party, two-party and multiparty systems.

But what is this "final solution" to the profound questions that have bedeviled political philosophers for thousands of years? Fortunately, it can be summed up quite quickly: in *The Green Book,* Gaddafi covers it in a mere three pages. His solution is to divide "the people" into "basic popular congresses," above which sit "popular congresses," above which sit "administrative people's committees," which are intended to replace the government administration. The committees will run state utilities and execute the policies emerging from the basic popular congresses. There are also syndicates and unions, and from this interlocking set of entities, the will of the people shall emerge and receive final expression in a General People's Congress. Or not quite, because drafted laws must return to the committees and other assorted bodies before action can be taken.

Clear? Don't worry, because Gaddafi provides a helpful chart:

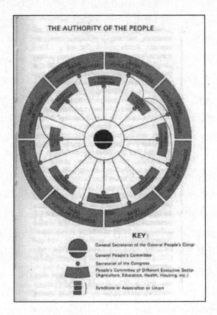

Through this system—which is not that new but actually strongly reminiscent of tribal councils, only on a giant scale—everybody will participate in everything, and the masses will be empowered, owning and managing all the resources of the state and managing the country directly. The people will thus solve their own problems and live free of tyranny. And that's it.

In 1978, GADDAFI published part 2 of *The Green Book*: "The Solution of the Economic Problem." In this tome, he reveals that any type of work carried out in exchange for wages is slavery and that everybody should share in the national wealth. Only by partnering in the means of production can workers be liberated from exploitation.

Exactly how this can be achieved is somewhat confusing, despite Gaddafi's best efforts. He is clear that working for money is bad on the grounds that "the wage-worker is like a slave to the master who hires him." Meanwhile, although Gaddafi sees some differences between public and private ownership, whenever a worker is paid in wages, the result is the same: slavery. Obviously the solution is to abolish the "wage system" and return to conditions that existed before the emergence of classes, government, man-made laws, etc. Gaddafi continues at length in this vein, progressing from the history of iron ore to the transition from camel to factory, to the conclusion that the problem can be fixed by making the worker a partner in production rather than a toiler for wages. And let's not forget that advances in science will reduce the need for tedious work.

Gaddafi nevertheless manages to balance his advocacy of socialist ideas with a belief in private property, at least insofar as it provides for basic needs. Thus it is good to own housing but it is bad to own a second home as renting it out would be to subjugate your neighbor; likewise, using a second car as a taxi also leads directly to exploitation. As Gaddafi puts it, "Man's freedom is lacking if somebody else controls what he needs." Land cannot be owned, although everyone has a right to use it. And nobody is allowed to hire servants.

And so Gaddafi resolves the contradictions of both capitalism and communism, providing the human race with a "Third Way" that should "set oppressed peoples free everywhere."

PUBLISHED IN 1979, the concluding section of *The Green Book*, "The Social Basis of the Third Universal Theory," is the most entertaining of Gaddafi's works and also the most frequently quoted (for reasons that shall soon become obvious). Gaddafi begins by straining at the same theoretical tone as before ("The relationship between an individual and a group is a social relationship, i.e., the relationship between the members of a nation"), and the publisher promises that the text "presents the genuine interpretation of history, the solution of man's struggle in life and the unsolved problem of man and woman."

So far, so good. Alas, *The Green Book* then rapidly dissolves into an almost stream-of-consciousness tour of the colonel's musings on assorted grand subjects that never makes much sense, nor even attempts to mimic a logical progression. Nevertheless, Gaddafi tries something new, quite possibly because while he is sure that this section should exist, he isn't so sure what should be in it. Having abused a "theoretical" style in the previous installments, Gaddafi now writes in what he imagines is a more scientific mode, presumably to demonstrate the scope of his knowledge. When seeking a metaphor for the nation, he gazes upward to the night sky, and finds great clunkiness amid the stars:

> Nationalism in the human world and group instinct in the animal kingdom are like gravity in the domain of material and celestial bodies. If the sun lost its gravity, its gasses would explode and its unity would no longer exist. Accordingly, unity is the basis for survival. The factor of unity in any group is a social factor; in man's case, nationalism. For this reason, human communities struggle for their own national unity, the basis for their survival.

He is at his most magnificent, however, when he addresses the problem of men and women. Here Gaddafi is so naïve, so bizarre, and so lacking in self-awareness that he reaches transcendent levels of bathos. Certainly, the contrast with the sophisticated ramblings of his idol Nasser could not be more striking. "It is an undisputed fact that both man and woman are human beings," Gaddafi declares sagely, and then continues:

> Women are females and men are males. According to gynaecologists, women menstruate every month or so, while men, being male, do not menstruate or suffer during the monthly period. A woman, being a female, is naturally subject to monthly bleeding. When a woman does not menstruate, she is pregnant. If she is pregnant, she becomes, due to pregnancy, less active for about a year, which means that all her natural activities are seriously reduced until she delivers her baby. When she delivers her baby or has a miscarriage, she suffers puerperium, a condition attendant on delivery or miscarriage. As man does not get pregnant, he is not liable to the conditions which women, being female, suffer. Afterwards a woman may breast-feed the baby she bore. Breast-feeding continues for about two years. Breast-feeding means that a woman is so inseparable from her baby that her activity is seriously reduced. She becomes directly responsible for another person whom she assists in his or her biological functions; without this assistance that person would die. The man, on

the other hand, neither conceives nor breast-feeds. End of gynaecological statement!

The abrupt and awkward climax of this remarkable passage suggests that even Gaddafi senses he may have gone too far—and yet evidently incapable of self-editing, he kept it in there. He also predicts that "BLACK PEOPLE WILL PREVAIL IN THE WORLD," on the vague grounds that since (so the colonel informs us) "the Blacks" are less fixated on work and are unlikely to use birth control, they will reproduce in greater numbers. While discussing the arts, Gaddafi reveals himself to be a pioneer in the struggle against "cultural appropriation," although he roots his opposition in a Lamarckian approach to genetics, claiming that because "sentiment" can be passed on through the genes, this means that "people are only harmonious with their own arts and heritage." When it comes to educa-tion, Gaddafi dreams of a "universal cultural revolution that frees the human mind from curricula of fanaticism which dictate a process of deliberate distortion of man's tastes, conceptual ability and mentality." He then dismisses the performing arts, citing the superior attitudes of nomadic Arabs such as himself:

> Bedouin peoples show no interest in theatres and shows because they are very serious and industrious. As they have created a serious life, they ridicule acting. Bedouin societies also do not watch performers, but per-form games and take part in joyful ceremonies because they naturally recognize the need for these activities and practise them spontaneously.

. . . before climaxing with a denunciation of boxing and wrestling as "savage."

And that's it for *The Green Book*.

THE GREEN BOOK was an embarrassment to Gaddafi and to Libya. Only, the colonel was not embarrassed. On the contrary, he was perfectly earnest about his philosophy and sincerely regarded the text as a direct blueprint for his new state. Whereas all Lenin had to offer the reader were mere assur-ances that the state would wither away, Gaddafi provided the details. Short and simplistic as it was, *The Green Book* did include a plan for the creation of popular congresses; there was also that handy diagram. The book thus offered a pathway leading to the introduction of "direct democracy." All that was left was to implement it—and the work on that began before Gaddafi had even completed all three volumes of *The Green Book*.

Dawn rose on Gaddafi's era of the masses on March 2, 1977. Fellow dictator Fidel Castro was guest of honor at the declaration, adding a dash of global revolutionary cachet to the occasion. Libya now acquired the somewhat awkward name the Socialist People's Libyan Arab Jamahiriyya, and Gaddafi's system of congresses was established across the land (with himself at the head of the Secretariat, needless to say). Meeting halls designed to resemble Bedouin tents sprang up in every town, wage labor was abolished, entrepreneurs and traders were denounced, and the poor benefited from new policies mandating the redistribution of wealth. Industries were subject to the control of "basic production committees," and farmers were permitted to lease only the land that was essential to them. Mysteriously, however, the oil and banking industries were left untouched.

And so the ideas in *The Green Book* rapidly moved from the page into the physical world. But when paradise failed to erupt and Gaddafi's reforms met with indifference or opposition, he demonstrated a willingness to go beyond what was written between the covers of his masterpiece. In 1978 he revealed that revolutionary authority was a separate, higher power distinct from the people's authority. He resigned from the General People's Congress and assumed the title "Brother Leader." Officially he held no position but was in fact liberated to act as the supreme revolutionary, above everyone and guiding everything, free to interpret the revolution as he desired. This included introducing further innovations, such as the "revolutionary committees" (heavily staffed with his relatives) that eliminated opponents, enforced the revolution and controlled the People's Congress.

Meanwhile, Gaddafi took a step that no other dictator in the Islamic world had ever taken: he launched a direct attack on the holy texts themselves. Although Atatürk spent decades extirpating Islam from the public sphere and had little respect for its taboos, he never proclaimed that Allah was dead, desecrated the Quran or indulged in Soviet-style antireligious violence; nor did he attempt to supplant the Islamic sacred texts with his own canon of works. Religion under Atatürk was put in its place but then left in its place. As for Nasser, he was a believer and even rambles on about Islam a bit in his *Philosophy of the Revolution*, though he ruthlessly suppressed Islamist groups such as the Muslim Brotherhood.

Ironically enough, Gaddafi was probably the most devout of the three, and yet he would brook no competition for *The Green Book*. Well, he might accept some competition from Allah, but only from that source. There were far too many Islamic texts, Gaddafi thought, and some of them contradicted his law: something had to be done. In 1978 he delivered a speech in which he stated that only the Quran was holy, that the hadith (collections of the words and deeds of the prophet) were man-made, and that Islamic laws no longer applied to the social, economic or political questions in modern society. There was another book now, and it was green, and it had the answers to problems that the immense body of texts Muslims had accumulated over the centuries did not.

Further extending his authority over religious matters, Gaddafi redefined time in late 1978. Until this moment, Libyans had used the same Islamic calendar as other Muslims, beginning with Muhammad's migration from Mecca to Medina. Gaddafi overruled this: from now on, the era had begun at the moment of the prophet's death, ten years later. Religious leaders who had the temerity to express displeasure at these changes were arrested, or mysteriously vanished.

In this way, Gaddafi persisted in running Libya as his own private laboratory for social, cultural and political experiments, with *The Green Book* at the center of the madness. Libyans studied it in school and at universities, listened to recitations on TV, and attended conferences on its sublime mysteries. A "World Center for the Study and Research of *The Green Book*" was established in Tripoli, but it also had branches worldwide and oversaw the translation of Gaddafi's megatext into more than thirty languages. Scholarly monographs were composed; symposiums were held; millions were obliged to pretend that this most obvious confection of gibberish was a masterpiece.

But even as *The Green Book* remained constant, so Gaddafi proved to be mercurial, trying on different ideas for size. Pan-Arabism gave way to pan-Africanism, while the sponsorship of terrorism gave way to photo ops with Tony Blair, also a believer in a political "Third Way." Amid all these mutations, Gaddafi continued writing. In the 1990s he dabbled in "short stories," which were initially published in Libya in two collections: *Escape to Hell* (1993) and *Illegal Publications* (1995). These were not short stories in any conventional sense but actually brief prose feuilletons and pseudophilosophical streams of consciousness, far less disciplined than *The Green Book*—which was not in the least bit disciplined to begin with.

In these "stories," Gaddafi roams through a wide array of themes. He mocks Islamist obscurantists, although his prose is now filled with references to the Quran, unlike in *The Green Book*. He probes hidden history, revealing that it was an "Arab prince" and not Columbus who discovered America. He extolls the village and condemns the city as "a nightmare" where people watch cockfights and children die in the street or are abducted by criminal organleggers. In "Suicide of the Astronaut," he ridicules space travel as a lunar traveler returns to earth and discovers that his qualifications have left him unable to secure useful work. And in "Death," Gaddafi surpasses even Nasser levels of ruminatory navel-gazing as he tackles the pressing question: is death a man, and thus to be fought, or a woman to whose tender embrace we must surrender?

Then, one day, an angry mob pulled him out of a pipe where he was hiding. Gaddafi was sodomized with a bayonet, then shot in the head, the bullet fatally perforating the peculiar brain from which the Third Universal Theory had sprung. His corpse was disposed of in an unmarked grave, and *The Green Book* went the way of all suddenly unsacred texts that have been forced upon a population for a generation. Not every copy was burned or tossed in the trash, however: loyalists sought to keep *The Green Book* alive online, and today a sad website featuring a few free translations floats in cyberspace as a virtual tombstone for the colonel's grandiose ambitions.

Today Libya has to deal with the problem of Gaddafi's success. Unlike many dictators, he really did implement the vision he had spelled out in his book: by the time he was dead, there was neither a parliament nor political parties. There was, however, a yawning abyss, into which the nation fell. Cue war, radical Islam and great rivers of blood, flooding through the streets of towns and villages and out into the desert.

Dead Letters

What's that you say? I've written an autobiography?

The world created by the Russian Revolution of 1917 was moving beyond middle age and into its dotage. Both at the center and in the satellites, the leader-authors were edging ever closer to death. They were flabby, they were decrepit—more interested in preserving the status quo and their privileged place in it than in turning the world upside down. The ideological atmosphere around them had grown thin, and not because they had reached the top of the mountain. Rather, it was as if they were all trapped together on a long-distance flight to nowhere, breathing in the recycled air.

The withering away of revolutionary fervor did not mean that the aging leaders had stopped generating text. On the contrary, it was necessary to churn out books to prove continuity with the past, to demonstrate that they were still participating in a tradition started by the founders of the faith. Mostly these books were explorations in ultraboredom, although the world of communist letters was not yet entirely deathly. It was mostly deathly, yes, and always excruciatingly dull, but on the periphery of this vast epidemic of "theoretical" logorrhea, mutant forms could as yet be glimpsed, shadowy hunchbacks and three-tailed dogs running loose outside the city walls, not quite within reach of Moscow's authority.

In Romania, for instance, Nicolae Ceaușescu criticized his fellow Romanians for their prostration "before what is foreign" in his *July Theses,* while also inflicting his wife Elena's ghostwritten dissertation, *The Stereospecific Polymerization of Isoprene,* on the masses. But while Ceaușescu made a great performance of his autonomy from Moscow, he was careful never to challenge any of the central shibboleths of the communist faith, such as central planning or the one-party state, and there is little that was radical in the many volumes of his *Selected Writings.* For a more forceful and enduring expression of literary and political autonomy we must look farther east, to North Korea, where Kim Il-sung reigned from the capital, Pyongyang.

Born in 1912 to a family of Christian peasants who named him Kim Song-ju,* the future progenitor of a (so far) three-generation dynasty of tyrants spent much of his early life outside his homeland. Korea had been under Japanese occupation since 1910, and Kim's family fled to Manchuria when he was seven. He was to remain in China for the next twenty-one years (bar a two-year stint during his teens when he returned to Korea). He discovered the texts of Marx, Lenin et al. and joined the Chinese Communist Party in 1931. Kim thus became a practitioner of Mao-style guerrilla warfare and cut his teeth in combat against the Japanese before moving to the USSR, where he joined the Soviet Red Army in the Far East. This shift from China to the Soviet Union benefited his career enormously. After the war, Kim served Stalin as a loyal homunculus in the Soviet-backed provisional government in the northern half of Korea,

---

* Kim Il-sung, or "Be the Sun," was a revolutionary name that, he claimed, had been bestowed upon him by awestruck comrades despite his protestations of modesty.

and was rewarded with the post of leader when the Democratic People's Republic of Korea was officially founded in 1948.

Since he had spent most of his life elsewhere, Kim barely knew Korea except through stories and books and the memories of others. However, the years spent in China and the USSR had at least equipped him with a great understanding of how Mao and Stalin approached communism— essential knowledge indeed, given that North Korea shared borders with both China and the USSR. In the early days of the regime, he was truly dependent on his master Stalin. Soviet experts designed a personality cult for him using the techniques they had developed in the USSR, and in speeches and texts Kim was careful to pay homage to his master in the fawning style of the other homunculi. Yet he was never entirely submissive. Noting how freely Stalin rewrote history in his own books, Kim had asked his Soviet advisers if they could do a bit of that for him, by generating an alternative reality in which the anti-Japanese guerrilla faction to which he had belonged might be credited as participants in the liberation of Korea. It was a modest lie compared to the colossal lies of Stalin, an understandable sop to national pride, and it is easy to see why he wanted it—but the request was denied. Nevertheless, Kim could be persuasive when he wanted to be. After Korea was formally split into two countries in 1948, he won Stalin's backing for an invasion of the South that would reunite the entire peninsula under his command. Without heavy Soviet support and Mao's intervention on the North Korean side, Kim would have lost. Instead, the war ended in 1953 with millions dead and an inglorious stalemate that persists to this day.

Stalin died months before the end of the war, and so the Vozhd never had an opportunity to punish his acolyte for the bloody debacle. Kim remained in office, riding out the internal crisis through the application of the usual tactics: repression, intensification of the personality cult, and the propagation of lies—in this case, that the United States had started the war. It was a bold falsehood; backed as it was by the sword of the state, Kim's pen proved to be mightier than any other, and the lie endured.

It was not enough merely to lie, though, and with Stalin now safely dead Kim began to experiment with words and ideas that did not originate in Moscow. The word *juche*, which is usually translated as "self-reliance" but also carries connotations of "self-identity," first appeared in December 1955, in the speech "On the Need to Repel Dogmatism and Formalism and to Establish Juche in Carrying Out Ideological Programs," thus predating Khrushchev's "Secret Speech" by two months. The denuncia-tion of Stalin led to whatever nascent tension there may have been between Pyongyang and Moscow becoming slightly less nascent, as Kim had little interest in pursuing a Khrushchev-style path of liberalization or reform, or in abandoning his personality cult. Increasingly, he began to view China as an alternative model of communist development. When Mao launched the Great Leap Forward in 1958, Kim followed suit with an analogous "Chol-lima" campaign, named after a mythological horse that could race great distances in a short space of time.

Kim's ardor for both Mao and the Chinese model appears to have cooled somewhat during the Cultural Revolution, and it did not help when a group of Red Guards denounced him in print as a "fat counterrevolu-tionary pig." Kim took it personally. He retaliated not only through such conventional measures as the withdrawal of diplomatic staff but also deployed the "irritating neighbor" strategy of using loudspeakers to make a terrible noise for the purpose of aggravating the people next door. In this case, the terrible noise consisted of derogatory comments about Mao's regime that were blasted across the border. Although Kim's increas-ingly complicated relationships with his two powerful neighbors posed risks, they also offered opportunities. Unlike in the postwar period, when Soviet ideological watchdogs were everywhere, Kim now exercised control over the regime's texts. In state propaganda his guerrillas now took a star-ring role in the narrative of North Korea's liberation from Japan. In the late 1960s, the seed of *juche* planted over a decade earlier sprouted with a ven-geance, as Kim began to elaborate on its meaning in speeches that were quickly printed and bound and distributed to the masses.

What, then, is *juche*? In 1997, Hwang Jang-yop, the former head of Kim Il-sung University (and holder of many other grand titles) defected to the West, claiming to be the father of the state ideology; as a result, he is sometimes referred to as the "intellectual force" or "architect" behind *juche*. Even if his claims are true, those titles are a bit of an overstretch as *juche* is not, in fact, all that clever. Does a garden shed require an archi-tect? Does a pocketful of simple ideas that anyone could grasp require an "intellectual force"? Is it profound to state that 1) men are the masters of history, but that 2) they cannot attain revolution spontaneously and thus require a great leader to guide them to liberation?

Not really. The first statement isn't very Marxist, but then again, Mao's gospel was also heavy on the idea of salvation through hard work and sacrifice. As for the second statement, it is but a small step forward from Lenin's insistence on the need for a revolutionary vanguard, a step Stalin had taken decades earlier. *Juche* simply took long-standing trends, pushed them a bit further, and turned up the volume on the nationalism. Kim himself stressed the continuity by claiming that *juche* was not just Marxist but "the most correct Marxism-Leninism-oriented guiding philosophy designed to carry out our revolution and construction." Stylistically, too, *juche* was totally dependent on Marxism-Leninism, as *juche* texts were likewise replete with long sentences, bogus statistics, exaggerations, lies, bold declarations regarding "struggle," bold declarations regarding "the future," and lots of repetition, lots more repetition, and, finally, still more repetition.

From this indigestible word stew a more personal aspect does emerge. After two decades in power, Kim, the superhomunculus who achieved nothing without the support of Stalin and Mao, is liberating himself from the need to display reverence before his "senior officers." A recurring theme is the rejection of "flunkeyism," of bowing before "great powers and dogmatism." As to what this means, Kim is quite clear:

> Not following others blindly, approaching foreign things critically instead
> of mechanically copying or swallowing them whole; and striving to solve
> all problems according to the actual conditions of our country and on the
> basis of their own wisdom and strength.

Here Kim echoes Mao's insistence on adapting Marxism to "concrete conditions," but the implications are more profound. Mao and the Chinese communists were very interested in replacing the USSR at the forefront of a global revolutionary movement. But for all that Kim still had "Workers of the World, Unite" printed on the frontispiece of his books, by insisting on full political independence, he was abandoning the dream of the worldwide communist community under the leadership of a Marxist Jerusalem. "All nations are equal and have the solemn right of national self-determination of deciding their own destinies for themselves," Kim declared in *Let Us Embody More Thoroughly the Revolutionary Spirit of Independence, Self-Sustenance and Self-Defense in All Fields of State Activity.* "A nation can secure independence and freedom and attain welfare and prosperity only if it achieves complete political self-determination and exercises its rights[,] taking them firmly into its hands."

Kim allows that it is a "sacred duty" to help other socialist states, but maintains that the "decisive factor for victory in the struggle against imperialist reaction" is "in the internal forces of the country concerned." *Juche* is thus universal only insofar as it insists that all countries be allowed to follow their own path, which is essential for "all round efflorescence." Grand as that may sound, Kim has stripped away all sense of the inevitability of a millenarian proletarian paradise, and in other speeches *juche* degenerates into an insecure, chip-on-the-shoulder nationalism. In *Our Party's Policy Toward Intellectuals*, Kim rails against people who use Chinese words when there are perfectly good Korean alternatives, and denounces "a certain singer" who "insists on singing Italian songs, considering them the best in the world." In other speeches, Kim criticized Korean poets who drew inspiration from Pushkin, and musicians who liked Tchaikovsky. Jazz was also a Very Bad Thing: it was "fundamentally wrong" that Koreans should be "dancing naked on a stage" to American "jazz" (as he claimed had happened in Indonesia).

But Kim had not abandoned the transcendent aspirations of communism to replace them with complaints about jazz or vague talk about self-determination. He had something more primal, more visceral, to offer his people. Having spent much of his life outside Korea, he returned to find that his homeland was not whole. Now, over and over again in his texts, he picked at the psychic wound, casting it as a greater problem for the South than for the North. Just as Marxism offered acolytes all the psychological thrills of righteous hatred in its demonization of the diabolical bourgeoisie, so Kim relentlessly portrayed the U.S. "occupier" as a racist, imperialist aggressor guilty of monstrous cruelties. Although Kim's official prose style was among the worst of all communist despots, a life-giving hatred seethes in even the flattest *juche* texts. Worship of the leader was all very well, but the addition of ethnic pride and revenge fantasies added fire to the rituals, while the promise of terrible reprisals for dissenters provided the crucial ingredient of fear. Thus *juche* helped bind the nation together, and thus has this confection of nonsense endured for decades, surviving the collapse of communism and two changes of leader.*

---

* Decades later, the hate remains undimmed, as this extract from a North Korean schoolbook makes clear: "During the Fatherland Liberation War [North Korea's official name for the Korean War] the brave uncles of Korean People's Army killed 265 American imperialist bastards in the first battle. In the second battle they killed 70 more bastards than they had in

But if hatred breathed a life of sorts into *juche*, it also limited its appeal. In the late 1960s, Kim's regime dabbled in the global "anti-imperialist" struggle, and even formed an alliance with the Black Panthers. In the early 1970s, Kim went a little more mainstream, taking out ads in the *New York Times* to promote *juche* and Korean reunification.* Efforts were also made to export *juche* to Africa: between December 18 and 20, 1972, fifty delegates from sixteen countries descended upon Freetown, Sierra Leone, to attend a "pan-African seminar" on the application of Kim's great idea to their homelands. In the pamphlet published to commemorate the event, *The Great Idea Juche Mediates over the Revolutionary Struggles of the African Peoples*, it was claimed that the event was taking "place at a time when many, many heads of state are adopting the universal principles of *Juche* as basis for their own actions." As with almost everything else the regime and its reporters claimed, this wasn't true. *Juche* was for domestic consumption only, and so it remains.

For all his tirades against flunkeyism, Kim was still in thrall to communist convention. Even with the relative autonomy he had carved out for himself, he could not escape the conditions he had created. Like the officer in Kafka's story "In the Penal Colony," he was not only the warden of an isolated prison where people were tormented to death by a monstrous writing machine, but also in thrall to the device he had created.

In that story, a visitor to an island inhabited solely by convicts and their wardens is invited to the execution of a soldier caught sleeping while on duty. In typical Kafka fashion, the soldier never undergoes a trial, nor is he informed that he has been sentenced, as "guilt is never in doubt." Instead he is strapped naked, facedown, into an execution machine that resembles a four-poster bed. Death, the officer in charge explains, will come by an act of writing, as a "harrow" comprised of rows and rows of needles shall inscribe upon his flesh the message "Honor Thy Superiors," until the condemned man is able to read his crime through his own wounds. Once he is dead, the machine will dump him into a pit. The visitor senses that

---

the first battle. How many bastards did they kill in the second battle? How many American imperialist bastards did they kill all together?"

* Black Panther leader Eldridge Cleaver was especially enamored of North Korea. He visited twice, in 1969 and 1970, and even wrote the foreword to a U.S. anthology of Kim Il-sung's writings, entitled *Juche!* This fascination did not last, however: later Cleaver founded his own religion, Chrislam, which had a militant wing called the Guardians of the Sperm. Then he joined the Church of Jesus Christ of Latter-Day Saints and ended his days a political conservative.

the officer seeks his approval for this barbaric method of execution; when it does not come, he straps himself into the machine and submits to the carving of the harrow. Then, just as the machine is inscribing the message "Be Just" on his back, it breaks down and the officer dies.

For Kim, it wasn't quite so bad as all that. But at the same time, he couldn't just declare himself president for life and enjoy his palaces and concubines. He felt obliged to produce a "theory" and then publish a vast bibliography dedicated to expanding upon it ad nauseam. Captive to the same book-worshipping tradition as other communist dictators, he hired an army of ideological workers to produce reams of turgid copy. He then toured the country giving speeches, visiting factories and making declarations in which he repeated himself over and over and over again. Subject to neither Moscow nor Beijing, he was still stuck inside a country run according to a nonsense philosophy, and felt compelled to lie about it all the time to maintain the illusion. The harrow did not kill him; its needles weren't designed for that. It just worked away on his flabby back, giving him a compulsory massage that never ended.

WAS THERE NO way out, no liberation from the deluge of otiose, untrue words? In fact, there was not. As the distance in time from 1917 grew ever farther, and the failure of prophecy ever more obvious and the faith withered into a lifeless husk, so the writing continued. Kim at least had found a new spin on the tropes, and enlivened them with some hate. Most dictators just kept cranking out collected editions of dreary speeches. Then, in Albania—also a Stalinist state, albeit even more peripheral and isolated than North Korea—another mutation appeared in the genre of dictator literature. It was time for a turning within, to focus on the personal experience of the leader.

When Stalin thought about feelings, it was in order to engineer them. An emphasis on the inner world was not only Not Very Marxist; it was positively bourgeois. Communist leaders rarely kept diaries, and neither Lenin nor Stalin wrote memoirs. Among lesser dictator-authors, personal texts were also scarce, although there were a few instances of them. Before he was appointed Stalin's top stooge in the Comintern, and long before he became leader of communist Bulgaria, the superhomunculus Georgi Dimitrov published a collage memoir of his trial in Nazi Germany. Dimitrov mixes personal documents, letters and speeches to show how he successfully defended himself against accusations that he had participated in burning down the Reichstag. Written before his soul was completely corrupted, it is surprisingly readable.

In 1970, Khrushchev published the first volume of his memoirs, *Khrushchev Remembers*, although by that point he was out of power and one year away from death. Not only that, but the book was published in the West, not in the USSR.

It is telling therefore that the pioneering memoirist of communism-while-still-in-power, Enver Hoxha (1908–1985), leader of Albania, was also the last self-proclaimed Stalinist in the world. If even a fanatic like that could no longer keep riffing infinitely on Marxism-Leninism, but had to start mining his childhood and youth to meet his page count, then something was definitely wrong.

As for that childhood and youth, it is what you'd expect: provinces, religion (this time Islam), school, scholarship, Marx. This was followed by power, purges, Stalinist bootlicking and the ruthless pursuit of his nation's immiseration over the course of many decades. Hoxha's distinction is that he remained loyal to Stalin longer than anyone: he credited the Vozhd with preventing Albania's absorption into Yugoslavia, and his gratitude never waned. When Stalin died, Hoxha kneeled before the tyrant's bronze statue in Tirana and declared a two-week period of official mourning, longer even than that observed in the Soviet Union. When Khrushchev denounced Stalin, Hoxha made the appropriate noises—"Stalin made some mistakes which cost the Soviet peoples and the cause of socialism deeply"—but he did not follow them up with action. The monuments stayed on their plinths, and Stalin's birthday, December 21, remained a holiday. When Hoxha himself died in 1985, the bronze Stalin was still standing on Stalin Boulevard in Albania's capital, Tirana. It stayed there until 1990.

As loyal as Hoxha was to Stalin, so he was hostile to Khrushchev, whose 1955 rapprochement with Yugoslavia enraged the Albanian dictator. Hoxha sided with Mao following the Sino-Soviet split, and for a while he looked to China for inspiration. Between 1966 and 1969, Albania even enjoyed its own "cultural revolution," although in a much more tightly controlled form, and without the wild excesses of Red Guard leader worship. But this alliance also broke down and by 1978 Hoxha had led Albania into a state of extreme isolation. His heart still belonged to Stalin, and in some ways he was even more radical. Whereas Stalin had merely subjected believers to severe repression, Hoxha went one better: in 1967 he closed every mosque and church in the country, jailed all religious leaders, and declared Albania the "first atheist state in the world" (the announcement was made in a literary journal, of course). He took Stalin-esque paranoia to hallucinatory levels, ordering the construction of 750,000 bunkers (one for every four citizens), inspired by fear that an invasion was imminent. And, like Stalin, he was a bibliophile. Hoxha owned twenty-two thousand books, including memoirs and works of poetry and history; he also had a penchant for stories about vampires. Given his eminent status as the dictator of Albania, he managed to acquire several rare signed editions, among them books by such eminent communists as Chairman Mao and the French surrealist Louis Aragon.

And also like Stalin, he wrote—only, Hoxha was much more prolific. In his lifetime, he produced sixty-eight volumes of ideological fare, including the lyrically named *Eurocommunism Is Anticommunism* (1980). His unlucky subjects had to submit to studying his works in school, at university and in factories, Cultural Revolution–style. However, it was in the late 1970s, as he grew old and increasingly immersed in a state of radical isolation, that his work entered its new, more inward-looking phase: Hoxha produced thirteen volumes of memoirs, amounting to an impressive seven thousand pages of self-reflection.

Just like Kurtz in Conrad's *Heart of Darkness*, Hoxha knew no restraint. Then again, he was fast, and seems to have been one of those fortunate authors for whom writing came with little effort. He cranked out his memoirs in a mere seven years, at a rate of two every twelve months on average; on top of that, there was nobody to stop him. His wife, Nexhmije, was not only his editor but also the director of the Institute of Marxist-Leninist Studies, which published all his books. Despite the fact that he had no allies and represented an otherwise abandoned form of Marxism, Hoxha clung to the universalist tradition of communism with all the fervor of a true believer. There was close to zero demand for his writing, but still his books were translated into foreign languages and distributed abroad.

The titles of the memoirs themselves provide an outline of Hoxha's life:

The Childhood Years
The Youth Years
When the Party Was Born
Laying the Foundations of a New Albania

The Anglo-American Threat to Albania
The Titoites
The Khrushchevites
Reflections on China
Two Friendly Peoples

And so on. However, as an encounter with any one of his books makes clear, Hoxha wrote so many volumes not because he had a lot to say but because he was not that skilled a writer. In particular, he never compressed his material but rather reported every tiny detail. In *The Anglo-American Threat to Albania*, for instance, he repeatedly commits the basic error of filling pages with lots of reported dialogue. Most of it is stilted, although occasionally he rises to Stalin (if not Lenin) levels of invective:

> The Anglo-American imperialists, those savage and determined ene-
> mies of the Albanian people, have always used our country as a means
> of exchange in their international transactions . . . Britain wanted Italy to
> occupy Albania, because it planned to set Italian Fascism and German
> Nazism, which it was financing, like dogs to attack the Soviet Union.

Even that is a fairly generic expression of anti-imperialist hatred, however. Hoxha is the worst kind of storyteller: the bore who boasts about how he wins every fight, whose every anecdote ends with his vindication. Albania is the victim, Hoxha the virtuous and noble defender of her honor and interests. Although the memoir is ostensibly personal, it turns out that there isn't much personality left: celebrity is not the only mask that eats into the face.

Yet in *With Stalin*, published in 1979 to mark the one hundredth anniversary of the birth of Hoxha's idol, there is an element of the genu-inely personal, even a hint of tenderness, if not quite full-blown homo-erotic passion. Hoxha met Stalin five times between 1947 and 1951, and the book is subdivided into five chapters, one dedicated to each of these encounters. Hoxha is keen to defend his hero's honor, declaring, "No, Sta-lin was not a tyrant; he was not a despot." Reading it is akin to entering a parallel reality, in which the Albanian dictator (who was no stranger to exactly the kind of political violence Stalin committed) praises the Vozhd as ineffably kind, gentle, patient, etc. He is not only sincere but passionate:

almost thirty years after the tyrant's death, the flame of Hoxha's man crush blazes bright. He is "breathless" at the thought of encountering the "man of steel" in the flesh, and confesses to "dreaming night and day of meeting Stalin." There are moments of relaxed chitchat, as Stalin feigns curiosity about his guest's ethnicity and language, wondering whether Hoxha's Albanians are related to a people with the same name in the Caucasus and Crimea. Hoxha receives this act of politeness as a sign of the leader's great people skills, and the first meeting ends with him sitting close to his idol on a sofa, watching a stirring Soviet musical titled *Tractor Drivers*. This sense of Stalin's proximity and Hoxha's reference to his "warm voice" give the book a curiously intimate quality. Dictator bodies are usually made of bronze, or pickled and preserved: they don't sit next to you on movie night.

That said, this is no tell-all. Hoxha was not Stalin's confidant but instead a homunculus from the periphery of the Soviet Empire, and his approach to his subject is cloying and predictable. The usual incantations about forward movement, grateful workers, brotherhood and progress appear, and Hoxha romanticizes Stalin as a hero of communism while condemning Khrushchev as a nefarious villain who led Soviet youth away from the truth. Hagiography combines with hagiography as Hoxha slyly promotes his own cult alongside that of his hero. Occasionally he even preempts Stalin's judgments, assuming the role of apt pupil at the master's feet. The effect is to establish continuity between Stalin's USSR and his own rule, thus "proving" that his particular sectarian offshoot of communism is the "true" heir to the Russian Revolution, even if it is entirely marginal and without influence on world affairs.

As the book progresses, Hoxha dedicates fewer words to tender recollections of small talk with Stalin and more to diatribes against "imperialists," "monarcho-fascists," and apostate communists. Hoxha's world is a hostile place full of threats, where only Stalin can be trusted—and he is dead. There must be "physical liquidations," and Hoxha pledges that he will "wipe out" his foes. It is a dark, lonely place, and the book represents a howl from a dream that died, but from which its author cannot wake up. Outside Hoxha's window, 750,000 bunkers lurk in darkness, unoccupied, waiting for the crisis that never came, because nobody cared enough. Where to go, what else to do but climb inside the writing machine?

And so he did.

———————

OF THE MANY bodies strapped to the writing machine during this late phase of communism, the largest and most significant was that of Leonid Ilyich Brezhnev (1906–1982), general secretary of the Soviet Communist Party since Khrushchev's fall. His predecessor's proclamation that the USSR would have successfully constructed a communist society by 1980 was shelved. Brezhnev was content with more modest achievements. The state may not have withered away; in fact, it had grown much more bloated. But at least more people had TVs and washing machines and some had cars, even if they were inferior to the ones you could buy in the imperialist West. The good news was: communism was more moral than capitalism. Thus although the political elite still claimed to believe in Marxism-Leninism, and while professional theoreticians continued to toil away on refinements and revisions of ideology, it was clear from the actions and priorities of the men at the top that if they believed at all, it was rather tepidly.

Unlike Hoxha, who was a ruthless tyrant of the Stalin school, Brezhnev was in tune with the more relaxed mores of his era. He had wanted to be an actor but had wound up a metallurgist. His education was technical and administrative rather than heavily theoretical. He was not averse to repression; in 1968 he dispatched tanks to the streets of Prague to clamp down on an attempt by the local communists to introduce a reformed, more liberal vision of socialism. But he was not a drinker of blood. Brezhnev preferred to exile dissidents or have them declared insane rather than shot in a cellar or dispatched to the gulag. When he turned the screws, it was done not in homage to ideological purity and the dead Stalin but from a desire to preserve the stability of the system.

Stability interested him a great deal. Without it, how was he to live the easy life? Fat, complacent and lazy, Brezhnev enjoyed playing dominoes and liked to shoot bears, but couldn't be bothered to actually hunt them. Instead, he'd sit in a chair and enjoy a glass of vodka while lackeys drove his ursine prey in front of his gun. He was also a shameless hypocrite: he enjoyed riding around in his collection of luxury foreign cars,* even as ordinary Soviet citizens waited years to get a Lada, a metal box on wheels modeled on an old Fiat. Brezhnev's ascent to the

———————

* The garages in the Kremlin held more than thirty at the time of his death.

top was clear evidence that the history of the Soviet leadership was like an evolutionary chart in reverse, in which the general secretaries grew ever less intelligent, less charismatic and less healthy. Brezhnev even hated reading: mastering the sacred texts of Marxism-Leninism in order to rise through the party ranks must have been torture. Once in power, he was able to relax, as he could order his underlings to read documents aloud to him.

In 1974, a series of strokes left Brezhnev severely debilitated. Combined with the gout, heart disease and arteriosclerosis already ravaging his system, the now half-alive general secretary was able to work for only a few hours a day, and his health was so precarious that an ambulance followed his motorcade wherever he went. While a simulacrum "Brezhnev" carried on a vigorous life in the newspapers, on TV and in official biographies, basking in the glow of a personality cult and accumulating more honors than all his predecessors combined, the actual, physical Brezhnev was reduced to the status of an enormous meat puppet to be paraded before crowds and cameras at parades and state visits whenever necessary, and not more often than that. Behind the curtain, party technocrats were quietly running the USSR. Brezhnev played dominoes. Brezhnev wept. And yet even in this state of advanced decomposition he still lived by the communist law of publish or perish. With all his cars and privilege relative to ordinary citizens, even on the verge of death, he was not free: his mortal flesh remained strapped to the writing machine, and the harrow carved away on his back right until the end.

The merciful thing was that Brezhnev didn't really notice. He just lay there while teams of professionals worked to ensure that the steady flow of publications was uninterrupted. Nine volumes of speeches and articles appeared under his name during the 1970s, yet more explorations in ideological necrosis adding to the millions of other dead letters produced by his peers and predecessors. But then, just as Hoxha was turning to memoir, so too did Brezhnev. At the periphery and at the center alike, the faith had hollowed itself out, leaving a vacuum into which the personality (such as it was) of the leader was stuffed.

It was not, however, Brezhnev's idea to write a memoir, let alone four volumes of personal reminiscences. The general secretary did keep a diary, but it was hardly usable material. Although he was in theory the master of a great superpower, his entries reveal a minimal preoccupation with affairs of state, or Politburo machinations, or foreign policy, or even such personal matters as his daughter Galina's scandalous love affair with a circus performer. Instead, he wrote things like this:

> 16 May 1976: Went nowhere—rang no one, likewise no one me—haircut, shaved and washed hair in the morning. Walked a bit during the day, then watched Central Army lose to Spartak (the lads played well).

Admittedly, when excerpted in fragment form it does read a bit like the work of a midcentury absurdist such as Samuel Beckett: there could be an understated artfulness there, a wry commentary on the meaninglessness of existence. But when experienced as a succession of entries that run on and on without ever coming close to a point or insight or reflection the diaries read more like the scribblings of an imbecile.

That said, Brezhnev was not—or at least not yet—an imbecile. He was compos mentis enough to know that his memoirs existed, and he wanted the Soviet people to read them, but that was about the extent of it. According to the Soviet general and historian Dmitri Volkogonov, the next-but-one leader of the USSR, Konstantin Chernenko, helped drive the initiative, while the writing and the remembering of the first book, *Malaya Zemlya* ("Little Land"), was outsourced to Arkady Sakhnin, a journalist and editor at the newspaper *Komsomolskaya Pravda*. That initial slim volume appeared in 1978, four years after Brezhnev's first stroke, and two more ghosted volumes, *The Virgin Lands* and *Reconstruction*, followed in rapid succession. Remembering the leader's life on his behalf was starting to resemble a cottage industry: a volume of "autobiography" was published in 1981, the year before its "author" died.

Yet so poor was the source material that even in a ghosted memoir written by a professional granted great license to enhance the image of its protagonist, Brezhnev emerges as a mediocrity. The general secretary's war service was a major part of his cult and so in *Malaya Zemlya*, a hitherto little-known battle in a lost corner of Soviet Ukraine was retconned as a hugely significant part of the war effort. But Brezhnev was a political officer, not a combatant, so even in an idealized account of his past he doesn't see much action. At the start of the book a bomb explodes near his boat and launches him into the water—and it doesn't get much more exciting than that. Brezhnev's work required him not to kill Nazis but rather to produce and disseminate propaganda, enforce political correctness and keep an eye out for sedition (although that last aspect of his work is never mentioned in *Malaya Zemlya*). He was a generator of words and a witness to bravery. And witness he does, commemorating the fallen via death lists and by paying tribute to the "mass heroism" of the Soviet people. Brezhnev also cites by name particularly brave individuals, such as red-haired Maria Pedenko who "spared neither her youth nor her own life" in the struggle against fascism. Her role was to raise the men's spirits by writing propaganda articles and reciting poetry and speeches. Then there was the unnamed soldier who turned down his leave to stay with his unit at the front, and died as a result. Brezhnev would be a minor figure in comparison were it not for the Soviet tradition whereby the leader's act of producing words was transmuted into an act of heroism.

Thus just as Lenin's slogans were cited as epochal historic events in the *Short Course*, so "Brezhnev" recalls his important work talking to the men ("I always spoke the truth no matter how bitter"). He makes speeches, quotes Lenin, cites his own pamphlets approvingly, and stresses how eager the generals were to listen to him. In *Malaya Zemlya*, the production of text is central to victory, as it is through these words that an act of ideological alchemy takes place. So it was that "the political workers became the heart and soul of the armed forces."

Needless to say, some important details are omitted. There are no political executions, and Stalin's role is reduced to an appearance in a photograph. But it is not only the Vozhd who is absent from the text: Brezhnev's body is likewise conspicuous by its immateriality. In fact, aside from the opening scene in which he is sent flying into the water, Brezhnev becomes corporeal only twice: while fleeing from a falling explosive (he was the one to detect its approach, naturally) and when confronted by an advancing horde of Germans. At this point, Brezhnev locates his hands and seizes a machine gun, opening fire. This moment of action comes to a swift conclusion when Soviet troops arrive in the trench. "One of them touched my arm," says Brezhnev, reassuring us that he does indeed have substance, that he was there, that he is not merely the simulacrum on TV and in the papers. Brezhnev's body is absent because Brezhnev himself was absent from the production of the text. The ghostwriter knew official utterances but not his interior life, and so Brezhnev is much less present in his memoirs than Lenin was in his theoretical writings, or Stalin was in his late-period work on linguistics. Even Kim Il-sung, the supreme overlord of communist death prose, can be found in the resentment and hatred of *juche*.

Brezhnev's epic flatness was no obstacle to success, of course. The state machine guaranteed that *Malaya Zemlya* and his other books would enjoy huge print runs, and that they would be turned into set texts at schools and adapted into movies for the edification of the masses.* And so they were.

BREZHNEV ROTTED AT the top for eighteen years and then died. When his remains were moved to Moscow's illustrious Hall of Columns to lie in state, the deceased general secretary turned out to be so heavy that his body crashed through the coffin and landed on the floor. A new and improved casket with a metal base was procured, this one sturdy enough to contain the expanse of Brezhnev's dead flesh. His literary corpus turned out to be much less solid: it disappeared within a few years of his death when Mikhail Gorbachev denounced Brezhnev's reign as a period of "stagnation."† And so was set in motion the erasure of Brezhnev and his name from cities, factories, and school curricula, and a great forgetting engulfed the literary works of the hero of *Malaya Zemlya*.

FIRST STALIN, NOW BREZHNEV—AND over in China something similar was happening to the works of Chairman Mao. It was as if the words of the dictators were unwriting themselves, the books vanishing at an ever faster rate, with less effort required than before to make the dead weight of words slip into a limbo where they might safely dissipate. For all that the selected works of dictators were physically very heavy, these immense tomes suffered from an unbearable lightness of being. Without

---

* Decades later, Brezhnev's books are remembered in the former USSR with relative good humor. Compared to some of the other things Soviet citizens had to read, they were comparatively painless to plow through. No doubt this was because they were written by professionals and were largely bereft of theory.

† Gorbachev had not always been so critical, however. On May 6, 1978, while advancing up the greasy pole of the Communist Party hierarchy he published this review of *Malaya Zemlya*:

> Not long ago we opened the pages of Comrade L.I. Brezhnev's remarkable book *Malaya Zemlya*, in which the legendary heroes of the battles of the North Caucasus are portrayed in letters of gold. A short time has elapsed since its publication, but the memoirs have produced wide, truly national interest . . . In its number of pages *Malaya Zemlya* is not very large, but in the depth of its ideological content, in the breadth of the author's generalisations and opinions, it has become a great event in public life.

the repressive force of the state to keep them in print, they could not maintain their existence. There simply wasn't any demand for their "scientific truths." Only Lenin, dead now for sixty years yet still as dapper as ever, resisted the forces of dissolution: he continued to sleep undisturbed in his glass box by the Kremlin Walls, as well preserved as his body of work. But a mummy is hardly a symbol of health and vigor.

In 1979, communism was still supposed to last forever, even if in a highly degraded form. The prophecies had been disconfirmed, the books were obviously false, the high priests of the ideology resembled the living dead, but Brezhnev and Hoxha were still strapped to the writing machine, and the printing presses were still rolling and of course the nuclear warheads kept multiplying. It *seemed* alive, and Sovietologists were still predicting that the East/West divide would endure, almost as if it were a natural landmark, like the English Channel.

The scholars of communism were thus caught off guard when, in 1989, the Berlin Wall fell and the USSR blinked out of existence two years after that. They did not realize the extent to which the USSR had hollowed itself out. They should have paid closer attention to the texts of the leaders. In their mounting emptiness and futility, and in the increasing difficulty the books had in sustaining their existence, they were harbingers of extinction. Dead letters foretold a dead end.

6

Another Green World

If communism was a walking corpse, what new idea could offer salvation to humanity—and provide tyrants with material for their books?

In an ideal world, the answer would have been "none." After three-quarters of a century of rampant demagoguery and disastrous social and economic experiments, it was surely time to take a break from millenarian fantasies and scientistic follies. There were no supermen; there was neither shape nor structure to history; there were only humans, and frequently quite despicable ones, doing appalling things in the conviction that it would all be worth it in the end. After all, they had read in a book that it would; sometimes they had even written the book.

As we have seen, by the late 1970s, the state of dictatorial prose was parlous. The strongmen remained, but their ideas were in crisis. In China, the party was quietly retconning Maoism to remove its radical aspects, while in the Middle East, Nasser was dead, Gaddafi was absurd (if murderous) and the Turkish military was obliged to periodically stage coups to protect Atatürk's secular legacy. In Europe, Franco and Salazar were dead; Nazism and Fascism were ghosts. The assorted nationalisms and military regimes of Latin America were largely uninterested in the construction of vast theoretical bibliographies (although Chilean military dictator Augusto Pinochet dabbled and Fidel Castro could crank it out with the best of them). Radical guerrilla groups in Asia and Latin America operated out of theoretical playbooks written earlier in the century. Meanwhile, in the nontyrannical world, the United States was on the verge of electing Ronald Reagan, and the United Kingdom had already elected Margaret Thatcher. Cold warriors par excellence, their support of democracy inspired millions, but their free-market ideologies did not offer redemption on earth—although in their more radical forms these also had the whiff of unreality. Certainly, the promise that wealth would "trickle down" like some rivulet of liquid gold heading south along a drunkard's leg was not the kind of thing anybody was willing to die for.

But there was another idea awaiting its moment to turn the world upside down, another set of books lying in wait, containing fresh approaches to the solution of human misery. The problem was that after a century spent in pursuit of secular utopias, the politicians and analysts whose job it was to think about such things did not take this idea seriously when it materialized. They were constricted by their own prejudices, their own ways of thinking, by the secular myth of progress, even by how they had been taught to think about time. Take 1979, for instance: what did it mean? Nothing, really. It was a number without much resonance—in Western cultures at least. But for Muslims it was the 1,400th anniversary of Muhammad's pilgrimage to Mecca, the start of a new century, and, according to tradition, time for a *mujaddid* to appear in order to renew the faith.

Atatürk and those inspired by him had regarded religion as a retrograde force; the transformative energy was to be found elsewhere. By AH 1400, however, it was clear to many that the nationalists and socialists and modernizers had overturned tradition but had not brought into being the new world they had promised. In Iran, where secularization was almost as old as the Russian Revolution, Mohammad Reza Shah Pahlavi was reviled by millions as a tyrant and corrupt U.S. puppet, despite or because of his attempts at reform. When his regime collapsed, the books that had inspired frenzy in so many twentieth-century intellectuals turned out to have little purchase. It was time for a different set of texts: holy ones.

The new face of revolution stared out from beneath a turban, and it had a very long, very white beard.

IRAN HAS STRONG APOCALYPTIC TRADITIONS. In pre-Islamic times, the state religion was Zoroastrianism, according to which life is a battle between darkness and light that will ultimately conclude with the arrival of a savior and a last judgment. In the sixteenth century, a boy king named Ismail converted Iran to Shiism, which, with its intense longing for the return of the Hidden Imam, has a much more pronounced apocalyptic aspect than the majority Sunni strain of Islam. Ismail revealed a powerful messianic streak of his own in poetry dedicated to himself ("I am God's mystery . . . In me is prophethood and the mystery of holiness"), while a subsequent ruler always kept two horses at the ready so that when the Hidden Imam and Jesus (whose return is also anticipated) appeared to fight the battles of the end-time, they would not have to waste time hunting around for steeds. On occasion, prophets would tap into this deep longing and proclaim themselves the awaited Messiah; thus it was, for instance, that the Baha'i faith got its start in Iran in the mid-nineteenth century. By the time secular Marxist millenarianism was added to the eschatological mix, people in Iran had already spent around three thousand years waiting for the arrival of cosmic justice.

Little wonder, then, that when the Bolsheviks announced that the final stage of history had begun in 1917, Marxists in Iran, which shared a border with the USSR, swiftly attempted to ride the revolutionary momentum, establishing a Persian Soviet Socialist Republic in the province of Gilan in June 1920. This was during the period of frenzied faith in the Bolshevik Revolution, when radicals in Germany, Hungary, Slovakia and elsewhere were attempting to ride the lightning of postwar chaos all the way to world revolution. The Persian Soviet Socialist Republic was short-lived (it had ceased to exist by September 1921) but, even so, it lasted longer than any of the contemporaneous attempts at establishing Soviet states to the west of Moscow, none of which made it to a year. The USSR recognized the revolutionary potential of Iran's intellectuals and students, and supported the homegrown Marxist Tudeh Party, in anticipation of the moment when the workers of that ancient land would rise up.

Around this time the man who would eventually spearhead Iran's revolution sixty years later was studying in a seminary. Ruhollah Khomeini was fifteen years old when the Bolsheviks seized power to the north, and eighteen when the Persian Soviet Socialist Republic was declared. Britain and the USSR were playing Great Power games, and the government had largely lost control outside the capital. It was a time of turmoil and strife, providing ideal conditions for the rearing of a future dictator-author, and Khomeini does tick a lot of the right boxes. Born in the provinces? Check. Dead father? Check. Raised by his mother? Check. Religious education? Check. Comes of age in a once mighty imperial power fallen on hard times? Check. Imperialist powers prowling around for spoils? Check. Other empires in the vicinity collapsing? Check. Unpopular tyrannical rulers living in great opulence while the masses endured endemic poverty? Check.

But Khomeini also diverged significantly from the narrative: rather than abandon religious belief for the simplifications of Marxism or some other novel idea found in a Western book, he deepened his study of Islam. Rather than win a scholarship to Russia or France where he could immerse himself in radical ideas, he moved to the holy city of Qom.

Over the course of his religious studies, Khomeini immersed himself in a vast and interconnected universe of texts. Like communist theorists, he was trained not to think empirically but to seek the deep and manifold connections between words on paper, and to know what had been said about those connections in the past, what was a legitimate interpretation and what was an illegitimate interpretation. He studied Arabic and Persian, grammar, logic, rhetoric, jurisprudence, Islamic philosophy, Islamic science and Islamic history, and it was by demonstrating mastery of this written tradition that he established his authority as a religious guide— just as communists were obliged to commit public acts of theory to build careers in the party. However, whereas communists grew accustomed to a world of rigidly hierarchical bureaucratic power structures, Shiite Islam was less straightforward. Leaders could "emerge" only through recognition by the community; Khomeini had to be truly convincing when he spoke and when he wrote.

From his base in Qom, Khomeini taught, and preached, and wrote, and published, in both Arabic and Persian. He was especially highly regarded for his expertise in Islamic law and the far more theologically risky field of gnosticism. By the 1950s he was recognized as an ayatollah ("Sign of God"), a title that marked him out as an outstanding scholar and member of the religious hierarchy. By the early 1960s, he was a "Grand Ayatollah," one of the highest-ranking spiritual leaders in Iran. It had been a slow and steady advance, achieved without revolution or violation of the rules. He was not the leader of a political party or a coiner of slogans. He did not have an Islamic "Red Guard" at his command. He did not have an army. So what was it about his teachings and those books that had such impact?

As KHOMEINI WAS writing within a literary and theological tradition elaborated upon by a multitude of participants over the course of centuries, it is difficult for outsiders to grasp the meaning and context of his writings—that is, if they bother to read them at all. For most of us, thankfully, there is no more need to subject ourselves to a crash course in Khomeini's texts than there is to read the works of, say, Kim Il-sung. A problem arises only when individuals claiming to provide a certain expertise on Iran offer opinions that clearly demonstrate total unfamiliarity with Khomeini's published oeuvre.

You might reasonably expect that William Sullivan, the last U.S. ambassador to Iran, would have at least assigned a junior lackey to take a quick look at Khomeini's writings as the cleric's influence was surging in the late 1970s. Instead, he dashed off a quick memo to Washington in which he compared Khomeini to Gandhi. In Sullivan's defense, he was a busy man trying to keep abreast of the looming collapse of an important U.S. client regime. However, Richard Falk, a professor at Princeton who had actually met Khomeini and should definitely have known better, wrote an infamous op-ed for the *New York Times* in which he assured readers that Khomeini's circle was "uniformly composed of moderate progressive individuals," all of whom shared "a notable concern for human rights."*

Just as nobody took the Bolsheviks or the Nazis seriously until it was much too late, so Khomeini managed to advance toward power without raising many flags, even though he had produced an extensive bibliography that openly telegraphed, and in detail, his less than progressive views on a multitude of subjects. Attention was still focused on old ideological battles from earlier in the century. The idea that religion was a force to be taken seriously in politics was as alien to well-educated opinion formers as it is distasteful to them now.

All that said, we should not judge the naïfs of the 1970s too harshly, as the works of the ayatollah were written in Arabic and Persian, while the State Department was full of linguists trained in the tongues spoken

---

* In all fairness, Falk later changed his mind, and described Khomeini's regime as the "most terroristic since Hitler."

behind the iron curtain. Just how difficult it was to get a sense of what Khomeini stood for becomes clear when we consider that the first anthology of his work to appear in English did not do so until 1980, and it was hardly a model of scholarly research. Rather, it was a mass market paperback published by Bantam Books that bore the unwieldy (and not terribly grammatical) title *The Little Green Book The Astonishing Beliefs of the Man Who Has Shaken the Western World The Sayings of the Ayatollah Khomeini Political Philosophical Social and Religious* on the cover. (It was truncated to *The Sayings of the Ayatollah Khomeini* on the spine.)

The Sayings of the Ayatollah Khomeini was an English translation of a French translation of some of Khomeini's "greatest hits." It was also obviously a crass commercial cash-in that worked too hard to include every dictatorial trope known to man in the title via the invocation of American socialist and journalist Jack Reed, Chairman Mao and Gaddafi. Dip in, and the Khomeini who emerges from the slim volume's pages is a somewhat confused and confusing figure. There is the Khomeini who hates tyranny and injustice. He sounds a lot like Che Guevara—or perhaps Ali Shariati, an Islamic-Marxist writer and antimonarchical contemporary of Khomeini who was one of the ideologues of the Iranian Revolution, representing a path that was ultimately never followed:

> Islam is the religion of those who struggle for truth and justice, of those who clamor for liberty and independence. It is the school of those who fight colonialism.

Then there is the Islamic supremacist Khomeini ("Holy war means the conquest of all non-Muslim territories. Such a war may be declared after the formation of a government worthy of that name, at the direction of the Imam or under his orders"); and the stern opponent of male grooming Khomeini ("Shaving one's face, whether with bladed razors or electric apparatuses intended for the same purposes, is highly unacceptable"). In addition, there is the frothing anti-Semite Khomeini, the conspiratorial fantasist Khomeini, the Khomeini who denounces Western remedies for typhus, and so on. These Khomeinis were all real enough, but *The Sayings of the Ayatollah Khomeini* doesn't shed much light on them as the book is overwhelmed by another Khomeini: the one who is really obsessed with semen, sweat and the anus.

Indeed, Khomeini is very precise when it comes to such matters, viz.:

In three cases, it is absolutely necessary to purify one's anus with water: when the excrement has been expelled with other impurities such as blood, for example; when some impure thing has grazed the anus; when the anal opening has been soiled more than usual.

In all other cases, one may wash one's anus with water or wipe it with fabric or a stone. And this is as nothing compared to the detail in which *The Sayings of the Ayatollah Khomeini* quotes the man on the rights and wrongs of multiple sexual scenarios, including bestiality. Particularly illuminating is the set of instructions regarding what you should do with a camel that has experienced some vigorous thrusts from a male human's member in its anus.

The quotations are selected and organized in such a way that Khomeini sounds obsessive, fanatical and perverse. Yet something is wrong: the tone. Content notwithstanding, the ayatollah's voice is lucid, rational, and extremely solemn. This is simply not how a ranting maniac obsessed with filth and purity expresses himself. And missing entirely from the book is another Khomeini—the one who wrote poetry, including lines such as this:

Open the door of the tavern and let us go there day and night,
For I am sick and tired of the mosque and seminary.

Rather than help explain events in Iran, *The Sayings of the Ayatollah Khomeini* provided its readers with an opportunity to explain them away as sheer lunacy and barbarism. It's not that the text contains lies but rather that it is a sensationalistic compression of three separate, much longer works, which are themselves but a small selection of Khomeini's bibliography. By the time of the revolution he had published eighteen books, and it turns out that compressing the most salacious bits into a 125-page paperback just isn't very helpful as a guide to his beliefs—just as stripping away all the context from Mao's thought in his *Quotations* did not lead to enlightenment in China. And while it is certainly tempting to dismiss so unpleasant a figure as Khomeini, he was clearly a highly effective revolutionary leader. It is better to learn from his books than to ridicule them.

In fact, the strategy of caricaturing the ayatollah as a demented obscurantist had already failed in Iran. Agents of Iran's ruler, Mohammad Reza Shah Pahlavi, had also noticed the semen/anus/camel sodomy material in Khomeini's corpus and had extracted and disseminated appropriately amusing examples in 1977 and 1978 to discredit him. Instead, they exposed themselves and their disconnection from their own culture, as the quotations had been pulled from *A Clarification of Questions.* This was not a work expressive of Khomeini's inner soul but actually a detailed "purity code" of the sort that can be found in the Old Testament book of Leviticus, which also contains instructions on sexual relations with animals, relatives, members of the same sex, among many other matters. Khomeini's entry in the genre was more or less identical to those of other prominent ayatollahs who, since the 1950s, had followed a trend of publishing similar compilations of questions and answers. By demonstrating the breadth and depth of their religious scholarship, they heightened their authority as spiritual leaders. However, most ayatollahs left the actual work of creating the compilation to their juniors, and then applied their names to the finished product in the same way that Brezhnev did to his memoirs.

This points to another problem with focusing on camel molestation: whatever Khomeini's assistants felt was appropriate to include in a huge anthology on purity codes had absolutely nothing to do with his standing as a revolutionary leader. Exercises in the finer points of Islamic jurisprudence had helped Khomeini attain prominence as a teacher, but they were not what had turned him into the man who brought down the shah; nor had his refined mystical verse or his two books on commercial law. Rather it was his stubborn refusal to submit to the shah's secular authority when it contravened the law of God, and his willingness to place himself at risk by writing and preaching against it.

For Khomeini, Western ideas of progress and the Enlightenment were the creation of men, and their adoption could only distance Muslims from the creator. Yet for his entire adult life, the rulers of Iran had been pushing for "modernization." Following a military coup in 1925, an officer by the name of Reza Pahlavi had crowned himself shah. An admirer of Atatürk, Reza Shah had likewise pursued policies of modernization and nationalism until Soviet and British forces occupied Iran in 1941, forcing his abdication.* The shah's son Mohammad Reza Pahlavi was installed in his place, but he was a weaker man than his father, European educated and fond of parties and beautiful actresses.

Khomeini appears to have seized the moment of internal disorientation to write *The Revelation of Secrets*, his first political work, which was published anonymously in 1944. The book contains attacks on reformist clerics and proponents of Westernization. Here we see Khomeini expressing himself directly, raging against Iran's secular law ("emanating from the syphilitic brains of a certain bunch"), coeducational schools and the cinema, while proclaiming the totality of the divine law. However, he stops short of calling for resistance to the shah. The most senior religious leader in Qom, the Ayatollah Boroujerdi, believed that religion should be kept distinct from government business, and as stability returned to Iran, Khomeini contained whatever impulses he felt toward making criticisms of Mohammad Reza, who continued to pursue policies of reform and modernization.

The new shah was not personally hostile to Islam, but in his autobiography, *Mission for My Country* (1960), he makes strikingly few references to the "Moslem faith." After confessing to a "passionate belief" in the revelation of Muhammad, indications as to what that belief might entail beyond a quietist, internal piety are scant. By contrast, entire chapters are dedicated to such themes as "Westernization," "Nationalism," "The Rights of Women," "Education," and, of course, "Oil"—for it was Iran's oil that had brought vast wealth to the country, and which the shah intended to use to transform Iran into a "Great Civilization" by means of a "White Revolution." The emperor himself had his own book, and intended to lead from the top, Mao-style, combining land reform with massive development projects, literacy campaigns and the emancipation of women.

To Khomeini, this "White Revolution" was a violation of the eternal laws of God. In 1961, Ayatollah Boroujerdi died, and Khomeini became the most senior cleric in Qom. By this point his standing was so high that he had attained the status of *marja-e taqlid* ("a person to be imitated"), and Khomeini left little to the imagination as to the kind of behavior he wanted his followers to imitate. He had already raised the literary stakes

---

* Reza Shah (who owned a signed photograph of Adolf Hitler) had adopted a policy of neutrality toward Germany during the war, but Churchill and Stalin were having none of it.

(albeit quietly) by slipping a chapter on "Resistance to the Oppressor" inside an otherwise nonrevolutionary Islamic treatise, *Forbidden Sources of Income*, in which he openly declared that "to assist an oppressor in his oppression is forbidden without any question." But as the shah's White Revolution escaped the confines of ink on paper and began to overturn centuries of Islamic practice in Iran, so Khomeini's urge to resist the oppressor also slipped completely free of all restraints. In 1962 he led a protest of religious leaders against a proposed change to the law that would have allowed state officials to take their oath of office on "the holy book" rather than specifically stating "the Quran"—this seemed to place texts by Christians, Jews, Zoroastrians and even Baha'i on an equal footing with Shiite Muslims. Invoking (as he would many times over the years) the specter of the diabolical Jew, Khomeini thundered that this was a Zionist plot to take control of Iran. The government backed down, but Khomeini was just getting warmed up. The war of words intensified. As Khomeini stepped up his criticisms of the shah, the shah responded in kind, describing the religious opposition in Qom as "black reaction." Khomeini replied with greater force, accusing the shah of hostility to Islam and love of Israel, while suggesting that the Iranian people would be glad to see the back of him.

Khomeini was arrested, and riots ensued. The regime kept him in prison for almost a year and then released him. But no sooner was the ayatollah on the loose than he immediately resumed his attacks on the shah and his policies, rallying the faithful against the relentless change coming from the West. So Khomeini was arrested again, and deported to Turkey before finally settling in Najaf, a city sacred to Shiite Muslims situated about one hundred miles south of Baghdad. Although the beneficiary of an extremely expensive education at the ultra-prestigious Institut Le Rosey in Switzerland, the shah had clearly skipped the part of the curriculum that covered the history of the Russian Revolution: Khomeini now joined Marx and Lenin in the ranks of radicals who, through their writings, proved to be deadlier in exile than they would have been subject to restrictions at home.

THROUGHOUT THIS BOOK we have more than once seen dictator-authors discover that truths hitherto concealed from them were lurking in plain view within their sacred texts. Communists in particular were adept at finding that "scientifically proven" historical laws were rather less iron-clad than previously believed. Not that this is anything new: during the Crusades, hard-bitten warrior monks managed to find justification for stupendous acts of violence against the infidel despite Christ's rather overt statements regarding nonviolence in the Gospels.

Necessity, then, is the mother not only of invention but also of reinterpretation. As Khomeini sat in Najaf with his books, watching in horror as the White Revolution unfolded across the border, he began to reflect on the legal concept of "guardianship of the jurist." Traditionally this was understood to refer to the laws regarding an Islamic jurist's responsibility for the lives and property of orphans and widows. But Khomeini saw potential in the idea and would take it much further.

The ayatollah first presented his arguments in a five-volume legal treatise entitled *The Book of Sale*. As the title indicates, it is a work dedicated to the theme of Islamic laws of sale. Deep within its pages, however, Khomeini slyly slips in a scholarly discussion on the plight of orphans that represents a massive expansion of the Islamic jurist's powers. The jurist's duty of care, Khomeini explains, applies not only to a handful of specific family situations but extends to the entire state. It reaches beyond the mosque and into the political and social spheres; in fact, only those who are experts in Islamic law are qualified to lead an Islamic state—which should have an Islamic government and an Islamic legal system.

Khomeini had advanced from opposing the shah to providing the outline for a different model of government. Better yet, he could provide details while retaining all the advantages of arguing for a utopia the likes of which existed nowhere on earth. Unlike the Bolsheviks of 1917, Iranian communists had a real-time example of a communist state directly to the north to point to as a model, and it was obvious to anyone who was not a true believer that there was a lot wrong with it. Khomeini, by contrast, had a vast and precisely detailed corpus of Islamic law that he could point to, and upon which he was widely recognized as a major authority. At the same time, though, his example of applied Islamic government was taken from an idealized golden age, when the prophet Muhammad still walked the earth. It was a time known only from texts, and not based on empirical experience. It was, in short, ideal.

In exile, Khomeini elaborated upon his idea, which received full expression in *Islamic Government*. Like Stalin's *The Foundations of Leninism*, this book originated as a series of lectures developed for students. Khomeini, like Stalin, wanted to popularize his revolutionary idea. To do this, he had to equip his followers with a thorough understanding of the "guardianship of the Islamic jurist." He delivered the lectures in Najaf in 1970; a pupil transcribed them, and they were published in book form in 1971.

Now, a title like *Islamic Government* certainly sounds difficult and forbidding, especially when reading English-language discussions of it that insist on using the Persian *velayat e faqih* instead of "guardianship of the jurist" in the text. *Islamic Government* was the very last dictatorial work I read during my research for this book; I feared something even more abstruse than Mao's "theoretical" works, more so even, as *Islamic Government* is based on a deep reading of Islamic law rather than Stalin's *Short Course* and a handful of Lenin's greatest hits. Yet as I sat down to read it, I soon realized I had misjudged the ayatollah. It's not that *Islamic Government* is a relaxing beach read—far from it—but it is well constructed and clear; lucid, even. Within its pages, Khomeini is methodical and scholarly, but also deeply concerned with communicating clearly. He articulates his ideas with immense precision, carefully demonstrating the chain of reasoning leading to his conclusions. It is as if Khomeini actually wanted to *persuade* his readers rather than browbeat them into submission (Lenin), rant at them until they nodded in assent (Hitler), or conceal his own ignorance through forbidding jargon (Mao). Just as Marx had charged the philosopher with the task of changing rather than interpreting the world, so Khomeini now charged the jurist with the same responsibility. But if that were to happen, the idea would have to be understood. As a result, *Islamic Government* is surprisingly easy to follow.

Khomeini begins his book with a portrait of a nation that has drifted apart from God. He blasts Iran's constitution as a violation of the laws and system of government of Islam, which he declares recognizes neither monarchy nor the principle of succession. Khomeini then looks around and sees a nation corrupted by foreign laws and sexual vice (nothing a little flogging wouldn't help); he is unimpressed by the moon landings (conquering space does not solve social problems or relieve human misery) and laments that imperialist propaganda has gulled many into believing that Islam and politics should be separate ("It is in total contradiction with our fundamental beliefs").

The solution, according to Khomeini, is obvious. He points to the example of Muhammad, who was both a spiritual and a political leader. "It is self-evident," he writes, "that the necessity for the enactment of the law, which necessitated the formation of a government by the Prophet (upon whom be peace), was not confined or restricted to his time, but continues after his departure from this world." Furthermore, he adds, "The glorious Quran and the Sunna* contain all the laws and ordinances man needs in order to attain happiness and the perfection of his state." Khomeini tells his students that they must preach these truths, for "it is your duty to establish an Islamic government."

Khomeini stresses the urgency of this mission by pointing to a crisis not only in Iran, but throughout the Muslim world. The nation of Islam is "weak and divided," he says, and it is the lack of "a leader, a guardian and our lack of institutions of government that made this all possible." Jews, foreigners, minorities and imperialists are to blame. Khomeini demands a return to order and authority. Fortunately, there is a solution: the divine revelation of Muhammad, which, he stresses, has answers to *every* moral, social, and political question, making the business of statecraft much simpler. For instance, since all law comes from the Divine Legislator, then "a simple planning body takes the place of the legislative assembly that is one of the three branches of government." And since Islamic government is a government of law, it stands to reason that the ruler should be an expert in law free from any major sins, the supreme expert in the law, a figure who "must surpass all others in knowledge."

Having laid out his thesis, Khomeini makes a more detailed argument for Islamic government by citing precedents from Islamic history, while also methodically addressing potential objections. Toward the end, he takes a brief detour into conspiracy theory—apparently Jews have introduced errors into some editions of the Quran as part of their plan for world domination—before encouraging his students to lay the groundwork for this new system. By improving the quality of their preaching, they will bring more people back to the true path. Thus, for all the ayatollah's legalistic parsing of historical precedents, the basic ideas are extremely simple: he promises an escape from the chaos of modernity into a state of harmony as it was in the days when Muhammad walked the earth. Muslims have lost their way, but if they listen to the supreme expert—himself, by any chance?—the law will lead them to a better place. Oh, yes, and with God's help they shall "foreshorten the arms of the oppressors" and "root out all traitors to Islam and the Islamic countries."

---

* Legal and social customs and practice of the Islamic community.

However lucid Khomeini's explanation of Islamic government was, it did raise some troubling questions. If "guardianship of the jurist" was the only legitimate form of leadership, why had everybody thought it was about taking care of orphans until now? And what about all the religious teachers and leaders who had come before Khomeini, who had supported monarchic rule? After all those centuries of experts poring over the texts and writing commentaries, you'd think that somebody would have noticed the error. Nor did Iran's senior clergy welcome the sudden revelation that they and their predecessors had been wrong for centuries.

The response to Khomeini's book was not kind. Still, loyal followers continued to smuggle photocopies of his writings and cassette recordings of his sermons across the border into Iran. In 1971, *Islamic Government* was ahead of its time. Fortunately for Khomeini (if not for the shah or anyone who takes a dim view of theocracy), it was ahead by only eight years.

In 1971, Shah Reza Pahlavi celebrated 2,500 years of the Persian monarchy with a grand blowout in the ruins of Persepolis, the ancient capital of the Achaemenid Empire. He had recently had himself crowned Shahanshah ("King of Kings") and now desired that the world witness the glory of the new reality he was establishing in the East. No expense was to be spared as, through a combination of pomp, pageantry and party, he strove to demonstrate the connection between the great civilization of Iran's present and the great civilization of Iran's past.

Since Persepolis itself (while still magnificent) had seen better days, a temporary city of luxury tents kitted out with all modern conveniences was erected among the ruins so that the kings, queens, sultans, presidents, vice presidents and prime ministers who attended could enjoy the celebration in comfort. Persepolis's current inhabitants, a substantial population of scorpions and snakes, were expelled, while chefs from the highly exclusive Maxim's of Paris were flown in to provide fine dining in the desert. The event climaxed with a spectacular fireworks and light show, all of which was captured in a documentary film of exceptional pomposity narrated by no less a figure than Orson Welles (who used his fee to fund an adaptation of *Moby Dick* that never went anywhere). Has there ever been a more textbook case of hubris preceding nemesis? The guest list itself looks eerie in retrospect, as so many of the guests would soon either die, fall into disgrace, or look on impotently as their countries disintegrated. Nicolae and Elena Ceaușescu came to the party; both of them would die by the executioner's bullet. Haile Selassie of Ethiopia also turned up; he would lose power in a coup and then die by strangulation. U.S. vice president Spiro Agnew was there; he would soon resign in order to avoid a jail sentence. Moktar Ould Daddah of Mauritania was in attendance; he was destined to be deposed in a military coup. Mobutu Sese Soko of Zaire watched the fireworks; he would be overthrown in an armed uprising. Imelda Marcos of the Philippines dined on the French cuisine; she would be forced to flee her country following a revolution, leaving behind her precious shoe collection. And this is not to mention the prominent politicians from Yugoslavia, Czechoslovakia and the USSR who witnessed this orgy of self-glorification, blissfully unaware that in two decades' time their own countries would have ceased to exist.

Then, of course, there was the shah, whose Great Civilization was slated for total destruction. Not that he could have imagined such a thing were possible; quite the contrary. He believed that he was reestablishing Iran as a world power. It's not even as if the great celebration of Persepolis was his last act of hubris. In 1976, Iran replaced the Islamic calendar with an "imperial" calendar, its year zero being the coronation of the Persian emperor Cyrus the Great. All at once it was no longer 1355 but 2535, as though Iran had taken a great leap a millennium into the future. In reality, most people continued to live in the era of the prophet.

By this point, the shah was three years away from the end. The truth was that despite his reforms and modernization, he was widely reviled as a tyrant responsible for a corrupt and repressive state. And as dissatisfaction with his policies grew, he relied ever more heavily on the SAVAK, his secret police, to suppress the opposition that came from a mixed coalition of Marxists, nationalists, liberals and religious believers; from readers of both the Islamic-Marxist utopian Ali Shariati and the Islamic revolutionary Ayatollah Khomeini, whose incendiary sermons continued to leak across the border.

In 1975, Ali Shariati, the Marx-reading "Islamic Utopian" who had inspired many of Iran's intellectuals to oppose the shah, died in exile. Khomeini, however, was still very much alive, and intent on filling the gap left by his dead rival and expanding his influence. Alarmed by the spread of his ideas, the shah's regime put pressure on the government in Baghdad to eject the ayatollah from his base in Najaf. On October 6, 1978,

Khomeini was expelled from Iraq, but once again the shah had committed a strategic error. Khomeini moved to a suburb of Paris, where he not only continued to enjoy rude health but also discovered that he had access to all the benefits of a free society. The ayatollah now grew *more* influential. It was at this time that credulous Western writers and intellectuals who had never read a word Khomeini had written began to gather around the exotic holy man with the beard, believing that, because he was from the East, and religious, and opposed the shah's regime, he must be gentle and kind—like Gandhi, as William Sullivan put it. Among these tourists was Michel Foucault, who last appeared in these pages as a "useful idiot" of Chairman Mao's. Foucault traveled to Iran in September 1978, visited Khomeini in Paris in October, and then returned to Iran in November. Knowing very little about Islam or Iran, or Khomeini's hostility toward "the Jews"—or his tendency to say things like "We will export our revolution throughout the world . . . until the calls 'there is no god but Allah and Muhammad is the messenger of Allah' are echoed all over the world"—Foucault waxed lyrical about what Khomeini represented, which apparently was "a revolution of the spirit in an age without the spirit." He reassured his readers that "Islamic government" did not mean "a political regime in which the clergy would have a role of supervision or control" and that "minorities will be protected and free to live as they please on the condition that they do not injure the majority," while "between men and women there will not be inequality with respect to rights, but difference, since there is a natural difference." In reality, of course, it was a revolution that would lead to gay men like him being hung from cranes or forced to undergo sex changes—but there you go. Foucault's terminal credulity resulted in an intellectual failure so complete as to be almost impressive.

The crisis within Iran accelerated, and the center could not hold. On January 16, 1979, the shah ran for the hills—or, rather, exile in Egypt. His American allies had abandoned him, and his Great Civilization had blinked out of existence. Already terminally ill, he was dead within a year.

Khomeini returned to Iran a fortnight after the shah's flight in disgrace. A jubilant throng met him at Tehran airport, while millions lined the streets of the capital to welcome him home. And although he had reassured Western intellectuals and reporters that he had no interest in wielding power directly, it transpired that the things he had written in Iran and Iraq were a better guide to his intentions than the things he had said in Paris. Following a referendum on April 1, Iran was declared an Islamic Republic, and it soon turned out that the unparalleled expert in the law that Khomeini had been talking about in sermons and books such as *Islamic Government*, the one who should run the state, was—surprise, surprise—himself.

The guardianship of the jurist, first expounded in what was ostensibly a book about commercial contracts fifteen or so years earlier, and which had been rejected by many imams when Khomeini expanded upon it in *Islamic Government*, was now enshrined in the constitution. Not only that, but Khomeini was proclaimed Supreme Leader for life; not bad for a cleric from the provinces. And now that he was in power, his interpretation of the law prevailed, the Grand Ayatollah's books became required reading, and the Islamic Republic quickly proved itself move repressive and more violent than the regime it had replaced.

It was all in the texts, of course. But even then, as with the Bolshevik Revolution in 1917, the books were quickly found wanting. In *Islamic Government*, the ayatollah had denounced the constitution of Iran as a Western concept, but his new Islamic state acquired a constitution of its own. He borrowed other ideas from the West, such as an elected presidency and parliament and the separation of powers (although he retained final authority as the Supreme Leader), and he had long peddled a line in anticolonial, anti-imperialist rhetoric that owed more to Marx than Muhammad. The inadequacy of his arguments was also demonstrated in the failure of the guardianship of the jurist to take root in other Shiite communities, despite the dissemination of the ayatollah's books abroad. Without a repressive state machinery to impose the idea, it had no takers.

Nevertheless, his impact was immense. Not only had Khomeini vanquished the U.S.-backed shah, but he had renewed Islam as a political force, and demonstrated that it could be an alternative to the godless utopias that had seduced so many throughout the century. This was a foreshadowing of things to come. No longer would secular millenarians borrow from the religious books; religious millenarians would borrow from the secular, and combine the very old with the relatively new, developing constitutions and republics, and picking and choosing what they required in order to form new hybrids. The ayatollah was a harbinger of a world that is perpetually struggling to be born in blood and fire—and the struggle is far from finished.

Of course, Khomeini had another direct influence: as a literary critic. In

1989 he condemned Salman Rushdie to death for committing a supposed act of blasphemy in a novel the ayatollah had not read and would never read. As a British citizen and (lapsed) Sunni Muslim, Rushdie was in no way subject to the Iranian Supreme Leader's jurisdiction. Yet riots, murders and terrorism followed the *fatwah* calling for Rushdie's death, accompanied by hand-wringing equivocations from Western *bien pensants* who should have known better. Khomeini had demonstrated that Islamic blasphemy laws could be extended to the whole world, and to communities living by entirely different customs and mores than his own. It set a precedent, the depressing consequences of which we are all familiar with today. As in Iran, that which was unimaginable quickly became the reality; we all live in the ayatollah's shadow now.

DISSOLUTION AND MADNESS

1

Midnight in the
Garden of Ultraboredom

Blissfully oblivious to their imminent obsolescence, the leaders of the transnational empire of ultraboredom remained strapped to the writing machine and continued to generate immense quantities of unwanted and useless verbiage. The great men did not realize that they were walking dead men. They thought they still contained life, that the world they ruled still had a future, and that the texts they generated had a place in it, in libraries and homes and in the offices of state.

And so when Yuri Andropov succeeded Brezhnev at the top of the USSR in 1982, the new general secretary (and former head of the KGB) could point to a paper trail accumulated over years that demonstrated his wisdom and fitness to rule. Come and see—*Selected Speeches and Writings, Sixty Years of the USSR, Leninism Shows the Way Forward*—it's all there: the profundity, the page count. And when Andropov died a mere fifteen months into his reign, and Konstantin Chernenko replaced him as general secretary, this ex-homunculus who had masterminded the creation of Brezhnev's memoirs could point to his own substantial publication record to remind the people of the USSR that he, too, was a communist supergenius worthy of reverence. Whether or not anyone had read the likes of *People and Party United, Human Rights in Soviet Society, The Transformational Power of Leninism* or *The Vanguard Role of the Communist Party,* their existence could not be denied. Plans were even afoot to transform Chernenko into a literary character, as scenes from his life were dramatized in a work for the stage entitled *A Man Presents Himself, A Man Is Renowned.* But the play was shelved—it was deemed to be of insufficient quality—and then Chernenko died, after only thirteen months in office.

The communist world had become embalmed in the ideological form-aldehyde of its own deceptions. This was what they had betrayed friends and family for, this was the reason for all the bloodshed, this was the "scientific" conclusion of history. In East Berlin, they were still killing people for trying to cross the border nine months before the wall fell. Between the world and the word there now lay a contradiction so great that not even Mao could have parsed it. The prophecies had failed, the sacred texts were manifestly false. And yet the system lingered on—until, suddenly, it was no more.

The revolutions of 1989 resulted in the sudden collapse not only of the communist system, but also of the authority of its texts. The towering theoretical edifice of Marxism-Leninism, that "queen of sciences" upon which generations of scholars had so thoroughly wasted their intellectual energies, crashed to its foundations. Deprived of their aura of power, millions of volumes of *Complete Works* and *Collected Speeches and Writings* disappeared from hundreds of thousands of bookcases, slipping into the great forgetting with nary a squeak. It turned out that the scientific, immutable laws of history had been entirely imaginary all along. Pick up a copy of a dictator book today and it feels like a relic, like some centuries-old alchemical manual on the transmutation of base metal into gold, written in some lost hermetic language. Gather round, children: it was not so long ago that people still took these ideas seriously enough to kill for them. But what is truly striking is how willingly the leaders of the USSR let their imperium slip into the world of vanished empires. Previously, when the sacred texts were subject to erroneous exegesis at the margins, Moscow sent in the tanks lest the heresy spread. Why, this time, had they failed to move to shore up the faith of their fathers?

In fact, the faith had finally eaten itself—and the texts themselves had played a central role in their own undoing. With the old guard dead and moldering in their graves under the Kremlin Walls, a young reformer by the name of Mikhail Gorbachev became general secretary. Unfortunately for the new leader, he had come of age in a time of optimism, launching his career in the party just as Khrushchev's thaw was getting under way. This had seriously hampered his understanding of what made the USSR function. Gorbachev accepted Khrushchev's naïve good Lenin/bad Stalin dichotomy, and was for almost fifty years a close friend of the Czech communist Zdeněk Mlynář, one of the architects of the Prague Spring that Brezhnev had crushed in 1968. For half a century, Gorbachev and Mlynář shared many conversations regarding how communism could be liberalized and reformed from the inside. It was never the general secretary's intention to destroy the system; he wanted to return to the "true meaning" of the texts, in the hopelessly deluded belief that this would help it last forever. His chief of ideology, Alexander Yakovlev, also believed in a rejuvenation of the USSR via a return to the original intent of the founder, uncovered through a close study of his writings. For Yakovlev, the quasi-religious aspect was not all that quasi: he openly described Gorbachev's policy of perestroika ("reconstruction") as a "reformation," as if it were a purification of the faith, a return to true principles.

But Lenin had generated so much contradictory copy in his lifetime that it was possible to deploy him as an ideological weapon in the service of many different approaches to government. Stalin had grasped the danger in this from the start, which is why he seized control of the regime's new scriptures almost immediately and established himself as Lenin's "most faithful pupil," that none might challenge his authority. Gorbachev and his ideological allies were akin to liberal theologians overlooking all the obvious references to hell and the Last Judgment in the Bible in favor of the nice, socially acceptable material about love and helping others. It's not that the gentler material isn't there, but it is a mistake to deny the significance of the harder, darker message. Thus they promoted the idea of Lenin the liberator, who overthrew the tsar and freed the citizens of the empire, releasing the vast creative potential of the new Soviet nation, but whose work was tragically cut short by a premature death and the rise of the diabolical Stalin. Ignored was the Lenin who executed priests, waged a ruthless civil war and presided over a "Red Terror" in which enemies of the regime were tortured and murdered.

But Gorbachev lived in an intellectual echo chamber, surrounded by like-minded reformers whose grasp on reality had been similarly weakened by their fatal misreading of the sacred texts. He shuffled the party leadership, dabbled with market forces, and relaxed the state's death grip on the Word, while moving the USSR closer to a democratic system. No longer would the party rewrite reality through an endless stream of mendacious texts backed by the threat of violence. The sudden eruption of truth in a vast and inefficient state built upon lies, which was riven with deep economic crisis and ethnic tension, proved to be fatal. By the time Gorbachev and his fellow reformers understood what they had done—if they ever really did—it was too late. When Boris Yeltsin and the leaders of Ukraine and Belarus met in a country house in Belarus in December 1991 to sign the document officially abolishing the USSR, Gorbachev was powerless to prevent its dissolution. The old gods were dead, and their texts had lost all power; after seventy-four years of egregious falsehoods, it was time for some new words.

Then again, perhaps there would be no more. Such at least was the thesis of a U.S. State Department official named Francis Fukuyama, who in his 1992 book *The End of History and the Last Man* argued that humanity had reached the apex of its ideological development, and that beyond the triumph of capitalism and liberal democracy we simply could not go. But while teleological philosophies of history may make sense in the context of broader religious or metaphysical belief systems, it is difficult in the absence of those conditions to see any grounds whatsoever for believing that a bunch of hairless talking apes who are only on the planet because of a large explosion that occurred some thirteen billion years ago should expect so tidy a resolution to their time on earth.

It was not the End of History. It wasn't even the End of Dictator Literature. Old forms persisted, and strange innovations appeared, like the impossible yet hyper-real objects assembled on hazy-terminal beaches in Yves Tanguy paintings. These new works, written at the end of one century and the beginning of another, are less coherent and frequently more personal—even intimate—than those dating from the era of the great dictators and the lesser canon of their successors. Most of the time, they are the work of dictator-authors who began their careers in the age of great ideological conflicts, and who found themselves shipwrecked in the post–Cold War world, obliged either to push doggedly forward with new variations on old themes or to try to invent new systems of thought altogether. They are also, it must be said, often accessible only sporadically, and in translations that are poor even by the standards of the dictatorial canon. To build a complete picture of them is difficult.

Yet these are the books of this transitional era. Perhaps they point us to a way forward, or perhaps they represent dead ends. Regardless, these works exist, and the readerly suffering they represent for those obliged to engage with them is no less real than that of earlier generations of readers in the twentieth century. Let us press on and sample the texts of the era of dissolution and madness.

2

North Korea:
The Metafictions of Kim Jong-il

The Dear Leader checking to see that North Korea's journalists
are following the precepts outlined in his own landmark work
The Great Teacher of Journalists *(1983)*

Kim Il-sung was seventy-nine years old and forty-three years into his reign over the more unfortunate half of the Korean peninsula when the USSR ceased to exist. Now all that work establishing *juche* as an alternative ideology decades earlier really paid off. In 1992 all mention of Marxism-Leninism was deleted from the North Korean constitution as if it had never been there, and Kim—who by this point had a baseball-size goiter emerging from the back of his neck like a second, mutant head of state—carried on regardless.

That said, Kim was in his dotage, and he left the day-to-day running of North Korea to his eldest son, Kim Jong-il, the secretary for organizational affairs. Relieved of the burdens of leadership, the elder Kim was left with abundant time to recollect in tranquility a long life dedicated to the cause of revolution, and to follow the trail blazed by Enver Hoxha, as he gazed within to compose his memoirs, *With the Century*.

Or at least that's what it looked like from the outside. In reality, Kim I was following the path of Brezhnev. He outsourced the creation of his memoirs to a team of propaganda novelists from North Korea's April 15 Literary Production Group, who drew upon revolutionary novels and films to produce an idealized (and highly fictional) account of his life. In old age, Kim I was able to read and enjoy *With the Century*, losing himself in a vast and intricate reimagining of his life the way it should have been, which of course became the way it had been, given the primacy of text over reality in North Korea. Deleting references to Marxism-Leninism from the constitution had not erased the lessons learned from Stalin. Alas, Kim I never got to find out how his life story ended: only eight volumes of a projected thirty were complete by the time he died in 1994. He had been in power for forty-six years: it was enough. Now it was time for the Dear Leader to replace the Great Leader as his son Kim Jong-il (hereafter referred to as Kim II, because, well, why not?) took his place on the throne.

It was a smooth succession, one that Kim II had been planning for years, even if the North Korean *Dictionary of Political Terminologies* had in earlier times denounced hereditary succession as a "reactionary custom" belonging to "exploitative societies." Continuity rather than disruption was key. Kim II loyally maintained his father's cult after his death: there would be no Khrushchev-style tearing down of the predecessor, no quiet Chinese-style sidelining of the former leader's ideas. Quite the contrary: Kim I's mortal remains were embalmed, and his official residence was transformed into a mausoleum, the Kumsusan Palace of the Sun. In 1997 the calendar was revised so that the modern era began with his birth. In 1998 his corpse received a promotion, as the dead leader ascended to the giddy heights of "Eternal President." And of course his body of work remained in print. Kim II not only kept *juche* in place but burrowed deep into its vacuity and hatred and then returned, blinking in the sunlight, to deliver weapons-grade assaults on reality via violently untruthful antiprose.

In April 1991, during the death throes of the USSR, Soviet Georgia voted to secede from the union. Kim II knew which way the winds of change were blowing: less than one month later, he delivered a speech to party officials that was later published as *Our Socialism Centered on the Masses Shall Not Perish*. It was a defiant speech, but also a wholly unoriginal one. Kim II's explanation for why the North Korean version of socialism would not perish was simple: *juche*. His reasons for declaring the ultimate victory of *juche* were also more or less identical to the reasons his father had cited in the late 1960s. The power of *juche* was that it was "man-centered socialism" and that it represented a "man-centered outlook on the world." He elaborates further in a vertiginous spray of solipsism:

> It has clarified the essential qualities of man as a social being with independence, creativity and consciousness. It has, on this basis, evolved the principle that man is the master of everything and decides everything. The Juche idea has established the viewpoint and attitude of dealing with everything in man's interests and approaching all changes and developments on the basis of man's activities. The Juche idea has raised man's dignity and value to the highest level. Because it is the embodiment of the Juche idea, our socialism is a man-centered socialism under which man is the master of everything and everything serves him.

It is only through *juche* that the popular masses can realize their desire for independence, only through *juche* that the masses are protected against the imperialists, who are "working viciously to trample upon the sovereignty of the country and nation." And so on, and so on. Although a mere forty-six pages long, *Our Socialism Centered on the Masses Shall Not Perish* feels much longer, perhaps because it is in essence a continuation of a very long superspeech, an infinite text that had been generating itself for decades. Radical in its unoriginality, Kim II's text defies time, an effect heightened by the dehumanized language and stripping out of references to anything outside his closed rhetorical system (bar the timeless abuse hurled at evil imperialists in America). What crisis is he responding to here? Is there a crisis? Will the war ever end? A rhetoric developed by Stalin and his acolytes returns, reheated, recycled, reused, repurposed in a string of self-referential clusters of jargon and grandiose generalities that could be disassembled and reassembled and placed in a different sequence and still hold the same amount of meaning. Thus Kafka's harrow continued to carve away on the back of a prostrate nation.

It wasn't *all* repetition and continuity, however. Kim II also expanded the field of dictator literature. Unlike his father, who was a military officer before he was a Stalinist homunculus, Kim II was a PR man before he was the heir apparent. He was perhaps the most postmodern of all dictators, the knowing architect of his own elaborate structure of lies, who spelled out in his published oeuvre precisely how he created and maintained the deceits that ensnared North Korea's population.

This was more down to fate than to any arch literary cleverness on Kim II's part. In 1971, at the start of his career, he had led the Workers' Party's Bureau of Propaganda and Agitation, where it was his job to manage Kim I's personality cult—commissioning the construction of monuments, statues and portraits, and overseeing the industrial-scale production of his father's texts. Through the manipulation of words, music and the moving image, Kim II had daily asserted an ideal reality in defiance of the physical one the people of North Korea actually lived in. So when it came time to lay the grounds for succession, Kim II's works on the manufacturing of illusions were just sitting there waiting to be used to establish his authority as a genius without parallel.

Thus, while *Selected Works Volume 1, 1964–69* may contain such rote and uninspiring fare as "On Improving the Work of the Youth League to Meet the Requirements of the Developing Situation," it also includes multiple texts on aesthetics, narrative and the manipulation of fictions. In fact, of the forty-six chapters in the book, twenty-two are dedicated to literature, music and film. Kim II delivers general aesthetic advice in short pieces such as "The Structure of Multipartite Works and the Problem of Dramatic Flow" and also provides case studies of specific works of art he helped produce, as in the essay "On Completing the Film *The Family of Choe Hak Sin* and Making It a Masterpiece Which Contributes to Anti-U.S. Education."

Kim II also generated books on the art of journalism (*Kim Jong-il, the Great Teacher of Journalists*) and the opera (*On the Art of the Opera*). According to the Institute for North Korean Studies, by 1993 his writings on art and aesthetics had mushroomed to an astounding thirty published volumes out of a projected forty. Official figures place the numbers far higher. No doubt he had some "assistance" but, regardless, the direction of his interests was clear. Not since Stalin had there been a dictator as obsessed with aesthetics as the "Dear Leader."

To stress his refined take on the art of telling monumental lies, Kim II had changed the name of the Department of Propaganda and Agitation to the more elegant Literary and Artistic Department. He loved illusions, and the illusions that fascinated him above all were those that danced upon the screen as a play of shadow and light. Kim II was a film fanatic, and he would famously kidnap a South Korean director (and his ex-wife) in the hope that they might be able to help him boost the quality of North Korean cinema. This resulted in the notorious *Pulgasari*, a *kaiju** film set in the Middle Ages that featured a Godzilla-style monster and lots of oppressed peasants. Prior to this, Kim II had upgraded the Pyongyang Film Studio from a relatively bare-bones operation producing simple propaganda films about noble workers, virtuous peasants and the evil Japanese to a well-funded ten-million-square-foot lot where crews labored day and night to churn out propaganda films about noble workers, virtuous peasants and the evil Japanese at a rate of forty per year. Kim II was heavily involved in certain productions, which are known in North Korea as the "immortal classics." He (allegedly) wrote the libretto for the first immortal classic, an adaptation of the opera *Sea of Blood*, and made substantial contributions to *The Flower Girl*, which won the "Prix Special" at the 1972 Karlovy Vary Film Festival in Czechoslovakia. Based on a play attributed to Kim Il-sung, *The Flower Girl* committed to celluloid the story of a Korean peasant lass much tormented by Japanese imperialists until her brother, a member of Kim Il-sung's Liberation Army, arrives to save the day: Kim II not only contributed to the script but also worked on the casting, editing and staging. The Korean War was a perennially popular theme, too, although of course it was never mentioned that Kim I started it or that North Korea would have lost it had it not been for the USSR and China.

Kim II was not just a producer but also a theoretician of cinema. In his *On the Art of Cinema* (1973) he advances a comprehensive vision of filmmaking that ranges from technical advice, to the theory of drama and characterization, to how to ram immense quantities of propaganda down the viewer's throat without causing him to flee the movie theater in great

---

* Japanese term for movie genre in which men in rubber suits pretend to be giant monsters.

haste. Most of the time, however, he trades in banalities. For example, in the section headed *Exacting Standards Should Be Set in Filming and Art Design*, Kim II stresses that "a film's images must look good on the screen." Reading on, we learn that "cinema is a visual art" and that "when the images are attractive to look at, they can instantly draw people into the world of film." Obvious perhaps, but which editor would dare criticize the Dear Leader? Surrounded by yes-men, Kim II perhaps felt it necessary to spell out the basics. That said, he does eventually show a little more nuance. Here, for instance, he calls for a subtler application of music to a picture:

> Music has its own particular part to play in the scene's portrayal of the theme. Music plays its part in the general representation through its own peculiar language, and if it is used to explain the content of scenes in a straightforward manner or simply repeats it mechanically, then it is failing completely to meet the specific requirements of film as a collective art form.

When it comes to acting, Kim II endorses something approaching the Method, while allowing for a modicum of distance between performer and role:

> The actor should be well-versed in acting techniques which allow him to understand and assimilate in detail the diverse and subtle changes of the character's ideas and emotions in relation to a particular situation or event, so that the moment he goes on camera, he is quite naturally drawn deep into the world of the character's life.
>
> An actor who cannot genuinely enter into a character's state of feeling is not yet an actor. He must enter into this state in order to believe in the character as his own self and to act naturally, as though the scene were reality.

Kim Jong-il also notes that (like their imperialist counterparts) some North Korean directors "attempt to exploit the advantages of the wide screen by presenting nothing but large images of objects and crowding a lot of things into a single frame . . . thinking of nothing but the scale and form of the screen and ignoring the requirements of the content to be presented on it." This is an error, says Kim II, for:

[W]hen the form of a piece of work is regarded as good, it is because it matches the content, which has been expressed in an excellent and distinctive fashion, and not because the form itself has some appeal of its own apart from the content . . . A literary work is not regarded as a masterpiece because of its scale, but because of its content; in camerawork, also, it is not the physical scale but the expression of content that should be broad.

In fact, so intent on the primacy of story is Kim II that the first 111 pages of the book are dedicated to "Life and Literature," and it is only after he has established that "content is king" that he begins discussing how to turn that material into a cinematic experience. It's not exactly *Cahiers du Cinéma*, but Kim Jong-il's how-to book actually, well, *makes sense*.

Kim Jong-il died in December 2011 and was succeeded by his son Kim Jong-un. Kim III assumed the title of first general secretary as his dead father was elevated to the rank of eternal general secretary. Now there were two mummies in crystal boxes in the Kumsusan Palace of the Sun, but the regime rolled on without disruption: as Kim III resumed the generation of *juche* speeches and books, it was as if a single, continuously lying mouth had never stopped talking. So it was that in *The Cause of the Great Party of Comrades Kim Il-sung and Kim Jong-il Is Ever Victorious*, Kim III explained that the Workers' Party of Korea had developed into a *juche*-oriented revolutionary party, and that seven decades after the state's founding the revolution was still unfolding, and there were many tasks that needed to be done. Meanwhile, in *Let Us Hasten Final Victory Through a Revolutionary Ideological Offensive*, Kim III stressed the need to launch "a vigorous ideological offensive aimed at accelerating the struggle to defend socialism" by "concentrating all efforts in the Party's ideological work on establishing the Party's monolithic leadership system."

And on, and on, and on . . . and now floating online, so that anybody in the world with an Internet connection can read the words of the new leader. Under Kim Jong-un, North Korea remained dedicated to *juche*, the path of self-sufficiency, while mercilessly rehashing Stalinist formats abandoned practically everywhere else in the world. What else did the regime have to offer but the old lies reheated? In the dying days of world communism, an English doctor named Anthony Daniels passed through North Korea and wrote these words:

. . . within an established totalitarian regime the purpose of propaganda is not to persuade, much less to inform, but to humiliate. From this point of view, propaganda should not approximate to the truth as closely as possible: on the contrary, it should do as much violence to it as possible. For by endlessly asserting what is patently untrue, by making such untruth ubiquitous and unavoidable, and finally by insisting that everyone publicly acquiesce in it, the regime displays its power and reduces individuals to nullities. Who can retain his self-respect when, far from defending what he knows to be true, he has to applaud what he knows to be false— not occasionally, as we all do, but for the whole of his adult life?

They could just as easily have been written today.

3

Cuba: Castro's Maximum Verbiage

Fidel Castro, teetering on the brink of oblivion,
searches for le mot juste.

The implosion of the USSR also placed the Cuban dictator Fidel Castro in a difficult position. How would his three-decade-old regime survive into its fourth without the $4 to $6 billion it received annually in Soviet subsidies? Pundits quite reasonably foretold an imminent end to Castro's reign. And yet, like Kim Il-sung in North Korea, Castro refused to allow so small a thing as the complete failure of communism around the globe to persuade him to accept his obsolescence. He remained in power, standing monument-like amid the rubble of revolution, and would remain "Maximum Leader" for another seventeen years. Even after he had officially retired, he hung around in the background, looming over his little brother, Raúl, never quite able to let go, always ready to lambast the Americans in cranky old-man-style op-eds for the Cuban press. Only death could silence him—and death was a long time coming.

Until he received that visit from the Grim Reaper on November 25, 2016, however, Castro was a great survivor. One of the greatest, even—especially when you consider his penchant for provoking the heavily armed superpower a hundred or so miles to the north. For decades following his overthrow of the U.S.-backed dictator Fulgencio Batista in 1959, successive U.S. administrations, whether Democratic or Republican, raged against him. But Castro survived the debacle of the 1961 Bay of Pigs invasion, in which fourteen hundred CIA-trained Cuban commandos landed on a beach intent on destroying Cuba's meager air force and toppling the dictator. The problem was, they couldn't find any of Castro's planes and wound up surrendering en masse after less than twenty-four hours of fighting. A year later, Castro pulled off a much more impressive act of survival. By assenting to Khrushchev's suggestion that his island nation host long-range nuclear missiles aimed at the United States, Castro did his best to hasten the transformation of Cuba into 42,426 square miles of scorched forest, radioactive rubble and glass beaches while also bringing about the end of civilization in the process. Khrushchev never intended to use the missiles, and in the standoff that ensued he backed down rather than bring about an apocalyptic conflagration between superpowers. Castro, for his part, fired off a letter to Moscow proposing a preemptive nuclear strike on the United States to prevent an invasion of Cuba, which he believed to be imminent. But it was the noncrazed Khrushchev who was soon out of power, while the gung-ho-for-megadeath Cuban dictator remained in his office on Havana's Palacio de la Revolución.

And Castro just kept on surviving. According to Fabián Escalante, the former head of the Cuban secret service, the Maximum Leader survived over six hundred assassination attempts by the CIA during his many decades in power. Even allowing for exaggeration by a regime stooge, it is true that successive U.S. administrations attempted to dispose of the Cuban dictator via a bewilderingly cartoonish set of methods, ranging from weaponized cigars and seashells to botulism-laced milk shakes. The Castro regime was an existential irritant rather than a serious threat to U.S. power. Even so, it was quite the irritant, and the David and Goliath nature of the relationship scrambled the wits of many on the left, causing them to lose all sense of proportion. While the murderous U.S. ally General Pinochet was vilified for the repressions that followed his coup in Chile, praise for the still-more-murderous U.S. enemy Castro flowed from the pens of such highly privileged utopia tourists as Jean-Paul Sartre,* Pablo Picasso, Norman Mailer and Susan Sontag, not to mention less talented figures such as Abbie Hoffman, renowned in his day as the "clown prince of radical protest." Hoffman was particularly slavish in his praise: after witnessing Castro ride through Havana astride a tank on New Year's Day, he wrote this:

> . . . girls throw flowers at the tank and rush to tug playfully at this black beard. He laughs joyously and pinches a few rumps . . . The tank stops in the city square. Fidel lets the gun drop to the ground, slaps his thigh and stands erect. He is like a mighty penis coming to life, and when he is tall and straight, the crowd immediately is transformed.

Needless to say, the mighty penis come to life was cheerfully persecuting protesters, poets and intellectuals in his own country, while also imprisoning people for such crimes as being gay or enjoying rock music. By the 1990s, the mighty penis was looking decidedly flaccid, yet the mere fact that it was still hanging around enabled it to be repurposed as something that desiccated radicals, pseudointellectuals and authoritarian thugs could periodically pull out and wave in the face of American power. Thus in his dotage, Castro proved himself useful to both serious people such as Venezuelan president Hugo Chávez as well as exceedingly trivial people such as Oliver Stone and Sean Penn. And when he died, the tributes flooded in not only from the likes of Vladimir Putin and Bashar al-Assad—whom you might expect to respect a man who had managed to hold on to power for almost five decades—but also from the leaders of liberal democracies such as Spain, or the impeccably progressive prime minister of Canada, Justin Trudeau, who praised Castro's achievements in health care and education, apparently oblivious to the fact that many other countries manage quite well in these areas while also permitting free elections.

Constant throughout the existence of the Castro regime was the Maximum Leader's profound self-regard and love for the sound of his own voice. As Gabriel García Márquez put it, Castro was "addicted to the word"—although García Márquez, gifted with a Havana mansion and

---

* Last spotted in these pages praising Chairman Mao, you will recall.

control of a film institute by Castro, meant it as a compliment.* The dictator's first book, *History Will Absolve Me*, was put together by Castro in prison, as he wrote down from memory the four-hour-long speech he had delivered at his trial over the failed Moncada Uprising in 1953. But four hours was normal by Castro's standards. His capacity to extemporize at length was truly prodigious, as was his disregard for the patience of his listeners. On September 29, 1960, he treated an assembly of world leaders at the United Nations to a speech that clocked in at four hours and twenty-nine minutes, a world record for tedium even by the standards of that august body. But it was his captive domestic audience that suffered the most: in 1986, Castro subjected an audience of delegates at the Communist Party Congress in Havana to a speech that, at seven hours and ten minutes, was only slightly shorter than the working day.

Castro's status as Cuba's pontiff of pontification enabled him to utter into existence a large bibliography of pamphlets and books containing his addresses to the Central Committee of the Cuban Communist Party and to "the people," his thoughts on the "world economic and social crisis," his musings on the "betrayal of Cuba by China," etc. He also published things he had actually taken the time to sit down and write, such as collections of prison letters, newspaper columns and the occasional poem. Both before and after the collapse of the USSR, the authority of "the book" was repeatedly exploited to confer an illusion of sagacity upon assemblages of interviews, speeches and musings, continuing into the twenty-first century with publications such as *War, Racism and Economic Injustice: The Global Ravages of Capitalism* (2002), *Cold War: Warnings for a Unipolar World* (2003), and *Obama and the Empire* (2011).

Castro's gift for stultifying extemporization also led to the generation of a "memoir" of Che Guevara in 1994 (updated in 2006), which is interesting only insofar as how uninteresting it manages to be. Fortunately for Castro, Che's premature death made him a martyr, which, combined with his capacity to look good on posters and T-shirts, only enhanced his value as a symbol of the Cuban Revolution—a fact that Castro mercilessly

---

* García Márquez, a Colombian, was quite generous when it came to slathering unctuous praise upon his patron. Consider for instance this description of what it felt like to listen to one of those very long speeches: "It is inspiration, an irresistible, blinding state of grace, which is only denied by those who have not had the glorious experience of living through it."

exploits over and over again in the speeches collected in the book, which progressively descends ever deeper into propagandistic pabulum.

Having spent decades speaking books filled with his public utterances into existence, in 2006 Castro published an oral autobiography of an ostensibly more intimate nature. Based on over one hundred hours of interviews conducted by the Spanish journalist Ignacio Ramonet, *My Life* is clearly intended to serve as a kind of last testament, in which the then third-longest-serving head of state in the world (after Queen Elizabeth II of the United Kingdom and King Bhumibol of Thailand) would sum up all he was willing to admit about his experience leading Cuba for almost five decades. The timing was right: after a long period in the political tundra, Castro had benefited from a political shift in Latin America that brought leftist governments to power in Venezuela (1999), Brazil (2003), Argentina (2003) and Bolivia (2005). He was suddenly relevant again, a grand statesman rather than a preposterous relic in a military uniform.

Alas, Castro's autobiography is disappointing. Although nowhere near as stilted as the memoirs of Brezhnev, Hoxha or Kim Il-sung, it is nevertheless unrelentingly disciplined in its self-editing and self-presentation. The act of speaking for one hundred hours does not lead to any accidentally revealing slips—or, if it did, Castro edited them out. Thus, although Ramonet describes Castro's speech as a "verbal avalanche" that he always "accompanies with the dancer like gestures of his expressive hands," the dictator remains fully in control and in character throughout. In Cuba, representations of living leaders are forbidden, but since Castro speaks like a very long-winded socialist-realist painting of himself and was on TV all the time, it is clear that all such representations were unnecessary. He had fully merged with his persona, becoming his own living, breathing monument.

And so the book shows us a Castro who throughout his life always takes the greatest risks to spare others the fallout should things go wrong, who always follows the most ethical path, never does anything dishonorable, and becomes leader only because nobody else would do it. Placing Soviet missiles on Cuban soil was not an act of wild recklessness but "absolutely legal, legitimate, even justified." When Ramonet does ask a difficult question, Castro is always prepared with a ratiocination; internment camps for homosexuals become "Military Units to Aid Production," while postrevolutionary executions were merely a result of the people's demand for justice, and so on.

Castro also projects his political and historic consciousness back into early childhood. Apparently his upbringing as the son of a wealthy land-owner equipped him with a profound understanding of the common man, while also giving him the benefit of a quality education. At nine years old he is developing a detailed understanding of the geopolitical situation by following the progress of Mussolini's Italo-Ethiopian War in trading cards that came free with some biscuits. Before he is even a teen-ager, Castro is taking care of the illiterate peasants, as he reads reports on the Spanish Civil War to the family cook, a fire-breathing Republican. He is also the heroic rebel, rejecting "French manners" at the dinner table, or using a slingshot to throw pebbles on the roof of a teacher he disliked—these acts are reported by the fanboyish Ramonet as harbingers of future rebellion.

That said, the book is not entirely a work of auto-hagiography. Ramonet begins *My Life* with a description of Castro's personal office. There is "[a]n immense bookshelf on one wall, and before it, a long, heavy desk covered with books and documents." Castro was a prodigious reader, and through-out the memoir he refers to the books that made an impression on him, from the works of Marx, Lenin and the Cuban revolutionary José Martí (without whose writings he "could not even have conceived of a revolu-tion"); to those of French authors such as Victor Hugo (whose *Les Misérables* he enjoys discussing with Hugo Chávez), Balzac and Romain Rolland (Castro has read all ten volumes of the novel *Jean-Christophe*); to the works of Dostoyevsky, Tolstoy, Benito Pérez Galdós, Régis Debray, Mikhail Sholokhov, Rachel Carson (the mother of the contemporary environmentalist movement) and André Voisin,* author of *Soil, Grass, and Cancer* (1959). Mao, he claims, had less of an influence on him, although he is keen on Cervantes, as well as Arthur Schlesinger's nine-hundred-page book on the Kennedy assassination. Indeed, Castro proclaims him-self "almost nostalgic" for the years he spent in prison, where he could read for fifteen hours a day.

It is when he talks about Hemingway that he finally lets the mask slip. Castro met Hemingway twice, and a signed photograph of the author sat on his desk. But what is the appeal to the Cuban dictator of the macho American author who shot himself? His short sentences? His

---

* Yet he mysteriously neglects to mention the editions of Mussolini's works that sat on his shelves while he was a student.

man-of-action persona? His participation in the Spanish Civil War? None of those things.

"I've read some of his novels more than once," says Castro. "And in a lot of them—*For Whom the Bell Tolls*, *A Farewell to Arms*—he always has his main character talk to himself. That's what I like best about Hemingway—the monologues, when his characters talk to themselves."

4

Iraq: The Historical Romances
of Saddam Hussein

Although today Saddam Hussein may be remembered primarily for his wars, despotism, kitsch palaces and the magnificent beard he was wearing when pulled out of a hole by some GIs in 2003, his name was not always a byword for hirsute evil. In the 1980s, the Reagan administration provided his regime with intelligence and military hardware to aid it in its war with Iran, while in the 1970s, Hussein had talked the talk of secularism, liberation and revolution as a leading member of Iraq's ruling Ba'ath Party ("the Party of the Resurrection"), which was founded in the 1940s by two Syrian schoolteachers, one Christian, the other a Sunni Muslim.

The Ba'ath Party represented a separate strand of Arab nationalism from Nasser's, although Ba'athists too spoke of unity, liberation and socialism and dreamed of a single Arab nation. Hussein himself was yet another autodidact from the provinces who had discovered politics as a teenager. A minority Sunni Muslim in a majority Shia country, he was attracted to the party's message of transcendent Arab unity, and through coups, exile and prison Hussein made a career in politics, finally entering Iraq's government when Ahmed Hassan al-Bakr became dictator following a coup in 1968. Hussein was just thirty-one, but he soon established himself as the power behind the throne. After a decade or so, he stepped forward to establish himself as the actual power *on* the throne: al-Bakr retired due to "ill health" in 1979.

Although Hussein was adept at parroting the language of revolution and liberation, and had not entirely wasted Iraq's oil revenues (standards of living were high for the region, while he had also developed industry, education and health care), it was clear from the start of his dictatorship that he was not a very nice man. George H. W. Bush and George W. Bush were both wont to compare him to Hitler, but the Ba'athist leader had another dictatorial model, and one he was not even shy about. He openly emulated Stalin, and not just in the sense that he wore a thick mustache and had a fondness for military titles despite never having served in the military. Shortly after becoming president, Hussein declared that the Ba'athists had entered their "Stalinist era" and announced his intention to "strike with an iron fist against the slightest deviation or backsliding." And strike he did, accusing sixty-eight high-ranking party members of treason at a party assembly one week after coming to power. Twenty-two were executed *pour encourager les autres*, and purges, torture, and political murder would become hallmarks of his regime.

Then there was the florid personality cult,* the paranoia, the repression of minorities, the pretend closeness to the people—Hussein had a direct telephone line to the presidential palace installed in the 1980s—and the books, so many books, although Hussein, like Stalin, did not claim to be an ideological innovator but rather the "best pupil" of the party's chief ideologue (in this case, Michel Aflaq). His own works were flat, dull and serious, and the illusion of a substantial bibliography was fostered by the (now thoroughly standard) dictatorial sleight of hand of collecting speeches, repackaging long interviews, and appending the preposition *on* to collections of banalities in order to create the impression of theory.† So it was that such classics as *On History, Heritage, and*

---

* Statuary representing Hussein was remarkably diverse in its themes: he appeared dressed as a businessman, a soldier, a sportsman, a pilgrim kneeling in prayer, a loving father, the wise father with his son on his knee, etc. In propaganda posters, he might appear alongside the Ancient Babylonian king Nebuchadnezzar in his chariot; he also liked to be compared to Saladin while court poets sang the praises of the "Shaper of History" and credited him with the creation of a "new Arab man."

† Literary aspiration ran in the family: in the early 1980s, one of Hussein's uncles published a book titled *Three Whom God Should Not Have Created: Persians, Jews, and Flies*. Persians were defined as "animals God created in the shape of humans." Jews were "a mixture of the dirt and leftovers of diverse people." Flies, "[w]hom we do not understand God's purpose in creating," were the least troubling of the three.

Religion (1981), *Our Policy Is an Embodiment of the Nation's Present and Future* (1981), *Thus We Should Fight Persians* (1983), and *America Reaps the Thorns Its Rulers Sowed in the World* (2001) became physical objects that existed in the world. It was a generic oeuvre: at least two of those titles could easily be appended to texts by Fidel Castro or any North Korean leader of the last seventy years. Some of it was even quite reasonable: *The Revolution and Woman in Iraq* (1977) contains lots of progressive words about the importance of educating women and getting them into the workforce. A society cannot be free until women are free, says Hussein, and a "revolution is not a true revolution if it does not contain the liberation of women." As for the forces holding them back, Hussein uses coded language, referring only to "chains of backwardness imposed by the past" rather than to specific Islamic laws or customs. Even the Butcher of Baghdad knew when to watch his words.

That was Saddam Hussein in his modernizing heyday. In the 1980s, however, a religious element erupted in his rhetoric and cult. Facing off against the theocratic dictator of Shiite Iran, Hussein began to identify himself and Ba'athism with the defense of Sunni Islam against the nefarious Persians, whom he accused of using religion as a smoke screen for what was really a war of revenge for the Arab conquest a millennium and a half earlier. As the years passed and his troubles multiplied, Hussein leaned ever more heavily on Islam and the glorious military history of the Arabs for his personality cult. For instance, he produced "proof" of his descent from Muhammad, and named his private plane *al-Buraq*, after the miraculous horse on which the prophet rode from Mecca to Jerusalem in a single night, while a poet acclaimed him "Lord" Saddam, who had "brought the light of God / to the Arab tribes / And broken their idols / In long times past." Toward the end of his regime, following the disaster of the First Gulf War and the ensuing years of U.S. sanctions, Hussein even commissioned a hemoglobin-Quran written in his own blood as a sign of his dedication to Islam.

Meanwhile, Hussein's own writings entered a new phase. Whereas his previous publications had been somewhat rote exercises in dictator literature offering little in the way of innovation, he now began a radical experiment. He would use prose not as an expression of the personality cult, but of the personality itself, and attempt to communicate directly with "the people." In other words, he began to write like a "real" author, and in the process of doing so became the first sitting dictator to author a work of fiction since Franco had knocked out *Raza* in a couple of weeks in 1941. However, Hussein's novel, a historical-philosophical romance entitled *Zabiba and the King*, was more ambitious and much more personal than Franco's stiff melodrama. By no means is it good, but it is at least the work of a man rather than a monument, and, in comparison to most other works in the dictatorial canon, very honest.

According to Sa'adoon al-Zubaydi, who was for many years Hussein's English interpreter but who ended his years of service as his de facto editor, *Zabiba and the King* is the most autobiographical of the dictator's works. Hussein began writing the book in 2000, after falling in love with the twenty-four-year-old daughter of one of his advisers. A mere thirty-nine years his junior, she became his fourth wife and, says al-Zubaydi, gave the besieged and disillusioned dictator renewed "inspiration" and "vitality"—and even "encouraged him to pick up pen and paper." Thus inspired by this sensation of renewed passion, Hussein descended from his plinth and became a vulnerable mortal again as he sat down to crank out the tragic story of an isolated, alienated pagan king and the beautiful young Muslim woman who loves and dies for him. Although biographical, the book is not an autobiography; nor is it a direct allegory for the relationship between Iraq and the evil, imperialist United States, although such an interpretation is defensible. No: *Zabiba and the King* is altogether wilder and much more interesting than that.

Unlike many twentieth-century dictators who could write professionally enough—at the level of a journalist, at least—Hussein is an amateur. But he is an amateur in the most interesting sense, in that he can't quite control his words* or his subject matter, and he certainly can't control his book's structure. This gives his novel something of the quality of a work of outsider art in prose form.

He begins with a long preamble loftily invoking the glory of Iraq before switching to the story-within-a-story framing device familiar from such works as *The Arabian Nights*. However, he immediately alerts the reader to the fact that this will be no work of adventure, humor or scandalous eroticism but something much weightier. Dictators are the enemies of laughter, after all, and although many enjoy interesting sex lives in pri-

---

* In an interview with *Ha'aretz*, al-Zubaydi complained, "When he stumbled upon a new word, especially a complicated one, he would become fascinated with it and use it again and again, almost always inappropriately."

vate, they almost always impose puritanical moral codes on their subjects. And so Hussein stresses that the book will be serious, as "in Iraq it
is not customary to tell vain tales and jokes." Then, to double down, he
makes the narrator not a beautiful princess seeking to evade death at the
hands of a capricious and sex-crazed tyrant but a man retelling a story he
heard as a boy from an elderly grandmother in Tikrit (not coincidentally
Hussein's own birthplace). Yet Hussein the author is as reluctant to relin-
quish control as Hussein the dictator; no sooner has the grandmother
squeezed out a couple of paragraphs than he interrupts her with a string
of anguished interjections on the inner turmoil of the ruler.

> Did not the soul of the one who had surrounded himself with a multitude
> of useless things become burdened by the intricate maze of his palaces,
> their furniture and thick walls? Had not his soul died as a result, having
> completely lost its aesthetic sense?

Only on page 8 does Hussein's narrator relent on the dictatorial cries
for help and permit the grandmother to take over and tell the story of a
powerful, proud king who "wanted kings who ruled in the far reaches of
the world to submit to him." Then the story begins, as the king stumbles
upon a palace almost as big as his own while out riding one day. Living in
a hut on the outskirts of the estate (which belongs to a merchant named
Hiskil) are Zabiba and her elderly father. Dazzled by her beauty and wisdom, the king invites her to his palace, where he learns her tragic back-
story: economic necessity forced her father to marry her off to her brutish
cousin, a member of Hiskil's gang.

Then something strange happens. Rather than have the cousin killed
and make Zabiba his concubine—as you might reasonably expect a
seventh-century pagan monarch to do—the king instead opts to spend
his evenings and nights in chaste discussions with her about leadership
and statecraft. In these conversations, it is Zabiba who schools the king,
seeking to bring him closer to his subjects, delivering herself of insights
like this: "You need to become a living particle of the people, its conscience,
thoughts and deed."

Sometimes Hussein inserts elements of his own life story into the
novel. When the king explains to Zabiba how, as a boy, he was ejected from
his mother's house to live with an uncle and then summoned back to live
among relatives who despised him, this fits closely with Hussein's own

experience. Most of the time, however, the parallels are less direct, and if the king is intended as a self-portrait, then it is an exceedingly unflattering one. (Although if read as a before-and-after tribute to Hussein's new young wife, the book is extremely flattering.) Until he meets Zabiba, the king is a detached, remote ruler who does not understand his people. He is not a Muslim but a bumbling, accident-prone pagan who complains about losing the key to the closet where he keeps his god; it is Zabiba who teaches him about Islam.

Also, the king is very stupid. After Zabiba snatches away a cup of poisoned chamomile tea from her beloved's lips, she whispers:

I fear that this may be a new poisonous arrow, which is intended to kill you and me as well.

To which the impossibly dense king replies:

But a chamomile brew is not an arrow!

After which Zabiba patiently explains:

I am speaking figuratively, only using the arrow as a comparison . . .

Sometimes the narrative rises above somniferous political discourse and clumsily executed plot devices. Hussein's king is trapped in a loveless marriage and comes to yearn for more than just Zabiba's musings on statecraft. In a poetic evocation of the anguish of separation, Hussein declares the king jealous "of the air and the water and even of every morsel of food in her mouth." At other times, the king laments his awful isolation with such intensity that you can almost hear Hussein himself bleating in his bedroom at night as he hides out at yet another undisclosed location, alone again (naturally).

Surrounded by plotting courtiers, relatives, and servants, not to mention a hostile wife, the king explains that it was his yearning for human contact that caused him to fall in love with Zabiba:

I fell in love with you so that my soul would not wither and so that I would not depart from real life. I wanted to remain close to the people, so that I could be a part of it and lead it after me. I do not want to become one of the gods that stand in the holy places and who receive promises from those presenting their requests. I want to live with you, and among you and meet sunrises with you.

In the physical world, Hussein ruled by inspiring fear. In the world he created on paper, the king loves and is loved back. In the perfunctory fight scene that ends the novel, Zabiba hurls herself in front of a sword aimed at the king, whose name (she finally reveals) is "Arab." Love inspires both Zabiba and the people to rise up in defense of their leader and their land from a depraved foreign invader. Allegory takes over. America loses; the Arabs win, and in spite of the tragedy of Zabiba's death things will only get better.

Hussein's amateurism shines through in this idealized ending. He is not yet in total control of the narrative, and through his incompetence as a storyteller inadvertent revelations emerge. It is striking that the climactic battle scene is over in precisely two paragraphs, and that the king is almost completely absent from the combat scenes—until you remember that Hussein never served in the military and had no experience of combat. Unable to imagine a thing he had never experienced, Hussein becomes as bodiless as Brezhnev when confronted by war.

When it comes to rape and sexual abuse, however, Hussein is lavish in his detail. Zabiba complains early and often about the loveless sex her husband forces upon her: "I am dead in my house, and my corpse is decaying when I am in bed with my husband." Necrophilia is an insufficiently potent metaphor for Hussein, so he combines it with bestiality as Zabiba complains that her husband uses her as a ram might a sheep, interested only in the frequency of his performance and not in her sexual pleasure. Then, in one of the strangest passages in dictator literature, Zabiba spins a tale of man-bear love, which Hussein appears to think is a thing in northern Iraq. Zabiba contrasts her husband's seduction techniques unfavorably with those of the polymorphously perverse honey eaters:

Even an animal respects a man's desire, if it wants to copulate with him. Doesn't a female bear try to please a herdsman when she drags him into the mountains as it happens in the North of Iraq? She drags him into her den, so that he, obeying her desire, would copulate with her? Doesn't she bring him nuts, gathering them from the trees or picking them from the bushes? Doesn't she climb into the houses of farmers in order to steal some cheese, nuts and even raisins, so that she can feed the man and awake in him the desire to have her?*

Well . . . no, actually.

The degradation escalates as Zabiba reveals that her husband participates in rape orgies that his patron, Hiskil, arranges for emirs, ministers, and noblemen, not to mention "large, small and medium scale pimps." A popular game is "Tearing in the woods":

The game was played like this: Everybody would run out of the palace into the garden and yard, and then the men would try to take the women. Any woman could be "Torn apart" by any man and they had no previous agreement. A woman could defend herself using only her hands, while the man would try to take her, till he overcame her by force. Or they would pretend to defend themselves.

If the women refuse to participate, then their men divorce them. Only Zabiba, "the daughter of the people and its conscience," manages to hold herself aloof, even as drunken emirs fall at her feet and sinister foreigners with fair skin and blue eyes show up. At this point, Hussein reveals rather too much about himself, as it is only after hearing these tales of rape games that the king finally consummates his relationship with Zabiba. We are a long way from the book's origins as a child's tale spun by a kindly grandmother, although the long philosophical conversations throughout have already established substantial distance. And yet, intriguingly, it's at this climactic moment in the narrative, when the king penetrates Zabiba, that Hussein suddenly remembers his original narrative device. After 120 pages, the kindly grandmother suddenly reappears and addresses the young boys in her audience:

The old woman continued: "Some lust to have the King's concubines, their wives and daughters. Isn't that very lust, in a way, the beginning of

---

* In a footnote, the translator of the English edition suggests that the bear is a metaphor for Russia, but Russia is not Iraq's neighbor to the north. And so it remains mysterious.

a yearning to acquire something which is not at all possible? In that case, how is lust different from yearning?"

Following these profound philosophical musings, she then alerts one of the older boys to the danger of nocturnal emissions: "If you start thinking of them, at night you will dream you have taken one of them." A page or two later, she reappears to describe in graphic detail how, as Zabiba is riding home from the palace, she is knocked from her horse, bound, gagged, raped, and raped again—all by her husband, who is wearing a mask and whose throat she tears at with her teeth. As the narrator puts it, "I knew that Grandmother always found stories with a moral for us."

Thus, like all great novels, even though it is actually a terrible novel, *Zabiba and the King* has a life of its own. It reveals, and conceals, and plays games with its reader. In the final days of his rule, Saddam Hussein became a bona fide writer. He wasn't just a political figure brutalizing his subjects with crude mendacities; he was a man seeking to tell the truth about his own experience through narratives. If it wasn't quite the whole truth, and if he distorted things and exaggerated and even lied at times, then doesn't that make him all the more a novelist?

So dedicated was Hussein to this new career that, according to al-Zubaydi, he neglected his duties as dictator in the last years of his regime, instead "shutting himself up in his office and writing." In novels such as *Walled Fortress, Men and the City,* and the stirringly titled *Get Out, You Damned One!* Hussein wove yet more tales of kings and princes, and of love, invasion and betrayal. Although he published these books anonymously ("a novel written by its author"), it was no secret in Iraq or anywhere else in the world who was responsible for these thrilling volumes, and if there had been, the obvious lack of craft was enough to dispel suspicions professional ghostwriters were involved.

The books were so personal, so important to Hussein that he worked on them right up until the end of his rule. He finished *Get Out, You Damned One!* right before the Battle of Baghdad in 2003. Editing continued throughout the fighting, and the presidential publisher Al-Hurriah ("Freedom") completed printing of the book mere hours before fighting ceased and the United States cemented its conquest of the city. The title of this last novel was a direct rebuke to the invading American forces, the same forces who dragged him out of the hole where he was hiding and handed him over to his people.

These were the same people to whom he had addressed *Zabiba and the King*, and to whom he had bared his soul again and again, in novel after novel, in a desperate effort to connect.

Reader, they hanged him.

5

Post-Soviet:
Comrade Zoroaster

In Russia, the 1990s represented a transitional era, a groping in chaotic darkness toward a state not yet born. Almost overnight, the desiccated linguistic rituals practiced for seventy years crumbled to dust. Those who sought to make a career in the era of bandit capitalism ceased to be "comrades" or to speak of five-year plans and production quotas, or to seek apposite quotes from Lenin to illustrate their points. Instead, they attempted to conjure up a new reality based on a different set of incantations. Now words such as *oligarch, privatization, loans-for-shares* and *shock therapy* held all the sacred mystery.

In this context, the Soviet practice of generating "theory" seemed like a quaint and almost inexplicable superstition from a simpler and more naïve time. The dictator book, symbol of a failed and vanished empire, had lost its status, and it was no longer necessary even to pay lip service to the works of Lenin and his successors. That was left to the likes of Gennady Zyuganov, the mediocrity who took over leadership of the Communist Party of the Russian Federation in 1993, and who has led it ever since in its long, futile winter. He published a book about Stalin as late as 2009, as if the Marxist-Leninist tradition still mattered and the accretion of words was still a crucial step in a political career. In truth, it was an empty act of ancestor worship.

This is not to say that the words of the leader had lost all significance. Russian book worship predated the Soviets, and the new, democratically elected president Boris Yeltsin still published volumes with his name on them, but he did so after the fashion of a democratic, Western politician— that is to say, his books were not works of ideology or even faux ideology but merely self-justifying memoirs, composed by a professional ghost-writer, through which he hoped to fatten his bank balance. Yet as ephemeral and unnecessary as Yeltsin's books may have been, they still had a great (if indirect) impact on the future of the country. When his second volume of memoirs, *Notes from a President*, did not generate the million dollars in foreign royalties Yeltsin had hoped for, the notorious oligarch Boris Berezovsky stepped in to "fix" the situation. Berezovsky arranged for the book's publication in Russia and later claimed that he had paid millions of dollars in "royalties" into Yeltsin's bank account, stuffing the president's pockets to a more acceptable degree. Having performed this service to Russian letters, Berezovsky gained access to the president's inner circle, and it was in his role as éminence grise of the Kremlin that he would later push for the appointment of an ex-KGB colonel named Vladimir Putin to serve as Yeltsin's successor.

Within a year of Putin's election, Berezovsky would be living in exile, as it turned out that his chosen puppet was much less easy to dupe than Yeltsin. And as Putin steadily consolidated and expanded his power, it became clear that he had less interest in covering himself with literary glory than any Russian leader since Tsar Nikolai II. Despite his concern with identifying a "national idea" for post-Soviet Russia, he did not start cranking out essays on the topic, and even if he liberally sprinkled references to philosophers throughout his speeches, he did not collect those speeches into fat hardcover volumes that every local satrap was obliged to display in his office. He resurrected Soviet symbols and the old national anthem (albeit with new lyrics) and replaced the word *Volgograd* with *Stalingrad* at the Eternal Flame by the Kremlin Walls, but he was considerably less interested in the sacred texts of the old regime. His concern was to control television rather than print, and so instead of publishing incredibly long speeches between covers, once a year he participated in incredibly long phone-in chats with the nation instead. Meanwhile, his own PR people introduced something new to Russian propaganda: a Mussolini-style emphasis on the dynamic, living body of the leader.

Whereas Stalin had placed a carcass at the heart of the USSR, Putin flew planes and frolicked with tigers, posed shirtless on horseback and splashed about in the water with a hunting rifle. What texts he did issue were few in number and pragmatic. *First Person*, based on over twenty-four hours of interviews, was published in 2000 to introduce him to the world: its most interesting passage may be a brief discourse from Putin on the lessons he learned observing a cornered rat.* His next book, *Judo: History, Theory, Practice* (2004), stressed his credentials as a vigorous yet highly disciplined man of action—in stark contrast to his bloated, alcoholic predecessor. An actual honest-to-god bona fide judo manual complete with lots of drawings of men in pajamas grappling with each other, *Judo: History, Theory, Practice* may yet reveal some insights beyond its apparently simple purpose. In particular, the exploration of *kuzushi*, judo's art of unbalancing, surely reveals much about Putin's strategy in international politics, where he often turns an apparent weakness into an advantage against a theoretically stronger foe.

It was not until 2015, when Putin was a decade and a half into his rule, that anything appeared with his name on it that fit the conventions of the dictator book and—even then—there were significant differences. *Words of a Changing World* was a collection of nineteen speeches and articles attributed to Putin. By this point, a Soviet dictator would have managed to fill at least ten volumes with this type of material, but restraint was not the only difference. As a literary object, *Words of a Changing World* looked completely different from any dictator book that had preceded it. Printed on glossy paper and filled with colorful photographs and memorable quotes, it resembled not so much a solemn tome of theory as a shiny hardcover prospectus prepared by a marketing team to be handed out at international conventions.

---

* "There, on that stair landing, I got a quick and lasting lesson in the meaning of the word *cornered*. There were hordes of rats in the front entryway. My friends and I used to chase them around with sticks. Once I spotted a huge rat and pursued it down the hall until I drove it into a corner. It had nowhere to run. Suddenly it lashed around and threw itself at me. I was surprised and frightened. Now the rat was chasing me. It jumped across the landing and down the stairs. Luckily, I was a little faster and managed to slam the door shut in its nose."

IF DICTATOR LITERATURE had withered away in the former New Jerusalem, the tradition received new life in the Central Asian republics of the former USSR. In the explicitly authoritarian regimes of Kazakhstan, Uzbekistan, Tajikistan and Turkmenistan (and even in the less authoritarian regime of Kyrgyzstan), the ideal of the leader-genius persisted, as did the compulsion to demonstrate that genius by writing things. The disappearance of the unifying Marxist-Leninist ideology had created a greater vacuum in Central Asia than in Russia, which at least had its long imperial past to fall back on as an alternative to its Soviet identity. The nations of Central Asia, by contrast, were patchwork amalgamations of ethnicities, ancient city-states, and warring tribes that had been stitched together in the 1920s by Soviet "experts," overwriting a complex history that stretched back millennia.

These "experts" had not only drawn up the borders, at times dividing ancient communities (for instance, assigning ancient centers of Tajik culture to Uzbekistan), but also introduced the very concepts of "nationality" and "socialism" as replacements for clan and tribal loyalties. Soviet nation builders had torn off veils, suppressed Islam and waged a decades-long war against rebels who eventually surrendered or disappeared over the border into Afghanistan. Meanwhile, they had imported a newly minted socialist written culture to replace the much older, primarily oral local cultures. Literacy campaigns produced millions of new readers, and under Stalin, Russian "engineers of the soul" were dispatched to the region to train local writers and artists in how to write novels, plays and poetry in the socialist-realist style.

The instant nullification of all of that in 1991 left the ex-communist presidents of these newly independent states searching for new justifications for their authority. If the goal was no longer the defeat of imperialism, the triumph of the proletariat and the dream of "full communism," then what was it? More to the point, how to unite the disparate nationalities and clans over whom they now had dominion? And how to justify that dominion?

To a man, the new presidents of Central Asia were the intellectual products of the Soviet Union, and Stalin-style they displayed a freewheeling disregard for accuracy in interpreting what had actually happened in the territories they now controlled. Instead, they projected national identities that were inventions of the communist era into the ancient past. Stripped of Marxist-Leninist content, the forms nevertheless endured. In Uzbekistan, Timur the Magnificent was reborn as a national hero rather than as the leader of a pan-Islamic empire; he replaced Lenin on plinths. Kazakhstan's Nursultan Nazarbayev laid claim to the great medieval philosopher and poet al-Farabi; he replaced Lenin on currency. Tajikistan's Emomali Rahmon went one better and recast the prophet Zoroaster, founder of the ancient religion of the Persian empire, as a Soviet-style ethical superman to be emulated by all Tajiks.

Lenin and Stalin were gone, but they cast long shadows—as did their bibliographies. It was not enough merely to find heroes in the past; new heroes had to be created, too, and the Central Asian dictators used books to establish their authority and buttress their own personality cults. However, they attempted to adapt their published works to the new era, writing in a style better attuned to the modes and mores of the age. In order to signal to the world that they were reliable business partners and ready for investment, some of them adopted the tropes of responsible enlightened capitalism, of democracy and liberalism. That said, the authoritarianism was never that far from the surface—there was the domestic audience to consider, after all.

A good case study is Nursultan Nazarbayev, the president of Kazakhstan. This is a vast, resource-rich state with a nominally Muslim Kazakh majority but which also has sizable populations of practically every other nationality in the former USSR, with Russians being the largest group and especially heavily represented in the country's Soviet-era capital Almaty. Nazarbayev flirted with Kazakh nationalism and Islam, but also portrayed himself as a modernizer and unifier, a wise leader tolerant of all faiths, intent on economic development and maintaining good relations with other countries in the world (all the while making it patently clear that he would never risk loosening his grip on power).

In his post-independence publications, Nazarbayev inclined toward a late-Soviet approach. He was unshocking, reassuring and fundamentally unrevolutionary, although also eager to demonstrate his psychological freedom from Marxist-Leninist taboos and signal his readiness to make deals and do business. Reading his books, you'd think the decades he had spent mouthing socialist platitudes had never happened. The very titles were bland and soothing in an almost Clintonian or Blairite "Third Way"* fashion.

Who, after all, could take issue with something called *The Critical Decade: A Strategy for the Development of Kazakhstan as a Sovereign State*, or *Kazakhstan on the Threshold of the 21st Century*? And if a reader did dip inside, he or she would find no radical ideas, no verbal assaults on imperialism or cries of solidarity with the global oppressed but rather Nazarbayev's musings on policy, development and the economy, as well as lots of nice words about maintaining harmonious relationships between nationalities and religious groups. Nazarbayev was particularly keen to stress his credentials as a man able to see beyond Cold War conflicts, who had done his bit to reduce the risk of nuclear Armageddon. Thus in *Epicenter of Peace*, published on the tenth anniversary of Kazakhstan's independence, Nazarbayev reminded his people (and the world) of his willingness to give up the vast arsenal of atomic weapons that the nation had inherited from the USSR. He had also closed the Semipalatinsk Test Site, where the USSR had detonated more than 450 bombs over a forty-year period. Through his ever-expanding bibliography, Nazarbayev (who styled himself the First President) has continued to stress his credentials as a civilized, kindly type, a combination of wise father and shrewd CEO of Kazakhstan Corp. His was a new, bland, Davos man style of dictator literature.

However, as the years passed, so Nazarbayev grew more extravagant and more ambitious. Stupendous oil and gas revenues enabled him to pursue immense vanity projects, the foremost of which was the construction of an entirely new capital, Astana ("Capital"), in the center of the country. Among the futuristic structures erected in the windswept steppes was a two-hundred-foot-high glass pyramid designed by Norman Foster with the grandiose name the Palace of Peace and Reconciliation. Here Nazarbayev staked his claim to higher, transnational ideals: the palace was intended to represent all the planet's religions as well as every ethnic group in Kazakhstan, and came with a fifteen-hundred-seat opera house. Of course, as far as messages to the planet go you can do a lot worse, and Nazarbayev the dictator-unifier also expressed his enlightened ideals in print. In 2009 he issued *A Strategy of Post-industrial Society Formation and the Partnership of Civilizations*, which was followed by a sequel, *Radical*

---

* As opposed to the Third Way of Italian Fascism, or Gaddafi's Third Universal Theory, of course.

Renewal of Global Society (2010). In these books, the planet healer with 91.5 percent of the vote revealed his thoughts on development in the postindustrial era and relationships between "global civilizations"—while also throwing in bonus musings on the environment, energy security and technology to further aid humanity on its voyage into the future:

> The twenty-first century that we are now entering is a period which will scc a dcepening of integration between the various communities on the planet and an intensification of their dialogue and partnership in order to resolve the new range of problems facing mankind as a whole. I think we can be confident in saying that the contemporary world at the beginning of the twenty-first century is one of local societies which display the variety of our historical experience and the contemporary life of the communities which constitute them. It is only by preserving and developing this variety within the framework of partnerships that societies can hope to flourish in the future, and make possible the avoidance both of conflict between them and of the threat posed by accumulated stockpiles of weapons.

And there's a lot more where that came from. Nazarbayev may have excised the Marxism-Leninism, but he still retained the ability to generate sententious statements about world peace in the classic Soviet style.

There does seem to be something personal about this flood of text, however—as if Nazarbayev truly does believe that his experience of steering multifaith, multiethnic Kazakhstan through the post-Soviet period without significant violence really does qualify him as a sage with serious teachings for a troubled planet. In 2014, Nazarbayev appropriated the U.S. tradition of opening a presidential library dedicated to himself while still alive. It contained not only his official archive but also, in a nod to his Soviet precursors, his personal library—some twenty thousand books amassed since the 1960s. Nazarbayev thus presented himself as not only an exceptional leader but also a super reader and man of knowledge. And alongside treasures from his personal collection—such as a Quran that spent time in outer space and a rare book of sketches by Leonardo da Vinci—Nazarbayev's own collected works occupy plenty of shelf space. In addition, the entire presidential corpus is freely available online for the entire species (or at least the part with an Internet connection) to read, that we all may learn from Nazarbayev's wisdom and begin to heal.

———

Two other Central Asian presidents generated books with a similarly bland, pro-stability, pro-market, pro-development tone. President Askar Akayev of Kyrgyzstan, who prior to his ascent to power had authored scientific works with titles such as *Optical Information Processing Methods* (1988), produced *Thinking About the Future with Optimism* (2004), even though he was about to be chased out of the country following a coup. In next-door Uzbekistan, notorious strongman Islam Karimov combined acts of violent repression with a publishing slate that featured books with upbeat titles such as *Uzbekistan: The Road of Independence and Progress* (1992) and *Building the Future: Uzbekistan—Its Own Model for Transition to a Market Economy* (1993), as well as *Uzbekistan on the Threshold of the 21st Century* (1997). Karimov was less successful than Nazarbayev at passing himself off as a modern chief executive. In the early twenty-first century, he won U.S. favor by offering his services in the war on terror, but the relationship soured after a widely reported massacre in the city of Andijan made the relationship untenable. Karimov carried on regardless, torturing his enemies, tossing "extremists" into penal colonies and eventually placing his own daughter under house arrest while continuing to publish books with optimistic titles. In 2009, he issued *The Global Financial-Economic Crisis, Ways and Measures to Overcome It in the Conditions of Uzbekistan*, while in 2015, the year before his death, he produced *Serving in the Path of Happiness and Great Future of Our Motherland Is a Top Value*. Even as he strove to throw off the Soviet past and provide the Uzbeks with an alternative identity, Karimov nonetheless ensured that another aspect of Stalin's literary technique endured into the twenty-first century: the use of incredibly flat yet upbeat prose to exclude the possibility of holding any discussion of what was actually happening in the world.

Explicit in the texts of Nazarbayev, Akayev, and Karimov was an awareness of another reality: the Western way of life, with its money, comfort and consumer goods. In order to gain access to that reality, they knew they had to adopt its language and mimic its ideas—up to a point. But what if you couldn't attract Western investment, or weren't that interested in it due to the concessions you would have to make? What if you were ruling a war-torn land next door to Afghanistan and still relied on military support from Russia?

Such was the scenario faced by the Tajik dictator Emomali Rahmonov (subsequently "Rahmon" after a bout of decolonization that saw Russian suffixes removed from all Tajik names). An ex–collective farm boss, Rahmon had seen his nation torn apart in a vicious civil war between the Soviet successor regime and radical Islamist forces that lasted from 1992 until 1997. Between 60,000 and 100,000 people died in the conflict, while another 730,000 were displaced. Already the poorest of the Central Asian states, Tajikistan suffered a further $7 billion in damage due to the war.

With his country ravaged by conflict and bereft of the natural resources that enabled some other Central Asian states to fund titanic construction projects, Rahmon did not have an upbeat message of togetherness for the planet, Nazarbayev-style. His priority was to find a new, unifying identity to impose on the Tajiks from above. The importance of this mission is obvious from the timing of his book *The Tajiks in the Mirror of History* (1997), which was issued just as the nation was emerging from the war. In this work, Rahmon portrays the history of the Tajiks as one of perpetual struggle and existential terror, in which "the Tajik nation has been confronted by all sorts of vehement opponents who doubted its very existence." Faced as he was with severe ontological challenges, how could Rahmon write about such trivialities as "global development"?

Obviously he couldn't. So rather than talk about the future and Tajikistan's shining place in it, he turned to the past. As a communist apparatchik, he had been reared on the Marxist myth of the coming workers' paradise; now he turned it on its head, replacing it with its older ancestor, the lost golden age. Rahmon travels deep into antiquity in pursuit of Tajik identity and dignity, finding precursors in the ancient Central Asian states of Bactria and Sogdiana, while the Samanid state of AD 819–999 stands out as the best period in Tajik history. In this narrative, socialism barely registers, while Islam is revealed to be an alien belief system imposed upon the Tajiks by Arab conquerors, severing their connection with their ancient Zoroastrian heritage.

According to Rahmon, the prophet Zoroaster was born in the territory of Tajikistan. However, he is not very interested in Zoroaster the prophet who conversed with Ahura Mazda, the lord of light, instead reimagining him as a transmitter and exemplar of Tajik moral values, virtuous and noble, like the hero of a Soviet factory novel beamed thousands of years into the past. Intriguingly, Rahmon's Zoroaster is a fighter against "atheism," which is generally considered not to have been a major problem 2,500 to 3,000 years ago; he also declares that the ancient Tajiks were always "patriotically minded . . . ready to defend the principles of progress and enlightenment." Rahmon likewise notes approvingly that the holy book of Zoroastrianism, the Avesta, is superior to the works of Homer because it is older and has more words (two million versus 345,000) and argues that it serves as an "ethnographic Klondyke," a guide to past Tajik greatness.

And so Rahmon metaphorically disinters Zoroaster, removes the parts he doesn't need, embalms the remains, and places the mummy in a glass box for the edification of the nation. Yet for all that Rahmon is more concerned with matters of the spirit and identity than Nazarbayev or his other post-Soviet peers, *The Tajiks in the Mirror of History* (1997) remains a fundamentally rationalist project. Rahmon does not believe in Ahura Mazda and does not expect his subjects to do so either. He flirts with religion but is really only interested in finding an idea that will bring stability and unity to his country. At no point does he set himself up as a man-god, or proclaim his book holy. It is, almost reassuringly, quite, quite boring.

To the west, in Turkmenistan, it was a very different story. Here was a country already damaged by Soviet books that was about to receive new suffering from an exceptionally virulent example of dictator literature, *The Rukhnama*, or "Book of the Soul."

6

Turkmenistan: Post-Everything

*Monument to the Rukhnama in Ashgabat, Turkmenistan. A smaller
version was blasted into space, that aliens might enjoy it, too.*

And so we end this voyage through the history of dictator literature
where—for me, at least—it began. One Sunday morning early in the
twenty-first century, I was channel surfing in my Moscow apartment
when all of a sudden I stumbled upon a transmission from a parallel universe. There, on the tiny screen of my TV, I beheld a bizarre monument,
exquisite in its tastelessness. It was a great big pink-and-green book, and
what was obviously a golden dictator head in profile dominated the cover.
But who was this dictator? I had no idea. What was the title of the book?
I didn't catch it. The camera then cut to a group of Turkic women in traditional dress (although no tradition I recognized), who were studying the

book in a brightly lit schoolroom; then to some immense white marble towers and gleaming cupolas that fused Stalinist Neoclassicism with an opulent Orientalism into a new, bombastic and hallucinatory architectural style; then to the head that had provided the model for the golden portrait on the cover of the giant book.

In its living, moving, three-dimensional form, the head was actually a solid, fleshy block crowned with a tenuous black fuzz that was failing to project an image of youth, and beneath which a pair of beady eyes scanned a roomful of sycophants. Below this slab of face-meat, an extra-large white shirt was draped over the evidence of a profoundly Epicurean lifestyle. There were gold rings on his fingers—or maybe I'm projecting those backward in time from a framed photo I saw later. I do remember this, though: the narrator kept repeating a single, alien word, *Rukhnama*.

In fact, this was no transmission from a parallel universe but rather a broadcast from Turkmenistan, a country that until recently had been part of the USSR. Here, a former Communist Party boss by the name of Saparmurat Niyazov had carved out a singular career in the post-Soviet era. Assuming the name Turkmenbashi ("Father of All Turkmen"), he had used the nation's immense gas reserves to finance the construction of a phantasmagorical capital of grandiose buildings and fountains and vast, empty freeways. He had also fostered a personality cult extreme enough to rival that of Kim Jong-il, although it received far less attention. Turkmenbashi had declared Turkmenistan "eternally neutral," and since he stayed out of geopolitical conflicts, few outside the country cared or even knew about what he was doing.

Central to Turkmenbashi's cult was the book I had seen on my TV screen, *The Rukhnama*, or "Book of the Soul." It was this text that suddenly seized my imagination. I had known about *Mein Kampf* and Mao's *Little Red Book* since I was a child and I had visited many Russian apartments where dusty volumes of Lenin cluttered up bookcases. This, however, was the first time I had witnessed the phenomenon of the *living* dictator book. Until that moment, I had treated them with the same dismissive disinterest as everybody else. Despite years of living in Moscow, I'd never felt tempted to take Lenin off the shelf and *actually read him*. Yet within days of watching that broadcast, I was spending hours downloading via dial-up an English translation of *The Rukhnama* from a Turkmen government site. The complete text was very long, and yet with what great eagerness did I begin to read. Then I stopped. It was awful.

Within a year or two, the words and deeds of Turkmenbashi had begun to attract interest from Western news outlets. He was not the most cruel, nor the most belligerent, nor even the most geopolitically significant of dictators, but he was the most *colorful* since Gaddafi, and perhaps he outdid even the colonel on that score. Who else had banned gold teeth and lip synching, and the ballet and opera, and the circus and smoking? Who else had renamed the month of January after himself and bread after his mother? Who else had a golden statue that stood atop a tripod with its arms held aloft, revolving throughout the day so that the sun was always in its grasp?

And who else had authored a book that was not only required reading for a driving test but that also sat next to the Quran and the Bible in the entrances to mosques and churches? Who else had authored a book that, if read from start to finish three times, guaranteed entrance to paradise? Who else had authored a book that was so sacred that excerpts were inscribed on the minarets of the biggest mosque in all of Central Asia? Who else had authored a book of such time-quaking importance that the month of September was renamed in its honor? And who else had authored a book that had been translated into so many languages by so many cynical corporations hoping to flatter their way into juicy business contracts?*

Nobody, that's who. Not even Kim Jong-il had gone this far.

The idea that the Turkmen needed a "Book of the Soul" was first floated in October 1991, as the USSR teetered on the brink of extinction. A prominent historian proposed compiling an anthology of folklore and traditions that would reconnect the Turkmen to their past after seven decades of Soviet rule. Prior to the revolution the Turkmen had been a nomadic people with a primarily oral rather than written culture, and according to Soviet sources, between 97 and 99 percent of the population was illiterate when the Turkmen Soviet Socialist Republic was founded in 1925. Thus the history of the nation was a Marxist-Leninist fable in which the Turkmen played the role of a backward people propelled into the glorious future by a revolution, which had originated at the old imperial center. It is easy to see why a corrective was deemed necessary, and the book was

---

* Siemens, DaimlerChrysler, Caterpillar, and John Deere were among the many multinational corporations that discovered a passion for sharing the wisdom of Turkmenbashi with the nations of the world.

commissioned—but Niyazov outsourced the production of this first itera-tion of *The Rukhnama* to a committee. So low was it on his list of priorities at this time that the book appeared under the name of his press secretary, who had overseen the project.

But *Rukhnama* Mark 1 was swiftly withdrawn from circulation as not fit for purpose, and work began instead on *Rukhnama* Mark 2. This time, a poet, a historian and a few heavy-drinking Soviet authors were at the helm. This version got no farther than the outline. By now it was the mid-1990s and Niyazov had mutated into Turkmenbashi, god-king and Father of the Nation. No longer did he answer to masters in the Kremlin; he understood well the leverage that comes of sitting atop the world's fourth-largest reserves of natural gas. These days, he spoke with Bill Clinton as one president to another. Turkmenistan was internally stable and had no enemies. His regime was awash in money. He had done great things; he would do more. He would write the Turkmen "Book of the Soul" himself.

It is immediately clear when you open *The Rukhnama* that this is something new in the world of post-Soviet dictator letters, and perhaps dictator literature more generally. The subtitle, *Reflections on the Spiritual Values of the Turkmen*, leaves no doubt as to the type of thematic terrain Turkmenbashi intends to cover. He had indicated his interest in spiritual matters early in his career as president of independent Turkmenistan; in 1992 he became the first Central Asian leader to visit Mecca. Even so, it comes as a bit of a surprise when the former Communist Party boss starts his epic with the proclamation, "In the name of Allah, the most exalted!"

While Nazarbayev has mutated into a national CEO, and Putin writes like a judo coach, Turkmenbashi addresses his "beloved people" as if he were some kind of prophet:

> This book, written with the help of inspiration sent to my heart by the God who created this wonderful universe and who is able to do whatever He wills, is Turkmen *Rukhnama*.

Fascists and Catholic nationalists of the 1920s and '30s were also prone to pontificating about the spirit, but they never claimed direct inspiration from the heavens. Nor for that matter had Khomeini, whose oeuvre was built upon interactions with other texts rather than upon per-sonal communication with God. Turkmenbashi by contrast writes like a poetic mystic with a direct channel to the Almighty. Yet what follows is still profoundly Soviet in its freewheeling attitude to the relationship between words and facts. When facts don't fit the narrative, they are suppressed, and more convenient ones are invented. Turkmenbashi is quite unrestrained in his mythic fantasizing, inventing in a couple of pages a history for the Turkmen that reaches back five thousand years through the establishment of seventy states to "the Prophet Noah" himself.

Reading Turkmenbashi in the context of almost a century of Soviet and post-Soviet prose is a profoundly disorienting experience. Although he must have mastered the complicated rhetoric of Marxist-Leninist pseudoscience to advance in his career, here he offers the reader a cod-religious narrative of extraordinary simplicity. Nor is it merely simplistic; it's also very, very lazy. Turkmenbashi gives no indication that he is familiar with the details of Noah's story: there is no mention of a message of doom or an ark, although these are part of the Islamic narrative as well as the Christian one. Instead, Noah is a lawgiver and moral exemplar, a bit like Emomali Rahmon's Zoroaster, only without the historical research conducted by other people on the dictator's behalf. For Turkmenbashi, Noah is a convenient literary glove puppet, who instructs the Turkmen to love their homeland and to respect their parents while also advising women to cover their mouths, but not their faces. Helpfully, Noah also offers tips on grooming ("wear clean and decent clothes") and interior design ("the decoration of the home, its order, cleanliness and appearance should be good)." In *The Rukhnama*, Noah is exactly who Turkmenbashi wants him to be, and Turkmenbashi wants him to be a tool for conferring immense historical and spiritual dignity on his people, even if that dignity is based on claims that an eight-year-old would think twice before making. Turkmenbashi did not care. Liberated from Soviet hegemony he would create a new reality and a new spirituality that suited him.

There were only four mosques in Turkmenistan during the Soviet period, and as a child raised in a state orphanage Turkmenbashi likely did not spend much or any time in them, or learning the Islamic scriptures, for that matter. Thus in *The Rukhnama*, he refers frequently to prophets and sacred texts, but not so much about what any of them said, probably because he didn't know. Having spent his youth studying Lenin and works of Russian and Soviet literature, he was also detached from Turkmenistan's folk religious traditions. But the entire nation had been similarly deprived, and the void in historical, religious and cultural knowledge that the original *Rukhnama* had been intended to overcome was now ruthlessly exploited by Turkmenbashi as he spun his simple narratives.

He asserts that the Turkmen believe in the Quran, the "Old Testament," and the Psalms, but he does not mention the hadith, which are essential texts in the corpus of Islamic belief. And so, according to Turkmenbashi, bits of the Hebrew Bible may be more relevant than actual Islamic scripture, which is a somewhat heterodox stance for somebody professing to be a Muslim, to say the least.

But even if Turkmenbashi is short on concrete details, he does claim to believe in the sanctity of the word:

> The Word is the most sacred gift that God gave to human beings
> The Word is the fruit of people, but it is given to human beings by God.

In particular, he believes in his own word. Although he denies that *The Rukhnama* is sacred, he does strongly imply that it's as close as you can get. Turkmenbashi dwells on the significance of *his* text at much greater length than he does on those written by any mere prophet. Answering his own question "What is this *Rukhnama*?" he enters a linguistic hall of mirrors and solipsism.

The Rukhnama is . . .

- "a source of power that will keep hearts alert"
- "the book of unity and togetherness"
- "the veil of the Turkmen people's face and soul"
- "the Turkmen people's first and basic reference book"
- "the total of the Turkmen mind, customs and traditions, intensions [*sic*] doings and ideals"
- "the visit made to the heart of the Turkmen"
- "a sweet spiritual fruit grown in this territory"
- "a book opening the spring of the mind and meeting the thirst of the dry intellect"
- [the means by which Turkmenbashi can] "string the past, present and future on a single rope"
- [a "courier" that] "transmits the past's secret and necessary news to the future"
- "a new worldview in the sense that it is a spirit that stimulates nature, society and people to work"

- "a light and a guide on [the Turkmen nation's] journey towards its goal"
- "the centre of [the] universe [that is the spirit of the Turkmen]. In this universe, all the current and future cosmic matters should go on spinning, in Rukhnama's attraction, centripetal force and orbits"

And so on. What he neglects to mention is that *The Rukhnama* is also a poorly structured, highly repetitive confection of unverifiable historical assertions, found texts, fabrications and bad poetry. Nevertheless, as the text proceeds, Turkmenbashi attempts in truly freewheeling fashion to write a new Turkmen identity into being. It contains digressions on etymology, ethics, religion (the Turkmen love God but are basically secular), music (Turkmen music is different from other types in that it has been wrought with deep philosophy), melons (Turkmen melons are very good), the rights of women (they should be free to work), rugs (Turkmen rugs are the best), policies, and treaties with other states (Turkmen are eternally neutral and have lots of friends), not to mention great Turkmen inventions (apparently we have the Turkmen to thank for the invention of the wheel, which "precipitated the scientific progress of the world").

Turkmenbashi's nonsensical litany of national achievements appears alongside cut-and-pasted extracts from genealogies that are biblical in length and mythological in nature but that are presented to the reader as fact. He casually tosses off some radical theological innovations, including the claim that the Turkmen's ancestor Oguz Khan is a prophet and that the Turkmen themselves have been monotheists for five thousand years ("O brother for fifty centuries the Turkmen have been living . . . with the belief of Allah"). This is considerably longer than the Jews, Christians, Muslims or anyone else for that matter.

But as much as *The Rukhnama* is an absurd historico-religious phantasmagoria, so too is it a profoundly personal work, right up there with Saddam Hussein's romance novels and Hitler's *Mein Kampf*. Intent on demonstrating the authenticity of his message, Turkmenbashi intersperses throughout the text facsimiles of his own handwritten manuscript. Aside from children, all his readers had lived their lives in the USSR, where it was well known that the leaders had little to do with the books to which their names were attached. Turkmenbashi sets out to overcome any possible skepticism regarding his authorship of *The Rukhnama* by "proving" that his hand wrote the words. More than that, he also demonstrates authenticity through the confessional aspect of his narrative, as he speaks nakedly about his own life experience to his people in a way that no Soviet leader ever did. Turkmenbashi lays bare his own personal trauma and then inserts it into the history of the nation, placing his autobiography at the center of history.

Here, at least, Turkmenbashi is not exaggerating. Saparmurat Niyazov *did* suffer immense trauma as a child. He was born in 1940 in the Turkmen village of Gypjak, which his father, Atamurat, left soon afterward to fight for Stalin in the Red Army; he would vanish at the front. In 1948, Niyazov's mother and siblings died in an earthquake that devastated Ashgabat. Father Stalin, whose portrait watched over Niyazov in the orphanage where he spent his formative years, died when he was thirteen. Eventually Niyazov landed in Leningrad, where the state taught him engineering. He then returned home to work for the party, which he served faithfully until the collapse of the USSR. Many of these details turn up in *The Rukhnama*, but in strikingly raw form. On page 8, Turkmenbashi speaks of his grief at the loss of his mother and father:

> No human being who has not experienced what I lived through can understand me.
>
> Your father who is supposed to support you in hard times is dead in an unknown, foreign place!
>
> Your dear mother is lying with your two sisters under Karakum. You are alone in Leningrad. You have no one behind you who is asking about you and writing a letter to you.
>
> I was sick and asked my supposedly close relatives to take care of me. They wrote to tell me that they had forgotten about me, let alone helping me.
>
> There was no one other than The One, Allah Almighty, to seek refuge in and no one to ask for help other than my Allah. The whole country was crying that there is no Allah. Oh, Allah!

At this point, so great is Turkmenbashi's anguish, so profound his torment, that it brings him to the verge of "maddness [*sic*]." Unable to suppress his feelings any longer, he erupts in a poem addressed to "Jygalybeg," a mythic warrior-leader, which I reproduce at length because it is so entertainingly overwrought:

I have powerful Turkmen thoroughbred, would you groom it, Jygalybeg?
I have also a broken and uneased heart, would you groom it, Jygalybeg?
My bowers are shackled, my Chandybil is a grieved country now,
And our ill-fortune never awakens, unless you, unless you . . . ,
    Jygalybeg!
Where are the mountain-like valiants who rose against the black
    mountain?
Alas, sorrowing are the stately variants that fought against the bad lot!
Many heroic and wise fell martyred, so that I was left behind lonely,
    abandoned,
Even the dessert bent double with pain, moaning. Can you hear,
    Jygalybeg?
The prosperous wealthy men were collected, suffered, and sent to exile
    in Siberia,
The lion-hearted brave fell as martyr in the fight and already became
    graves,
Your orphan cried bitterly, left all alone, no strength, patience, endurance,
My land weep and my folk bewailed, the country in disorder, Jygalybeg!
I have powerful Turkmen thoroughbred, would you groom it, Jygalybeg?
I have also a broken and uneased, heart, would you groom it, Jygalybeg?
Lend me Gorogly's curved sword and your spear to me, Jygalybeg!
No fear! I shall fight to death. Give me your own crown, Jygalybeg! . . .

Turkmenbashi then tells a story about "an old Russian" he met in Leningrad who knew his father, and was present when he died by German machine-gun fire in North Ossetia. Turkmenbashi provides a lot more detail on his father than on his own years in the orphanage or in Leningrad, which are glossed over as if that pain were still unresolved. It all comes together in the end, however, as Turkmenbashi reveals that the very instruction to create *The Rukhnama* came from no less a figure than the "prophet" Oguz Khan:

The Soul of Oguz Khan said: Write! The place where your nation came into existence will be the route; the place which your nation favors will be the territory; the wishes of your nation will be realized.

The personal thus fuses with the historical, the mythological, the religious and the political, giving birth to the megatext of *The Rukhnama*.

It was a hugely ambitious project, perhaps the most ambitious of all dictator books. Rather than take a preexisting theory and explain it, Turkmenbashi conjured something new out of everything he saw lying around that he felt he could use, and not only that but he did it while running a totalitarian state. In addition, he followed *The Rukhnama* with a sequel while also cranking out books of poetry and history. In all this, Turkmenbashi was striving to create not merely an ideology but a new history, a new mythology for his nation: by means of long discourses on Turkic clans, a child's take on religion and history, and sheer narcissism, he sought to restore dignity to the desert people who had been colonized by the Russians and stripped of their culture by the Soviets. It would have been a monumental task for a very great author, but Turkmenbashi was not even a mediocre author. He was a very, very bad one. With *The Rukhnama*, he aimed for the stars but ended up in the landfill.

So AWFUL WAS *The Rukhnama* that it took me three years to finish it, which I did while traveling through Turkmenistan's Karakum Desert. It was necessary to have all possible distractions removed in order to make it to the end of the green-and-pink book with the golden head on the cover. This was in March 2006: by this point Niyazov had reached peak notoriety, and journalists were banned from entering the country. I got in because my first book had not yet been published, and a Google search turned up no results for my name. The plan was to spend a month traveling the length and breadth of the land and then to return to Moscow, where I would interview dissidents and exiles. After reading every book about Turkmenistan available in English (not a very long reading list) and whatever interesting curios I could track down in Russian, I would write the definitive work on Turkmenbashi's regime. But shortly after my interviews were complete, Niyazov had the temerity to die. For a couple of months, I deluded myself into thinking that the plan might still work—hadn't the great Ryszard Kapuściński published his book on the shah's regime years after the Iranian Revolution? Yet deep inside—or maybe not even that deep inside—I knew my book was dead. It was also around this time that I read an article exposing Kapuściński as something of a fabulist himself who, like Turkmenbashi, had never admitted exactly how much of his oeuvre he had made up. Perhaps his was not an example to emulate.

The truth was that I had been struggling with the book even before

Turkmenbashi took the great leap into oblivion. For some reason, it was difficult to articulate exactly what it was that I had seen there. Nor was it just me. A few months after the trip I met with one of my traveling partners, and he confessed to the same problem. He didn't know how to think about Turkmenistan, or how to describe it. I recall that the solidity of his eighteenth-century stone house, the walls of which had borne witness to the lives of multiple generations of dead English people, contrasted heavily with the ephemeral, almost hallucinatory nature of our trip. It was as if we had spent a month trapped inside somebody else's dream, and now that we had awoken from it, talking about it in a way that made any sense at all to those who had not been subject to Turkmenbashi's waking psychosis was as challenging as explaining the most personal and subjective of our own individual dreams. We had seen the monument to *The Rukhnama* and the golden statue of the leader that revolved to meet the sun. I had bought myself a box of baby food with Turkmenbashi's mother's face on it. I had visited an empty nightclub where the owner sang along to George Michael's "Careless Whisper" with a crazed intensity. So what did it all mean? Where was I in that flux?

I now realize that at the time it meant nothing, or nothing that wasn't already quite obvious. But ten years later, and having reached the end of a different book, it has acquired meaning, and I at last understand what I saw: the moment before the great unremembering that engulfs and erases almost all trace of the sacred text once the leader dies. I saw the epiphenomena, the effervescent surface of the cult and its rituals, the moment when the book is alive and impossible to escape. I felt the effect of the forced consensus that gives the book life for as long as the force is in place to maintain it.

This subjective moment is the most elusive aspect of the study of dictator literature. In Turkmenistan in 2006, however, the text was as yet a vigorous and virulent presence that forced itself on your consciousness with the full backing of a police state. For the first couple of weeks in particular—until my brain adjusted to the sensory overload—it was intensely present: a hallucination I could touch, a lucid dream in pink and green and gold that wouldn't end. Close my eyes and I can still see it all today: the moment, luminous and awful and unending, everywhere I went.

It was there in the giant monument to *The Rukhnama* that suddenly leapt from my TV screen and into the actual world as I traveled from the airport to the hotel. Ominous and immense and exceedingly kitsch in the desert night, I could see it through the window of my room, hovering in the darkness like a fluorescent mirage. The giant book was supposed to open by itself, to reveal a double-page spread of Turkmenbashi's wisdom each night—but it never did. The mechanism had broken, and nobody repaired it.

It was there on my first full day in Ashgabat, when I visited a bookshop in the city center (I never found another one) and saw dozens of copies of *The Rukhnama* facing outward on the shelves in multiple languages—Turkmen, English, Russian, German, Italian—all of them pink and green and gold, like a really badly designed children's book published by the most cynical vanity press in the world. *Rukhnama 2* was also there, hot off the presses, along with other key texts of Turkmenbashi, such as his book on national heroes and his volume of poetry, *Turkmenistan, My Happiness*. But none of those had yet been rendered in English. Aside from the complete works of the leader, there wasn't much else to buy: a coffee table photography book on horses and another on shiny marble buildings and something about the Turkmen military, and that was it. Except . . .

It was there in the curious survival of a select handful of once "great" Soviet authors as under-the-counter material. Thus was I offered a thirty-year-old, two-volume Russian-language edition of *The Decisive Step*, by Berdi Kerbabayev, the "Turkmen Sholokhov." The sales assistant assured me it was a great book, while pointedly not attempting to upsell me on any of Turkmenbashi's works.

It was there in the absence of works by contemporary Turkmen writers in the same shop; Turkmenbashi would brook no rivals.

It was there in my quest to find the ruins of the old circus, closed since Turkmenbashi issued his edict banning this insufficiently Turkmen art, which led me deep into a network of residential streets. There I found a library, one of the few still open in the country, and stepped within to find a *Rukhnama* reading room immediately to my left. Inside were neatly arranged rows of desks and a portrait of the president on the wall. A young girl was bent over a copy of *The Rukhnama*, studying furiously. The librarian smiled and beckoned us to enter.

It was there in the hotel where I watched a televised concert that consisted entirely of young men and women standing onstage in a giant hall, taking turns reading aloud from *The Rukhnama* in Turkmen, English, French, German and Russian. The audience sat in rapt attention as the text, repeatedly described as "holy," was intoned in their general direction.

It was there in the only other bookshop I found in Turkmenistan, the one in the city of Mari, which I explored alone while my friends were visiting the ruins of the ancient city of Merv. It was even emptier than the one in Ashgabat, in that it didn't have the same selection of coffee table photo books or quite so many foreign-language editions of *The Rukhnama.*

And it was there in the ancient episode of *Benny Hill* that I watched in the truck stop café afterward.

It was there in the abandoned underground car park of the immense "Mosque of Turkmenbashi's Soul" and in the inscriptions from *The Rukhnama* on the minarets, surely an act of stupendous blasphemy—yet nobody seemed to care, even as in next-door Afghanistan they were killing people over some cartoons that had lately been published in Denmark. The mosque was as empty as the car park, bar a few women who went to the front to pray, and nobody cared about that either.

It was there on the way to Kunya-Urgench, in the billboards for Turkmenbashi's books by the side of quiet roads, and in the white stones in distant hills that spelled out "Rukhnama."

It was there at the foot of the mountain where they had found the perfectly preserved footprints of the "Turkmenosaurus." There, in the home of the head of the village, I sat where Turkmenbashi had once sat, in an earlier period of his rule, when he was as yet a man of the people, making the rounds of the country and talking to regional leaders. Our guide mentioned that it was Turkmenbashi's birthday—and it was there in the silence that followed.

It was there in the national museum where the young guide wore a Turkmenbashi pin in his lapel. When I asked him for his take on *The Rukhnama*, he replied with great enthusiasm that it was "very great," and yet he could not articulate why, only that it was "profound" in some indefinable way. And it was also there when I asked him about *Rukhnama 2*, which was also "very great"; and it was there in the sheepish expression he wore when I asked him what was in it. "More of the same," he replied.

And it was there more than anywhere in the apartment we rented in the godforsaken oil town of Balkanabat, in the stench of crude in the air and in the local disco with its diverse selection of Russian, Ukrainian and Kazakh (but not Turkmen) whores, and in the cheerful friendliness of our temporary landlady's eleven-year-old daughter, and in the absence of the girl's father, and in the hard, hard lives that stretched ahead of both the girl and her mother, and in the books of Turkmenbashi on display behind the glass of a Soviet-era cabinet, although the woman was no government official, and this was no office but rather a private home, and she had nothing to gain by putting them there—and yet there they were, in all their depraved banality.

It was there, and I was there; and then I wasn't there, and then it wasn't there, either. With Turkmenbashi's death, the process of unremembering began.

THE DICTATOR'S SUCCESSOR was a dentist turned deputy prime minister who rejoiced in the name Gurbanguly Berdymukhammedov. In U.S. diplomatic cables leaked by WikiLeaks in 2010 he is described as "not a very bright guy," yet he was shrewd enough to know that he would have to advance cautiously if he were to survive the transition to power. His predecessor's personality cult was comparable in scale to Stalin's and could not be dismantled overnight without causing great disruption. And so the infestation of golden statues of Turkmenbashi was cleared from the landscape—but gradually. The notorious Arch of Neutrality, with its giant rotating Turkmenbashi who always held the sun between his palms, was moved from the center to the outskirts of Ashgabat—but not until 2010. (The giant Turkmenbashi stayed, but never again would he keep pace with the sun.) Likewise, *The Rukhnama* steadily lost its place at the center of the Turkmen universe, but it was not until 2012 that it finally vanished from school curricula and university courses. This did not mean that the five million inhabitants of Turkmenistan were suddenly liberated. Although initially somewhat coy, Berdymukhammedov soon grew to enjoy the power his predecessor had accumulated in the office of the president. And lo, the Golden Age of Turkmenbashi, the "Father of All Turkmen," soon gave way to the revival of the Arkadag, their "protector."

A new era needed new books of course, and now the process of generating great works began all over again, as the Turkmen discovered that they were truly cursed, that they were still strapped to Kafka's writing machine, that there was no escape from the prison house of (dictator) language, and that nowhere on earth was the tradition begun by Lenin more enduring. Karl Marx, wrong about so many things, was right about this:

> Men make their own history, but they do not make it as they please; they do not make it under self-selected circumstances, but under circum-

stances existing already, given and transmitted from the past. The tradition of all dead generations weighs like a nightmare on the brains of the living.

Marx's vision is tragic and confers dignity in suffering upon the human race, damned to labor under this terrible and inescapable burden. But while the history of dictator literature is certainly tragic, its trajectory is more in the direction of black farce. It's not as though Stalin was an improvement upon Lenin, or that Mao represented a sophisticated development of totalitarian thought, or that Hitler was a refinement upon Mussolini—but their texts demanded to be taken seriously. Now, however, the dictator book was a joke in poor taste, repeated ad nauseam. Relentlessly bleak in his *1984*, Orwell demonstrated that he, like Marx, didn't quite get it. Yes, every now and then a devil in human form appears to commit acts of monstrous evil, and in the twentieth century there were several of them, and they spread their ideological contamination through diabolical texts. But satanic majesties are rare; most of the time we have to put up with small demons, bumptious idiots, cruel cretins. Pace Orwell, the sorry truth for our species is this: "If you want a picture of the future, imagine a clown shoe stamping on a human face—forever."

Nowhere is this demonstrated more clearly than Turkmenistan in the era of the Arkadag. After all, this was not the Turkmen people's first visit to the infernal library of dictator literature: it was their ninth, and there did not appear to be any way out. Berdymukhammedov proved to be less talented than every dictator-author who had come before him, including even his immediate predecessor. The texts he inflicted on his people maintained all the myths and misreadings of history perpetrated by Turkmenbashi, but lacked the entertainingly bad poetry and monumental ambition. Instead of fusing all of history into one colorful tome, Berdymukhammedov generated a series of dry books on different aspects of Turkmen folk culture, as if he had returned to the original conception of *The Rukhnama* only to multiply it across a horde of (quite obviously ghostwritten) books.

An early instance was *Akhalteke: Our Pride and Glory* (2008), in which "Berdymukhammedov" recounts the history of Turkmenistan's signature horse breed, the "national pride and glory" that has become "a terrestrial embodiment of a unity of the cultural space of the world and left fond memories of itself throughout historical epochs." The sustained dullness of the prose is enough to leave the reader longing for the days of Turkmenbashi's anguished soul-searching. Berdymukhammedov advances through the history of the horse and modern breeding techniques before inflicting upon the reader an incredibly long catalogue of 132 horses from his own stable (modestly titled "the superstrain of the akahltekke breed") complete with photographs, names and vital statistics. The book then concludes with a few tips on horse riding and advice on gear for the devotee of equestrian sports.

Evidently pleased with this first venture into writing about horses, Berdymukhammedov followed it up with a still more banal coffee table book titled *The Flight of Celestial Racehorse*. But the dictator was only getting started, and soon a veritable deluge of prose would be attributed to the new president. In 2009 the Turkmen delegation at the Moscow Book Fair unveiled the first of a projected ten-volume series titled *Medicinal Plants of Turkmenistan*, while other books on topics as varied as carpet weaving, music, history and ethnography followed in rapid succession. Berdymukhammedov also tried his hand at fiction, launching his debut novel, *The Bird of Happiness*, at an event in the city of Dashoguz in October 2013.

The Arkadag next extended his tentacles into verse and popular music, occasionally appearing on television with a guitar or a synthesizer to accompany popular singers at New Year's Eve concerts. In August 2015 his interest in both art forms came together as his poem "Only Forward" was set to music and performed by a choir of 4,166 patriotic Turkmen, winning Berdymukhammedov a place in the *Guinness Book of Records* as the author of the song performed by the most people singing in the round.

Nearly ten years into his reign, and there were few aspects of Turkmen culture to which he had not dedicated at least one book. In early 2016, Radio Free Europe reported that Berdymukhammedov had generated no fewer than thirty-five masterpieces at a rate of around three and a half a year. Nor was there any sign of his slowing down. That January he released an anthology of Turkmen proverbs and sayings entitled *Wisdom Source*, while a mere two months later he published *Tea: Healing and Inspiration*. The cover depicts a pot of tea, a loaf of bread and a rug. State television showed Berdymukhammedov presenting the book to state officials, who kissed it and raised it to their foreheads as if it were the holy of holies.

And why not? For, as Berdymukhammedov said, "Every Turkmen

knows there is nothing tastier than tea brewed in water from a mountain stream and boiled on an open fire in a traditional teapot."

So it was that in 2016, the most prolific dictator-author of the twenty-first century had at last answered Lenin's question, the fundamental problem that stands at the heart of the tyrant's canon: what is to be done?

Why—make a cup of tea, of course.

---- PHASE IV ----

DEATH IS
NOT THE END

Conclusion

The psychopath never dates:
Mein Kampf *in Arabic c. 1995.*

Looking back over more than a hundred years of dictator literature, it is difficult to resist the conclusion that, as with monotheism, philosophy or classical music, the great peaks have already been formed and everything that now follows will exist in their shadow. Do we really expect another

Christ or Muhammad or Plato or Bach to emerge? No: and so it is with the great tyrants and their toxic texts. Today's dictators offer us only lesser, derivative works.

This is not to say that the foundational works of the previous century are especially healthy or virulent. Like all canons, the dictatorial version is less read than it is revered—or, in this case, feared. And if these books are ever read, then it is in a new context and through interpretive prisms that are very different from those of the original readership. With that in mind, let us take a look at the critical status of the five "classics" of dictator literature in the second decade of the twenty-first century.

LENIN

Today Lenin remains in print both in Russia and in many other countries around the world, but he no longer has any direct connections to significant mass movements claiming to act in his name.

In Russia, his corpse still lies in its glass box on Red Square, a dark and grotesque reminder of an earlier, simpler reality about which many people still demonstrate conflicted feelings. For two decades now, the leaders in the Kremlin have resisted calls to bury the Father of the World Proletariat, as if this final repudiation of the Russian Revolution would amount to admitting that, yes, the twentieth century was a disaster and that generations of Russians suffered and died in vain. That said, uncritical admirers of Lenin are rare, and the notion that Putin wants to restore the Soviet Union is a naïve (or cynical) fantasy of hack journalists and Beltway think tank warriors sniffing for grant money. It is the heroic deeds of the Soviet people rather than the texts of its founders that Putin is interested in, and at official events he poses beside church leaders and generals rather than "great theoreticians."

Thus Lenin's body remains trapped in limbo, while interest in his body of work has dwindled to become the preserve of historians of Russia and revolutions, the occasional campus pseudoradical and pockets of Marxist-Leninist cultists online. Despite this, of all the texts I read for this book, Lenin's seemed to me the most vital in terms of applicability. If you can read past the reductionist scientism and the tedious arguments with long-dead socialists then some truths for the ages—"eternal verities," if you will—emerge. So long as you are an amoral seeker after power, that is.

For these are not nice or reassuring truths: Lenin's texts do not heal or ennoble. Rather, they show you how to do bad things. The strategies and tactics he advocated for running a clandestine organization, his alertness to the ebb and flow of the historical moment, his grasp of how to seize and maintain power in a moment of crisis and his desire to smash a corrupt state are all still instructive today, for those who would seek to learn from the master.

Why then aren't more people reading his books? Perhaps it's the association with a defunct ideology; perhaps it's the absence of context. It may also be that Lenin was just too successful. Leninist theory can be interpreted only in the broader framework of Marxist pseudoscience, but Leninist tactics can be used by ideologues of all kinds, whether they reside in Egypt, Iran, China or corporate boardrooms across the United States. Why plow through *Materialism and Empiriocriticism* if you don't have to? Lenin's intellectual heirs may be Leninists without ever having opened one of his books. But it was in those books that his ideas first appeared, and from the pages of which they went forth to infiltrate psyches around the world.

STALIN

Although Stalin's critics in the Bolshevik Party were foolish to write him off as an intellectual mediocrity, they were correct in their assessment that he was not a terribly good or original writer (youthful poetry aside, perhaps).

Stalin's greatest literary skill was as an editor of others, rather than as a creator of his own texts. His prose was coherent but drab, his structure methodical but repetitive, and his assorted expostulations on nationality, "socialism in one country," Leninism and linguistics have all long since passed their expiry date. The once ubiquitous *Short Course* is today a curio, and the socialist-realist literature generated in response to his dictum that the writer is the engineer of the human soul has mostly disappeared, although some of the more prominent practitioners, such as Nobel Prize winner Mikhail Sholokhov, remain in print and may even still have readers.

This disappearance is telling. While a close study of Stalin's *deeds* can teach would-be criminal masterminds a great deal, the texts themselves —which were refinements upon Lenin generated to suit the ideological needs of the moment or concatenations of lies that concealed what Stalin was really up to—have already served their dismal purpose.

This is not to say the books do not live on in zombified form; they do. Such is Stalin's notoriety that his texts continue to enjoy an attenuated literary afterlife. You can read the Vozhd's collected works for free online or, if you so choose, pay for them. The Russian publisher Eksmo spotted a market for Stalin-era nostalgia in the mid-2000s and began pumping out physical books to meet demand and so generate profits: such are the leaden ironies of history.

MUSSOLINI

As for Mussolini, the afterlife of his texts began not long after his battered body was cut down from the lamppost and subjected to further desecration. One account has it that the nurses at his autopsy played Ping-Pong with his organs, tossing Il Duce's liver, lungs and heart back and forth in a giddy, giggling act of body horror outdoing even the scenes in his own *The Cardinal's Mistress*.

Despite the total and absolute collapse of the Fascist regime, interest in Il Duce was still strong enough to sustain the publication of a thirty-six-volume collected works that started to roll off the presses in 1951; the most complete collection runs to forty-four volumes. Nor was the interest in Mussolini's texts entirely historical/archival. There was demand for fresh material, which the dictator himself was kind enough to supply from beyond the grave, or at least such was the claim of a certain "Piero Caliandro," whose *Benito Mussolini Without Fascism: 12 Conversations from the Other Side* was published in Milan in 1952. In this book the shade of Mussolini informs his coroner that "these are not the imaginings of someone who is dead. I here am in possession of the truth; you, instead, examine putrefying matter of that which has hardened in formaldehyde or alcohol." Ghost Mussolini then appeals to all Italian patriots to form a new party and so revive the Italian nation.

The Italian nation was revived, but not by followers of the dead dictator. Although Mussolini's granddaughter sat in the Italian Senate and is today a member of the European Parliament, a full-blown Fascist revival has been striking only by its absence. Mussolini's birthplace in Predappio remains a site of pilgrimage for admirers of the Fascist dictator, and apocryphal texts and lost works attributed to him have continued to appear into the twenty-first century, but they no more represent a coherent body of ideas now than they did in the 1920s and '30s. Without the charismatic presence of Il Duce to breathe life into them, they are simply units to be sold.

HITLER

In Germany, Hitler's corpse vanished and *Mein Kampf* went out of print, although yellowing copies of the book continued to haunt used-bookstores for years after the war had ended. Following a police raid on Berlin bookshops in 1960, the trade in ideological poison was subjected to restrictions. Hitler's magnum opus could be sold to "a limited number of specialist libraries," but buyers had to be able to demonstrate "legitimate professional interest," although fewer restrictions were placed on *Mein Kampf*'s original enthusiasts, who with a few notable exceptions continued to hold political office, run large companies and occupy seats in the civil service into the 1980s.

Yet *Mein Kampf* was never banned outright in Germany as it was in some other European countries. Rather, the state of Bavaria controlled the copyright and prevented new copies from appearing. The situation changed when the book entered the public domain on December 31, 2015. A group of scholars at the Institute of Contemporary History in Munich had a plan, however: they would release a new, two-thousand-page scholarly edition filled with commentary that would demonstrate once and for all that Hitler's magnum opus really was the badly written, vile confection of anti-Semitism it had always appeared to be. Published in 2016, *Mein Kampf: Eine Kritische Edition* came laden with thirty-five hundred scholarly footnotes and annotations that pointed out all Hitler's distortions, lies and grotesqueries. Although the institute originally planned to print a mere four thousand copies, preorders raised the total to fifteen thousand. By the end of the year, eighty-five thousand copies had been sold and Hitler had spent thirty-five weeks on *Der Spiegel*'s bestseller list.

But while the impulse to confront bad ideas rather than wish them away through a ban is admirable, it is hard to resist the conclusion that the existence of this annotated *Mein Kampf* indicates an unawareness of a simple truth on the part of its highly educated editors—that arguing with a fanatic is almost always a waste of time. According to the book's distributors, most of the new readers were academics or people with a general interest in history: in other words, educated, thoughtful people unlikely to be converted to Nazism. But it was clear to most of its earliest reviewers in 1924 and 1925 that *Mein Kampf* was a travesty, and even Hitler would come to regret his grievous act of authorship. It has long since attained a symbolic power that transcends its origins as a printed object. *Mein Kampf* does not need to be read; it is difficult to read. To provoke unease, fear, hatred and terror, it need only exist.

Outside Germany, Hitler's *magnum excrementum* has done just that, as it has enjoyed a vigorous afterlife since 1945. After the war, Spanish, Portuguese, English, Brazilian and Arabic editions started rolling off the presses in places as far afield as Mexico, Beirut, Portugal, Brazil and the United States with nary so much as an interruption. In some countries publishers kept *Mein Kampf* in print simply to make money—in the United States, for instance, the eminently respectable house of Houghton Mifflin quietly collected proceeds on it for decades.* In some other territories, however, publishers had a more ideological interest in the dissemination of Hitler's text.

In another of history's leaden ironies, *Mein Kampf* is perhaps most popular today in countries populated by peoples Hitler regarded as *Untermenschen*. The Nazis first disseminated copies in the Middle East during the war—*Mein Kampf* can be translated into Arabic as *My Jihad*—and it has since spread throughout the Islamic world, selling at bookstalls alongside the likes of *The Protocols of the Elders of Zion*. Journalists found editions on sale in the Palestinian territories, Egypt, Iraq, India† and Bangladesh, while in 2005 the *Guardian* reported that *Mein Kampf* was doing a roaring trade in the bookstores of NATO member and U.S. ally Turkey, where one hundred thousand copies were sold in two months.

Such is the book's power that its readers overlook its obvious implications for their races and extract from it what they want: an explanation for their own resentments found in a modern articulation of the ancient hatred of the Jew, that diabolical master of conspiracies, the source of all miseries, the eternal scapegoat.

---

* Since 2000, Houghton Mifflin has donated all proceeds from the sale of *Mein Kampf* to organizations combating anti-Semitism.
† According to a BBC report, Indian readers regard *Mein Kampf* as an inspirational self-help book for entrepreneurs, which is a curious interpretation of a memoir by a hate-filled paranoiac who killed himself after committing world-historical crimes and leading his adopted country to disaster.

MAO

In 1979, the CCP was confronted with a dilemma. Chairman Mao had been safely dead for three years, and the party, under the leadership of Deng Xiaoping, was beginning to implement market reforms that would open up China to foreign trade and transform the country into an economic powerhouse. This was all very distant from the ideas behind the Great Leap Forward and the Cultural Revolution. And so what was to be done about the mummified leader-meat occupying the crystal display cabinet in the mausoleum on Tiananmen Square? And what about the hundreds of millions of unsold copies of his works that were taking up valuable shelf space in bookstores and warehouses across China?

The party leadership considered burying the Chairman but ultimately decided to leave him in his box to maintain symbolic continuity with the past, even as they pursued policies he would have abhorred. As for his writings, they too were maintained, albeit subject to restrictions. In February 1979, the Department of Propaganda ordered the withdrawal from sale of both Chinese and foreign-language editions of *Quotations of Chairman Mao* and of posters, portraits and pamphlets dating back to the Cultural Revolution. The book that had cured cancer and made the blind see was now pulped en masse, going from ubiquity to scarcity (alongside hundreds of millions of unsold copies of works by Marx, Engels, Lenin, and Stalin). The party then undertook a thorough review of Mao's opus, and in 1981 an official list of forty-three "canonical" works to be kept in print was drawn up. The first four volumes of Mao's *Selected Works*, covering the years leading to the foundation of the communist state in 1949, made the cut, but volume 5, which reveals what Mao did next, was deemed too radical and was withdrawn in 1982.

Despite these lacunae, Mao stands today as the only dictator of the Big Five with an official canon that is still endorsed by the state he once ruled. Yet as the years have passed, doubts as to how much of his oeuvre he actually wrote have only deepened.

In 1993, reports appeared in Hong Kong claiming that, after five years of party-sponsored research into Mao's bibliography, scholars had found that of the 470 speeches, reports and other texts they had analyzed, fewer than half of them were actually the Chairman's own work. Even as an editor Mao was much more hands off than Stalin: scribbling "I agree" or "good" in the margins was often the extent of his involvement. It turned out that Chen Boda, who had enjoyed a reputation as the foremost authority on Mao Zedong Thought, was actually the primary author of quite a lot of it, while other leading party members, such as the general Zhu De and the Chinese premier Zhou Enlai, had also pitched in to bolster the Chairman's bibliography. Meanwhile, of 120 texts related to military matters it transpired that Mao had written only 12. This use of ghost-writers had been going on since 1949, while in 1962 the Chairman had formally assigned a group of five writers the task of generating Mao Zedong Thought.

Despite this, Mao's texts continue to be repurposed for the new era. *Quotations of Chairman Mao* returned to print and enjoyed a second life as tourist tat, and in 2013, on the eve of the 120th anniversary of the Chairman's birth, a scholarly new edition was released, overseen by a senior colonel at the Academy of Military Science. The product of two years' work, this revised version was stripped of quotations falsely attributed to Mao, while also drawing upon texts not included in the original version. But alongside serious scholarly attempts to rejuvenate Mao's political legacy, a parallel Chairman enjoys a more commercial afterlife. Today young Chinese entrepreneurs study "his" military writings for guidance on how to conquer their competitors in much the same way that Sun Tzu's *The Art of War* has for decades provided fodder for books and articles on business strategy.

Regardless of whether Mao's second act as a business guru takes hold, his ability to coin a rousing slogan is not in doubt. Mao more than any dictator succeeded at infiltrating his language into the speech not only of his own people, but of millions more around the world. Phrases such as "A revolution is not a dinner party" and "Political power grows out of the barrel of a gun" are more resonant—and true—than the vast majority of advertising slogans. Linguistically, the Chairman continues to conquer.

So THE DICTATOR books are defanged and declawed in the present, safely quarantined in faraway lands of which we know little, or dead and gone and stranded in that other country, the past. In this reduced state we can surely feel confident that the Infernal Library could never open up a branch office in the United States.

Well, maybe. It's not that I *expect* it to happen here, but nobody expected it to happen in Russia, Italy, Germany or China, either. Yet a century ago a terrible new world emerged from the chaos of war and the ruins of empire, as intellectuals claimed that this or that absurd idea represented the final revelation providing the answer to the most fundamental problems of existence facing humanity. Democracy was out; utopian fantasies were in; tyranny and mass murder ensued. It was the worst of times, and it was the worst of times. Today we are also living in an era of disintegration, albeit of a less dramatic sort. There is no great, continent-spanning conflagration. But the post–Cold War order is breaking down with global repercussions: beliefs and pieties that went for the most part unquestioned for decades are now under attack from both left and right.

Things fall apart. And when they do, they tend to fall apart quickly— and few are the sages who see it coming. Lenin went from writing *What Is to Be Done?* in exile in Munich to changing the course of history from an office in the Kremlin in a mere sixteen years. Mao went from writing about the importance of exercise for *New Youth* magazine to uniting the world's most populous country under his leadership in thirty-two years. Hitler and Mussolini rose from obscurity to dominance even faster. The dictatorial canon emerged not in small or peripheral countries but in once mighty empires, ancient lands and advanced nations that were home to many of history's greatest writers, philosophers, scientists, artists and musicians. There was no shortage of good books in Russia, Italy, Germany or China. Yet in a short space of time, hundreds of millions of people found themselves compelled to read very bad books.

It couldn't happen here? Why not? It happened there.

Certainly the United States has a long, deep experience with the millenarian hopes and apocalyptic terrors that, in mutant form, played an important role in the rise of the twentieth century's great dictators. When the Puritans sailed over from England, they brought with them a firm belief that they were living in the end-time. Their arrival in the New World was itself a fulfillment of the prophecy in Matthew 24:14: "And this gospel of the kingdom shall be preached in all the world for a witness unto all nations; and then shall the end come." The image of America as a "city upon a hill" providing an example to the world goes all the way back to a sermon (also based on a passage from Matthew's Gospel) preached in 1630 by the Puritan John Winthrop, before he had even set foot on American soil. Thus the dream of a New Jerusalem in the New World, the conceptualization of America as a unique land, providing a home for a new society that would serve as a guiding beacon for the rest of humanity, long predates the similarly millenarian conceits of Manifest Destiny and "American exceptionalism," while as an image and an ideal it has enjoyed a vigorous secularized afterlife in its own right.

The United States is also an intensely logocentric nation, in that it defines itself not as a community built on linguistic or ethnic ties but by words written on paper by a group of intellectuals who had read a lot of books that were at the cutting edge of philosophy around 250 years ago. But while the Declaration of Independence and the U.S. Constitution are clearly contingent documents conceived by individuals as subject to the intellectual limitations of their age as the rest of us, we in the early twenty-first century still revere them as texts that are eternal and transcendent. In other countries such documents come and go, and sometimes with great regularity—France has had sixteen constitutions or draft constitutions since the eighteenth century, for instance. In the United States, such a thing is inconceivable: if there is only one thing everybody is agreed upon it is that the society we live in should be governed through the framework of those texts. We may disagree on matters of hermeneutics, but without the word, who or what would we be?

A heightened sense of awe for the power of the written word can easily be found in other contexts, at the most elite levels of society. At Amherst College in 1963, John F. Kennedy delivered his celebrated eulogy for Robert Frost, who two years earlier had become the first poet ever to read at a presidential inauguration (that is, Kennedy's). The president's inspiring words are still widely quoted today:

> When power leads men towards arrogance, poetry reminds him of his limitations. When power narrows the areas of man's concern, poetry reminds him of the richness and diversity of existence. When power corrupts, poetry cleanses.

. . . even though they are quite obviously false. Stalin read poetry; Mussolini read poetry; Mao read poetry; they were not reminded of their limitations, nor were they cleansed. Even poets who have no access to the levers of political power are not purified by their constant exposure to verse. Ezra Pound was a great poet and editor, but he still became a cheerleader for Fascism, and Edgar Allan Poe wrote verse with necrophiliac undertones and ended his days wandering the streets of Baltimore in a delirium. The list goes on. No: what's actually interesting about JFK's speech on poetry is how close it comes to Stalin's conception of the author as "engineer of the soul," granted an uncanny power to shape the inner lives of morals via the pleasing organization of words on the printed page.*

Jump forward a few decades, and things are little better—or possibly slightly worse. In 2008, Barack Obama was elected. A gifted orator and writer, he had inspired many people over the course of his first electoral campaign. Some were inspired a little too much, however—as we can see in the following passage, where a well-educated commentator who should have known better labors over a biblical allusion to deliver a worshipful paean to the transcendent power of the leader's speech that wouldn't look at all out of place in a totalitarian society:

> Obama's finest speeches do not excite. They do not inform. They don't even really inspire. They elevate. They enmesh you in a grander moment, as if history has stopped flowing passively by, and, just for an instant, contracted around you, made you aware of its presence, and your role in it. He is not the Word made flesh, but the triumph of word over flesh, over color, over despair. The other great leaders I've heard guide us towards a better politics, but Obama is, at his best, able to call us back to our highest selves, to the place where America exists as a glittering ideal, and where we, its honored inhabitants, seem capable of achieving it, and thus of sharing in its meaning and transcendence.

Obama himself dabbled with vaguely messianic language about planetary healing during this period, but he never lost his composure or sense of proportion: it was rhetoric. The preceding outburst, published in a serious intellectual magazine, is a whole other matter. Yes, the embarrassingly overcooked prose is eye-watering to read, but at a deeper level it represents a sudden and spontaneous eruption of the millenarian view of American history, rooted not in rational analysis but in deep cultural undercurrents beyond our control, which lie in wait for the moment when they can break through to the surface.

So could it happen here? Certainly, we have all the right ingredients.

---

* The CIA agreed. For decades it funded magazines and translations of literary novels that were smuggled into the East in the hope that mass exposure to *Dr. Zhivago*, say, might somehow weaken the Soviet system. But the written word is a lot slipperier than that, and nothing of the sort happened.

What we lack is the catalyst. After all, countries that experience revolutions and upon whose people dictatorial bibliographies are subsequently inflicted also tend to be countries in deep crisis. They are war ravaged and impoverished, places where the people cannot live as they are living and where the government cannot continue governing. It is in situations of societal breakdown and profound despair that demagogues and false prophets find themselves best positioned to seize power and impose their texts on the rest of us. And right now the United States, for all its troubles, does not come close to replicating those conditions. It remains the wealthiest and most powerful nation on earth, where most of the population enjoys a standard of living far higher than that found in most other places on the planet. There is rage and anxiety, and the nation is increasingly divided against itself, but there are also streaming video services and smartphones and lots of jobs, even if they don't pay as much as we would like, and even if the people at the top make far more money than the rest of us combined. More than that, there is also a lack of serious engagement with any alternative to the current political status quo. Words such as *socialism* and *fascism* are tossed about freely, but there is little evidence that those using them are very familiar with the actual content of those ideologies, or that they have the intellectual discipline to engage with them. The demagogues of our era are much less well read than those of the past.

I moved to the United States from Putin's Russia in 2006, but to take American political rhetoric at face value, you would think I had made a terrible mistake. Putin is cynical and unpleasant and authoritarian, but compared to the people who ran Russia for much of the twentieth century he is moderate. The gulag will not reopen; the Red Terror will not return. In the United States, however, it seems that we are forever standing at the edge of a political precipice, that a new Hitler or Stalin is forever waiting in the wings to impose tyranny as soon as he is able. The carelessness with which extreme historical analogies are drawn and the frequency with which apocalyptic prophecies are uttered might be amusing were they not so exhausting, and did these jeremiads not have so detrimental an effect upon thinking about what is actually happening in the world.

This is a phenomenon that has been exacerbated by the Internet and social media. For some time I wondered how to fit new technologies of the word into this book, or if I could fit them in. What impact would the radical democratization of the means of communication have upon the dictator book? Could such a canon, predicated upon centralized control of the media, exist in an age when social media platforms make everybody a publisher with global reach?

The revolutions of the Arab Spring happened about two years into my research into dictator literature. At the time, it was widely reported that social media had played a critical role in bringing about the downfall of at least some of the dictators toppled during those heady days in early 2011. These uprisings were not just expressions of popular rage at oppressive regimes; they were "Twitter revolutions," representing something new in human affairs. And yet, if true, it is curious indeed that social media were powerless to prevent the counterrevolution in Egypt, and hopeless as tools of resistance to the Bahrain crackdowns, and quite useless when Bashar al-Assad proved willing to unleash an army against protesters. In fact, dictatorial regimes also know how to use social media. Both the Ayatollah Ali Khamenei of Iran and Emomali Rahmon of Tajikistan have Twitter accounts, as does Vladimir Putin: autocrats are perfectly capable of tweeting their deep thoughts in 140 characters or fewer.

In fact, the impact of social media is felt most not in dictatorships, where it has become another channel for the dissemination of flat prose attributed to the leader, but in liberal democracies. The now familiar phenomenon of public shaming, in which a public or private figure utters something deemed unacceptable and is then hounded out of his job and/ or compelled to deliver groveling self-criticism by an online mob, has obvious parallels with totalitarian societies, where those who did not adhere closely enough to the state ideology were subject to the same treatment. Stalin and Mao were adept at organizing campaigns of public persecution against writers, scientists and politicians who had crossed a line. In our enlightened times, such campaigns happen spontaneously, rather than as a result of a directive from a tyrant.

Public stonings and witch burnings are venerable forms of mass entertainment, and as Aldous Huxley observed, to "be able to destroy with good conscience, to be able to behave badly and call your bad behavior 'righteous indignation'" is indeed "a delicious moral treat." So there is nothing new here; Stalin and Mao and their ilk were merely tapping into deep and unpleasant currents of human psychology for their own benefit. What *is* interesting is the way in which the explosion of voices, which truly is without precedent in history, has been a case not so much of "letting a hundred flowers bloom" as of relentlessly homogenizing and hardening reductive viewpoints, resulting in springtime for yet another era of terrible simplifications. Who would have imagined that toppling the gate-keepers who once kept such a tight control over the word and giving every-body the means to become a publisher would have led to such a narrowing of minds, to so much unjustified certainty, to so much shrill and intoler-ant self-righteousness? For the radicals and would-be dictators of the past, the underground printing press was not only a means through which they spread the word to their followers, but also a means through which the self was amplified as they wrote themselves into the great ideological battles of their times. In the twenty-first century, new technologies make this so much faster, and cheaper, and easier.

And, of course, such battles are only truly exciting when they are framed as part of an apocalyptic showdown between the forces of good and evil. With the stakes so high, it is a simple thing to demonize your enemies, to divide the world into the righteous and the damned, to suc-cumb to paranoia and fear of conspiracies, and to wage war against such terrors through the medium of text. But in doing so, we replicate in our-selves the mentality and approach to the word and the world of a Lenin, so confident in his beliefs, raging against diabolical enemies from the comfort of his chair and hurling texts at a small group of like-minded comrades, all of whom believed they were engaged in a battle of world-historical importance.

We should all know by now where that type of thinking can lead. But as Aleksandr Solzhenitsyn—who knew a thing or two about the nature of tyranny and evil—observed:

> If only it were all so simple! If only there were evil people somewhere insidiously committing evil deeds, and it were necessary only to separate them from the rest of us and destroy them. But the line dividing good and evil cuts through the heart of every human being. And who is willing to destroy a piece of his own heart?

ACKNOWLEDGMENTS

The Infernal Library is the result of many years' labor and research, and along the way a number of fine people helped me take it from the realm of implausible ideas and into reality. To make a book like this requires the support of people with vision, and these are in short supply in any age. I was fortunate enough to find several.

First I must thank Sarah Crown, the inspired ex-editor of the *Guardian*'s online book pages who accepted my proposal for a series of blogs about books by dictators, thus setting in motion the chain of events that brought this book into being. Little did I know what I was letting myself in for. Then I must thank Aaron Schlechter, who not only connected me with agent extraordinaire Jim Rutman, but also planted a vital seed at Holt. Jim made me think deeply about the ultimate form and content of *The Infernal Library* during the proposal stage, and so prevented much wailing and gnashing of teeth once work began in earnest. Not only that, but he expertly steered it into the hands of Sarah Bowlin, who proved to be an enthusiastic and sympathetic editor. Michael Signorelli picked up the baton from Sarah when she departed for the West Coast and did sterling work preparing this book for the world. In addition, thanks go out also to Jim Gill at United Agents; Alex Christophi and Jon Bentley-Smith at OneWorld; Mike Harpley and Henry Jeffries, both formerly of OneWorld; not to mention Brian Egan; Kanyin Ajayi; Kelly S. Too; the scholar and gentleman Mr. Nik White; and Camilla Hornby, who was so instrumental in launching my career as an author over a decade ago now.

But wait, there's more:

All of these people helped make *The Infernal Library* a reality, even if a few of them were not aware at the time: Marc Bennetts, Erin Osterhaus, Lenka Duskova, Kacper Pobłocki, Piotr Siemion, Masha Timofeeva, Ed Nawotka, Vadim Staklo, Victoria MacArthur, Andrew Gauld, Scott Stein, Sema Balaman, Alptekin Tanir, Joe Davies, Mariano Mamertino, Marc Adler, Semyon Stankevich, Masha Lipman, Sandy Carson, Craig Borowski, Daniel Harris, Nancy Humphries, Nathaniel Humphries, Joy Humphries, David Humphries, Roy Humphries, Elizabeth Humphries. There are too many people to name from my time spent living in Moscow; I thank them. Likewise I am grateful to the Star Coffee Co. of Round Rock, Texas, and the staff of the libraries at the University of Texas, Austin. Finally, my family showed extraordinary patience as I entombed myself in the study of the worst books in the world. Now it really is done.

Austin–Leander–Georgetown–Round Rock, 2009–2017.

Amen.

SELECTED BIBLIOGRAPHY

Abrams, Bradley, *The Struggle for the Soul of the Nation: Czech Culture and the Rise of Communism*, Rowman and Littlefield, Lanham, MD, 2004.

Alexander, Anne, *Nasser*, Haus, London, 2005.

Alexandrov et al. (eds.), *Iosif Vissarionovich Stalin: Kratkaya Biografiya*, State Publishing House of Political Literature, Moscow, 1948.

Anderson, Kevin, *Marx at the Margins: On Nationalism, Ethnicity, and Non-Western Societies*, University of Chicago Press, Chicago, IL, 2010.

de Andrade, Jaime, *Raza*, Planeta, Barcelona, 1997.

Andrew, Mitrokhin, *The Mitrokhin Archive*, Basic Books, New York, 2000.

Anonymous (ed.), *Documents and Deliberations of the Seminar/Preparatory Committee of the Pan-African Seminar on the Juche Idea of Comrade Kim Il Sung*, Dar al-Talia, Beirut, 1973.

Anonymous (ed.), *The True Story of Kim Jong-Il*, The Institute for South-North Korea Studies, Seoul, 1993.

Ansary, Tamim, *Destiny Disrupted*, Public Affairs, New York, 2009.

Apor, Balazs (ed.), *The Leader Cult in Communist Dictatorships: Stalin and the Eastern Bloc*, Palgrave Macmillan, New York, 2004.

Appelbaum, Anne, *Iron Curtain*, Doubleday, New York, 2012.

Ayoub, Mahmoud, *Islam and the Third Universal Theory: The Religious Thought of Mu'ammar al-Qadhdhafi*, KPI, London, 1987.

Bacon, Edwin, and Mark Sandle (eds.), *Brezhnev Reconsidered*, Palgrave Macmillan, New York, 2002.

Banerji, Arup, *Writing History in the Soviet Union: Making the Past Work*, Social Science Press, New Delhi, 2008.

Barmé, Geremie, *Shades of Mao: The Posthumous Cult of the Great Leader*, ME Sharpe, Armonk, NY, 1996.

Bawden, Charles R., *The Modern History of Mongolia*, Praeger, New York, 1968.

Berdymukhammedov, Gurbanguly, *Akhalteke Our Pride and Glory*, Türkmendöwlethabarlary, Ashgabat, Turkmenistan, 2008.

Berdymukhammedov, Gurbanguly, *The Flight of Celestial Racehorses*, Turkmen State Publishing Service, Ashgabat, Turkmenistan, 2011.

Billington, James H., *The Icon and the Axe*, Alfred A. Knopf, New York, 1966.

Blok, Alexander, *Selected Poems*, Eyre & Spottiswoode, London, 1970.

Bogdanov, Alexander, *Red Star*, Indiana University Press, Bloomington, IN, 1984.

Bohachevsky-Chomiak, Martha, and Bernice Glatzer Rosenthal (eds.), *A Revolution of the Spirit: Crisis of Value in Russia, 1890–1924*, Fordham University Press, New York, 1990.

Boor, Jakim, *Masoneria*, Fundacion Nacional Francisco Franco, Madrid, 1981.

Borghi, Armando, *Mussolini, Red and Black*, Freie Arbeiter Stimme, New York, 1938.

Bosworth, R. J. B., *Mussolini* (new ed.), Bloomsbury, London, 2010.

Bosworth, R. J. B., *Mussolini's Italy*, Allen Lane, London, 2005.

Breen, Michael, *Kim Jong-il: North Korea's Dear Leader* (rev. and updated ed.), Wiley, Singapore, 2012.

Brezhnev, Leonid, *Trilogy*, Progress Publishers, Moscow, 1980.

Burleigh, Michael, *Sacred Causes*, HarperPress, London, 2006.

Burleigh, Michael, *The Third Reich*, Macmillan, London, 2000.

Caesar, Julius, *The Civil War*, Penguin Books, London, 1967.

Cardoza, Anthony L., *Benito Mussolini: The First Fascist*, Pearson Longman, New York, 2006.

Castro, Fidel, *Che: A Memoir by Fidel Castro*, Ocean Press, Victoria, 2006.

Castro, Fidel, and Ignacio Ramonet, *My Life: A Spoken Autobiography*, Scribner, New York, 2008.

Cazorla Sánchez, Antonio, *Franco: The Biography of the Myth*, Routledge, London, 2014.

Cecil, Robert, *The Myth of the Master Race: Alfred Rosenberg and Nazi Ideology*, Dodd Mead, New York, 1972.

Chatterjee, Kingshuk, *Ali Shariati and the Shaping of Political Islam in Iran*, Palgrave Macmillan, New York, 2011.

Childs, David, *The GDR: Moscow's German Ally*, George Allen & Unwin, London, 1983.

Choibalsan, Khorloogiin, *Izbrannie Stati i Rechi*, Foreign Literature Publishing House, Moscow, 1961.

Clark, Katerina, *The Soviet Novel: History as Ritual* (3rd ed.), Indiana University Press, Bloomington, IN, 2000.

Clark Katerina, and Evgeny Dobrenko (eds.), *Soviet Culture and Power*, Yale, New Haven, CT, 2007.

Commission of the Central Committee of the CPSU (ed.), *History of the Communist Party of the Soviet Union (Bolsheviks)*, International Publishers, New York, 1939.

Cook, Alexander (ed.), *Mao's Little Red Book: A Global History*, Cambridge University Press, Cambridge, 2014.

Cook, Michael, *The Koran: A Very Short Introduction*, Oxford University Press, Oxford, 2000.

Courtois, Stéphane (ed.), *The Black Book of Communism*, Harvard University Press, Cambridge, MA, 1999.

Daniels, Anthony, *Utopias Elsewhere*, Crown Publishers, New York, 1991.

Davies, R. W., *Soviet History in the Gorbachev Revolution*, Macmillan, London, 1989.

Davin, Delia, *Mao: A Very Short Introduction*, Oxford University Press, Oxford, 2013.

De Meneses, Filipe Ribeiro, *Salazar: A Political Biography*, Enigma Books, New York, 2009.

Demick, Barbara, *Nothing to Envy: Ordinary Lives in North Korea*, Spiegel & Grau, New York, 2009.

Dikotter, Frank, *Mao's Great Famine*, Walker & Co., New York, 2010.

Dimitrov, Georgi, *The Diary of Georgi Dimitrov, 1933–1949*, Yale University Press, New Haven, CT, 2003.

Dimitrov, Georgi, *Dimitroff's Letters from Prison*, Gollancz, London, 1935.

Dimitrov, Georgi, *The Guarantee of Victory*, Workers Library Publishers Inc., New York, 1938.

Dimitrov, Georgi, *Selected Works*, Foreign Languages Press, Sofia, 1967.

Dobbs, Michael, *Down with Big Brother: The Fall of the Soviet Empire*, Bloomsbury, London, 1996.

Dobrenko, Evgeny, *The Making of the State Writer: Social and Aesthetic Origins of Soviet Literary Culture*, Stanford University Press, Stanford, CA, 2001.

Dobrenko, Evgeny, *Stalinist Cinema and the Production of History*, Edinburgh University Press, Edinburgh, 2008.

Edgar, Adrienne Lynne, *Tribal Nation*, Princeton University Press, Princeton, NJ, 2004.

Elsie, Robert, *Historical Dictionary of Albania* (2nd ed.), Scarecrow Press, Lanham, MD, 2010.

Engelstein, Laura, *Castration and the Heavenly Kingdom*, Cornell University Press, Ithaca, NY, 1999.

Farrell, Nicholas, *Mussolini: A New Life*, Weidenfeld & Nicolson, London, 2003.

Felshtinsky, Yuri, *Lenin and His Comrades: The Bolsheviks Take Over Russia 1917–1924*, Enigma Books, New York, 2010.

Fevziu, Blendi, *Enver Hoxha: The Iron Fist of Albania*, IB Tauris, New York, 2016.

Figes, Orlando, *A People's Tragedy*, Jonathan Cape, London, 1996.

Figes, Orlando, *The Whisperers*, Metropolitan Books, New York, 2007.

Fischer, Paul, *A Kim Jong-Il Production*, Flatiron Books, New York, 2015.

Fitzpatrick, Sheila, *Education and Social Mobility in the Soviet Union 1921–1934*, Cambridge University Press, Cambridge, 1979.

Fitzpatrick, Sheila, *Everyday Stalinism*, Oxford University Press, Oxford, 1999.

Franco, Francisco, *Pensamiento político de Franco*, Ediciones del Movimiento, Madrid, 1975.

Franco, Francisco, *Textos de Doctrina Política; Palabras y Escritos de 1945 a 1950*, Publicaciones Españoles, Madrid, 1951.

Gaddafi, Muammar, *Escape to Hell and Other Stories*, Blake Publishing, London, 1999.

Gaddafi, Muammar, *The Green Book*, Tripoli, 1979.

Geifman, Anna, *Death Orders*, Praeger, Santa Barbara, CA, 2010.

Gill, Graham, *Symbols and Legitimacy in Soviet Politics*, Cambridge University Press, Cambridge, 2011.

Gomulka, Wladyslaw, *On the German Problem*, Kisiazka i Wiedza, Warsaw, 1969.

Goodwin, James, *Confronting Dostoevsky's Demons*, Peter Lang Publishing, New York, 2010.

Gottwald, Klement, *Selected Writings*, Orbis Press, Prague, 1981.

Gottwald, Klement, *Statement of Policy of Mr. Gottwald's Government*, Czechoslovak Ministry of Information, Prague, 1946.

Gottwald, Klement, *Vojenská politika KSČ. Sborník,* Naše vojsko, Praha, 1972.

Gray, John, *Black Mass*, Allen Lane, London, 2007.

Griffith, William E., *Albania and the Sino-Soviet Rift*, MIT Press, Cambridge, MA, 1963.

Hamann, Brigitte, *Hitler's Vienna: A Dictator's Apprenticeship*, Oxford University Press, New York, 1999.

Hann, Chris, *The Postsocialist Religious Question: Faith and Power in Central Asia and East-Central Europe* (Halle Studies in the Anthropology of Eurasia), LIT Verlag, Berlin, 2006.

Harrold, Michael, *Comrades and Strangers: Behind the Closed Doors of North Korea*, John Wiley and Sons, Hoboken, NJ, 2004.

Hellbeck, Jochen, *Revolution on My Mind*, Harvard University Press, Cambridge, MA, 2006.

Herwig, Holger H., *The Demon of Geopolitics: How Karl Haushofer "Educated" Hitler and Hess*, Rowman & Littlefield, Lanham, MD, 2016.

Hiro, Dilip, *Inside Central Asia: A Political and Cultural History of Uzbekistan, Turkmenistan, Kazakhstan, Kyrgyzstan, Tajikistan, Turkey and Iran*, Overlook, NY, 2009.

Hitler, Adolf, *Hitler's Secret Book*, Grove Press, New York, 1961.

Hitler, Adolf, *Mein Kampf*, Houghton Mifflin, Boston, 1943.

Hoberman, John M., *Sport and Political Ideology*, University of Texas Press, Austin, TX, 1984.

Hollander, Paul, *Political Pilgrims* (4th ed.), Transaction Publishers, New Brunswick, NJ, 2009.

Hoxha, Enver, *The Anglo-American Threat to Albania*, The 8 Nentori Publishing House, Tirana, 1982.

Hoxha, Enver, *The Artful Albanian: Memoirs of Enver Hozha*, Chatto & Windus, London, 1986.

Hoxha, Enver, *With Stalin*, The 8 Nentori Publishing House, Tirana, 1979.

Hughes-Hallett, Lucy, *Gabriel d'Annunzio: Poet, Seducer and Preacher of War*, Alfred A. Knopf, New York, 2013.

Hussein, Saddam, *La Revolucion y la Mujer*, Lausana, Sartec, Baghdad, 1977.

Hussein, Saddam, *Zabiba and the King*, VBW Publishing, College Station, TX, 2004.

Huxley, Aldous, *Crome Yellow*, Chatto & Windus, London, 1921.

Jang Jin-sung, *Dear Leader*, Atria Books, New York, 2014.

Johnson, Paul, *Intellectuals*, Weidenfeld & Nicolson, London, 1988.

Jones, Derek (ed.), *Censorship: A World Encyclopedia*, Fitzroy Dearborn Publishers, Chicago, 2001.

Jones, J. Sydney, *Hitler in Vienna, 1907–1913*, Stein and Day, New York, 1983.

Karsh, Efraim, *Islamic Imperialism*, Yale University Press, New Haven, CT, 2007.

Karsh, Efraim, and Inari Rautsi, *Saddam Hussein: A Political Biography*, Grove Press, New York, 2002.

Kemp, Geoff, *Censorship Moments: Reading Texts in the History of Censorship and Freedom of Expression*, Bloomsbury Academic, London, 2015.

Kershaw, Ian, *Hitler, 1889–1936 Hubris*, W. W. Norton, New York, 1999.

Khomeini, Ruhollah, *A Clarification of Questions*, Westview Press, Boulder, CO, 1984.

Khomeini, Ruhollah, *Islam and Revolution*, Mizan Press, Berkeley, CA, 1981.

Khomeini, Ruhollah, *Sayings of the Ayatollah Khomeini: Political, Philosophical, Social and Religious*, Bantam Books, New York, 1979.

Khrushchev, Nikita, *Khrushchev Remembers*, Little, Brown, New York, 1970.

Khrushchev, Nikita, *Speech to 20th Congress of the C.P.S.U.*, Marxists.org, 1956.

Kihl Young Whan and Kim Hong Nack (eds.), *North Korea: The Politics of Regime Survival*, M. E. Sharpe, Armonk, NY, 2006.

Kim Il-sung, *Juche! The Speeches and Writings of Kim Il-sung*, Grossman, New York, 1972.

Kim Il-sung, *On Juche in Our Revolution*, Foreign Languages Publishing House, Pyongyang, 1975.

Kim Il-sung, *With the Century*, vol. 1, Foreign Languages Publishing House, Pyongyang, 1992.

Kim Il-sung, *Works*, Foreign Languages Publishing House, Pyongyang, 1971.

Kim Jong-il, *On the Art of Cinema*, Foreign Languages Publishing House, Pyongyang, 1989.

Kim Jong-il, *Our Socialism Centered on the Masses Shall Not Perish*, University Press of the Pacific, Honolulu, 2003.

Kim Jong-il, *Selected Works*, Foreign Languages Publishing House, Pyongyang, 1992.

Kim Jong-un, *The Cause of the Great Party of Comrades Kim Il-sung and Kim Jong-il Is Ever Victorious*, Foreign Languages Publishing House, Pyongyang, 2015.

Kim Jong-un, *Let Us Hasten Final Victory Through a Revolutionary Ideological Offensive*, Foreign Languages Publishing House, Pyongyang, 2014.

Kotkin, Stephen, *Stalin Volume 1: Paradoxes of Power 1878–1928*, Penguin Press, New York, 2014.

Kovrig, Bennet, *Communism in Hungary from Kun to Kadar*, Hoover Institution Press, Stanford, CA, 1979.

Kraus, Richard C., *The Cultural Revolution: A Very Short Introduction*, Oxford University Press, Oxford, 2012.

Kukushkin, Vadim, *From Peasants to Labourers*, McGill-Queen's University Press, Montreal, 2007.

Kunetskaya, Mashtakova, *Lenin, Great and Human*, Progress Publishers, Moscow, 1979.

Landau, Jacob (ed.), *Ataturk and the Modernization of Turkey*, Westview Press, Boulder, CO, 1984.

Landes, Richard (ed.), *Encyclopedia of Millennialism and Millennial Movements*, Routledge, New York, 2000.

Landes, Richard, *Heaven on Earth: The Varieties of the Millennial Experience*, Oxford University Press, New York, 2011.

Lane, David, *Leninism: A Sociological Interpretation*, Cambridge University Press, Cambridge, 1981.

Lankov, A. N., *The Real North Korea*, Oxford University Press, Oxford, 2013.

Lattimore, Owen, *Nationalism and Revolution in Mongolia*, Oxford University Press, New York, 1955.

Leese, Daniel, *Mao Cult: Rhetoric and Ritual in the Cultural Revolution*, Cambridge University Press, Cambridge, 2011.

Leites, Nathan, *The Operational Code of the Politburo*, McGraw-Hill, New York, 1951.

Lenin, V. I., *Collected Works*, Progress Publishers, Moscow, 1962.

Lenin, V. I., *Essential Works of Lenin: "What Is to Be Done?" and Other Writings*, Bantam Books, New York, 1966.

Lenin, V. I. (ed. Robert C. Tucker), *The Lenin Anthology*, W. W. Norton, New York, 1975.

Lenin, V. I. (ed. S. Zizek), *Revolution at the Gates: Selected Writings of Lenin from 1917*, Verso, London, 2002.

Levitsky, Alexander (ed.), *Worlds Apart*, Overlook, New York, 2007.

Lew, Christopher R., and Edwin Pak-wah Leung, *Historical Dictionary of the Chinese Civil War* (2nd ed.), Scarecrow Press, Lanham, MD, 2013.

Lewis, Paul H., *Authoritarian Regimes in Latin America: Dictators, Despots and Tyrants*, Rowman & Littlefield, Lanham, MD, 2006.

Leys, Simon, *Chinese Shadows*, Viking Press, New York, 1977.

Li Zhisui, *The Private Life of Chairman Mao*, Random House, New York, 1994.

Ludwig, Emil, *Talks with Mussolini*, Little, Brown, Boston, 1933.

Luzzatto, Sergio, *The Body of Il Duce*, Metropolitan Books, New York, 2005.

MacFarquhar, Roderick, and Michael Schoenhals, *Mao's Last Revolution*, Belknap Press of Harvard University Press, Cambridge, MA, 2006.

Margolius, Ivan, *Reflections of Prague: Journeys Through the 20th Century*, Wiley, Hoboken, NJ, 2006.

Marks, Steven G., *How Russia Shaped the Modern World*, Princeton University Press, Princeton, NJ, 2003.

Maser, Werner, *Hitler's Mein Kampf: An Analysis*, Faber & Faber, London, 1970.

Mayakovsky, Vladimir, *Selected Poems*, Northwestern University Press, Evanston, IL, 2015.

Mayakovsky, Vladimir, *Selected Works 2: Longer Poems*, Raduga, Moscow, 1986.

McDermott, Kevin, *The Comintern: A History of International Communism from Lenin to Stalin*, St. Martin's Press, New York, 1996.

McLoughlin, Barry, and Kevin McDermott (eds.), *Stalin's Terror: High Politics and Mass Repression in the Soviet Union*, Palgrave Macmillan, New York, 2011.

Megaro, Gaudens, *Mussolini in the Making*, George Allen & Unwin, London, 1938.

Miłosz, Czesław, *The Captive Mind*, Alfred A. Knopf, New York, 1953.

Minh, Ho Chi (Walden Bello, ed.), *Down with Colonialism!* Verso, London, 2007.

Minh, Ho Chi, *The Prison Diary of Ho Chi Minh*, Bantam, New York, 1971.

Molavi, Afshin, *Persian Pilgrimages*, W. W. Norton & Company, New York, 2003.

Montefiore, Simon Sebag, *Young Stalin*, Weidenfeld & Nicolson, London, 2007.

Mottahedeh, Roy, *The Mantle of the Prophet: Religion and Politics in Iran* (2nd ed.), Oneworld, Oxford, 2000.

Mount, Ferdinand (ed.), *Communism: A TLS Companion*, University of Chicago Press, Chicago, 1993.

Mugabe, Robert Gabriel, *War, Peace, and Development in Contemporary Africa*, Indian Council for Cultural Relations, New Delhi, 1987.

Mussolini, Benito, *The Cardinal's Mistress*, Albert & Charles Boni, New York, 1928.

Mussolini, Benito, *The Fall of Mussolini: His Own Story*, Farrar, Straus, New York, 1948.

Mussolini, Benito, *John Huss*, Albert & Charles Boni, New York, 1929.

Mussolini, Benito, *My Autobiography*, Scribner, New York, 1928.

Mussolini, Benito, *My Autobiography* (rev. ed.), Hutchinson & Co., London, 1939.

Mussolini, Benito, *My Diary 1915–1917*, Small, Maynard and Company, Boston, 1925.

Mussolini, Benito, *Opera Omnia*, La Fenice, Firenze, 1951.

Mussolini, Benito, and Giovanni Forzano, *Napoleon: The Hundred Days*, London, Sidgwick & Jackson, 1932.

Naimark, Norman, and Gibianskii, Leonid (eds.), *The Establishment of Communist Regimes in Eastern Europe, 1944–1949*, Westview Press, Boulder, CO, 1997.

Naipaul, V. S. *Among the Believers*, Andre Deutsch, London, 1981.

Nasser, Gamal A., *The Philosophy of the Revolution*, Dar al-Maaref, Cairo, 1955.

Nasser, Gamal A., *Speeches and Press Interviews*, Information Department, Cairo, 1963.

Nazarbayev, Nursultan, *The Critical Decade*, First, London, 2003.

Nazarbayev, Nursultan, *Epicenter of Peace*, Hollis Publishing Co., Hollis, NH, 2001.

Nazarbayev, Nursultan, *Radical Renewal of Global Society*, Stacey International, London, 2010.

Nolan, Adrianne, "'Shitting Medals': L. I. Brezhnev, the Great Patriotic War, and the Failure of the Personality Cult, 1965–1982," M.A. thesis, University of North Carolina at Chapel Hill, 2008.

Nova, Fritz, *Alfred Rosenberg, Nazi Theorist of the Holocaust*, Hippocrene, New York, 1986.

Onon, Urgunge (ed.), *Mongolian Heroes of the Twentieth Century*, AMS Press, New York, 1976.

Orizio, Riccardo, *Talk of the Devil*, Walker and Company, New York, 2003.

Orwell, George, *The Collected Essays, Journalism and Letters of George Orwell*, vol. 2, Secker & Warburg, London, 1968.

Ostrovsky, Arkady, *The Invention of Russia*, Viking, New York, 2016.

Overy, R. J., *The Dictators: Hitler's Germany and Stalin's Russia*, W. W. Norton, New York, 2004.

Pahlavi, Reza Shah, *Mission for My Country*, McGraw-Hill, New York, 1961.

Pantsov, Alexander, and Steven I. Levine, *Mao: The Real Story*, Simon & Schuster, New York, 2012.

Pargeter, Alison, *Libya: The Rise and Fall of Qaddafi*, Yale University Press, New Haven, CT, 2012.

Passmore, Kevin, *Fascism: A Very Short Introduction*, Oxford University Press, Oxford, 2002.

Payne, Robert, *Marx*, Simon & Schuster, New York, 1968.

Pipes, Richard, *Communism: A History*, Modern Library, New York, 2001.

Pipes, Richard, *Three "Whys" of the Russian Revolution*, Vintage Books, New York, 1996.

Pipes, Richard, *The Unknown Lenin*, Yale University Press, New Haven, CT, 1996.

Plokhy, Serhii, *The Last Empire*, Oneworld, London, 2014.

Pomper, Philip, *Lenin's Brother*, W. W. Norton, New York, 2010.

Pound, Ezra, *Ezra Pound and "Globe" Magazine: The Complete Correspondence*, Bloomsbury, London, 2015.

Preston, Paul, *Franco: A Biography*, Basic Books, New York, 1994.

Priestland, David, *The Red Flag*, Grove Press, New York, 2009.

Prifti, Peter R., *Socialist Albania Since 1944*, MIT Press, Cambridge, MA, 1978.

Putin, Vladimir, *Slova Menyaiushie Mir*, Set, Moscow, 2015.

Putin, Vladimir, Nataliya Gevorkyan, Natalya Timakova, and Andrei Kolesnikov, *First Person: An Astonishingly Frank Self-Portrait by Russia's President*, PublicAffairs, New York, 2000.

Putin, Vladimir, Vasily Shestakov, and Alexy Levitsky, *Judo: History, Theory, Practice*, Blue Snake Books, Berkeley, CA, 2004.

Quirk, Robert E., *Fidel Castro*, W. W. Norton, New York, 1993.

Radzinsky, Edvard, *Alexander II*, Free Press, New York, 2005.

Radzinsky, Edvard, *Stalin*, Doubleday, New York, 1996.

Rappaport, Helen, *Stalin: A Biographical Companion*, ABC-Clio, Santa Barbara, CA, 1999.

Ridley, Jasper, *Mussolini*, Constable, London, 1997.

Robert, Cecil, *The Myth of the Master Race: Alfred Rosenberg and Nazi Ideology*, Dodd, Mead, New York, 1972.

Rosenberg, Alfred, *Memoirs of Alfred Rosenberg*, Ziff-Davis, Chicago, 1949.

Rupen, Robert Arthur, *How Mongolia Is Really Ruled: A Political History of the Mongolian People's Republic, 1900–1978*, Hoover Institution Press, Stanford University, Stanford, CA, 1979.

Ryback, Timothy W., *Hitler's Private Library: The Books That Shaped His Life*, Alfred A. Knopf, New York, 2008.

Salazar, Antonio de Oliviera, *Doctrine and Action*, Faber and Faber, London, 1939.

Salazar, Antonio de Oliviera, *Salazar Prime Minister of Portugal Says*, SPN Books, Lisbon, 1939.

Sandag, Shagdariin, and Harry Kendall, *Poisoned Arrows: The Stalin-Choibalsan Mongolian Massacres, 1921–1941*, Westview Press, Boulder, CO, 2000.

Schoenhals, Michael, *Doing Things with Words in Chinese Politics*, University of California at Berkeley, Center for Chinese Studies, Research Monograph no. 41, Berkeley, CA, 1992.

Seldes, George, *Sawdust Caesar: The Untold History of Mussolini and Fascism*, Harper & Brothers, New York and London, 1935.

Service, Robert, *Comrades: A World History of Communism*, Macmillan, London, 2007.

Service, Robert, *Lenin: A Biography*, Macmillan, London, 2000.

Service, Robert, *Stalin: A Biography*, Macmillan, London, 2004.

Shubin, Daniel H., *A History of Russian Christianity*, vol. 4, Algora Publishing, New York, 2006.

Siegelbaum, Lewis, and Andrei Sokolov, (eds.), *Stalinism as a Way of Life*, Yale University Press, New Haven, CT, 2000.

Simons, Geoff, *Libya: The Struggle for Survival* (2nd ed.), Macmillan, London, 1996.

Spence, Jonathan, *God's Chinese Son: The Taiping Heavenly Kingdom of Hong Xiuquan*, W. W. Norton, New York, 1996.

Sperber, Jonathan, *Karl Marx*, Liveright, New York, 2013.

Stalin, J. V., *Collected Works*, Foreign Languages Publishing House, Moscow, 1954.

Stalin, J. V., *Foundations of Leninism*, International Publishers, New York, 1939.

Stalin, J. V., *Marxism and Linguistics*, International Publishers, New York, 1951.

Stalin, J. V., *Problems of Leninism*, International Publishers, New York, 1934.

Stalin, J. V. (M. R. Werner, ed.), *Stalin's Kampf*, Howell, Soskin & Company, New York, 1940.

Stalin, J. V., *Two Speeches*, Co-operative Publishing Society of Foreign Workers in the USSR, Moscow, 1935.

Stern, Carola, *Ulbricht: A Political Biography*, Frederick A. Praeger, New York, 1965.

Stone, Norman, *The Atlantic and Its Enemies*, Basic Books, New York, 2010.

Su, Yang, *Collective Killings in Rural China During the Cultural Revolution*, Cambridge University Press, New York, 2011.

Sworakowski, Witold S., *World Communism: A Handbook 1918–1965*, Hoover Institution Press, Stanford, CA, 1973.

Szczygel, Mariusz, *Gottland*, Melville House, Brooklyn/London, 2014.

Taubman, William, *Khrushchev: The Man and His Era*, W. W. Norton, New York, 2003.

Terrill, Ross, *Mao: A Biography*, Stanford University Press, Stanford, CA, 1999.

Thompson, Damian, *The End of Time*, Sinclair-Stevenson, London, 1996.

Thrower, James, *Marxist-Leninist "Scientific Atheism" and the Study of Religion and Atheism in the USSR*, Mouton Publishers, Berlin, 1983.

Tismaneau, Vladimir, ed., *Stalinism Revisited: The Establishment of Communist Regimes in East-Central Europe*, Central European University Press, Budapest, 2009.

Tito, Iosip Broz, *The Essential Tito*, St. Martin's Press, New York, 1970.

Tito, Iosip Broz, *The Yugoslav People's Fight to Live*, The United Committee of South-Slavic Americans, New York, 1944.

Toland, John, *Adolf Hitler: The Definitive Biography*, Doubleday, New York, 1976.

Trotsky, Leon, *My Life*, Pathfinder Press, New York, 1971.

Tsapkin, N., *Mongolskaia Narodnaya Respublika*, State Publishing House of Political Literature, Moscow, 1948.

Tucker, Robert, *Stalinism: Essays in Historical Interpretation*, W. W. Norton, New York, 1977.

Tumarkin, Nina, *Lenin Lives! The Lenin Cult in Soviet Russia*, Harvard University Press, Cambridge, MA, 1997.

Turkmenbashi, Saparmurat, *Rukhnama*, State Publishing Service, Ashgabat, Turkmenistan, 2005.

Ulbricht, Walter, *On Questions of Socialist Construction in the GDR*, Verlag Zeit Im Bild, Dresden, 1968.

Ullrich, Volker, *Hitler: Ascent*, Bodley Head, London, 2016.

Urban, George, *The Miracles of Chairman Mao*, Tom Stacey Ltd., London, 1971.

Vandewalle, Dirk, *A History of Modern Libya*, Cambridge University Press, Cambridge, 2006.

Verdery, Katherine, *National Ideology Under Socialism: Identity and Cultural Politics in Ceaușescu's Romania*, University of California Press, Berkeley, 1991.

Volkogonov, Dmitri, *Lenin: A New Biography*, Free Press, New York, 1994.

Volkogonov, Dmitri, *The Rise and Fall of the Soviet Empire*, HarperCollins, London, 1998.

Von Geldern, James, and Richard Stites (eds.), *Mass Culture in Soviet Russia*, Indiana University Press, Bloomington, 1995.

Vorontsov, V. V., *Words of the Wise: A Book of Russian Quotations*, Progress, Moscow, 1979.

Weber, Eugen, *Apocalypses*, Harvard University Press, Cambridge, MA, 1999.

Weber, Thomas, *Hitler's First War: Adolf Hitler, the Men of the List Regiment, and the First World War*, Oxford University Press, Oxford, 2010.

Wesson, Robert G., *Lenin's Legacy*, Hoover Institution Press, Stanford, CA, 1978.

Westerman, Frank, *Engineers of the Soul*, Overlook, New York, 2011.

Wheen, Francis, *Karl Marx: A Life*, Fourth Estate, London, 1999.

Yedlin, Tovah, *Maxim Gorky: A Political Biography*, Praeger, Westport, CT, 1989.

Zbarsky, Ilya, and Samuel Hutchinson, *Lenin's Embalmers*, Harvill, London, 1998.

Zedong, Mao, *Mao Tse-tung on Literature and Art* (3rd ed.), Foreign Languages Press, Beijing, 1967.

Zedong, Mao (ed. S. Zizek), *On Practice and Contradiction (Revolutions)*, Verso, New York, 2007.

Zedong, Mao (ed. M. Rejai), *On Revolution and War*, Anchor Books, Garden City, NY, 1970.

Zedong, Mao, *The Poems of Mao Zedong*, Harper & Row, New York, 1972.

Zedong, Mao (ed. S. Schram), *The Political Thought of Mao Tse-tung*, Praeger, New York, 1969.

Zedong, Mao, *Quotations from Chairman Mao Tse-tung*, Foreign Languages Press, Beijing, 1966.

Zedong, Mao, *Selected Military Writings*, Foreign Languages Press, Beijing, 1963.

Zedong, Mao, *Selected Works*, Foreign Languages Press, Beijing, 1961.

Zedong, Mao, *Selected Works of Mao Tse-tung*, Harper & Row, New York, 1970.

Zyuganov, Gennady, *Stalin i Sovremenost*, Molodaya Gvardia, Moscow, 2009.

I also benefited from access to declassified documents from the Stalin archive of the Russian State Archive of Social and Political History (RGASPI) hosted at Yale University Press's Stalin Digital Archive.

INDEX

ABOUT THE AUTHOR

DANIEL KALDER was born and raised in Fife, Scotland. In 1997, he moved to Moscow, Russia, and spent the better part of the next ten years working, living and traveling in and around the former Soviet Union. This experience led to two books, *Lost Cosmonaut* (2006) and *Strange Telescopes* (2008), and an enduring fascination with dictator literature, which now culminates in the volume you hold in your hands. He has also published journalism in many venues, and written and presented for BBC Radio. He lives in Austin, Texas.

DATE DUE

**This item is Due on
or before Date shown.**

MAR – – 2018